W9-BXR-973

DEVELOPING CONNECTIONS

FREE PROFESSIONAL COPY

COPY
PROFESSIONAL
FREE

DEVELOPING CONNECTIONS
A Writer's Guide
with Readings

JUDITH A. STANFORD
Rivier College

Mayfield Publishing Company
Mountain View, California
London • Toronto

For Cynthia Hervey

Copyright © 1995 by Mayfield Publishing Company
All rights reserved. No portion of this book may be reproduced in any form
or by any means without written permission of the publisher.

LIBRARY OF CONGRESS CATALOGING–IN–PUBLICATION DATA
Stanford, Judith A.
    Developing connections : a writer's guide with readings / Judith A.
Stanford.
        p.   cm.
    Includes index.
    ISBN 1-55934-309-5
    1. English language—Rhetoric.   2. College readers.   I. Title.
PE1408.S674   1994
808'.0427—dc20   94-13059
                                                                        CIP

Manufactured in the United States of America
10 9 8 7 6 5 4 3 2 1

Mayfield Publishing Company
1280 Villa Street
Mountain View, California 94041

Sponsoring editor, Janet M. Beatty; production editor, April Wells-Hayes;
manuscript editor, Loralee Windsor; art director, Jeanne M. Schreiber; cover
design, Donna Davis; illustrator, Robin Mouat; manufacturing manager,
Aimee Rutter. The text was set in 11/12 Bembo by Thompson Type and
printed on 45# Restorecote Thin by the Maple-Vail Book Manufacturing
Group.

Cover image: *Symmetry Drawing E42.* © 1994, M. C. Escher/Cordon Art–
Baarn–Holland. All rights reserved.

Acknowledgments appear on pages 337–340, which constitute an extension
of the copyright page.

 This book is printed on acid-free, recycled paper.

PREFACE

"Only connect!" E. M. Forster's widely quoted injunction urges us. The passage from *Howards End* continues: "Only connect the prose and the passion, and both will be exalted, and human love will be seen at its height. Live in fragments no longer." This book takes its title and its philosophy from Forster's vision.

The structure, the apparatus, and the selections in *Developing Connections* encourage beginning writers to seek relationships: among the processes of reading, writing, and thinking; among the ideas and emotions expressed by the reading selections; among the cultures represented by these diverse pieces; and, most of all, between the reading, writing, and thinking students are doing and the process of their own lives.

Developing Connections does much more than simply provide a collection of short readings that represents the diversity of today's world. Because its audience is students who are in the process of building basic reading and writing skills, Part 1 provides five introductory chapters encouraging step-by-step progress in strategies essential for college-level reading, writing, and thinking. The first four chapters demonstrate three key reading strategies: responding, understanding, and evaluating. Integrated with the reading strategies in these chapters are carefully planned prompts that introduce various aspects of the writing process through short one- or two-paragraph assignments. The fifth chapter shows how these strategies lead to conceiving and writing longer essays, including approaches to discovery, drafting, and revising. Throughout the first five chapters abundant student responses—sample discussions, journal entries, summaries, and a paper in various stages of the writing process—exemplify possible ways of reading, writing, and thinking, both individually and collaboratively.

Following Chapters 1–5 on the reading and writing process, Part 2 provides seven chapters of thematically arranged reading selections. Themes include Arrivals, Roots, and Memories; Parents and Children; Ways of Learning; American Dreams and Creations; Men and Women; Rights and Responsibilities; and Questions of Language. Readings have been carefully chosen to challenge and interest beginning students while not overwhelming them with ornate organization or arcane vocabulary.

The writing apparatus that accompanies each selection involves students in a variety of roles and rhetorical situations. Each selection is introduced by a brief note on the author and the circumstances of the original publication, followed by a series of prereading prompts designed especially for journal writing, brief informal class writing, or discussion that will lead to thoughtful reading. Following each selection are a series of topics for writing and discussion as well as suggestions for longer papers related to the reading. At the end of each thematic section, "Suggestions for Making Connections" asks students to stretch their responses beyond a single selection. Every writing suggestion encourages students to read closely, carefully, and with an open mind and seeks to engage students in meaningful writing that raises questions rather than simply answering them.

Preceding each thematic section are several photographs related to the theme as well as brief quotations taken from the selections that follow. The instructor's guide provides questions that give students the opportunity to respond to these photographs and quotations as a means of introduction to the theme. The instructor's guide also includes detailed discussion of each selection and innovative and flexible suggestions for using the text with various semester or quarter schedules.

Selections have been carefully chosen to provide diversity in terms of both the voices and the types of discourse represented. Readers will find an intriguing mix of letters, essays, newspaper columns, speeches, short stories, and poems. Again, the emphasis is on connection; selections represent an extraordinarily wide range of cultures that extends *multicultural* to include accounts of immigrants, first-generation sons and daughters, the educated and the uneducated, the poor and the middle-class, white, gay, handicapped, male, young, and old.

ACKNOWLEDGMENTS

Once again, I wish to thank the Writing and Learning Center faculty as well as the English Department faculty at Rivier College for creating a working atmosphere that promotes sharing ideas, exploring new possibilities, and taking risks. I am especially grateful to colleagues who have used *Connections* in their classes and who have generously offered suggestions for approaches to this related textbook.

My colleague Lorraine Lordi deserves special mention for her astute advice on selections and, particularly, for her creative and wise contributions to the apparatus accompanying selections. Once again, she has also planned and written the main sections of the detailed instructor's guide. I appreciate her support, her humor, and most of all her constant devotion to the true purpose of education: enabling students to learn through joy as well as through hard work.

My husband, Don, as always, has provided a listening ear, a sympathetic heart, and the wisdom of his constant wide reading to help me through the project. My mother, Arline Dupras, continues to give me her full and generous support. Her editing, word processing, and proofreading are valued; but more important are the love of reading, the dedication to teaching, and the optimistic view of life that she has passed on to me.

I have dedicated this book to my sister, Cynthia Hervey, who now more than ever perfectly exemplifies the energy, strength, wit, and love required to "develop connections."

The reviewers of this text offered helpful and wise suggestions, which I greatly appreciate: Cathryn Amdahl, Harrisburg Area Community College; Leslie O. Bradley, Pennsylvania State University; Ann George, Pennsylvania State University; Scott Oates, Salt Lake Community College; Mary Sauer, Indiana University, Indianapolis; Marti Singer, Georgia State University; Alison Smith, Western Washington University; and Beckey Stamm, Columbus State Community College.

At Mayfield Publishing Company, April Wells-Hayes skillfully guided the book through production, while Loralee Windsor offered excellent suggestions for fine-tuning as she copyedited the manuscript. Julianna Scott Fein has my deepest thanks and admiration for her careful and thorough research on each author included in the anthology section. Pamela Trainer's patient and sensible approach to obtaining permissions has been both helpful and informative.

My editor, Jan Beatty, deserves more than a paragraph. Jan, I wish I could write a whole chapter to describe my admiration for your approach to publishing and for your entirely sensible and sensitive way of working with your authors and your books. At a time when textbook publishing seems far too often simply a footnote in the life of a giant corporation, you (and Mayfield) take care to plan each project carefully and to see each book and each author as unique. Your involvement in every step of the publishing process (from campus visits to the book cover selection), your wide reading (when do you find the time?), and your commitment to professional development make you an ideal editor. Your understanding of the human condition (joy, sorrow, strength, weakness) makes you an ideal friend. Thanks for all this and much more.

CONTENTS

A Russian immigrant recalls the wondrous and magical first weeks of life in America during the late 1800s. The novelty of even the most basic objects, from rocking chairs to street lamps, instills in this writer an early sense that freedom, above all the riches her family left behind, is the most valuable gift a person can possess.

Intertwined experience, reading, and emotions compel this young black man to change his world of apartheid with his writings. As Mathabane discovered, perhaps the greatest outcome of such writing was his deeper understanding of himself and his homeland, South Africa.

An old, gray stone Catholic church, Protestant neighbors, an agnostic Hollywood screenwriter, and an anonymous parish lady create a collage of one woman's Midwestern childhood.

READINGS ARRANGED
BY RHETORICAL STRATEGY*

*Please note that most selections are included in more than one category.

Illustration and Example

Definition

Classification and Division

Argument and Persuasion

Fiction and Poetry

WHAT DOES IT MEAN TO THINK MULTICULTURALLY? A LETTER TO THE READER

This text asks readers to think, read, and write in a multicultural context. While Chapter 1 includes a definition of culture and provides options for addressing the question "Why read and think to cross cultures?" I want to explore with you, the instructors and students who use *Developing Connections,* my own reasons for writing this book and its predecessor, *Connections.*

I find that I—and many people—think and learn best through storytelling. So, as I thought about writing this letter, stories about my own life came to mind. My first story takes place in 1962, when, as a senior in college, I thought seriously about what I wanted to do for the rest of my life. I arrived as a freshman intending to become a high school English teacher, yet as I settled more and more fully into campus life, I fell in love with the energy and the exhaustion, the order and the chaos, the elation and the frustration that comprise academia. Now I was puzzled: How could I reach my goal of high school teaching, yet stay part of the college world I loved so much? I solved my dilemma by fantasizing that I might someday meet and marry a man who would be a college professor! It simply did not occur to me that I myself might fill that role. In 1962 I believed that only unusual, extraordinarily brilliant women—who were willing to sacrifice a "normal" family life for a very long time—could pursue the paths to graduate school, law school, medical school. Not until the late 1970s did I start to think about gender-based assumptions. Only then did I see myself as a member of the culture group "women." Only then did I recognize that I had been profoundly affected by what I perceived to be the expected roles and behaviors of that culture group. I began reading works written by and about women with the "culture group" idea in mind, and my life began to change. One of those changes led me to graduate school and thus to work I love and a world that has opened to me in ways I never believed possible.

I began reading multiculturally when my interest in gender issues led me to recognize that there were many other culture groups I had previously not recognized or, more often, simply ignored. As I sought out and read works by African American, Asian American, Latino, Jewish, Catholic, homosexual, teenaged, and elderly authors (among many others), I was forced to confront my own narrowness of thinking. I learned new ways of looking at the world in which I live, and I discovered ambiguities, questions, and paradoxes that still intrigue, delight, and, often, disturb me. Rarely do I find answers in what I read, yet somehow I feel a great hopefulness from learning about everyday heroism, survival, and growth, not simply in the dominant culture in which I grew up but also in hundreds of hidden cultures I never knew about or acknowledged.

My final story provides an example of what I mean by hidden cultures. During my childhood years, I knew in a vague sort of way that my father's family was French Canadian. He told wonderful tales, passed down from his grandparents; his characters were sharp-witted ghosts, animals with uncanny wiles, and, most of all, heroes who were "short and small, but very smart and clever." Except for these stories, I knew nothing about the French Canadian side of my family and definitely did not consider myself part of that culture group. When my father dragged my sister and me to yet another funeral of a distant friend or previously unknown relative, we rolled our eyes at each other as he spoke a few words of French to the bereaved and then, in English, offered his comforting opinion of the corpse's appearance: "looks just like himself" or "looks like she's asleep." He always stayed away from the groups of people conversing in rapid French and told us, disparagingly, that those people were "old-fashioned." He never spoke French to us, and we were not surprised when he said he only knew "two or three words," remembered from childhood visits with his grandparents.

During his final years, my father suffered from a brain disease that led him to be confused, angry, suspicious, and mean-spirited. Whenever he was in a hospital or rehab facility he ranted and raved, telling us how awful everything was. Finally, exhausted and unable to care for him at home, my mother, my sister, and I found a nursing home willing to accept him. Fearfully we anticipated his usual anger and outbursts. But on my first visit, I was astonished to hear, "They are nice people here" and "They take good care of me." My father lived for a month, and each visit found him calm, able to recognize us, at peace. At the funeral, we wondered what had brought about the change. In my heart, I will always believe the answer came from the French Canadian Sister of Mercy, who worked at the nursing home and who came to tell us that she had visited Gilbert (she gave it the French pronunciation, Jil-ber) often. "He told me such stories, and all in French, too." Astonished, we asked, "In French? But he only spoke a few words." She looked surprised, "Ah, no! He was fluent! He told me of his mother. Sometimes, he was a very naughty boy, Gilbert!" I felt at that moment as if a key piece to a puzzle suddenly fell into place. My father had found a grace-filled way to die because he had quite literally found a way home to the language of his childhood, which he had denied but never lost. Even when much of his mind was gone, he knew those words "by heart."

Since then, I've started to read and think about the French Canadians who emigrated in such large numbers to New England. As I read, I discover things I never knew about the place where I grew up and about the people who were and are part of my "hidden culture." I've begun to find collections of French Canadian narratives, and I am not at all surprised to find that their heroes are often "short and small but very smart and clever."

Judith A. Stanford

DEVELOPING CONNECTIONS

Part 1

Critical Reading and Writing

1

Critical Reading and Thinking:
An Approach to Crossing
Cultures

Every day, each of us encounters customs, actions, beliefs, or values
that seem different from our own. On a city street, in an international
airport, on nightly television news programs, we see people who dress, talk,
and act in unfamiliar ways. As the population of our country—small towns
as well as large cities—grows increasingly diverse, thinking about the ways
we respond to difference becomes increasingly important.

As a way to begin, consider your responses as you read the following
sections of anthropologist Horace Miner's essay "Body Ritual among the
Nacirema." Miner offers a look at a people he describes as obsessed with the
idea "that the human body is ugly and that its natural tendency is to debility
and disease."

BODY RITUAL AMONG THE NACIREMA
Horace Miner

The anthropologist has become so familiar with the diversity of
ways in which different peoples behave in similar situations that he is
not apt to be surprised by even the most exotic customs. In fact, if all
of the logically possible combinations of behavior have not been found
somewhere in the world, he is apt to suspect that they must be present
in some yet undescribed tribe. . . . In this light, the magical beliefs and
practices of the Nacirema present such unusual aspects that it seems

desirable to describe them as an example of the extremes to which human behavior can go. . . .

Nacirema culture is characterized by a highly developed market economy which has evolved in a rich natural habitat. While much of the people's time is devoted to economic pursuits, a large part of the fruits of these labors and a considerable portion of the day are spent in ritual activity. The focus of this activity is the human body, the appearance and health of which loom as a dominant concern in the ethos of the people. While such a concern is certainly not unusual, its ceremonial aspects and associated philosophy are unique.

The fundamental belief underlying the whole system appears to be that the human body is ugly and that its natural tendency is to debility and disease. Incarcerated in such a body, man's only hope is to avert these characteristics through the use of the powerful influences of ritual and ceremony. Every household has one or more shrines devoted to this purpose. The more powerful individuals in the society have several shrines in their houses and, in fact, the opulence of a house is often referred to in terms of the number of such ritual centers it possesses. Most houses are of wattle and daub constructions, but the shrine rooms of the more wealthy are walled with stone. Poorer families imitate the rich by applying pottery plaques to their shrine walls.

Exercise 1

As you read these paragraphs, what is your initial response? Do the Nacirema seem similar to any group of people with whom you are familiar? Is your overall reaction to the Nacirema society negative or positive, so far?

After writing your response, continue to read the following passages from Miner's article.

The focal point of the shrine is a box or chest which is built into the wall. In this chest are kept the many charms and magical potions without which no native believes he could live. These preparations are secured from a variety of specialized practitioners. The most powerful of these are the medicine men, whose assistance must be rewarded with substantial gifts. However, the medicine men do not provide the curative potions for their clients, but decide what the ingredients should be and then write them down in an ancient and secret language. This writing is understood only by the medicine men and by the herbalists who, for another gift, provide the required charm. . . .

In the hierarchy of magical practitioners, and below the medicine men in prestige, are specialists whose designation is best translated as "holy-mouth-men." The Nacirema have an almost pathological horror of and fascination with the mouth, the condition of which is believed to have a supernatural influence on all social relationships.

Were it not for the rituals of the mouth, they believe that their teeth would fall out, their gums bleed, their jaws shrink, their friends desert them, and their lovers reject them.

The daily body ritual performed by everyone includes a mouth-rite. Despite the fact that these people are so punctilious about care of the mouth, this rite involves a practice which strikes the uninitiated stranger as revolting. It was reported to me that the ritual consists of inserting a small bundle of hog hairs into the mouth, along with certain magical powders, and then moving the bundle in a highly formalized series of gestures.

Exercise 2

As you read the additional passages from Miner's essay, did your response to the Nacirema change? Do you see their practices and beliefs as entirely different from your own? Or do you see some similarities?

Could you explain the Nacirema practices, beliefs, and rituals in a way that would make them seem more familiar?

Most readers encountering Miner's essay for the first time agree with his observation that these practices "strike the uninitiated stranger as revolting." These initial responses change, however, as the reader continues reading. The essay goes on to describe such details as the twice-yearly visit to the "holy-mouth-man" who engages in "unbelievable ritual torture" by enlarging "any holes which decay may have created in the teeth" and inserting "magical materials" into these holes. It soon becomes clear that Miner has been pulling the reader's leg by describing aspects of modern American (*Nacirema* spelled backward) culture in unfamiliar ways. With his exaggerations and distorted viewpoints, he gently pokes fun at what he sees as the American obsession with health and cleanliness. Perhaps more importantly, he insists that we examine our tendency to judge different customs, actions, beliefs, and values as strange, odd, or even "revolting."

WHAT IS CULTURE?

The title of Miner's essay, "Body Ritual among the Nacirema," leads us to expect that we will be reading about a culture different from our own. To understand the responses often triggered by such an expectation, we need to know what the word *culture* means.

Culture may be defined as the ideas, customs, values, skills, and arts of a specific group of people. Most of us belong not to one culture group but to several. For instance, our age places us in the culture of childhood, youth, middle age, and so on. We may be called "baby boomers," or "Generation X," and these phrases may trigger certain images or values in the minds of those who hear or read them. In addition, we are all either male or female, and various societies have traditionally created cultural distinctions between men and women. Another group we belong to relates to the country of our birth or to the country where our ancestors were born. We may be Norwegian, Japanese, or Native American, or we may be Irish American, African American, or even more complex combinations of ethnic roots. The selections in this book all look at some aspect of the various cultures that make up the United States.

WHY READ AND THINK TO CROSS CULTURES?

Learning to read and think critically in the context of different cultures is essential, not only to read this book but also to fully appreciate many other college courses. You also need these skills to work effectively in an increasingly diverse environment and to live, not just with tolerance but with real understanding, among the many groups of people who comprise the citizens of the United States and the world.

You will study aspects of other cultures in many other courses, including history, sociology, psychology, business, science, literature, art, music, and religion. In the future you will almost certainly work with people from different cultural groups who are making significant contributions to your chosen field. Developing the patterns of thinking encouraged in this book will help you communicate—read, speak, and write—as a fully aware citizen of the multicultural world in which we live.

STRATEGIES FOR READING AND THINKING ACROSS CULTURES

Reading cross-cultural selections thoughtfully and productively calls for both skill and courage—the skill to understand and evaluate a complex idea or issue and the courage to approach each writer's work with a mind open to multiple possibilities and points of view. You need to be willing to see and acknowledge differences and at the same time look for similarities and connections. Most of all, you should avoid hasty judgments, discard standard responses, and tolerate apparent contradictions.

To help you begin developing strategies for reading and thinking across cultures, the following exercises ask you to write paragraphs exploring your responses to your own culture groups as well as to other cultural perspectives. Before you respond to the exercises, you may want to consult the boxed guidelines that review the definition of a paragraph. As you read the guidelines, use this paragraph as a model:

Americans are a rootless people. Each year one in six of us changes residences; one in four changes jobs. We see nothing troubling in these statistics. For most of us, they merely reflect the restless energy that made America great. A nation of immigrants, unsurprisingly, celebrates those willing to pick up stakes and move on: the frontiersman, the cowboy, the entrepreneur, the corporate raider.
(from "Rootlessness" by David Morris, pp. 99–102)

Guidelines: Writing a Paragraph

1. A paragraph is a group of sentences that deals with one main idea.
   (In the example, the main idea is that Americans tend not to remain attached to the comfortable and familiar.)
2. A paragraph usually has a *topic sentence* that states the main idea (most often, the first or last sentence).
   (In the example, the topic sentence is the first: "Americans are a rootless people.")
3. A paragraph usually has several sentences that support and develop the main idea.
   (Each of the sentences that follows the topic sentence provides one or more examples of American rootlessness.)
4. Each supporting sentence within a paragraph should be written so that its relationship to the main idea is clear.
   (Each sentence clearly follows the previous sentence. For instance, sentence 3 analyzes the author's perceptions of the American people's response to the statistics given in sentence 2. Sentence 4 begins with the transitional phrase "for most of us," which connects the readers' reactions to the statistics and analysis provided in sentences 2 and 3.)
5. A paragraph that is too short often fails to develop its idea sufficiently.
   (The five sentences in this paragraph clearly develop its main idea.)
6. A paragraph that is too long often combines several main ideas and becomes confusing; it should be rewritten as two or more shorter paragraphs.
7. Paragraphs vary in length, but if you have written a paragraph of fewer than four sentences or more than ten sentences, check to see if you have either omitted needed support (too short) or tried to deal with too many ideas (too long).
8. Longer pieces of writing (such as essays, newspaper articles, and books) are made up of paragraphs that relate to one another.

Exercise 3

Read the following entry from a journal written by John Coleman during a 1973–74 sabbatical leave from his position as president of Haverford College. During this year, Coleman worked at a variety of blue-collar jobs. The people with whom he worked did not know about his academic or professional background. His experiences showed him how belonging to a particular culture group affected the way others treated him.

From BLUE-COLLAR JOURNAL
John Coleman

Tuesday, March 27

One of the waitresses I find hard to take asked me at one point today, "Are you the boy who cuts the lemons?"

"I'm the man who does," I replied.

"Well, there are none cut." There wasn't a hint that she heard my point.

Dana, who has cooked here for twelve years or so, heard that exchange.

"It's no use, Jack," he said when she was gone. "If she doesn't know now, she never will." There was a trace of a smile on his face, but it was a sad look all the same.

In that moment, I learned the full thrust of those billboard ads of a few years ago that said, "BOY. Drop out of school and that's what they'll call you the rest of your life." I had read those ads before with a certain feeling of pride; education matters, they said, and that gave a lift to my field. Today I saw them saying something else. They were untrue in part; it turns out that you'll get called "boy" if you do work that others don't respect even if you have a Ph.D. It isn't education that counts, but the job in which you land. And the ads spoke too of a sad resignation about the world. They assumed that some people just won't learn respect for others, so you should adapt yourself to them. Don't try to change them. Get the right job and they won't call *you* boy any more. They'll save it for the next man.

It isn't just people like this one waitress who learn slowly, if at all. Haverford College has prided itself on being a caring, considerate community in the Quaker tradition for many long years. Yet when I came there I soon learned that the cleaning women in the dormitories were called "wombats" by all the students. No one seemed to know where the name came from or what connection, if any, it had with the dictionary definition. *The American College Dictionary* says a wombat is "any of three species of burrowing marsupials of Australia . . . somewhat resembling ground hogs." The name was just one of Haverford's unexamined ways of doing things.

It didn't take much persuasion to get the name dropped. Today there are few students who remember it at all. But I imagine the cleaning women remember it well.

Certainly I won't forget being called a boy today.

Exercise 4

After reading Coleman's journal entry, do the following:
1. Make a list of as many cultural groups as possible to which you see yourself as belonging. These cultural groups may relate to your age, your ethnic background, your religious preference, your political beliefs, your current work status.
2. After making the list, choose one of the cultural groups to which you belong and write a paragraph describing the ideas, customs, values, skills, and arts of that group that you see as positive. When you write your paragraph, refer to the guidelines on page 7.

Here is one student's approach to the preceding exercise:

List of Culture Groups

age: "twenty-something"
Italian–American
waitress
student
daughter
Catholic
Democrat (but voted for Perot)

Paragraph: BEING A WAITRESS
I never thought of waitresses as a culture group until now. But after reading John Coleman's journal entry, I can see that I and the other women I work with have things in common that relate to what we do. We all value working hard to make good money. Serving food is not easy, but it gives you a good way to make more than minimum wage. We also have all come to appreciate good relationships with customers for more reasons than tips. If you exchange a pleasant word or two with the people you wait on, the evening goes faster and you feel less tired. You also feel as if you are making the customer's meal

more enjoyable. Even better than talking with customers, I like talking with the other waitresses. At the end of the evening, after we've cleaned our stations, we all sit together and have coffee or a Coke and talk about what happened. It's something we all look forward to because we can just be ourselves and not worry about keeping that happy smile on our faces.

Exercise 5

Write a paragraph or two responding to one of the following topics:
1. Describe something you read or heard in another class that gave you a view of a cultural perspective other than your own. What new ideas or possibilities did this perspective suggest?
2. Describe an incident from a television program or a film you have seen that showed you a cultural perspective different from your own. What new ideas or possibilities did this perspective suggest?
3. Describe an event from your work that showed you a cultural perspective different from your own. What new ideas or possibilities did this perspective suggest?

2

Reading to Respond

We read for many reasons. These students' responses to the question "Why do you read?" suggest just a few possibilities.

Mostly I read to get information. Maybe I want to know how to fix something or where I can buy something for the best price. *Janet Mathis (age 23)*

"Self-help" would sum up my main reason. I feel like I can get power over some parts of my life by reading about ways to solve problems and how other people have learned to solve their problems. *Amon Wilkuski (age 33)*

I read purely to escape the troubles I see. I want a book that will entertain me and sometimes make me cry, but always end with a smile. Because there's too much trouble in life. I like to read about something that gives me a dream to hope for. *Keren Pfirschbaum (age 18)*

Mostly I read what is assigned for school or what I have to read at work. I don't have time for a lot of reading, and it's not easy for me. So mostly I read only when I have to. *Tony Vladim (age 20)*

Exercise 1

Write a few sentences describing the main reason or reasons you read. If possible, discuss your reasons with other members of the class.

THE PROCESS OF RESPONDING

Sometimes—for instance when you read a daily newspaper to learn the main events of the day—you may read quickly, scanning the information once and not returning to reread. When you read for classes or in your personal search for deeper insights into your world, you use a more complex strategy. This process includes reading to respond, reading to understand, and reading to evaluate. This chapter, and the two that follow, discuss ways of developing these three ways of reading.

When you first read any fiction or nonfiction work, one of the best strategies is to skim through quickly. Be sure to pay attention to your responses as you move quickly from point to point. Being aware of your first responses is particularly important when you read across cultures. When you encounter unfamiliar ideas, images, and values, it's easy to feel overwhelmed by new vocabulary, unexpected examples, or different values.

During a first reading, try not to block out any of your responses, whether they be negative, positive, or neutral. On the other hand, no matter how much you may agree or disagree with what you are reading, try expressing some of your reactions in the form of questions or open-ended statements. Such questions and statements should lead to discussion rather than closing it off. By working with these structures, you'll keep an honest record of your thoughts and feelings. Better yet, you'll help yourself remain alert to many different possibilities and directions.

RESPONDING BY MAKING MARGINAL NOTES

As an example of initial responses, consider the notes one student, Alyssa Clark, wrote in the margins of her book as she read this excerpt. The passage comes from "What's American about America?" an essay by Ishmael Reed, a black American novelist, poet, and editor. The original version of this selection appeared in Reed's 1983 nonfiction book, *Writin' Is Fightin'*.

From WHAT'S AMERICAN ABOUT AMERICA?
Ishmael Reed

Were all these people U.S. citizens? Tourists? New immigrants?

① An item from the *New York Times,* June 23, 1983: "At the annual Lower East Side Jewish Festival yesterday, a Chinese woman ate a pizza slice in front of Ty Thuan Duc's Vietnamese grocery store. Beside her a Spanish-speaking family patronized a cart with two signs: 'Italian Ices' and 'Kosher by Rabbi Alper.' And after the pastrami ran out, everybody ate knishes."

Where do Islamic people usually live? (Not in Detroit?)

② On the day before Memorial Day, 1983, a poet called me to describe a city he had just visited. He said that one section included mosques, built by the Islamic people who dwelled there. Attending his reading, he said, were large numbers of Hispanic people, 40,000 of whom lived in the same city. He was not talking about a fabled city located in some mysterious region of the world. The city he'd visited was Detroit.

③ A few months before, as I was visiting Texas, I heard the taped voice used to guide passengers to their connections at the Dallas Airport announcing items in both Spanish and English. This trend is likely to continue; after all, for some southwestern states like Texas, where the largest minority is now Mexican-American, Spanish was the first written language and the Spanish style lives on in the Western way of life.

should Spanish be a second language in U.S.? Why? / Why not?

Do other airports do this? Other languages?

④ Shortly after my Texas trip, I sat in a campus auditorium at the University of Wisconsin at Milwaukee as a Yale professor—whose original work on the influence of African cultures upon those of the Americas has led to his ostracism from some intellectual circles— walked up and down the aisle like an old-time Southern evangelist, dancing and drumming the top of the lectern, illustrating his points before some Afro-American intellectuals and artists who cheered and applauded his performance. The professor was "white." After his lecture, he conversed with a group of Milwaukeeans—all of whom spoke Yoruban, though only the professor had ever traveled to Africa.

Why is he ostracized for this?

Why the quotes?

⑤ One of the artists there told me that his paintings, which included African and Afro-American mythological symbols and imagery, were hanging in the local McDonald's restaurant. The next day I went to McDonald's and snapped pictures of smiling youngsters eating hamburgers below paintings that could grace the walls of any of the country's leading museums. The manager of the local McDonald's said, "I don't know what you boys are doing, but I like it," as he commissioned the local painters to exhibit in his restaurant.

Great idea!

5

What makes him think this?

⑥ Such blurring of cultural styles occurs in everyday life in the United States to a greater extent than anyone can imagine. The result is what the above-mentioned Yale professor, Robert Thompson, referred to as a cultural bouillabaisse. Yet members of the nation's present educational and cultural elect still cling to the notion that the United States belongs to some vaguely defined entity they refer to as "Western civilization," by which they mean presumably, a civilization created by people of Europe, as if Europe can even be viewed in monolithic terms. Is Beethoven's Ninth Symphony, which includes Turkish marches, a part of Western civilization? Or the late-nineteenth- and twentieth-century French paintings, whose creators were influenced by Japanese art? And what of the cubists, through whom the influence of African art changed modern painting? Or the surrealists, who were so impressed with the art of the Pacific Northwest Indians that, in their map of North America, Alaska dwarfs the lower forty-eight states in size?

Meaning?

Who does he mean?

Yes—Examples here on campus students wear clothes from other cultures

Meaning?

Yes! Because it's mostly Western.

As Alyssa read this article, she jotted in the margin any question or observation that came to mind. While most people don't stop to analyze their responses, it may be helpful to look closely not only at the content of Alyssa's notes but also at the types of comments and questions she wrote. You'll notice that many of her marginal observations fall loosely into the categories listed in the following guidelines.

Guidelines: Marginal Notes

As you make marginal notes when you read, keep in mind the following possibilities.

1. Questions that ask about people (paragraph 1)
2. Questions that ask about places (paragraph 2)
3. Questions that ask about actions (paragraphs 3, 4)
4. Questions that ask about policies, laws, or customs (paragraph 4)
5. Questions that address the writer's style, including such things as choice of example, vocabulary, sentence structure, or even unusual punctuation (paragraphs 4, 6)
6. Questions or comments that challenge or call for closer examination of the writer's observations, judgments or evaluations, or inferences (paragraphs 5, 6)
7. Comments that affirm or expand on the writer's observations, judgments or evaluations, or inferences (paragraphs 5, 6)

While there are many more ways of responding to reading, this list suggests the wide variety of ways readers react when they encounter a text. As you form your first responses, never be afraid of these early reactions. Don't worry that your ideas, feelings, or questions will be "wrong" or "silly" or "simplistic." Of course it's true that you may later change your mind and decide to revise or even reject one or more of your original reactions. You'll base these revisions on rereading, on writing in response to reading, and, perhaps, on discussions with your fellow classmates and your instructor. These changes do not indicate that your first responses were unworthy or embarrassing; they demonstrate your willingness to apply critical thinking and remain open to new possibilities.

Exercise 2

Read the following essay written by Gloria Bonilla, who left her native El Salvador in 1981 and came to the United States. This essay was originally published in 1988 in *You Can't Drown the Fire: Latin American Women Writing in Exile.*

As you read, make notes in the margins. When you finish making notes, reread the Guidelines on page 14. Then evaluate your own notes to see whether any of them fit the categories described. Next, reread the article and make notes in the margins of any new questions, observations, or comments that come to mind.

LEAVING EL SALVADOR
Gloria Bonilla

January 4, 1988

I saw my friend Alicia this afternoon while I was at the post office waiting   1
in line. We began chatting of things, projects, etc. The book, her deadline. El Salvador. Incredible! It has been almost seven years since I left. I have not been back since.
—Write something, write about your feelings—
It is so difficult to write, to think, to reflect on it. My experience. It is still painful to remember.

I fled El Salvador, leaving behind my family and friends, my undergraduate studies, a job, and all short- and long-term personal goals, in April of 1981 to escape government persecution. In an effort to remain in the United States more than three months at one time, and map out bits and pieces of an unknown future, I was required to change my tourist visa to a student visa. Because the United States recognized then, and continues to recognize today, the government of El Salvador, I have been unable to enter the United States as a refugee, nor can I realistically expect to receive political asylum.

My story does not differ very much from the stories that most   5
Salvadorans tell. I consider myself more fortunate because I did not have to cross the Mexican border and enter the United States illegally. I was also able to maintain a legal status which allows me to continue my education in the United States.

I think, like my parents, I have learned through life quite a bit. My father used to say that we never stop learning in life. He did not go to college. I remember him very much because most of what he knew he had learned on his own. My first recollections of the history of El Salvador were through my father and mother. That history was not in print.

My trip to the United States was sudden, precipitous. I, like many other Salvadorans, finally realized that El Salvador was no longer a safe place to live.

I arrived in Washington, D.C., in April of 1981. When I arrived, my good friend, John, was waiting for me at the airport, carrying a heavy coat, assuming I would have no winter clothing. I met John in

El Salvador back in the seventies when he was a Peace Corps volunteer. After he came back to the United States, he kept in touch with me, until the political conditions in El Salvador reached serious and dangerous proportions. Then he invited me to come to the United States, an invitation which I did not decline, but which I postponed until I could no longer remain in El Salvador. One day, I called John from Guatemala to let him know I was on my way.

I knew no one in Washington except John, who sheltered me until I was able to support myself. John introduced me to his friends, some of whom are my friends still. As insiders, they helped me to become familiar with the United States. I am grateful for all their help.

A lot has happened since that moment on that spring day in 1981, 10 when I arrived in the United States.

I underwent a metamorphosis. I went from a period of mutiny, in which I encapsulated myself like a larva in a cocoon, to a period of awakening and rebirth. The process was painful and difficult. But I survived. Because I left El Salvador so quickly, I hardly had the chance to reflect on what was happening. When I came to the United States, I carried with me my past, which tied me to people and a land that I had to give up.

There is no medicine to take care of heartache and homesickness—not even here in the United States where there are drugs for almost everything, mostly for pain. I believe we unconsciously or consciously develop methods to cope with those ailments. So, I made up a prescription of my own to help me stay sane and survive in my new niche. I filled my hours, my days, without respite, so I had no time to think, cry or break.

I forced myself to learn English. I took intensive English courses from 9:00 A.M. to 2:00 P.M. I worked in the afternoons. Later, I got a full-time job and I enrolled at the university, finished college and went straight for a master's degree in sociology. I did it all in five and a half years.

I did not do it alone, but with the support of friends. I had moments of despair in which I felt lost, with little or no hope. My driving force was that I had no relatives in Washington to look after me. Therefore, I could not afford to lose my most precious commodity, my mind. Some call it pride; for others it is survival instinct. I experienced both.

The United States Immigration and Naturalization Service regu- 15 lates, controls, and restricts the free access of foreigners to society and subsequently to its benefits. For example, I had a legal status that allowed me to study and remain in the United States as long as I attended school full time. On the other hand, that same status forbade me to work and compete freely for jobs that I thought I was qualified for.

I maintained that legal status as long as I went to school full time. I paid my bills as long as I worked full time. I had no choice. My constant concerns were basic: food, shelter, education, legal status.

A legal status which allows an immigrant to work is an imperative. In my case, the choice was to apply for political asylum or for permanent residence. The best bet was permanent residence.

Political asylum, in the case of Salvadorans, becomes a dead end since U.S. immigration law requires the applicant to provide evidence of a well-founded fear of persecution. A subjective condition, when you think about it. For example, the army did not need any evidence to determine that I was a "suspicious individual," and to break into my home and my parents' home in 1981. Ironically, it is the same subjective reasoning used by a U.S. immigration judge that determines the non-eligibility of a Salvadoran for political asylum. Salvadorans in exile in the United States have been required to all but present a signed affidavit from their persecutors in order to prove their well-founded fear of persecution.

I believe I had good enough reasons to be granted political asylum back in 1981 if I had applied. But a U.S. judge might have disagreed with me, since I did not have concrete evidence of my fear of persecution. Worse, I came from a country whose government is friendly to the United States.

I eliminated the political asylum option from the very beginning. Salvadorans had, back in the early 1980s, little or no chance of having a political asylum application approved; later, it became pointless, since the Reagan administration had invested so much money "democratizing" El Salvador.

I am only an example of what Salvadorans could do if given the chance. In my case, maintaining a student visa gave me access to education, something most Salvadorans have not been able to attain. That is why Salvadorans in the United States hold occupations that require little or no formal education.

I think Salvadorans have tried their best to prove their worth. Our future in the United States does not look promising. Lawmakers had an opportunity to offer better conditions to Salvadorans. The Immigration Reform and Control Act proves it. The United States had a chance to review the law and to review the Central American question, but did not. I believe Salvadorans in the United States have been sentenced without trial. When you think about it, it is not very different from the way our people are treated in El Salvador.

RESPONDING BY WRITING JOURNAL ENTRIES

Another useful way of responding to reading is to keep a reading journal. Such journals take many different forms. You may keep a journal strictly as private writing that allows you to explore your responses. Or you may keep one as a course requirement. If you write a journal as a class assignment, the instructor may give you guidelines for the number of entries per week and their length. The instructor may also suggest topics or approaches to help you determine the focus of the entries.

Whether you are keeping a journal for yourself or as a requirement, writing entries in response to your initial readings can be a helpful way of thinking about the ideas and feelings the writer expresses. Here are several examples of journal entries that students wrote following their first quick reading of Ishmael Reed's "What's American about America?" (pp. 12–13):

1. I like the way the writer, I. Reed, looks at the positive side. His example of the quote from the *New York Times* in the first paragraph, for example, shows people from five different nationalities all getting along. On the other hand, this seems too ideal to me. From what I've seen and from what you see all the time on the television news, I think a situation like this festival would be a place for fights or at least name-calling. *Frank Pagiano*

2. He [Reed] just describes all these other people who live in these places, but he doesn't talk about the regular Americans. What I don't understand is why he keeps saying "Islamic," "Hispanic," and "Vietnamese." Aren't these people American? And why does he put quotes when he says "white"? Does he think only white people are real Americans? I can't really figure out his point, which he says in the title "What's American about America?" *Lee Ann Jamross*

3. When I read about hearing the announcements in Spanish and English, my reaction was Why should the announcements be in both languages? This is the United States and English is our language. Why should we have to have another language? I know in some places the ballots and other papers like that have to be printed in Spanish, and my question is Why? *Stan O'Brien*

4. The airport description made me think of traveling in other countries. My family is military, and we've lived in Germany, Italy, and Japan. At the civilian airports in major cities, the announcements are in many different languages. And English is always one that I am glad to hear when I am traveling. That's because I don't know the language of the country if it's not English. What I noticed was that in most other countries people know more than one language, and I think this is a good idea because it gives you more possibilities of ways to communicate. I think it would be a good idea in this country if we were more aware of other languages and maybe started to learn them in the early grades instead of one or two years in high school. *Danya Mielewski*

5. "Bouillabaisse." I circled this word as one I didn't know, and I had to look it up because it seemed to me to be important to what the paragraph was saying. Well, it means "a chowder made with several kinds of fish and shellfish, vegetables, and seasoning." At first I thought, well, this is like the "melting pot" that you hear used to describe this country. But then I thought, no, because in a melting pot everything just goes together and becomes one big mass and you can't tell the different parts. But in this "bouillabaisse," which Reed says Robert Thompson calls America, you would still see all the parts (like the different kind of fish and the different vegetables). So they would still be themselves, but they would be working together to make something different, too (the chowder). So I'm wondering if America is like this. Do all the different groups stay separate in some ways but work together in others? *William Ferguson*

As you can see from these journal entries, readers respond very differently to what they read. The following list briefly evaluates and comments on each of the entries:

1. Frank Pagiano identifies a detail that he admires in the essay and explains his reasons. However, he goes on to show some reservations he feels about the accuracy of this detail.
2. In her entry, Lee Ann Jamross asks many questions about the terms Reed uses to describe groups of people. Her final questions raise points concerning definition: She wonders exactly how Reed defines *Americans.*
3. Stan O'Brien's initial response is to challenge an assumption that Reed makes. O'Brien doesn't flatly reject Reed's point about the Spanish language announcements, but the tone of his questions show that he is not entirely convinced.
4. Taking a viewpoint quite different from Stan O'Brien's, Danya Mielewski addresses the same issue: the use of more than one language within the United States. Mielewski uses personal examples as a way of exploring the ideas that were inspired by Reed's essay.
5. William Ferguson focuses on one unfamiliar word in Reed's essay. Because this word seemed central to the meaning of the paragraph in which it occurred, and because he couldn't determine the meaning of the word from the context in which it was used, Ferguson used a dictionary to help him get started. After finding the dictionary definition, he spent time pondering the implications of the comparison Robert Thompson (cited by Reed) makes between the American culture and the chowder called bouillabaisse. By looking at language closely and refusing to be discouraged or put off by a word he didn't know, Ferguson discovered an idea he considered worth pursuing.

These five entries suggest ways of writing journal entries as initial responses to reading. Notice that many of the entries focus on questions and that most of them keep open many possibilities rather than seeking one simple, easy answer. These entries also reflect the way early responses often relate to the reader's own experiences and knowledge.

Two of the sample entries (3 and 4) disagree with each other, but each asks thoughtful questions and raises important issues. The point here is that there is no one "correct" way to respond to any piece of reading. In addition, when these students returned to Reed's essay to read it for a second or third time, many of them changed or modified their initial responses. Points that seemed puzzling during the first reading became clear during the second. Issues that seemed simple revealed complications that had not been noticed before. Some students even noticed that opinions they had believed to be true were not supported by evidence in the reading. The richness in reading—and particularly in reading across cultures—lies in the diversity and the possibilities it offers.

_____

Exercise 3

Reread Gloria Bonilla's essay, "Leaving El Salvador" (p. 15), as well as the notes you made while reading it (Exercise 2, p. 14). Then choose three of those notes and develop each of them into a paragraph explaining and exploring your response.

As you plan to write, consult the guidelines for writing paragraphs (p. 7). In addition, keep in mind the following guidelines for writing journal entries in response to what you read.

_____

Guidelines: Writing Journal Entries

As you think about topics for journal entries, consider the following possibilities:

1. *Write about a person.* (Perhaps you were struck by someone in the reading or the reading reminded you of someone.)
2. *Write about a place.* (Perhaps you find interesting, troubling, or pleasing a place the author described.)
3. *Write about an action.* (Perhaps the writer explains an action you find brave, cowardly, or strange.)
4. *Write about policies, laws, or customs.* (Maybe you can compare a custom the author talks about with a custom familiar to you.)
5. *Write to explain why you disagree with a particular point the author has made.* (Be sure to give specific reasons.)

6. *Write to explain why you agree with a particular point the author has made.* (Be sure to give specific reasons.)

7. *Write to ask the author a question.* (If you could speak directly to this writer, imagine what you'd ask, and explain why.)

8. *Write a personal example that relates in some way to something you have read.* (Perhaps the reading brought back an old memory.)

9. *Write to define a word in the reading that was unfamiliar.* (Give more than just a dictionary definition; choose a word with many possible implications to explore.)

10. *Write down an intriguing phrase or sentence from the reading, and then explain why you found it interesting.*

3

Reading to Understand

After exploring your first responses to something you have read, the next step is to return to the selection and reread carefully. During the first reading, it is easy to skip over key points, miss important evidence, or be overwhelmed by the emotions the piece arouses. Second and third readings help you understand what the writer is saying and see how the author gets the message across to readers.

Writing down and talking about your first responses and then returning to the text before making firm evaluations are essential parts of critical thinking. While these steps are part of any careful, thoughtful reading, they are particularly important for reading across cultures. When we read something written from a different cultural viewpoint, it's easy to jump quickly to unwarranted conclusions or fail to see the author's point clearly.

UNDERSTANDING UNFAMILIAR WORDS

As you first read and make marginal notes, you'll almost certainly notice unfamiliar words. Readers have different responses when they encounter words they do not understand. Some become frustrated and stop reading. Others pause at every unknown word to use the dictionary. Many experienced readers, however, have learned three useful strategies: (1) to read through words they do not know if those words do not seem essential to the author's meaning; (2) to use context clues to identify the definitions of new words; and (3) after applying the other two strategies, to use the dictionary. This process saves both time and frustration.

To develop the skill of identifying meaning from context clues, consider the following guidelines:

Guidelines: Identifying Meaning from Context Clues

1. Discover definitions through examples.
   Example:

   Unfamiliar word: affluence

   Context: "In our days of *affluence* in Russia we had been accustomed to . . . embroidered linens, silver spoons and candlesticks, goblets of gold . . ."
   (from *The Promised Land* by Mary Antin, p. 63)

   Explanation: Because Antin provides the examples of the beautiful linens and the silver and gold tableware, the reader knows that *affluence* must mean great wealth and luxury.

2. Discover meaning through the author's definition.
   Example:

   Unfamiliar phrase: Western civilization

   Context: "[T]hey refer to . . . *Western civilization,* by which they mean, presumably, a civilization created by people of Europe."
   (from "What's American about America?" by Ishmael Reed, p. 12)

   Explanation: By providing the definition ("a civilization created by people of Europe"), Reed clearly identifies the concept he is challenging.

3. Discover meaning through a contrast.
   Example:

   Unfamiliar word: hostility

   Context: "Ultimately, I would grow to love him and appreciate how he dealt with becoming a single parent at the age of 56, but at first our relationship was . . . full of *hostility.*"
   (from "The Teacher Who Changed My Life" by Nicholas Gage, p. 181)

   Explanation: By providing the contrasting clue of the love and appreciation he later felt, Gage indicates that his first reaction opposed those positive emotions. So readers can easily infer that *hostile* can mean hateful and angry.

4. Discover meaning through a synonym.
   Example:

   Unfamiliar phrase: tenement district

Context: "They form a *tenement district,* or, in the newer phrase, the slums of Boston."
(from *The Promised Land* by Mary Antin, p. 63)

Explanation: The author explains what she means by *tenement district* by providing the synonym *slums,* which she believes might be more familiar to her readers than the older term her family used.

Exercise 1

Choose one of the following selections from Part 2: *The Promised Land* (p. 63); "Mothers, Sons, and the Gangs" (p. 140); "I Just Wanna Be Average" (p. 169); "Rootlessness" (p. 99); or "Bilingual Education: The Key to Basic Skills" (p. 315). Then follow this process:

1. Read the first five paragraphs of the selection you chose.
2. Highlight or write down on a separate piece of paper any unfamiliar words.
3. Try to define as many of the words as you can from the context provided.
4. Look up the dictionary definitions of those words and compare your understanding with the dictionary definitions.
5. Write a paragraph or two using as many of the words as possible in your own context.

SUMMARIZING TO UNDERSTAND THE MAIN IDEA AND SUPPORTING IDEAS

As you identify and learn the meanings of unfamiliar words, you are also reading to discover the author's main idea. Look for the author's support for the main idea. At this point, you must work to understand fully what the writer is saying. Only then can you move from your first responses to a logical and carefully thought out evaluation of the writer's ideas.

To gain a clear sense of what the author is saying, try writing a summary of the selection. When you summarize, you move from your own first responses to an objective view of the writer's ideas. In a summary you briefly restate in your own words the author's main idea or ideas. You also restate the most important supporting points. You do not put your own responses into a summary. Useful summaries usually share the qualities listed in the following guidelines:

Guidelines: Writing a Summary

1. Identify the author's main point or points.
2. Identify the most important supporting points.
3. Make clear the relationship between the main point and the supporting points.
4. Condense these points without omitting important ideas.
5. *Use your own words!* If you do include a phrase or two of the author's words, enclose them in quotation marks and give credit to the author.
6. Do not include your own observations or evaluations; focus only on the author's ideas and feelings.

Here are sample paragraphs written by three different students who had read Gloria Bonilla's "Leaving El Salvador" (p. 15). Their instructor asked them to write a summary of what they had read. As you read these paragraphs, consider which one best demonstrates the qualities listed in the guidelines for writing a summary and note your reasons for making this judgment.

A. Gloria Bonilla left El Salvador to escape government persecution, and she had to change her tourist visa to a student visa. She learned the history of El Salvador from her parents. She came to Washington, DC, in April 1981, and she stayed with her friend John who she had called from Guatemala. She was homesick, but she forced herself to study and to get a job. She had the support of friends. She had trouble with the U.S. Immigration Service, and the army broke into her home in 1981. But she could not get political asylum. She explains why many Salvadorans have not done very well. Because they don't have the education. She also thinks immigration laws are unfair and that Salvadorans have been sentenced without trial.

B. The central idea of this essay is that the author came from El Salvador to the United States to try to find a better life. But all she does is complain about the different laws and problems. She got a college education here and even a master's degree, so I don't see what she is complaining about. It seems like she wants the United States to change the immigration laws, but she doesn't say why. Also, what does she mean by "it is not very different from the way our people are treated in El Salvador"?

C. In her essay "Leaving El Salvador," Gloria Bonilla describes the reasons she left El Salvador to come to the United States. She explains the problems and conditions in her native country, but the real central point of the essay is to describe the problems she encountered after she came here, to explain what caused the problems, and to tell how she tried to solve them. Although being homesick was a difficulty at first, the main obstacles Bonilla describes did not come from inside herself. They came from the regulations and rules established by the U.S. immigration service. She gives many examples of the many issues Salvadorans must face if they want to come to this country. For example, she argues that the only reason she was able to succeed was that she was able to go to college. To go to college she had to get a student visa, "something most Salvadorans have not been able to attain" (p. 17). She ends her essay with a statement that compares the way the U.S. Immigration Service treats Salvadoran immigrants to the way the government in El Salvador treated the same people when they were citizens of that country.

Example A does not fit the definition of a summary. First, this sample does not clearly identify the central point. Also it does not differentiate between main ideas and supporting ideas. Instead, it simply plows chronologically through the essay picking up details here and there. Some of the details are important points—for example, "Gloria Bonilla left El Salvador to escape government persecution." Yet in the same sentence, and given equal emphasis, is a much less important point: "she had to change her tourist visa to a student visa." In addition, several details in the summary, such as that included in the second sentence, "She learned the history of El Salvador from her parents," are not clearly related to Bonilla's main points.

Another problem with Example A shows up in this sentence: "She had trouble with the U.S. Immigration Service, and the army broke into her home in 1981." As written, the sentence implies that the U.S. army broke into her home. Careful reading shows, however, that Bonilla cites this detail as an example of her persecution by the government in El Salvador.

Finally, several sentences take words directly from the essay without enclosing them in quotation marks or providing correct documentation. For a clear example of this problem, note the final sentence, which takes the phrase "have been sentenced without trial" from the next-to-last sentence in the essay. In addition to using the words without quotations, the writer fails to provide a proper context. Bonilla uses the image of sentencing without trial as a way of describing how she believes Salvadorans have been treated by the U.S. Immigration Service. In the summary, however, the phrase seems to mean that they have actually been sentenced by a judge with no free trial.

This summary demonstrates problems that can arise from failing to read carefully to establish a clear overview of the author's ideas. It also shows that you must read closely to understand how the author uses details, reasons, and examples to support that idea.

Example B is not really a summary; it is a response. While responding freely to a text is a useful way to begin the reading process, a different process is required for summarizing. Without summarizing—or a similar clarifying strategy—the reader never moves from initial responses to carefully considered judgments.

The writer of Example B starts off with a sentence that might well start a summary since it does suggest Bonilla's main idea. The rest of Example B, however, expresses opinions and asks questions. While it's important to react and respond to what you read throughout the reading process, it's also essential to be able to set aside those responses at some point and look objectively at what the author is saying. You cannot evaluate the author's ideas—or your own responses to those ideas—until you understand the main and supporting points clearly.

Example C provides a useful summary of "Leaving El Salvador." In the opening sentence, the student provides a context by mentioning both the author's name and the title of the essay being summarized. The student also suggests one of the author's purposes. In the second sentence, the student moves from the initial purpose to the central idea of the essay. This sentence shows that he or she understands that the first section of the essay, which discusses leaving El Salvador and arriving in the United States, serves primarily as a long introduction to the author's main point: describing "the problems she encountered after she came here, [explaining] what caused the problems, and [telling] how she tried to solve them." Notice that this student has read through the entire essay and sees how the parts of the essay fit together. Rather than writing a summary that simply moves chronologically through the essay, the student provides an overview of what happens throughout (see sentence 2) and then offers examples that develop this overview.

This student correctly uses quotation marks and documentation to identify words taken directly from Bonilla's essay and refrains from making evaluations. The act of writing the summary, then, accomplishes at least two goals: It helps the student writer understand clearly what Bonilla is saying, and it provides time to think and thus avoid the rush to unconsidered judgments.

Exercise 2

Reread the excerpt from Ishmael Reed's "What's American about America?" (p. 12). Then read the following summaries of that excerpt. Consider the criteria given on page 26 and follow the process used in the evaluations on pages 27–28. Then state which summary you believe demonstrates the clearest understanding of Reed's observations. Explain the reasons for your choice.

A. In Ishmael Reed's article about "What's American about America?" he seems to wonder about all the different kinds of people in this country. He lists a lot of examples of the different kinds of people like Italian, Islamic, and Spanish. He is saying that announcements on speakers at airports should be in Spanish, too. He also wants professors to talk about other cultures even if they're white. But maybe if a professor was white, he wouldn't be as much of an expert on another culture, so I would say that this point is a problem.

B. In his article "What's American about America?" Ishmael Reed tells about an item he read in the *New York Times* that describes a festival attended by people of many different nationalities. He also talks about a poet who talked to Hispanic people in Detroit who were Islamic. While in Texas, Reed heard an airport announcement in both Spanish and English, and when he returned he listened to a Yale professor whose original work on African cultures has led to his ostracism from some intellectual circles. This professor was a white man.

Reed also went to a McDonald's and took pictures of kids eating hamburgers. Then he talks about a cultural bouillabaisse and about Beethoven's Ninth symphony, the cubists, and the surrealists.

C. In this excerpt from his essay "What's American about America?" Ishmael Reed gives a series of examples that illustrate the question he asks in the title. This question suggests that it is very hard to give a single definition of *American*. Instead, the examples show that America is made up of many different kinds of people from many different backgrounds. Some of the groups he mentions are religious, for example, Jewish and Islamic. Other groups relate to the country where these people or their ancestors came from, for example, Chinese, African, and Hispanic. All the examples lead to the final paragraph where Reed quotes the Yale professor Robert Thompson who calls the United States "a cultural bouillabaisse" (p. 13). This comparison reinforces the main idea by showing that the American culture is like a soup, made of many different ingredients. In this kind of soup each ingredient stays separate, but it also combines in an interesting way with the other ingredients.

Exercise 3

Choose one of the following selections from Part 2: "For My Indian Daughter" (p. 136); "The African Contribution" (p. 69); "Indians in Aspic" (p. 203); "Television Insults Men, Too" (p. 249); "Give Us Jobs, Not Admiration" (p. 280). Read the selection carefully, and then write a summary. As you write, keep in mind the examples you have just read and consult the guidelines for a summary (p. 26).

READING TO UNDERSTAND INFERENCES

Writing a summary helps you understand the writer's main and supporting ideas. To understand the writer's meaning fully, however, you have to go further. You have to learn to "read between the lines" and make inferences. When you make inferences, you use hints or suggestions to understand more completely what a writer or speaker is saying. For example, if you show your uncle the hiking boots you have decided to buy, he might note that the high tops of the boot will be uncomfortable on summer hikes. While your uncle has not stated that you should reconsider your decision, you can infer that meaning from his comment. To understand his advice, you have to go beyond understanding the words he has said and recognize the implications of those words.

In a similar manner, to understand fully what you are reading, you need to go beyond recognizing the author's main points and supporting points. You need to think more deeply so that you can see ideas, feelings, and values that are not directly stated but are implied.

When you make inferences, you use clues in what you read to understand more completely what the writer is saying. For instance, consider the excerpt from Ishmael Reed's essay "What's American about America?" (p. 12). He talks about listening to a Yale professor speak on "the influence of African cultures upon those of the Americas." Nowhere in that paragraph does Reed directly state his attitude toward the professor. Nor does he say how he feels about those he describes as disapproving of the professor. Yet the words and images he chooses allow the reader to infer that Reed admires the speaker and scorns those who fail to see the worth of his work. For example, he shows us the professor "dancing and drumming the top of the lectern." These activities would be interpreted by many readers as lively, energetic and, therefore, positive actions as opposed to the negative "ostracism" the professor encounters from some "intellectual circles." We can infer that these "intellectual circles" who shun the professor are probably white. Certainly they are not black, since in the next sentence Reed tells us that the professor is cheered and applauded by "Afro-American intellectuals and artists." From these details, the reader can infer Reed's disapproval of the white intellectuals' response, his affirmation of the Afro-American intellectuals', and his admiration for the professor.

When you read to make inferences, you dig deeply to learn what the writer suggests as well as what he or she actually states. As you develop your ability to make inferences, keep in mind the following guidelines:

Guidelines: Making Inferences

1. Note the writer's choice of words. Be aware of the connotation (the emotional associations of the words) as well as the denotation (the dictionary definition of the words).

2. Notice the examples the writer chooses to describe an individual or a place or to explain a point. Consider the responses these examples evoke from readers.
3. Notice any value judgments the writer makes and consider whether these stated judgments help you understand the writer's attitude toward other topics discussed in the selection.
4. Notice any preferences or prejudices the writer states and consider how these views might relate to the topics discussed.

Exercise 4

Reread Gloria Bonilla's essay "Leaving El Salvador" (p. 15). Carefully note her choice of words as she describes her experiences in her native country and in the United States. Note also the examples she chooses to illustrate these experiences.

Then make a list of the inferences you can make about (1) Bonilla's attitude toward El Salvador and (2) Bonilla's attitude toward the United States. Does she seem to admire one country more than the other? Or does she dislike (or like) them equally? Explain your reasons.

Finally, write a brief paragraph discussing the inferences you can make about Bonilla's feelings concerning her fellow Salvadoran immigrants. Remember to go beyond what is actually stated and consider what is implied. For instance, what does she imply about the way she believes many U.S. citizens view Salvadoran immigrants?

4

Reading to Evaluate

While the process of reading is highly complex and varies widely from individual to individual, most effective critical reading moves through the two stages described in Sections 2 and 3—responding and understanding—to a third stage: evaluating.

UNDERSTANDING THE DISTINCTIONS:
RESPONSE, SUMMARY, INFERENCE, AND EVALUATION

Before developing ways of making evaluations about what you read, it is important to understand the distinctions between responding, summarizing, inferring, and evaluating.

• **Responding** When you respond, you simply write down or think about any idea, feeling, or question that comes into your mind as you read. Responses begin with first impressions and are particularly important during the early stages of the reading process.

• **Summarizing** Summarizing is a strategy for understanding exactly what a writer says. When you make a summary, you briefly restate in your own words the author's main idea or ideas and, often, the most important supporting points. Unlike a response, a summary does not include your own opinions or reactions. When you are trying to understand objectively, you put your own feelings, thoughts, and questions aside.

• **Inferring** Sometimes you need to look beyond the stated facts and ideas for hints and suggestions that tell you more about what an author is saying. When you search for inferences, you study the evidence provided by the writer's words, but you also "read between the lines." Inferring, then, leads to more complete understanding. When you make inferences, you may find that you have new responses. It is important to be honest with yourself about the difference between what you truly believe the author is implying and your own feelings about the subject.

• **Evaluating** When you evaluate, you make judgments based on careful, fair-minded thinking. To evaluate what you read (and your responses), you need to think both about what the author states and about what the author implies. You also need to think about the way you first react to those statements and implications. When you are reading selections from a wide variety of cultural backgrounds, you have to work diligently to establish intelligent, fair criteria (standards) by which to evaluate what you have read and then use those criteria to make sensible, balanced judgments that you can successfully explain.

ESTABLISHING CRITERIA FOR EVALUATING

When you make judgments about anything, you begin by establishing your criteria. For example, think about the process of buying a new pair of shoes. Before you even begin looking, you have a list of criteria in your head. These criteria are, of course, affected by many circumstances and do not remain exactly the same for every pair of shoes you buy. For instance, what if you are buying shoes to wear to work at a job that requires standing on your feet for eight hours a day? In that situation your criteria might include comfortable fit, sturdy material, cushioned innersoles, and low cost. On the other hand, what if you are buying shoes to wear as part of a wedding party? Your criteria might change to include a formal style, a certain color, comfortable fit, and low cost. Notice that while some of the criteria change to suit the specific circumstances, others (comfortable fit and low cost) remain the same.

As you develop criteria to evaluate what you read, you'll find the process similar. Some criteria will remain important to you no matter what you are reading. Other criteria may need to be established to fit the particular selection you are reading. For instance, consider the process of reading an essay written by someone from a culture very different from your own. You may find that to make a fair judgment you have to revise or even discard some of your standards. You may need to look at such writing in a new way.

As you develop criteria for evaluating what you read, keep the following guidelines in mind:

Guidelines: Developing Criteria for Evaluation

1. *Consider the author.* What do you know about the author? (In this book, the headnotes before each selection give some information about the author.) Do the author's credentials give you

confidence in his or her knowledge of the selection's topic? Do you have any reason to expect bias in the selection?

2. *Consider the audience.* For whom was the author originally writing? (In this book, the headnote often provides this information by telling you where the selection was first published.) How successful do you believe the author would have been in communicating with this audience? For instance, how well does he or she seem to know *who the readers are,* considering such things as

age	religious beliefs
sex	occupation
ethnic background	economic status
political philosophy	

How well does he or she consider *what the audience might already know?* Consider such things as

level of education
experience with the topic
prejudices about the topic

To what extent do you believe this author is successful in communicating with you and your fellow students as an audience? (Consider the aspects of audience analysis listed above.)

3. *Consider the author's purpose.* While it's usually not possible to neatly ascribe one specific reason for an author's writing any given selection, keep in mind three broad aims:

Writing to express emotions, ideas, incidents, and observations. When authors write expressively, they are usually describing something, often by telling a true story that they have experienced or observed. Their purpose is to create a word picture that will show the reader a new way of looking at life.

Writing to explain. When authors write to explain, they convey information to prove a point about the subjects they explore. To accomplish their purpose, they may analyze, evaluate, synthesize, describe a process, make a comparison, define an unfamiliar concept, or explain the causes and effects of an action or a decision, or they may use a combination of these strategies.

Writing to persuade. When authors write to persuade, they offer evidence or make emotional appeals designed to convince the reader to accept the idea they are promoting. Often they also hope to move the audience to certain actions. Identifying the

(continued)

(*continued*)

author's aim allows you to establish criteria to determine how well he or she has accomplished that aim.

4. *Consider the author's use of details, reasons, and examples.* After you have identified the author's intended audience and purpose, you need to look carefully at the way he or she works to accomplish the purpose. Depending on the audience and purpose you have identified, you may want to consider either or both of the following:

Use of evidence: Does the author provide evidence that convincingly supports the points he or she is making? For instance, if the author uses statistics, does he or she clearly explain them, and do they come from sources you believe to be reliable? If the author quotes experts, are these individuals' qualifications mentioned so that you can determine their reliability?

Use of emotional appeals: Does the author use examples, **anecdotes** (brief stories), or specific words that appeal particularly strongly to the readers' emotions? If so, do these emotional appeals help the writer communicate effectively or are they a hindrance? Many readers find that emotional appeals help a writer's efforts when they seem honest. When emotional appeals seem planned simply to play on people's emotions, many readers resent them. There are no easy tests to separate "honest" use of emotion from "dishonest" use of emotion. You'll need to establish your own ways of making such judgments.

5. *Consider the values represented.* In addition to evaluating how effectively the author communicates with the audience, you may also analyze the values suggested by what he or she has written. You might, for example, believe a selection that communicates strongly but disagree with what the author has to say.

When you make judgments about an author's values, you also think about and explore your own values, which serve as criteria for evaluating the writer. As you read selections written by writers who may share some, but not all, of your values, you'll often need to rethink both the author's views and your own. This rethinking is the most challenging, and often disturbing, part of reading critically. It is challenging because it requires you to examine what you believe to be true about the way humans should interact with each other, their institutions, and their environment. It is often disturbing because, as you read the thoughts and feelings of writers who hold different views from yours, you may find yourself questioning some of your own beliefs and ideals. The process may be less distressing if you consider that changing an opinion or a belief—or affirming in a new way an old opinion or belief—is an essential part of becoming an educated man or woman. If you pass through college entirely untouched by what you read or hear, you are wasting a great deal of time and money.

USING CRITERIA TO EVALUATE: JOURNAL ENTRIES

Once you have thought about the criteria you are using to evaluate a selection, you need to apply them. Writing journal entries is one way to do this.

An explanation of journal writing and several models of journal entries appear on pages 17–21. While these samples show students' responses rather than evaluations, the process is basically the same. You simply sit down and put on paper the evaluations that come to your mind as you are considering your criteria. In a journal entry, you are not worrying about formal aspects of writing such as organization, style, and mechanics; instead, you are using writing as a way of thinking. Here are two sample journal entries evaluating aspects of Gloria Bonilla's "Leaving El Salvador" (p. 15):

> As I read Gloria Bonilla's essay, I noticed that she uses a lot of examples to convince you that the U.S. legal system should have treated her better. As part of her point, she says that she believes she "had good enough reasons to be granted political asylum back in 1981." The thing is that when I looked at her examples closely, most of them had to do with what happened to her after she got here. Only one that I could find really talked about what happened to her in El Salvador and that was that the army broke into her house. She doesn't give enough information for me to be convinced that she should have been given political asylum, and it seems to me that leaving this out weakens the case she is making. How can she say it is as bad here as in El Salvador when she doesn't really show much of what happens there? *Cathy Lively*

> What I noticed was that Bonilla uses a lot of comparisons to describe what happened to her. For me, they really make her picture come to life. For instance, she compares herself to a "larva in a cocoon" and you can picture that she stayed in there and then emerged gradually and became the beautiful butterfly who is her current self. She is now well educated and a successful author who has had her essay published in a book. Also she talks about "heartache and homesickness" as though they were diseases and then she says she wrote her own "pre-

scription." This is a comparison that explains how and why she filled her days with work. For me, these comparisons make her story come to life, and I think she uses them effectively to tell about the changes she has lived through. These images remind me of my own feelings when I first came to this country and make me sympathetic with her experience. *Amy Ishigami*

These journal entries look at Bonilla's essay in markedly different ways, yet both make evaluations. Cathy Lively bases her evaluation on the evidence Bonilla offers to support her contention that she should have qualified for political asylum. Amy Ishigami, on the other hand, considers Bonilla's use of language as the main criterion for making a judgment. Lively's entry is somewhat critical of Bonilla's essay while Ishigami's entry indicates approval. Just as there is no single correct response to a reading selection, so also there is no single correct evaluation. Evaluations differ according to the criteria used and the way the person doing the evaluating applies those criteria.

USING CRITERIA TO EVALUATE: DISCUSSIONS

Discussing what you have read with others provides another way to explore your responses and develop evaluations. An instructor may ask you to participate in class discussions or small group discussions, or you may form your own group with other students to talk about what you have read. You may also explore ideas through conversations with friends, family members, or co-workers. The great advantage of discussion is that it provides many viewpoints. These different viewpoints help you stay open to revising your original responses and evaluations. That is, you often find yourself developing new ideas or changing old ideas in reaction to what you hear. As an example of the way discussions can help readers discover and explore ideas, consider the following transcript that records the comments and questions of several students who had read and written journal entries responding to Ishmael Reed's "What's American about America?" (p. 12).

Frank: He's just not realistic—he doesn't—I don't think—he doesn't see the bad side to all this together stuff. To me, this fiesta or festival—whatever—couldn't happen today.

Lee Ann: But that's just one example. He doesn't—well, I don't think he's saying that this happens all the time because here in—in this paragraph here (paragraph 5)—he shows about the "ostracism," as he says, of the white professor. So he does see that conflict and that's realistic, I think.

Stan: He's realistic about the so-called intellectual circle—and you can see they're white—or they're not black, anyway because of paragraph 4, about the "Afro-American intellectuals." But he's not realistic about expecting announcements to be in two languages.

Danya: Everybody keeps saying "realistic" but what exactly do you mean? Does it have to be something that really happens all the time? Does it have to be something like—what I'm wondering is—like an actual current fact everywhere to be worth reading about it? Is that what it has to be for it to be realistic? I mean it could be like the "I Have a Dream" that they play all the time on Martin Luther King's birthday. Which is something that is what you hope for but it may not be happening everywhere—or maybe it's going to happen in the future.

William: But if it's like a dream—so it isn't realistic—then what about all the examples he gives? They're supposed to be real, as far as I can see. I mean, he doesn't—there's no place where he says, "I wish this would happen."

Lee Ann: Well, maybe not a dream like future fantasy or something but like looking at the best possible case—in his opinion that is. So like maybe "idealistic" is the word instead of "realistic" or "dream."

In this short sample discussion, the participants express their own ideas and also listen carefully to what others have to say. Not only do they state opinions, but they also ask questions and indicate an openness to change. For example, they start out working with the idea of realism as a possible way to describe (and perhaps evaluate) the essay. As the discussion moves along, they try the possibility of seeing Reed's ideas as a dream. Then they consider the term *idealistic* as perhaps a better description. The discussion is by no means finished. It's easy to see that there are many different directions it could take. It's also important to note that a discussion like this need not have as its goal finding one "right answer." Groups working together do not always have to agree. In fact, rather than insisting on compromise and decision-making, the most fruitful discussions usually value the way multiple voices open fresh possibilities and raise new questions.

When you discuss what you read with others, keep the following guidelines in mind:

Guidelines: Discussing

1. Before the discussion read thoughtfully and carefully, making notes that record your questions and observations.
2. When you come to the discussion, bring notes, summaries, journal entries—anything you've written that may help ideas flow.
3. Respect your own ideas and come prepared to support them with specific references to what you have read.
4. Respect the ideas of others and listen with full attention. Do not, for example, turn off your hearing because you are planning what you are going to say next.

(continued)

(continued)

5. Remember that disagreeing with what someone else says or offering a different viewpoint is a legitimate—and useful—part of discussion.
6. Ask for clarification whenever you are not sure what a person means. (For example, if someone uses a term like *courage, duty,* or *patriotic,* you might want to ask for a definition.)
7. Encourage quiet participants to enter into the conversation— perhaps by asking them their opinion on a specific point.

Exercise 1

Read one of the following selections from Part 2: "Crossing the Border" (p. 90); "I Show a Child What Is Possible" (p. 187); "A Brother's Dreams" (p. 224); "'Real' Men and Women" (p. 252); "What's Fair in Love and War" (p. 284). As you read, make notes in the margins and then write a journal entry describing an initial response to the selection.

Reread the selection carefully, identifying the main idea and the primary supporting ideas. Then write a summary of no more than two paragraphs showing that you understand the main and supporting ideas.

Return to the selection to see if you can find inferences you might have missed. Remember to "read between the lines." Use the introductory material and the topics that follow the selection to help you think about what you are reading.

Finally, consider ways to evaluate what you have read. If possible, discuss the selection with other students. Then write a journal entry that evaluates some aspect of the selection.

As you do this exercise, keep in mind the following summary of the critical reading process. Remember that these approaches are not locked into place. For example, many readers make inferences as they first read and respond, and most readers develop new responses throughout the reading process, not just when they first encounter a text.

Summary: A Critical Reading Process

1. Initial response
2. Second response (responding to responses)
3. Clarification of meaning (summarizing, making inferences)
4. Evaluation (establishing criteria; forming judgments)

5

A Writing Process

Like reading, writing is a complex activity. People write for many reasons and in many ways. Both active reading and thoughtful writing require many strategies and stages rather than a single rigid approach. For instance, Sections 2 through 4 provide examples of paragraphs written for various purposes. These paragraphs respond to, summarize, or evaluate something that the writer has read. This chapter will look more closely at purposes for writing and at a process for writing papers for any purpose.

WRITING FOR A PURPOSE

Writing takes many different forms, but most forms share the broad purpose of conveying new information to readers. Writers use a variety of approaches that cannot be neatly labeled and are rarely used in isolation. It's helpful, however, to understand some possible ways to present new ideas or offer fresh ways of looking at familiar ideas.

Informing

When writers seek to inform, they are usually concerned mainly with providing facts: offering details, statistics, brief stories, and so on that readers did not know. An essay that is strictly informative almost always tries to be objective. That is, the writer does not offer an opinion about the information but simply provides it, usually ending with a brief summary. Readers then have the chance to draw their own conclusions or determine the implications of the new information. Articles in scientific journals are often written primarily to inform. A set of directions telling someone how to get to a previously unvisited location is one example of informative writing.

Defining

Writers who think about a complex concept may explain their ideas about that concept by developing a detailed, extended definition. Obviously, such essays go far beyond the brief information found in dictionaries. Essays that explain through defining explore complexities and apparent contradictions. They offer examples and details that help the reader see the richness of the subject being discussed.

In "Black Music in Our Hands," (p. 213), Bernice Reagon's thoughtful consideration of her own changing and developing views of black music provides an example of an essay that focuses on defining.

Analyzing

Analysis means looking at the parts of something to see how they work together to create the whole. To write an analysis, writers look closely at the aspects and qualities that make up such things as a place, a person, an idea, an emotion, a work of literature, or an object of art. Then they focus on those aspects or qualities that seem most significant and explain what they have discovered. It's particularly important to note that the purpose of analysis is not simply to see the parts of a whole. A useful analysis must also see the significance of those parts as they relate to each other.

A practical example of analysis is the process most of us go through when we are trying to fix something that isn't working. Consider, for example, a photocopier that refuses to make clean, clear copies. To solve the problem, we consult the owner's manual. After identifying the parts of the copier, we recognize that the paper tray, the power plug, and the front cover cannot be sources of the problem. However, the instructions tell us to check the glass, the chargers, and the toner box. We consider how these parts should be working together to produce a readable copy. If our analysis is successful, we learn what we need to do to get the whole process working smoothly once again.

Writers who make analyses may look at a complicated principle, a common belief, or, perhaps, a distinguished and unusual person's life. By looking at the parts that make up any of these (or many other) subjects, writers discover new and significant ideas and possibilities. They then explain these ideas and possibilities to the reader. Examples of selections that analyze include "Rootlessness" (p. 99); "Chinese Puzzle" (p. 129); "Where I Come From Is Like This" (p. 235); and "Television Insults Men, Too" (p. 249).

Synthesizing

The ability to synthesize information, ideas, and observations is essential for anyone truly interested in learning and growing. This process is particularly important for thinking, reading, and writing across cultures because when you synthesize, you look for connections, contradictions, differences, and similarities. What is more important, you look for the significance of the comparisons and contrasts you have observed. Writers who explain through synthesis work to see relationships among apparently different people, places, ideas, concepts, and emotions.

We all use the process of synthesis when we meet a new person who will be significant in our lives (co-worker, roommate, supervisor, in-law). Of course we observe differences between ourselves and these people, and we work to discover how to address those differences. But we also look for similarities and for ways to make connections with those who are important to us.

You can see an excellent example of synthesis in "The Right to Life: What Can the White Man Say to the Black Woman?" (p. 271). In this essay, Alice Walker observes mainly disjunctions and contrasts, yet explains her ideas by synthesizing the past experiences of black women with the present challenges and obstacles faced by the same women.

Evaluating

When writers evaluate, they provide readers with information about a particular person, place, idea, action, or theory. Then they go on to define or imply criteria for judging the subject they are discussing and to apply those criteria (see Section 4). Making an evaluation requires writers to form an opinion about the subject and provide evidence to convince the reader that the opinion deserves attention. An evaluation may be as straightforward as judging a book or film. For example, when you recommend a particular movie to a friend and then offer reasons why you think that movie is worth the time, money, and effort required to see it, you are making and expressing an evaluation.

A more complex, yet equally common, way of evaluating is to define a problem and then explain what you see as the significant causes or effects of that problem. An evaluation of a problem may also include suggestions for solving the problem. Selections that provide evaluations include "Rootlessness" (p. 99); "Mothers, Sons, and the Gangs" (p. 140); and "Just Walk on By: A Black Man Ponders His Power to Alter Public Space" (p. 244).

Persuading

Sometimes, as an extension of explaining, a writer will try to persuade readers. The main goal of such writers is to convince an audience to see a particular point of view as important and valid. As you read persuasive essays, notice the way the writers seek your agreement that their evaluation is worth adopting as your own. Most writers use a combination of facts and opinions that you must think about carefully. In judging the evidence the writer provides, ask yourself the following questions:

1. Has the writer provided sufficient evidence?
2. Has the writer used only evidence that clearly relates to the argument?

3. Has the writer used qualifying words like *some, most,* or *in many cases,* rather than using exaggerated generalizations that often begin with *all, every,* or *each?*
4. Has the writer successfully avoided logical fallacies?

In addition to judging a writer's use of rational appeals, when you read a persuasive essay, you should also pay close attention to the way the writer appeals to your emotions.

Emotional appeals cannot be evaluated as easily as rational appeals. Some people believe that any appeal to the emotions is somehow dishonest. Yet as humans, we base most of the decisions in our lives not only on what our minds know to be true, but also on what our emotions lead us to see as valid. Most of us agree that a balance between intellect and emotion is a good thing. Few of us would want to live in a world controlled solely by thought or solely by feelings. The problem, then, is to recognize how a writer appeals to our feelings and reject false manipulation. On the other hand, we do not want to ignore the claims of emotions we see as genuine and worthy of our response.

Examples of persuasive writing include "Give Us Jobs, Not Admiration" (p. 280); "Bilingual Education: The Key to Basic Skills" (p. 315); "Bilingual Education: Outdated and Unrealistic" (p. 319); "A Question of Language" (p. 324); and "What's Wrong with Black English?" (p. 328).

DEVELOPING A WRITING PROCESS

As you think about purposes for writing, you'll recognize that most of your own writing tasks require explanation of one kind or another. For example, professors may ask that you write a review or critique of an article, essay, book, or chapter. Such an assignment calls for evaluating and sometimes for persuading. Many essay exams require you to compare various aspects of the course's subject matter. Although the exam may not directly state that you are to give the significance you see in the similarities and differences, you are usually expected to synthesize the information you have discovered. The instructor expects you to provide a useful conclusion rather than just a list of things that are alike and things that are not alike. Another purpose for writing is to investigate causes and effects. For example, a history instructor may assign a consideration of the causes and effects of the French Revolution or the Great Depression, a writing task that can be accomplished only through analysis. Or a philosophy course that focuses on a semester-long exploration of a concept such as truth or love may require a final paper defining the complexities of the concept.

To write papers that explain requires that you develop a process for exploring ideas, gathering effective data, and formulating a clear thesis (central idea) that will serve as your focus. Whatever approach you take to explaining—informing, defining, analyzing, synthesizing, evaluating, or persuading—you need to keep in mind that your primary purpose is to convey new information or a new way of thinking to your reader. To convince readers that this new information or new way of thinking is worthy of their attention and consideration, you need to provide details, reasons, and examples that will show—not just tell—them what you want them to think about. Also remember that when you write to explain, you rarely use one approach exclusively. For instance, a paper that analyzes may also include an extended definition of an important term, and an essay that synthesizes two apparently different ideas may also evaluate the significance the writer sees in newly discovered similarities between these two ideas. And any of these papers might also try to persuade the reader to adopt a new point of view or a new approach to a problem.

A SAMPLE WRITING PROCESS

As an example of a writing process, consider Harue Hashimoto's approach to the following assignment:

> After reading Harry Dolan's "I Remember Papa," write an essay that explains a contradiction you have observed or experienced in the relationships between parents and children. As you write, keep in mind that your writing should lead the reader to see the significance you attribute to this contradiction.

(Before you continue, read "I Remember Papa" [p. 122].)

Discovering and Exploring Ideas

FREEWRITING After reading Dolan's essay several times, making notes in the margins, and participating in a discussion of the essay, Harue and her fellow students spent the final ten minutes of class doing a freewriting in response to the topic the instructor suggested.

Freewriting is a process that encourages writers to explore the far corners of their minds by writing without stopping (usually for a given period of time). This process can help writers get past a "blocked" feeling and can lead to new ideas and approaches at any stage in the writing process. For instance, as you begin a writing project, you might use freewriting to discover or narrow a topic; later, you may freewrite again to find details and examples that will successfully develop a weak or thin section of your draft.

Sometimes freewriting begins with whatever thought first pops into the writer's mind; sometimes it begins with a question, observation, or assignment. When you have a specific topic or assignment in mind, the strategy is called **focused freewriting.** Here's part of the focused freewriting Harue worked on as she began thinking about her topic.

> So—write about contradiction and do not stop—do not stop—contradict contradict mother says "do not contradict"—father just

silent—mother and father I do not understand why mother and father get along—big gap—father simple old Japanese character—shy, vague, conservative—thinks about World War II—"demons"—people who spoke English—mother modern/open-minded—liberal ideas/wanted to study in U.S. Mother wanted English for us—problem with Japanese school system—severe strict—my mother's teaching—feel like a race horse—just being trained to run a race and win for owner—mother-as-owner/but father, too? He wanted the other side—traditional culture/calligraphy/flower arrangement/tea ceremony—confusion—confusion—where am I going here?—keep writing—keep writing—confusion—confusion with English—loved English—radio—American songs—language like rhythmical music—problem with grades/not as good as my older sister—turned away from mother's dream to live through the daughters—father delights to teach Japanese culture/to encourage Japanese womanhood—still no answer—what about these two parts????

As Harue looked at the freewrite, she saw contradictions between her father's and mother's points of view. She decided to sort out and explore these differences by using another discovery strategy called **mapping.**

MAPPING   Mapping is a process similar to freewriting. Mapping encourages a visual picture of your ideas, rather than a strictly verbal exploration. There are no hard-and-fast rules for mapping, but usually you start out with a particular subject, perhaps a word or phrase, in the middle of a blank sheet of paper. From there, you try to come up with several possible subdivisions of that idea. You circle these new possibilities and attach them to the original circled idea with lines. Mapping helps you discover what you know about a topic and organize the information to write a rough draft.

Harue created two maps, one beginning with the word *father* and one beginning with *mother.* You can see these maps on the opposite page.

After looking back at her freewrite and studying her maps, Harue saw that the purpose of her paper would be to explore the differences she saw between her mother and father and the effects those differences had on her relationship with them. In addition, she was interested in the effects those differences had on the way she understood herself and her goals.

To expand further on what she had learned through freewriting and mapping, Harue used another discovery strategy called **listing.**

LISTING   Harue made two lists: one for her father and one for her mother.

Father

1. shy—values quiet contemplation
2. conservative—does not like change
3. speaks only Japanese—very patriotic

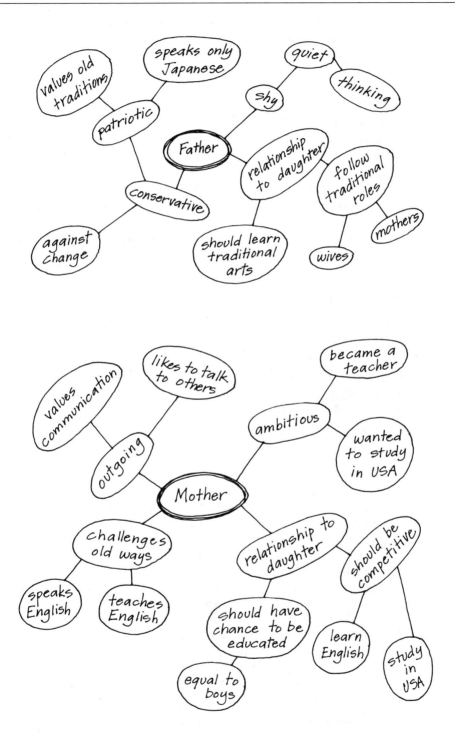

4. thinks daughters (and all girls) should learn Japanese arts—takes traditional approach
5. goal for daughters: to follow traditional roles of Japanese women—wives, mothers

Mother

1. outgoing—values communication, talking to others
2. wanted to study in the United States—ambitious
3. challenges old way of doing things—became a teacher (not a mother who stays at home)
4. speaks English as well as Japanese (teaches English)
5. thinks daughters (and all girls) should have a chance to be completely educated (same subjects as boys)
6. goals for daughters: to be competitive, to learn English perfectly (sister better than I am), to study in the United States

Making these lists allowed Harue to sort out some of her ideas, to discover new points, and to expand on thoughts she had already found through freewriting and mapping. These lists led to a third list, which pointed the way to some of the evaluations she thought she might include in the conclusion of her paper.

Evaluations (Conclusions)

1. First tried to please mother.
2. Then felt like failure in languages.
3. Next tried to please father.
4. Now trying to find my own way.

Planning and Writing a Draft

After making these lists, Harue was still not sure what her thesis would be, but she knew that her purpose would be to explain the contradictions and conflicts she saw between her mother's values and her father's values and to evaluate the effects of these conflicts on her. She decided to write a **discovery draft** (a draft that would explore the ideas she wanted to explain even though those ideas were not yet clearly focused or fully organized).

As she wrote, she knew she needed to keep her audience in mind. Of course, her instructor was part of the audience, but she would also be working in class with other students as peer editors, so she knew she had to consider them too. As she thought about audience, Harue used the following suggestions provided by her instructor:

Suggestions for Thinking about Audience

1. *Keep in mind how much your audience knows about your subject.* Consider what information, explanations, and definitions you need to

provide. You do not want to insult readers by telling them things they already know, but you do not want them to be puzzled because your subject matter or approach is entirely unfamiliar.

2. *Keep in mind your readers' values.* You determine your readers' values in many different ways. Sometimes you have talked with your readers, and they have told you that, for instance, they consider getting an education absolutely essential or that they believe practical experience is more important than theories learned in formal schooling. Sometimes you can guess at readers' values if you know such things as their political attitudes or their religious beliefs (or rebellion against religious beliefs). While it's dangerous to make generalizations without recognizing exceptions, you can guess that a group whose motto is "Save the whales" will hold considerably different values from a group who sums up their philosophy with the phrase "Save jobs not owls." If you are writing a paper on environmental issues, knowing that most of your readers belong to one or the other of these groups will certainly affect the way you approach your topic.

   If the values you are explaining are significantly different from those of your readers, consider how you can approach your discussion so that your audience will not immediately become angry or dismiss your ideas because they are looking only at the difference and not at the significance of the difference. You need to help your readers see possible connections with their own values.

3. *Keep in mind that your audience will probably not be a single, easily defined group.* Occasionally you may write for readers who all have nearly the same level of knowledge about your subject and hold similar values relating to your subject. More often, however, you'll be writing for people who, although they may be alike in some ways, are dramatically different in others. For instance, introductory writing classes often include students whose ages, ethnic background, work experience, and previous education vary widely. When you are writing to such a mixed audience, you have to decide how to meet the needs of as many readers as possible without making your paper a mishmash that fails to communicate clearly because it is trying to be all things to all people.

Harue knew that most people in her class were somewhat familiar with Japanese culture, but she decided that she needed to explain certain aspects of the Japanese education system. She also knew that some students might be uncomfortable with her discussion of her father's views toward his daughters' education and with her own agreement with some of those views. At first she thought about making a detailed explanation of her father's background, including many details about his childhood and his relationship with his parents. After thinking about this possibility, she decided not to take that approach. She made this decision for two reasons: (1) She was afraid it would lead her too far away from her original subject, and (2) she did not want her paper to sound like an apology.

Here is Harue's first draft:

MY FRUSTRATION

I do not understand why my mother and father get along with each other because certainly there is big gap between them. My father is a simple old Japanese character, shy, vague and conservative. Because of a long period of isolation from the rest of the world, Japanese have joined together to protect the original race. That is why Japanese think that group harmony is very much more important than the individual opinions, and they are concerned about what people think about them. My father, especially, experienced World War II, and at that time he thought the people who spoke English were demons.

On the other hand, my mother is more open-minded. She has been interested in English since she was a university student. Once she worked at a foreign embassy as an interpreter. In addition, when she was a student, she had a chance to study abroad, but her parents, who are also old type Japanese, opposed it. My mother gave up this chance, but she became an English teacher and still now she teaches junior high school students. She can speak her opinion openly and had very liberal ideas.

My mother began to teach me English when I was in the fourth grade. I was filled with the delight of knowing a language totally different from Japanese. English allowed me to have a bright, new world. I was very happy to share the same thing with my mother. I was excited to learn some English letters and words which were like mathematical signs to me. My mother always listened to the English radio station. I still remember that the sound of English speaking was a kind of rhythmical music to me. When I entered junior high school, I really began to study English. I did very good unexpectedly. So I was so awfully delighted with it. My friends who were around me took it for granted because I was the daughter of an English teacher. In addition, even my mother expected me not to disgrace her occupation. The only thing I had to take care of was to keep good grades in English. It invaded the relationship between my mother and me. English was then becoming a burden for me, because I thought that English alone was the glue to connect between us.

The Japanese educational system is very severe, strict, and competitive, because the academic background decides the way people are valued in society. That is why Japanese parents hope their children will enter a prestigious university. My mother was no exception. Without thinking of their children's feelings, adults compare their children as either better or inferior to others. I studied so as not to disappoint my mother's expectation and to be superior to others in this vehement competition. I was like a racing horse. I lost myself because I was driven by my purpose, but I still did not have any security. My mother began to seem not like a mother to me but like a Japanese woman with an American mask on her face. I now began to hate English.

My older sister has been so smart that she can speak English without   5 difficulty. I thought that my mother loved her more because she was the daughter my mother expected. Before I was aware, my English grades went down. I was very lonely, and in my loneliness, I turned to my father's way of thinking. It is his belief that daughters be educated to the old ways. Thinking about his view, I tried to adopt Japanese traditional cultures such as calligraphy, flower arrangement, and doing tea ceremonies instead of learning English. Through practicing those things, I recognized the Japanese spirit. This isolated island, my homeland, had created such a sensitive race and elegant and refined culture. My father was very delighted to teach me about it.

I can see now that the big gap between my mother and father is that of new ideas versus the old ones. I cannot argue which is better except that there is a large frustration in trying to reconcile them. Right now, as a Japanese woman, I see conflicts because I value my home culture, including the isolation from others, yet I also see how much modern Japan has learned from other cultures all over the world. For instance, although my father still remembers World War II and thinks of the United States as an enemy, my mother points out that behind today's Japanese prosperity, there has been American relief. Also, here I am in America where my mother often dreamed to go for study. Although I came with some reluctance, I think again that this country is great. It provides me with relief from the frustration I felt in Japan of having to choose between my mother's view and my father's view. From the time I was a young girl, I wanted only to please one parent or to please the other. Now, in this country, I see young people who do what they want to do. Now I understand real liberty means not following someone else's ways. Here I can become educated but also value my traditions. I don't have to be my mother or my father. This is my life and I am me.

Revising

After Harue finished writing her discovery draft, she put it away for several days. When she read it again, she immediately noticed several points of concern. To help in the revision process, she jotted down the following questions and observations to use as she worked with peer editors in class workshop sessions. She also used these revision notes when she visited the campus writing center for tutoring and when she consulted with her professor during office hours.

Revision Notes

1. What is my central idea? Should I focus on contradictions between the Japanese education system and the American education system and way of life?
   On the contradiction between my mother's and father's values?
   On the contradiction between what my mother wants for me and what I want for myself?
2. Do all the paragraphs relate to my general subject of contradiction? (Example: Does paragraph 5 get off topic by talking about my sister?)
3. I talk more about my mother and her ideas than about my father and his ideas, but the aim of the paper is to compare them and the influence of them in my life. Should I talk about both the same amount?
4. Does my conclusion say enough? Does it follow from the stories and examples I have given in the paper?
5. I have the same ideas in different places. Do I repeat too much?
6. Is it all right that I use *I* in this paper? In my English classes before I was told not to, but the essay we read in the textbook ("I Remember Papa" [p. 122]) did use *I.*
7. Do I use *is* and *was* too much? I did this on my last paper. How can I change these words?
8. Do I use apostrophes and commas right? I have problems with this.
9. Do I change the tense of the verbs when this is not necessary?

Harue's revision notes fall into three categories. Her first five questions address **global** issues. These questions look at the content and meaning of her essay. When writers revise, they notice many aspects of their writing. Most experienced writers try to focus on the larger, global issues before they move to issues of **style** (which questions 6 and 7 address) or issues of **grammar** and **mechanics** (which questions 8 and 9 address). As you revise your own work, you may want to consider the following checklist, which suggests global issues as well as issues of style, grammar, and mechanics:

Guidelines: A Revision Checklist

GLOBAL ISSUES

1. Have you focused on a subject that is specific enough to allow full treatment in a paper of the length you've been asked to write?
2. Do you have a clear understanding of the purpose of your paper? Do you communicate the purpose of your paper to your

---

readers? (You can do this through a **thesis statement**—a sentence or two that not only gives your subject but also tells what you intend to say about that subject.)

3. Have you organized the ideas, information, and descriptions you are presenting so that they make sense to your audience?

4. Does each paragraph deal with one main idea, and does each paragraph logically follow the paragraph before it?

5. Does every paragraph offer sufficient information (details, examples, reasons) to support the idea it expresses?

6. Do all the paragraphs relate clearly to the purpose of your paper?

7. Have you analyzed and evaluated your audience, considering their abilities, beliefs, values, opinions, knowledge, and interest? Have you written with your audience analysis in mind?

8. Have you provided an opening paragraph that catches the interest of your audience and makes them want to read further?

9. Have you written a concluding paragraph that provides an original analysis, evaluation, solution, option, or insight? (A strong conclusion usually does more than simply summarize what you've already said.)

10. Does every paragraph in the paper lead logically to the conclusion?

ISSUES OF STYLE

1. Have you used a variety of sentence structures to avoid sounding dull and monotonous?

2. Have you chosen words carefully, considering both **denotation** (the dictionary meaning) and **connotation** (the emotional overtones readers attach to words)?

3. Have you avoided **repetition** (unless, of course, the repetition is used for emphasis)?

4. Have you avoided **passive voice** (sentences in which the subject is acted upon rather than acting)?
     Example: Passive voice The map was read by the visitor.
     Active voice The visitor read the map.

5. Have you avoided using long, ornate words when a shorter, more concise word will convey your meaning just as accurately?

6. Have you avoided using unnecessary words (for example, saying "due to the fact that" when you could just as easily say "because")?

(continued)

(continued)

ISSUES OF GRAMMAR AND MECHANICS

1. Does each sentence express a complete thought?
2. Have you avoided joining two complete thoughts with no mark of punctuation or with only a comma?
3. Do your **modifiers** (descriptive words or phrases) relate clearly to the word or words they are intended to describe?
4. Do all subjects and verbs agree?
5. Does every pronoun have a clear **antecedent** (a noun to which it refers)?
6. Do all pronouns agree with their antecedents?
7. Is the **tense** (time reference) of verbs consistent throughout the paper except when you intend to indicate a change in time?
8. Are commas, semicolons, and other punctuation marks used correctly?
9. Are possessives formed correctly, using apostrophes with nouns (the girl's book; two girls' books) but not with personal pronouns (the book is hers; its cover is torn)?
10. Are all words spelled correctly?

After Harue talked with other students, with her tutor, and with her instructor, she realized that she did need a clearer focus. Her paper definitely had a purpose—to explain the contrasts she saw between her mother's values and her father's values—but her introduction didn't make clear why Harue saw these conflicting values as important. She realized that although her mother and father were essential to the idea she was explaining, it was her own conflict that was really the subject of the essay. She tried writing a list of several possible thesis statements and finally settled on this one:

> From the time of my earliest memory, I've always tried to understand why I am a person who is determined to go forward yet who always feels drawn back toward the past. Recently, as I was thinking about this question, I realized that the conflict I feel within myself is reflected in my mother and father and the values they hold.

As Harue considered how she would use this idea to focus her paper, she at first thought she would take out references to her sister and to the Japanese education system because they didn't seem to be clearly related to her own conflict. After trying this approach, she realized that she would lose parts of her paper she really liked and that she knew were important to the significance she saw in parents' differences. She then decided not to drop the story of her sister and the evaluation of the Japanese education system. Instead, she would provide transitions that would connect these points more clearly with her central idea.

Harue agreed with her readers that there was no problem with her discussing her mother more than her father because, as her revised conclusion notes, her mother's values are the ones that motivated her most strongly, as well as the ones she most needed to rebel against.

In addition to making the large revisions outlined here, Harue also worked on correcting punctuation and on using more active verbs rather than relying so heavily on forms of the verb *to be.*

After writing several drafts, Harue wrote the following final copy of her paper.

MY FRUSTRATION

From the time of my earliest memory, I've always tried to understand why I am a person who is determined to go forward yet who always feels drawn back toward the past. Recently, as I was thinking about this question, I realized that the conflict I feel within myself reflects the values my mother and father hold. I do not understand why my mother and father get along with each other because certainly a big gap exists between them, which can be represented by the way each one thinks about the English language.

My father is a simple, old Japanese character, shy, vague, and conservative. Like many other Japanese people, he thinks that group harmony is very much more important than individual opinions, and he worries about what other people think about him. He thinks that preserving the old ways is best, and he doesn't try to see things in a new way. For example, he and many of his friends experienced World War II, and at that time they thought the people who spoke English were demons; my father still does not speak English and does not like to hear any of his family speak English.

On the other hand, my mother thinks with a more open mind. She has been interested in English since she was a university student. Once she worked at a foreign embassy as an interpreter. In addition, during her student days, she had a chance to study in the United States, but her parents, who are also old type Japanese, opposed it. To please her parents, my mother gave up this chance, but she became an English teacher, and now she teaches junior high school students. She speaks her opinion openly and has very liberal ideas.

From my early years, I knew my father's beliefs, but my mother was the one who took care of me most of the time. In one way, at least, I was like my father from the beginning: I really cared what other people thought of me. I wanted my mother to think well of me; I wanted to please her. She began to teach me English when I was in the fourth grade, and I was filled with the delight of knowing a language totally different from Japanese. English allowed me to have a bright, new world and to develop an interest I was very happy to share with my mother. I was excited to learn some English letters and words, which were like mathematical signs to me.

During those years, I remember my father often leaving the house while my mother listened to the English radio station. I still can picture myself listening with her. To me the sound of English speaking was a kind of rhythmical music. When I entered junior high school, I really began to study English. Although my mother never said anything directly, I could tell from some hints that she expected me not to disgrace her profession. I started my English class with some dread, but to my delight I did very well with it. As I continued to study, however, I found I lost the pleasure of hearing enjoyable music in the English language. The only thing I had to take care of was to keep good grades. This pressure for high marks invaded the relationship between my mother and me. English was then becoming a burden for me, because I thought that English alone was the glue to connect us.

My mother realized that the Japanese educational system is very severe, strict, and competitive, and she knew that the academic back-ground decides the way people are valued in society. That is why, like other modern Japanese parents, she hoped her children would enter a prestigious university. Without thinking of their children's feelings, my mother and her friends and colleagues compared their children as either better or inferior to others. I studied so as not to disappoint my mother's expectation and to be superior to others in this vehement competition. I was like a racing horse. I lost myself, and my own pleasure in English, because I was driven by my purpose, but I still did not have any security. My mother began to seem not like a mother to me but like a Japanese woman with an American mask on her face. I now began to hate English.

To make things worse, my mother began talking to me more and more about my older sister who was so smart that she learned to speak English without difficulty. As I heard my mother make more and more of these comparisons, I thought that she loved my sister more because she was the daughter my mother expected. Before I was aware, my English grades went down and my mother was very unhappy with me. She did not scold me, but no longer did we share the harmonies of the American radio programs.

One day when she turned on the radio, I was feeling very lonely. In my loneliness, I followed my father out the door as he left to take a walk. For the first time, I listened to him talk about his thoughts about English language. He explained that for a long time Japan was isolated from other countries and that we had to depend on ourselves. Even now, we had to preserve our culture. I saw myself as that isolated island, and I turned to my father's way of thinking. It is his belief that daughters be educated to the old ways so that when they are wives and mothers they may carry on our customs. Thinking about his view, I tried to adopt Japanese traditional cultures such as calligraphy, flower arrangement, and tea ceremonies instead of studying English. Through practicing those things, I recognized the Japanese spirit. I saw that this isolated island, my homeland, had created such a sensitive race and an elegant and refined culture. My father was very delighted to teach me about it.

Now I had my father's approval, but I was still not happy. I saw that I was giving up one important part of myself—studying English—just because I was angry at the pressure my mother put on me. When I told my father I was going to study English again, I could see that he was sad. But I let him know that I was not going to forget all the Japanese culture I had learned. He said he did not see how that was possible, but still when my mother urged me to accept the chance to study in the United States, he did not try to keep me behind.

I can see now that the big gap between my mother and father is that of new ideas versus the old ones. My frustration came from trying always to think which was best. Right now, as a Japanese woman, I see conflicts because I value my home culture, including the isolation from others, yet I also see how much modern Japan has learned from other cultures all over the world. For instance, although my father still remembers World War II and thinks of the United States as an enemy, my mother points out that behind today's Japanese prosperity, there has been American relief. Also, here I am in America where my mother often dreamed to go for study. Although I came with some reluctance, I think that this country is great. Here I find relief from the frustration I felt in Japan of having to choose between my mother's view and my father's view. From the time I was a young girl, I wanted only to please one parent or to please the other. Now, in the United States, I see young people who do what they want to do. Now I understand real liberty means not following someone else's ways. Here I can become educated and study English language but also value my traditions. I don't have to be my mother or my father. This is my life and I am me.

Guidelines: Suggestions for a Writing Process

1. As you are prewriting, keep in mind the many purposes for writing: informing, defining, analyzing, synthesizing, evaluating, and persuading.
2. As you explore your ideas, use different discovery strategies such as freewriting, mapping, and listening.

(continued)

(continued)

3. As you think about your subject and plan your draft, consider your audience's knowledge, interests, concerns, and values.
4. As you write the opening paragraph, remember that your audience needs to understand your purpose. Readers need to know the subject of your essay as well as what you are going to say about that subject. A standard way to convey this information is in a thesis statement.
5. As you develop your ideas, remember that your purpose is to inform readers of a new idea or a new way of looking at the world. To accomplish this purpose, you'll need to provide plenty of specific details, reasons, and examples. You want to show your readers what you are talking about rather than overwhelming and perhaps confusing them with unsupported generalizations.
6. As you develop your ideas, remember that your audience needs to see clearly how you have organized your thoughts. Readers also need to understand the connections between your thoughts.
7. As you write your conclusion, remember that it should follow logically from the information you have given your reader in the rest of the essay. Remember, too, that the conclusion should do more than summarize. It should provide an original analysis, evaluation, solution, option, or insight.
8. As you consider what you have written, remember the three approaches to revision: global, stylistic, and mechanical-grammatical. Use each approach as it is needed.

Part 2

Anthology

6
Arrivals, Roots, and Memories

Previews: ARRIVALS, ROOTS, AND MEMORIES

Education was free. That subject my father had written about repeatedly, as comprising his chief hope for us children, the essence of American opportunity, the treasure that no thief could touch, not even misfortune or poverty. It was the one thing that he was able to promise us when he sent for us; surer, safer than bread or shelter.

From: *The Promised Land,* MARY ANTIN

I knew that Africa, despite its many and serious problems, despite the Western tendency to stereotype it, remained a place of immense natural and cultural beauty, and that its diverse, proud, brave, resilient, and beautiful peoples are descended from some of the oldest civilizations on earth, which have made valuable contributions to literature, art, music, dance, science, religion, and other fields of human endeavor.

From: *The African Contribution,* MARK MATHABANE

I was here for two months before I started working, and then my uncle got me a job, first in the celery fields, picking celery, washing it, packing it, and later picking prunes. Then, all of a sudden, one day the Immigration showed up, and I ran and I hid in a river that was next to the orchard. The man saw me and he questioned me, and he saw I didn't have any papers.

From: *Crossing the Border,* MIGUEL TORRES

Americans are a rootless people. Each year one in six of us changes residences; one in four changes jobs. We see nothing troubling in these statistics. For most of us, they merely reflect the restless energy that made America great.

From: *Rootlessness,* DAVID MORRIS

MARY ANTIN

The Promised Land

Born to an affluent Russian Jewish family in 1881, Mary Antin saw her family lose their wealth and security to the growing oppression of czarist Russia. This selection shows Antin's optimistic view of the immigrant experience. Neither the journey in steerage nor the difficult living circumstances in her family's crowded Boston apartment dampen her hope for a new and better life. In her 1912 book The Promised Land, *from which this excerpt is taken, Antin describes her family's move from the Russian ghetto to the "New World." She explains her immigration to the United States as an emergence into a new life, "I was born. I have lived. I have been made over."*

Antin was thirteen years old when she boarded the steamer that took her from a restrictive, fear-ridden life in Russia to new possibilities, particularly for education, in the United States. As you read this selection, keep in mind Antin's age when she first arrived, as well as the circumstances of this country in 1912 when, as an adult, she published her highly successful book. At that time, serious doubts were being raised about unlimited immigration policies. The Dillingham Commission to Congress argued in its 1911 report that people entering the United States from eastern and southern Europe constituted a dangerous threat to the country's stability, unlike their earlier predecessors from northern and western European countries. Conservatives pointed to immigrant slums as the basis for social problems such as drug use, organized crime, and joblessness. Into this dismal, fear-ridden atmosphere came Antin's reassuring book, answering with the story of her own optimistic, hardworking, and ultimately successful family the early twentieth-century challenges to the vision of the American Dream.

Pre-Reading and Journal-Writing Suggestions

1. Think back to your earliest memories when life was still full of mystery and magnificence. Describe from this childhood vantage point one specific change and your response to that change. This change should be one that was exciting and positive for you. Include as many details as you can to bring this experience to life for your readers (suggestions: moving to a new neighborhood, taking a trip to a new place, getting a new possession, or being given a new privilege).
2. Describe and explain the significance of a place that may appear ordinary to others but is special to you.

Anybody who knows Boston knows that the West and North Ends   *1*
are the wrong ends of that city. They form the tenement district, or, in the

newer phrase, the slums of Boston. Anybody who is acquainted with the slums of any American metropolis knows that that is the quarter where poor immigrants foregather, to live, for the most part, as unkempt, half-washed, toiling, unaspiring foreigners; pitiful in the eyes of social missionaries, the despair of boards of health, the hope of ward politicians, the touchstone of American democracy. The well-versed metropolitan knows the slums as a sort of house of detention for poor aliens, where they live on probation till they can show a certificate of good citizenship.

He may know all this and yet not guess how Wall Street, in the West End, appears in the eyes of a little immigrant from Polotzk. What would the sophisticated sight-seer say about Union Place, off Wall Street, where my new home waited for me? He would say that it is no place at all, but a short box of an alley. Two rows of three-story tenements are its sides, a stingy strip of sky is its lid, a littered pavement is the floor, and a narrow mouth its exit.

But I saw a very different picture on my introduction to Union Place. I saw two imposing rows of brick buildings, loftier than any dwelling I had ever lived in. Brick was even on the ground for me to tread on, instead of common earth or boards. Many friendly windows stood open, filled with uncovered heads of women and children. I thought the people were interested in us, which was very neighborly. I looked up to the topmost row of windows, and my eyes were filled with the May blue of an American sky!

In our days of affluence in Russia we had been accustomed to upholstered parlors, embroidered linen, silver spoons and candlesticks, goblets of gold, kitchen shelves shining with copper and brass. We had featherbeds heaped halfway to the ceiling; we had clothes presses dusky with velvet and silk and fine woollen. The three small rooms into which my father now ushered us, up one flight of stairs, contained only the necessary beds, with lean mattresses; a few wooden chairs; a table or two; a mysterious iron structure, which later turned out to be a stove; a couple of unornamental kerosene lamps; and a scanty array of cooking-utensils and crockery. And yet we were all impressed with our new home and its furniture. It was not only because we had just passed through our seven lean years, cooking in earthen vessels, eating black bread on holidays and wearing cotton; it was chiefly because these wooden chairs and tin pans were American chairs and pans that they shone glorious in our eyes. And if there was anything lacking for comfort or decoration we expected it to be presently supplied—at least, we children did. Perhaps my mother alone, of us newcomers, appreciated the shabbiness of the little apartment, and realized that for her there was as yet no laying down of the burden of poverty.

Our initiation into American ways began with the first step on the new soil. My father found occasion to instruct or correct us even on the way from the pier to Wall Street, which journey we made crowded together in a rickety cab. He told us not to lean out of the windows, not to point, and explained the word "greenhorn." We did not want to be "greenhorns," and gave the strictest attention to my father's instructions. I do not know

when my parents found opportunity to review together the history of Polotzk in the three years past, for we children had no patience with the
subject; my mother's narrative was constantly interrupted by irrelevant
questions, interjections, and explanations.

The first meal was an object lesson of much variety. My father produced several kinds of food, ready to eat, without any cooking, from little
tin cans that had printing all over them. He attempted to introduce us to a
queer, slippery kind of fruit, which he called "banana," but had to give it up
for the time being. After the meal, he had better luck with a curious piece
of furniture on runners, which he called "rocking-chair." There were five
of us newcomers, and we found five different ways of getting into the
American machine of perpetual motion, and as many ways of getting out of
it. One born and bred to the use of a rocking-chair cannot imagine how
ludicrous people can make themselves when attempting to use it for the first
time. We laughed immoderately over our various experiments with the
novelty, which was a wholesome way of letting off steam after the unusual
excitement of the day.

In our flat we did not think of such a thing as storing the coal in the
bathtub. There was no bathtub. So in the evening of the first day my father
conducted us to the public baths. As we moved along in a little procession,
I was delighted with the illumination of the streets. So many lamps, and
they burned until morning, my father said, and so people did not need to
carry lanterns. In America, then, everything was free, as we had heard in
Russia. Light was free; the streets were as bright as a synagogue on a holy
day. Music was free; we had been serenaded, to our gaping delight, by a
brass band of many pieces, soon after our installation on Union Place.

Education was free. That subject my father had written about repeatedly, as comprising his chief hope for us children, the essence of American
opportunity, the treasure that no thief could touch, not even misfortune or
poverty. It was the one thing that he was able to promise us when he sent
for us; surer, safer than bread or shelter. On our second day I was thrilled
with the realization of what this freedom of education meant. A little girl
from across the alley came and offered to conduct us to school. My father
was out, but we five between us had a few words of English by this time.
We knew the word school. We understood. This child, who had never seen
us till yesterday, who could not pronounce our names, who was not much
better dressed than we, was able to offer us the freedom of the schools of
Boston! No application made, no questions asked, no examinations, rulings,
exclusions; no machinations, no fees. The doors stood open for every one
of us. The smallest child could show us the way.

This incident impressed me more than anything I had heard in advance
of the freedom of education in America. It was a concrete proof—almost
the thing itself. One had to experience it to understand it.

It was a great disappointment to be told by my father that we were not   *10*
to enter upon our school career at once. It was too near the end of the term,

he said, and we were going to move to Crescent Beach in a week or so. We had to wait until the opening of the schools in September. What a loss of precious time—from May till September?

Not that the time was really lost. Even the interval on Union Place was crowded with lessons and experiences. We had to visit the stores and be dressed from head to foot in American clothing; we had to learn the mysteries of the iron stove, the washboard, and the speaking-tube; we had to learn to trade with the fruit peddler through the window, and not to be afraid of the policeman; and, above all, we had to learn English.

The kind people who assisted us in these important matters form a group by themselves in the gallery of my friends. If I had never seen them from those early days till now, I should still have remembered them with gratitude. When I enumerate the long list of my American teachers, I must begin with those who came to us on Wall Street and taught us our first steps. To my mother, in her perplexity over the cookstove, the woman who showed her how to make the fire was an angel of deliverance. A fairy godmother to us children was she who led us to a wonderful country called "uptown," where, in a dazzlingly beautiful palace called a "department store," we exchanged our hateful homemade European costumes, which pointed us out as "greenhorns" to the children on the street, for real American machine-made garments, and issued forth glorified in each other's eyes.

With our despised immigrant clothing we shed also our impossible Hebrew names. A committee of our friends, several years ahead of us in American experience, put their heads together and concocted American names for us all. Those of our real names that had no pleasing American equivalents they ruthlessly discarded, content if they retained the initials. My mother, possessing a name that was not easily translatable, was punished with the undignified nickname of Annie. Fetchke, Joseph, and Deborah issued as Frieda, Joseph, and Dora, respectively. As for poor me, I was simply cheated. The name they gave me was hardly new. My Hebrew name being Maryashe in full, Mashke for short, Russianized into Marya (*Mar-ya*), my friends said that it would hold good in English as *Mary:* which was very disappointing, as I longed to possess a strange-sounding American name like the others.

I am forgetting the consolation I had, in this matter of names, from the use of my surname, which I have had no occasion to mention until now. I found on my arrival that my father was "Mr. Antin" on the slightest provocation, and not, as in Polotzk, on state occasions alone. And so I was "Mary Antin," and I felt very important to answer to such a dignified title. It was just like America that even plain people should wear their surnames on week days.

As a family we were so diligent under instruction, so adaptable, and so *15* clever in hiding our deficiencies, that when we made the journey to Crescent Beach, in the wake of our small wagon-load of household goods, my father had very little occasion to admonish us on the way, and I am sure he was not ashamed of us. So much we had achieved toward our American-ization during the two weeks since our landing.

_____

Suggestions for Writing and Discussion

1. In one sentence, how would you describe Antin's experience in this new country?
2. This selection contains several words that may be unfamiliar. Using strat-egies suggested in the Guidelines on page 24, give your definition of each italicized word.
   A. "They form a *tenement district,* or, in the newer phrase, the slums of Boston."
   B. "Anybody who is acquainted with the slums of an American *metrop-olis* knows that this is the quarter where poor immigrants *foregather,* to live. . . ."
   C. "The well-versed *metropolitan* knows the slums as a sort of house of detention for poor *aliens,* where they live on *probation* till they can show a certificate of good citizenship."
   D. "In our days of *affluence* in Russia we had been accustomed to *uphol-stered* parlors, embroidered linens, silver spoons and candlesticks, gob-lets of gold. . . ."
   E. ". . . We children had no patience with the subject; my mother's narrative was constantly interrupted by *irrelevant* questions, *interjec-tions,* and explanations."
   F. "To my mother, in her *perplexity* over the cookstove, the woman who showed her how to make the fire was an angel of deliverance."
   G. "I found on my arrival that my father was 'Mr. Antin' on the slightest *provocation,* and not, as in Polotzk, on state occasions alone."
   H. "As a family we were so *diligent* under instruction, so *adaptable,* and so clever in hiding our *deficiencies.* . . ."
3. If, as a child, you had had to wait a summer in order to go to school, would you have regarded the delay as "a loss of precious time"? What is the author's attitude toward education? Why do she and her family con-sider education a valued gift, a privilege? To what extent do you share her views? How does your own view of education contrast with hers?
4. Antin writes that in the United States even "light was free." List, as quickly as you can, all the things in your daily life that are "free." As far as you know are these things "free" in other countries? Can you think of things that are free in other countries that are not free here?
5. Antin writes that her new Americanized name gives her a "dignified title." Why does this matter to her? Why is it so important that she and her family discard their original names? Have you ever changed your name in any way? Why did you make the change and how did you feel about it? If you have never changed your name, would you consider doing so? Explain.

6. Compare the values of the Antin family with those of modern American families as portrayed on television or in films. What similarities do you see? Differences? As you write your response, imagine that your readers are members of a historical society that is publishing a newsletter focusing on changing family values.

Suggestions for Extended Thinking and Writing

1. Compare the way you saw something as a child to the way you see it today. What do the similarities and differences you see tell you about the ways you have stayed the same and the ways you have changed?
2. Write an essay describing the steps necessary to begin something new. Base this essay on your own experience with a new project. Where did you start? What obstacles did you face? Where did you find support? What did you have to learn? What did you have to change?
3. Interview someone in your family or someone you know who has experienced a major trip or move. (The move does not have to be to another country; it could be to another state or town or perhaps to a new job or a new school.) Try to uncover the major changes the person encountered and what impact the move had on him or her.

MARK MATHABANE

The African Contribution

Born in South Africa in 1960, Mark Mathabane grew up under the harsh strictures of the apartheid system. The term apartheid *was first used in 1947 to describe the white South African government's policy of separating the country into two groups: black and white. Under apartheid, black Africans were forced to live in the least desirable areas of the cities and countryside. They had separate schools, restaurants, buses, and toilets. In addition, they were forced to carry passbooks so that the government—particularly the police force—could keep track of their location. Under apartheid, thousands of the government's opponents were jailed and tortured. Only in the past few years has apartheid in South Africa been successfully challenged, and the resistance to change is still violent and strong.*

Mathabane's first book, Kaffir Boy *(1989), explains and evaluates his childhood experiences growing up under this repressive system. Explaining his title, Mathabane notes that* kaffir *is a slang term used by some South African whites to degrade blacks. This selection comes from his second book,* Kaffir Boy in America *(1989), written to describe his life as a student in the United States on a tennis scholarship. In an interview with* Time *magazine (12 Nov. 1990), Mathabane described his arrival, alone, at age eighteen, headed for Limestone College in South Carolina: "When I came to the U.S. in 1978, I believed that America had long since solved its racial problems. . . . Then I discovered to my horror that not much had changed in people's hearts. . . . The black world in America resembled the world I had left—the poor buildings, the bad roads, the hopelessness, rage, frustration on the faces of the black boys and girls I met." On the other hand, Mathabane holds great hope for the future, believing that education is the catalyst for positive changes and hoping to communicate to his readers his dedication to the values his parents taught him: "self-reliance, self-motivation, self-confidence, discipline, and responsibility"* (Writers' Voices, *1986).*

Pre-Reading and Journal-Writing Suggestions

1. Explain your experience with a book that you "couldn't put down"— one that engulfed you, kept you reading, made you hope that the last page would never come.
2. Explain your process as you study something new. (This need not be formal study in school; it might relate to work, family life, or a hobby.) You might think of a past learning experience, as well as a more recent experience, to use as examples as you explain your process.

In the library one afternoon, having completed my homework, I be-   *1*
gan browsing among the bookshelves. I came upon a paperback copy of
Black Boy, Richard Wright's searing autobiography. My attention was arrested by the title and by the following defiant words on the back cover of
the book: "The white South said that it knew 'niggers,' and I was what the
white South called 'nigger.' Well, the white South had never known me—
never known what I thought, what I felt."

I mentally replaced "white South" with "white South Africa," and
"nigger" with "Kaffir," and was intrigued by how Richard Wright's feelings
mirrored my own. I immediately sat down in a chair by the window and
began reading the book. I was overwhelmed; I could not put the book
down. I even missed my economics class because I was so engrossed. When
the library closed I was three-quarters of the way through the book. Bleary-
eyed, I went back to my room and read the rest.

The next day I went back to the library and asked the head librarian—
a good-natured Franciscan priest with white hair and a charming smile—if
the library had more books by black authors. He guided me to the treasure.
I checked out Richard Wright's *Native Son,* Eldridge Cleaver's *Soul on Ice,*
W. E. B. Du Bois's *Souls of Black Folks, The Autobiography of Malcolm X,* Franz
Fanon's *The Wretched of the Earth,* Claude Brown's *Manchild of the Promised
Land,* James Baldwin's *The Fire Next Time* and *Notes of a Native Son,* Maya
Angelou's *I Know Why the Caged Bird Sings,* James Weldon Johnson's *The
Autobiography of an Ex-Colored Man,* and the autobiography and incendiary
speeches of Frederick Douglass. I devoured the books with relish.

After this momentous discovery I knew that my life would never be
the same. Here were black men and women, rebels in their own right, who
had felt, thought, and suffered deeply, who had grown up under conditions
that had threatened to destroy their very souls; here they were, baring their
bleeding hearts on paper, using words as weapons, plunging into realms of
experience I had never before thought reachable, and wrestling with fate
itself in an heroic attempt to make the incomprehensible—man's inhu-
manity to man—comprehensible. Most astonishing was that these men and
women had written about what I felt and thought, what I had been through
as a black man, what I desired, what I dreamed about, and what I refused to
compromise.

"These are soul mates," I said to myself, "these are my true brothers   *5*
and sisters." Where had they been all those years when I was lost in the
wilderness, feeling so alone, wondering why I was being misunderstood by
the world, why I seemed so at odds with complacent reality? I had to learn
to write like them, to purge myself of what they had purged themselves of
so eloquently. Here was a way through which I could finally understand
myself, perform the duty I'd pledged to my countrymen and to my mother.

Inspired by these black writers, I bought myself a pair of notebooks
and sat down one evening and began to write. I chose as a topic an issue of
which I had only superficial knowledge, but one which appealed to my

fancy. Words came very easily to the pen, but when I paused to evaluate what I had written and compared it to the masters I was determined to emulate, I found my effort ridiculous. The language was verbose, the ideas vague and incoherent. What was I doing wrong? Maybe I needed some expert advice. One day Mr. Allan, my English teacher, asked us to write a short story.

My story—a vivid, fictional description of Africa—was considered the best by Mr. Allan, who was a hard-to-please but excellent critic and teacher of English. He was stingy with A's, no matter how well the job was done. I received an A for my essay; my previous assignments had merited C's and B-minuses.

I carefully analyzed the essay to determine what exactly had so impressed the scrupulous teacher. I came up with the following answer: to write well, write about what you know, for experience is the best teacher, and writing is a means of self-expression.

Flushed with confidence from writing the essay, I jotted down ideas for more essays and possibly novels. I filled notebooks with descriptions and characters and plots. Maybe writing is my calling in life, I thought. Determined to hone my skills, I went back to my favorite writers for tips on how to go about the arduous task of learning how to move the world with the right word and the right accent. Every one of the writers I admired had been a voracious reader of books. I was already one. They had felt deeply. I felt deeply, too. They possessed an inborn obsession to share with the rest of humanity, through the written word, their innermost feelings, their vision of life, its agony and ecstasy, its manifold pains and sorrows and joys, its loves and hatreds—all of which they had extracted by looking deeply and with compassion into the human heart.

Such a temperament I believed I still lacked because I had yet to   10 acquire a sound liberal arts education. The college library had an impressive record collection of Shakespeare's plays; the dramas of Sophocles, Euripides, and Aristophanes; the *Dialogues* of Plato; the poems of Milton; and the plays of Dryden and Goldsmith, read by such giants of the stage as Paul Robeson, Claire Bloom, Sir Laurence Olivier, Anthony Quayle, Richard Burton, Sir John Gielgud, and Paul Schofield, among others. I checked out these records at the rate of three a day, and listened to them over and over again. The head librarian expressed pleasure at seeing me madly in love with Shakespeare and soon I was being talked about.

I took an English course with Professor Ann Klein. She instantly detected my enthusiastic love for poetry and helped me improve my taste and understanding of Keats, Shelley, Wordsworth, Coleridge, and Byron. Whereas heretofore my enjoyment of classical music had been visceral, I enrolled in a piano class out of a belief that the best way to understand classical music was to play an instrument.

Other subjects I now enjoyed were economics and philosophy. In the latter, taught by the easygoing, amiable Father Lucan, I was introduced to the brilliant ideas and provocative arguments for greater liberty, toleration, and individuality by Locke, Rousseau, and John Stuart Mill. The notably eclectic course Personal and Moral Life merely mentioned in passing their great ideas, but I went out in search of the complete works and read them avidly. I was fascinated by Rousseau's *The Social Contract,* especially his famous assertion "Man is born free, and everywhere he is in chains. One thinks himself the master of others and still remains a greater slave than they." But I found some of his arguments elliptical and contradictory. Mill and Locke became my favorite philosophers. I was amazed to discover, with repeated readings of their seminal works, that they basically confirmed what I had believed instinctively about the nature of freedom, individuality, and natural and civil rights. Locke's "Treatise on Toleration," his "Second Essay on Government," and Mill's *On Liberty* and *The Subjection of Women* left a decisive influence on my mind. This immersion in books alleviated the stress of constantly worrying about the condition of my mother and family.

Once again my love affair with the world of books landed me in trouble. I now walked about with a mind pregnant with thoughts inspired by reading. I longed to live only in the world of the imagination and ideas because physical reality suddenly seemed artificial, cold, dead. I became absentminded. Some of the black students on campus wondered why I no longer came to their parties, why I occasionally sat alone in the cafeteria, deep in thought.

"He's too proud," someone said.

"He's trying to be white," another said.

"He thinks he is better than us."

"He's stir-crazy."

They never understood my need for solitude, that "to fly from, need not be to hate, mankind." They never understood why I found great pleasure in watching squirrels racing up and down trees, in walking down to the Mississippi River and spending the afternoon staring at its murky waters, at the falling autumn leaves along its banks, at clouds sailing across the sky, and at the sleepy town of Hannibal on the other side, where Mark Twain was born. They never understood why I loved memorizing poetry, why I used quotations from books to illustrate a point, or why I urged them to become more politically active on campus so they could better protect their interests and make their presence felt as blacks. I tried establishing ties of solidarity with them, given our common experiences growing up in the ghetto, but we kept drifting apart because of our divergent attitudes. I was eager to fight, to protest, as black Americans had done in the 1960s, during those unforgettable days of Martin Luther King, Jr., Malcolm X, and Stokely Carmichael's misunderstood credo of Black Power. They were eager to accommodate, to live for the moment, to make their peace with the status quo, to wallow in apathy and self-pity. At times it appeared that I had come to America a generation too late. In fairness to many of these black students, they were concerned that an activist attitude might lose them their athletic scholarships or financial aid.

15

In celebration of black history month, in February 1980, I wrote the following poem, entitled "Longing for My Roots." It was a nostalgic poem, inspired by thoughts of home and of my ailing mother.

when I was a little child
living amidst innocence among
the chaste hills
and the pure forests and purer
streams
i never for a single moment paused
to think
that there might come a
time
when all i would have to live with
was to be just a memory

all the enchanting silhouettes of
the africa
i used to so lovingly know
all the natural beauty of her
beasts
the magnificent plumage of her
wild birds
the blithesomeness of her
black people
the eternal feeling of freedom
among singing titihoyes
the rivers that seem to eddy whirl
their courses
through hills and plains

all the everlasting elegance of
the springbok
the gentle tip-tappering of
summer's rain
the haunting murmur of
the windsong
the thundering of hooves
upon the serengeti

all that i am now without
all that boundless joy
i once so much cherished
i have prematurely left behind
to die and to decay

yet an african still am i
a proud man as such
i am black (soot black)
a handsome black warrior as such
i am still the proud possessor
of that undaunted spirit
reminiscent of endless freedom
among the misty hills
where the zebra used to cry
with ecstatic joy

i still remember the kraal
the grassy citadel of
my forefathers
i still can smell
the scent of fresh cowdung
and in hours of solitude
i still can hear
the bewitching sound of cowhide drums
and see through the haze of time
valiant, plumed warriors
as they leap and fall
while others
fall
never to leap again

even now
far, far away from home
oceans of water away
i still can see the misty hills
i can still hear mama's voice
echoing through the valley of
a thousand hills
calling me to come home
for supper around the fireside

I showed the poem to several black students. Some of them, apparently [20] ignorant or ashamed of their heritage as African-Americans, regarded it as confirmation of Africa's primitiveness. But I was proud of it. I knew that Africa, despite its many and serious problems, despite the Western tendency to stereotype it, remained a place of immense natural and cultural beauty, and that its diverse, proud, brave, resilient, and beautiful peoples are descended from some of the oldest civilizations on earth, which have made valuable contributions to literature, art, music, dance, science, religion, and other fields of human endeavor.

Suggestions for Writing and Discussion

1. From this piece, describe Mark Mathabane's views about learning, himself, life, and others. What values do these views suggest? Do you share the same values? Or do you see Mathabane's goals and ideals as distinctly different from your own?
2. Can you explain why Mathabane was so overwhelmed by the writings of black American authors?
3. Mathabane embarks on a pilgrimage to learn how to write more effectively. Can you relate to this type of zealous quest? Explain.
4. As Mathabane sees it, what was the major difference between his past writing assignments (on which he earned B's and C's) and his story about Africa (on which he earned an A)? Have you ever made similar evaluations of your own writing? Choose a piece of your own writing that you particularly like and explain its strengths.
5. What did Mathabane's favorite writers have in common? What didn't he find in their backgrounds that he, perhaps, had experienced in his own?
6. What does Mathabane mean when he says that his "love affair with the world of books" got him in trouble? Would you define his experiences as trouble? Why or why not? In what ways does a book's power differ from a visual or real-world experience? Can one be valued over the other?
7. What might Mathabane mean by "At times it appeared that I had come to America a generation too late"? What happened in this past generation? Why might Mathabane just now be recognizing this new way of thinking?
8. Read Mathabane's poem, slowly, out loud. Then reread it silently, to yourself. Jot down the images that move you the most. What do you now know about Africa that you didn't know before? What do you know about Mathabane? What do you know about yourself?

Suggestions for Extended Thinking and Writing

1. Write a piece in which you try to convince the members of this class that they should read your favorite book. Convince them that this book would be worth their while!
2. Read a book, essay, short story, or poem by a black author whose works you have never read before. (The list in paragraph 3 of "The African Contribution" provides some possibilities; consider also the writings of Alice Walker, Toni Morrison, Toni Cade Bambara, Paule Marshall, June Jordan, Ishmael Reed, and Gloria Naylor.) While reading the selection you choose, keep a response journal. At the end of your reading, review your response journal. Write an essay in which you synthesize and analyze your responses to this work.
3. Read a book, essay, short story, or poem by an author who is rooted in your own family's culture. For example, if your ancestors were from

Poland, find a Polish writer to study and read. If your ancestors were Puerto Rican, find a Puerto Rican author to read. (Of course many people have roots in several cultures; that opens many possibilities.)

As in suggestion 2, keep a response journal for this reading. Write an essay, perhaps along the lines of Mathabane's piece, in which you analyze what you learned and how the reading has affected you.

PATRICIA HAMPL

Parish Streets

Born in 1946, Patricia Hampl first won recognition for A Romantic Education, *her memoir about her Czech heritage, which was awarded a Houghton Mifflin Literary Fellowship in 1981. She has also published two collections of poetry, and in 1987 she published* Spillville, *a meditation about Antonín Dvořák's summer in Iowa. Hampl is now a professor of English at the University of Minnesota. She has written extensively of her early experiences growing up in a Roman Catholic family in the Midwest, and her most recent book is* Virgin Time, *a memoir about her Catholic upbringing and an inquiry into contemplative life. She has also recently edited an anthology of sacred poetry of the West, including poems relating to Islam, Judaism, and Christianity. Speaking about her writing, Hampl once said, "I write about all the things I intended to leave behind, to grow out of, or deny: being a Midwesterner, a Catholic, a woman."*

Pre-Reading and Journal-Writing Suggestions

1. Your journal can be a place for private and somewhat complex thoughts. Respond to the words *Religion* and *God* for five to ten minutes. Now reread your responses and write for another ten minutes; respond to your responses!
2. Write about the "holiest" person you have ever known. (You'll need to think about your definition of *holy* as you write.)
3. Write about how your family spent a typical Sunday when you were a child.

Lexington, Oxford, Chatsworth, continuing down Grand Avenue to   1
Milton and Avon, as far as St. Albans—the streets of our neighborhood had an English, even an Anglican, ring to them. But we were Catholic, and the parishes of the diocese, unmarked and ghostly as they were, posted borders more decisive than the street signs we passed on our way to St. Luke's grade school or, later, walking in the other direction to Visitation Convent for high school.

We were like people with dual citizenship. I *lived* on Linwood Avenue, but I *belonged* to St. Luke's. That was the lingo. Mothers spoke of daughters who were going to the junior-senior prom with boys "from Nativity" or "from St. Mark's," as if from fiefdoms across the sea.

"Where you from?" a boy livid with acne asked when we startled each other lurking behind a pillar in the St. Thomas Academy gym at a Friday night freshman mixer.

"Ladies' choice!" one of the mothers cried from a dim corner where a portable hi-fi was set up. She rasped the needle over the vinyl, and Fats Domino came on, insinuating a heavier pleasure than I yet knew: *I found my thrill . . . on Blueberry Hill.*

"I'm from Holy Spirit," the boy said, as if he'd been beamed in to stand   5
by the tepid Cokes and tuna sandwiches and the bowls of sweating potato chips on the refreshments table.

Parish members did not blush to describe themselves as being "from Immaculate Conception." Somewhere north, near the city line, there was even a parish frankly named Maternity of Mary. But then, in those years, the 1950s and early 1960s, breeding was low-grade fever pulsing amongst us unmentioned, like a buzz or hum you get used to and cease to hear. The white noise of matrimonial sex.

On Sundays the gray stone nave of St. Luke's church, big as a warehouse, was packed with families of eight or ten sitting in the honey-colored pews. The fathers wore brown suits. In memory they appear spectrally thin, wraithlike and spent, like trees hollowed of their pulp. The wives were petite and cheerful with helmetlike haircuts. Perkiness was their main trait. But what did they say, these small women, how did they talk? Mrs. Healy, mother of fourteen ("They can afford them," my mother said, as if to excuse her paltry two. "He's a doctor."), never uttered a word, as far as I remember. Even pregnant, she was somehow wiry, as if poised for a tennis match. Maybe these women only wore a *look* of perkiness, and like their lean husbands, they were sapped of personal strength. Maybe they were simply tense.

Not everyone around us was Catholic. Mr. Kirby, a widower who was our next door neighbor, was Methodist—whatever that was. The Nugents across the street behind their cement retaining wall and double row of giant salvia, were Lutheran, more or less. The Williams family, who subscribed to the *New Yorker* and had a living room outfitted with spare Danish furniture, were Episcopalian. They referred to their minister as a priest—a plagiarism that embarrassed me for them because I liked them and their light, airy ways.

As for the Bertrams, our nearest neighbors to the west, it could only be said that Mrs. Bertram, dressed in a narrow suit with a peplum jacket and a hat made of the same heathery wool, went *somewhere* via taxi on Sunday mornings. Mr. Bertram went nowhere—on Sunday or on any other day. He was understood, during my entire girlhood, to be indoors, resting.

Weekdays, Mrs. Bertram took the bus to her job downtown. Mr.   10
Bertram stayed home behind their birchwood Venetian blinds in an aquarium half-light, not an invalid (we never thought of him that way), but a man whose occupation it was to rest. Sometimes in the summer he ventured forth with a large wrench-like gadget to root out the masses of dandelions that gave the Bertram lawn a temporary brilliance in June.

I associated him with the Wizard of Oz. He was small and mild-looking, going bald. He gave the impression of extreme pallor except for small, very dark eyes.

It was a firm neighborhood rumor that Mr. Bertram had been a screenwriter in Hollywood. Yes, that pallor was a writer's pallor; those small dark eyes were a writer's eyes. They saw, they noted.

He allowed me to assist him in the rooting-out of his dandelions. I wanted to ask him about Hollywood—had he met Audrey Hepburn? I couldn't bring myself to maneuver for information on such an important subject. But I did feel something serious was called for here. I introduced religion while he plunged the dandelion gadget deep into the lawn.

No, he said, he did not go to church. "But you do believe in God?" I asked, hardly daring to hope he did not. I longed for novelty.

He paused for a moment and looked up at the sky where big, spreading   15
clouds streamed by. "God isn't the problem," he said.

Some ancient fissure split open, a fine crack in reality: So there *was* a problem. Just as I'd always felt. Beneath the family solidity, the claustrophobia of mother-father-brother-me, past the emphatic certainties of St. Luke's catechism class, there was a problem that would never go away. Mr. Bertram stood amid his dandelions, resigned as a Buddha, looking up at the sky which gave back nothing but drifting white shapes on the blue.

What alarmed me was my feeling of recognition. Of course there was a problem. It wasn't God. Life itself was a problem. Something was not right, would never be right. I'd sensed it all along, some kind of fishy vestigial quiver in the spine. It was bred in the bone, way past thought. Life, deep down, lacked the substantiality that it *seemed* to display. The physical world, full of detail and interest, was a parched topsoil that could be blown away.

This lack, this blankness akin to chronic disappointment, was everywhere, under the perkiness, lurking even within my own happiness. "What are you going to do today?" my father said when he saw me digging in the backyard on his way to work at the greenhouse.

"I'm digging to China," I said.

"Well, I'll see you at lunch," he said, "if you're still here."   20

I wouldn't bite. I frowned and went back to work with the bent tablespoon my mother had given me. It wasn't a game. I wanted out. I was on a desperate journey that only looked like play. I couldn't explain.

The blank disappointment, masked as weariness, played on the faces of people on the St. Clair bus. They looked out the windows, coming home from downtown, unseeing: Clearly nothing interested them. What were they thinking of? The passing scene was not beautiful enough—was that it?—to catch their eye. Like the empty clouds Mr. Bertram turned to, their blank looks gave back nothing. There was an unshivered shiver in each of us, a shudder we managed to hold back.

We got off the bus at Oxford where, one spring, in the lime green house behind the catalpa tree on the corner, Mr. Lenart (whom we didn't know well) had slung a pair of tire chains over a rafter in the basement and hanged himself. Such things happened. Only the tight clutch of family life ("The family that prays together stays together.") could keep things rolling along. Step out of the tight, bright circle, and you might find yourself dragging your chains down to the basement.

The perverse insubstantiality of the material world was the problem: Reality refused to be real enough. Nothing could keep you steadfastly happy. That was clear. Some people blamed God. But I sensed that Mr. Bertram was right not to take that tack. *God is not the problem.* The clouds passing in the big sky kept dissipating, changing form. That was the problem—but so what? Such worries resolved nothing and were best left unworried—the unshivered shiver.

There was no one to blame. You could only retire, like Mr. Bertram, 25 stay indoors behind your birchwood blinds, and contemplate the impossibility of things, allowing the Hollywood glitter of reality to fade away and become a vague local rumor.

There were other ways of coping. Mrs. Krueger, several houses down with a big garden rolling with hydrangea bushes, held as her faith a passionate belief in knowledge. She sold *World Book* encyclopedias. After trying Christian Science and a stint with the Unitarians, she had settled down as an agnostic. There seemed to be a lot of reading involved with being an agnostic, pamphlets and books, long citations on cultural anthropology in the *World Book*. It was an abstruse religion, and Mrs. Krueger seemed to belong to some ladies' auxiliary of disbelief.

But it didn't really matter what Mrs. Krueger decided about "the deity-idea," as she called God. No matter what they believed, our neighbors lived not just on Linwood Avenue; they were in St. Luke's parish too, whether they knew it or not. We claimed the territory. And we claimed them—even as we dismissed them. They were all non-Catholics, the term that disposed nicely of all spiritual otherness.

Let the Protestants go their schismatic ways; the Lutherans could splice themselves into synods any which way. Believers, nonbelievers, even Jews (the Kroners on the corner) or a breed as rare as the Greek Orthodox whose church was across the street from St. Luke's—they were all non-Catholics, just so much extraneous spiritual matter orbiting the nethersphere.

Or maybe it was more intimate than that, and we dismissed the rest of the world as we would our own serfs. We saw the Lutherans and Presbyterians, even those snobbish Episcopalians, as rude colonials, non-Catholics all, doing the best they could out there in the bush to imitate the ways of the homeland. *We* were the homeland.

Jimmy Guiliani was a bully. He pulled my hair when he ran by me on 30 Oxford as we all walked home from St. Luke's, the girls like a midget army in navy jumpers and white blouses, the boys with the greater authority of free civilians without uniforms. They all wore pretty much the same thing anyway: corduroy pants worn smooth at the knees and flannel shirts, usually plaid.

I wasn't the only one Jimmy picked on. He pulled Moira Murphy's hair, he punched Tommy Hague. He struck without reason, indiscriminately, so full of violence it may have been pent-up enthusiasm released at random after the long day leashed in school. Catholic kids were alleged, by public school kids, to be mean fighters, dirty fighters.

Jimmy Guiliani was the worst, a terror, hated and feared by Sister Julia's entire third-grade class.

So, it came as a surprise when, after many weeks of his tyranny, I managed to land a sure kick to his groin and he collapsed in a heap and cried real tears. "You shouldn't *do* that to a boy," he said, whimpering. He was almost primly admonishing. "Do you know how that feels?"

It's not correct to say that it was a sure kick. I just kicked. I took no aim and had no idea I'd hit paydirt—or why. Even when the tears started to his eyes and he doubled over clutching himself, I didn't understand.

But I liked it when he asked if I knew how it felt. For a brief, hopeful moment I thought he would tell me, that he would explain. Yes, tell me: How *does* it feel? And what's *there*, anyway? It was the first time the male body imposed itself.

I felt an odd satisfaction. I'd made contact. I wasn't glad I had hurt him, I wasn't even pleased to have taken the group's revenge on the class bully. I hadn't planned to kick him. It all just *happened*—as most physical encounters do. I was more astonished than he that I had succeeded in wounding him, I think. In a simple way, I wanted to say I was sorry. But I liked being taken seriously and could not forfeit that rare pleasure by making an apology.

For a few weeks after I kicked him, I had a crush on Jimmy Guiliani. Not because I'd hurt him. But because he had paused, looked right at me, and implored me to see things from his point of view. *Do you know how it feels?*

I didn't know—and yet I did. As soon as he asked, I realized obscurely that I did know how it felt. I knew what was there between his legs where he hurt. I ceased to be ignorant at that moment. And sex began—with a blow.

The surprise of knowing what I hadn't realized I knew seemed beautifully private, but also illicit. That was a problem. I had no desire to be an outlaw. The way I saw it, you were supposed to know what you had been *taught*. This involved being given segments of knowledge by someone (usually a nun) designated to dole out information in measured drams, like strong medicine.

Children were clean slates others were meant to write on.

But here was evidence I was not a blank slate at all. I was scribbled all over with intuitions, premonitions, vague resonances clamoring to give their signals. I had caught Mr. Bertram's skyward look and its implicit promise: Life will be tough. There was no point in blaming God—the Catholic habit. Or even more Catholic, blaming the nuns, which allowed you to blame Mother and God all in one package.

And here was Jimmy Guiliani drawing out of me this other knowledge, bred of empathy and a swift kick to his privates. *Yes, I know how it feels.*

The hierarchy we lived in, a great linked chain of religious being, seemed set to control every entrance and exit to and from the mind and heart. The buff-colored *Baltimore Catechism,* small and square, read like an owner's manual for a very complicated vehicle. There was something pleasant, lulling and rhythmic, like heavily rhymed poetry, about the singsong Q-and-A format. Who would not give over heart, if not mind, to the brisk nannyish assurance of the Baltimore prose:

Who made you?
God made me.

Why did God make you?
God made me to know, love and serve Him in this world, in order to be happy with Him forever in the next.

What pleasant lines to commit to memory. And how harmless our Jesuitical discussions about what, exactly, constituted a meatless spaghetti sauce on Friday. Strict constructionists said no meat of any kind should ever, at any time, have made its way into the tomato sauce; easy liberals held with the notion that meatballs could be lurking around in the sauce, as long as you didn't eat them. My brother lobbied valiantly for the meatball *intactus* but present. My mother said nothing doing. They raged for years.

Father Flannery, who owned his own airplane and drove a sports car, *45* had given Peter some ammunition when he'd been asked to rule on the meatball question in the confessional. My mother would hear none of it. "I don't want to know what goes on between you and your confessor," she said, taking the high road.

"A priest, Ma, a *priest,*" my brother cried. "This is an ordained priest saying right there in the sanctity of the confessional that meatballs are OK."

But we were going to heaven my mother's way.

Life was like that—crazy. Full of hair-splitting, and odd rituals. We got our throats blessed on St. Blaise day in February, with the priest holding oversized beeswax candles in an X around our necks, to ward off death by choking on fishbones. There were smudged foreheads on Ash Wednesday and home May altars with plaster statuettes of the Virgin festooned with lilacs. Advent wreaths and nightly family rosary vigils during October (Rosary Month), the entire family on their knees in the living room.

There were snatches of stories about nuns who beat kids with rulers in the coat room; the priest who had a twenty-year affair with a member of the Altar and Rosary Society; the other priest in love with an altar boy— they'd had to send him away. Not St. Luke's stories—oh no, certainly not— but stories, floating, as stories do, from inner ear to inner ear, respecting no parish boundaries. Part of the ether.

And with it all, a relentless xenophobia about other religions. "It's *50* going to be a mixed marriage, I understand," one of my aunts murmured about a friend's daughter who was marrying an Episcopalian. So what if he called himself High Church? What did that change? He was a non-Catholic.

And now, educated out of it all, well climbed into the professions, the Catholics find each other at cocktail parties and get going. The nun stories, the first confession traumas—and a tone of rage and dismay that seems to bewilder even the tellers of these tales.

Nobody says, when asked, "I'm Catholic." It's always, "Yes, I was brought up Catholic." Anything to put it at a distance, to diminish the presence of that grabby heritage that is not racial but acts as if it were. "You never get over it, you know," a fortyish lawyer told me a while ago at a party where we found ourselves huddled by the chips and dip, as if we were at a St. Thomas mixer once again.

He seemed to feel he was speaking to someone with the same hopeless congenital condition. "It's different now, of course." he said. "But when we were growing up back there. . . ." Ah yes, the past isn't a time. It's a place. And it's always there.

He had a very Jimmy Guiliani look to him. A chastened rascal. "I'm divorced," he said. We both smiled: There's no going to hell anymore. "Do they still have mortal sin?" he asked wistfully.

The love-hate lurch of a Catholic upbringing, like having an extra set of parents to contend with. Or an added national allegiance—not to the Vatican, as we were warned that the Baptists thought during John Kennedy's campaign for president. The allegiance was to a different realm. It was the implacable loyalty of faith, that flawless relation between self and existence which we were born into. A strange country where people prayed and believed impossible things. *55*

The nuns who taught us, rigged up in their bold black habits with the big round wimples stiff as frisbees, walked our parish streets; they moved from convent to church in twos or threes, dipping in the side door of the huge church "for a little adoration," as they would say. The roly-poly Irish-born monsignor told us to stand straight and proud when he met us slouching along Summit toward class. And fashionable Father Flannery who, every night, took a gentle, companionable walk with the old Irish pastor, the two of them taking out white handkerchiefs, waving them for safety, as they crossed the busy avenue on the way home in the dark, swallowed in their black suits and cassocks, invisible in the gloom.

But the one I would like to summon up most and to have pass me on Oxford as I head off to St. Luke's in the early morning mist, one of those mid-May weekdays, the lilacs just starting to spill, that one I want most to materialize from "back there"—I don't know her name, where, exactly, she lived, or who she was. We never spoke, in fact. We just passed each other, she coming home from six o'clock daily Mass, I going early to school to practice the piano for an hour before class began.

She was a "parish lady," part of the anonymous population that thickened our world, people who were always there, who were solidly part of us, part of what we were, but who never emerged beyond the bounds of being parishioners to become persons.

We met every morning, just past the Healys' low brick wall. She wore a librarian's cardigan sweater. She must have been about forty-five, and I sensed she was not married. Unlike Dr. and Mrs. Harrigan who walked smartly along Summit holding hands, their bright Irish setter accompanying them as far as the church door where he waited till Mass was over, the lady in the cardigan was always alone.

I saw her coming all the way from Grand where she had to pause for the traffic. She never rushed across the street, zipping past a truck, but waited until the coast was completely clear, and passed across keeping her slow, almost floating pace. A lovely, peaceful gait, no rush to it. `60`

When finally we were close enough to make eye contact, she looked up, straight into my face, and smiled. It was such a *complete* smile, so entire, that it startled me every time, as if I'd heard my name called out on the street of a foreign city.

She was a homely woman, plain and pale, unnoticeable. But I felt— how to put it—that she shed light. The mornings were often frail with mist, the light uncertain and tender. The smile was a brief flood of light. She loved me, I felt.

I knew what it was about. She was praying. Her hand, stuck in her cardigan pocket, held one of the crystal beads of her rosary. I knew this. I'd once seen her take it out of the left pocket and quickly replace it after she had found the handkerchief she needed.

If I had seen a nun mumbling the rosary along Summit (and that did happen), it would not have meant much to me. But here on Oxford, the side street we used as a sleepy corridor to St. Luke's, it was a different thing. The parish lady was not a nun. She was a person who prayed, who prayed alone, for no reason that I understood. But there was no question that she prayed without ceasing, as the strange scriptural line instructed.

She didn't look up to the blank clouds for a response, as Mr. Bertram did in his stoic way. Her head was bowed, quite unconsciously. And when she raised it, keeping her hand in her pocket where the clear beads were, she looked straight into the eyes of the person passing by. It was not an invasive look, but one brimming with a secret which, if only she had words, it was clear she would like to tell. `65`

Suggestions for Writing and Discussion

1. After reading this piece, make a list of memories that this piece might have stirred in you. Use the following categories as a guide:

   Church   Neighbors

   Family Rituals   Childhood Questions

   Teachers

2. How would you describe Hampl's childhood? Were the experiences she relates unhappy ones? Magical moments? Something else?

3. Hampl describes her experiences in St. Luke's Church as ritualistic and "crazy" (paragraph 48). Do you think her assessment is exaggerated or slanted in any way? Please explain.
4. What do you think of Mr. Bertram? Why do you think Hampl mentions him here? How about Jimmy Guiliani? Why is he included, too?
5. Toward the end of this reading, we meet a "parish lady." Look back to paragraphs 58–65; perhaps read them out loud. What mood does Hampl create with this character? Why do you think Hampl mentions this nameless character last?
6. In paragraph 50, Hampl notes "a relentless xenophobia about other religions." What does *xenophobia* mean? Explain why you think Hampl's essay either promotes or argues against religious xenophobia.

Suggestions for Extended Thinking and Writing

1. Based on this reading and your own experiences, write an essay in which you persuade your classmates that they should or should not join an organized religion.
2. Hampl introduces us to several "minor" characters in this piece. Choose any one character and write more about the person. Use your imagination to create sensory descriptions and vivid details to make this character come alive.
3. Write about any personal "religious" insight you have had, either recently or in your childhood.
4. Write a piece in which you compare your view of God or religion when you were a child and your viewpoint now.

TOSHIO MORI

The Woman Who Makes Swell Doughnuts

Toshio Mori began writing for publication in his late teens, finding time to continue this work even when he became a professional baseball player. He has done extensive research on the Japanese-American experience, conducting many interviews with Japanese-Americans who lived in the United States during the 1930s and 1940s.

Many of his interviews focus on individuals who, like Mori and his family, were interned at a Relocation Center during World War II. These were hastily built, crowded camps where the American government required Americans of Japanese descent to live out the war years. Making the best of this horrifying experience, Mori helped to found a newspaper and served as camp historian during the years he was forced to stay there. His essays have appeared in many journals, magazines, and anthologies, including Best American Short Stories of 1943, Writer's Forum, *and* New Directions. *In addition, he has published several books, including* Yokohama, California *(1949),* The Chauvinist and Other Stories *(1979), and* The Woman from Hiroshima *(1979). Mori's writings are best known for depicting with sensitivity and stunning clarity the ordinary, everyday incidents and people whose lives made up the Japanese-American community in California during the 1930s and 1940s.*

Pre-Reading and Journal-Writing Suggestions

1. Write about your favorite food. Aim to write for twenty minutes on this topic, but feel free to go off on any tangents to which the topic leads you.
2. Write about a special childhood memory you have of an older person.
3. What food are you most like? Have some fun as you create this analogy!

There is nothing I like to do better than to go to her house and knock *1* on the door and when she opens the door, to go in. It is one of the experiences I will long remember—perhaps the only immortality that I will ever be lucky to meet in my short life—and when I say experience I do not mean the actual movement, the motor of our lives. I mean by experience the dancing of emotions before our eyes and inside of us, the dance that is still but is the roar and the force capable of stirring the earth and the people.

Of course, she, the woman I visit, is old and of her youthful beauty there is little left. Her face of today is coarse with hard water and there is no question that she has lived her life: given birth to six children, worked side by side with her man for forty years, working in the fields, working in the house, caring for the grandchildren, facing the summers and winters and also the springs and autumns, running the household that is completely her little world. And when I came on the scene, when I discovered her in her little house on Seventh Street, all of her life was behind, all of her task in this world was tabbed, looked into, thoroughly attended, and all that is before her in life and the world, all that could be before her now was to sit and be served; duty done, work done, time clock punched; old-age pension or old-age security; easy chair; soft serene hours till death take her. But this was not of her, not the least bit of her.

When I visit her she takes me to the coziest chair in the living room, where are her magazines and books in Japanese and English. "Sit down," she says. "Make yourself comfortable. I will come back with some hot doughnuts just out of oil."

And before I can turn a page of a magazine she is back with a plateful of hot doughnuts. There is nothing I can do to describe her doughnut; it is in a class by itself, without words, without demonstration. It is a doughnut, just a plain doughnut just out of oil but it is different, unique. Perhaps when I am eating her doughnuts I am really eating her; I have this foolish notion in my head many times and whenever I catch myself doing so I say, that is not so, that is not true. Her doughnuts really taste swell, she is the best cook I have ever known, Oriental dishes or American dishes.

I bow humbly that such a room, such a house exists in my neighborhood so I may dash in and out when my spirit wanes, when hell is loose. I sing gratefully that such a simple and common experience becomes an event, an event of necessity and growth. It is an event that is a part of me, an addition to the elements of the earth, water, fire, and air, and I seek the day when it will become a part of everyone.

All her friends, old and young, call her Mama. Everybody calls her Mama. That is not new, it is logical. I suppose there is in every block of every city in America a woman who can be called Mama by her friends and the strangers meeting her. This is commonplace, it is not new and the old sentimentality may be the undoing of the moniker. But what of a woman who isn't a mama but is, and instead of priding in the expansion of her little world, takes her little circle, living out her days in the little circle, perhaps never to be exploited in a biography or on everybody's tongue, but enclosed, shut, excluded from world news and newsreels; just sitting, just moving, just alive, planting the plants in the fields, caring for the children and the grandchildren and baking the tastiest doughnuts this side of the next world.

When I sit with her I do not need to ask deep questions, I do not need to know Plato or The Sacred Books of the East or dancing. I do not need to be on guard. But I am on guard and foot-loose because the room is alive.

"Where are the grandchildren?" I say. "Where are Mickey, Tadao, and Yaeko?"

"They are out in the yard," she says. "I say to them, play, play hard, go out there and play hard. You will be glad later for everything you have done with all your might."

Sometimes we sit many minutes in silence. Silence does not bother 10 her. She says silence is the most beautiful symphony, she says the air breathed in silence is sweeter and sadder. That is about all we talk of. Sometimes I sit and gaze out the window and watch the Southern Pacific trains rumble by and the vehicles whizz with speed. And sometimes she catches me doing this and she nods her head and I know she understands that I think the silence in the room is great, and also the roar and the dust of the outside is great, and when she is nodding I understand that she is saying that this, her little room, her little circle, is a depot, a pause, for the weary traveler, but outside, outside of her little world there is dissonance, hugeness of another kind, and the travel to do. So she has her little house, she bakes the grandest doughnuts, and inside of her she houses a little depot.

Most stories would end with her death, would wait till she is peacefully dead and peacefully at rest but I cannot wait that long. I think she will grow, and her hot doughnuts just out of the oil will grow with softness and touch. And I think it would be a shame to talk of her doughnuts after she is dead, after she is formless.

Instead I take today to talk of her and her wonderful doughnuts when the earth is something to her, when the people from all parts of the earth may drop in and taste the flavor, her flavor, which is everyone's and all flavor; talk to her, sit with her, and also taste the silence of her room and the silence that is herself; and finally go away to hope and keep alive what is alive in her, on earth and in men, expressly myself.

Suggestions for Writing and Discussion

1. What's your initial impression of this piece? Did you like it? Find it boring? Something else?
2. Why are these doughnuts so special to the author? Is he writing this piece to explain how good the doughnuts tasted or for some other reason?
3. In what way might the experience of eating doughnuts be "an event of necessity and growth" (paragraph 5)? Do you feel the author is perhaps exaggerating here? Why or why not?
4. What do you think of Mama? Have you ever known anyone like her? Explain.
5. In paragraph 10, the author indicates that being able to be silent in another person's company is a sign of a special relationship. Using your own experience, do you believe this is true? If so, why, do you think, is it so difficult for people to be comfortable in silence?
6. What do you think the doughnuts "keep alive" (paragraph 12) within the author?

Suggestions for Extended Thinking and Writing

1. Write an essay in which you describe the oldest person you know. Concentrate on physical details and such aspects as voice and actions.
2. In what ways might Mama be described as a teacher? Compare the experiences described here with the experiences Judith Ortiz Cofer describes in the selection from *Casa* (p. 157). To an audience of parents who are anxious to educate their children well, explain what teachers such as Mama and the older women described in *Casa* can contribute to a child's growth and development.

MIGUEL TORRES

Crossing the Border

> At the time Miguel Torres told his story to an interpreter, he was twenty
> years old and was employed in a mushroom plant in California. He told the
> interviewer that he had entered the United States illegally four times during the
> past year. His story is representative of the many illegal aliens from various
> countries who take great risks to find the employment in the United States that
> they believe will bring them better lives. It is important to note, however, that a
> survey published by Time magazine in November 1993 showed that while
> 64 percent of Americans believed that most immigrants come into the country
> illegally, the actual figures demonstrated that 76 percent of immigrants arrive
> legally; only 24 percent come in illegally.

Pre-Reading and Journal-Writing Suggestions

1. Describe the circumstances under which you would leave your home
   and your country for a foreign land.
2. In your journal, describe your ideal country. Do any parts of your ideal
   seem possible in this country? What parts seem improbable?

I was born in a small town in the state of Michoacán in Mexico. When
I was fifteen, I went to Mexico City with my grandmother and my mother.
I worked in a parking lot, a big car lot. People would come in and they'd
say, "Well, park my car." And I'd give them a ticket and I'd park the car and
I'd be there, you know, watching the cars. I got paid in tips.

But I wanted to come to the United States to work and to earn more
money. My uncle was here, and I thought if I could come to him, I could
live with him and work and he would help me.

It's not possible to get papers to come over now. So when I decided to
come, I went to Tijuana in Mexico. There's a person there that will get in
contact with you. They call him the Coyote. He walks around town, and if
he sees someone wandering around alone, he says, "Hello, do you have
relatives in the United States?" And if you say yes, he says, "Do you want to
visit them?" And if you say yes, he says he can arrange it through a friend. It
costs $250 or $300.

The Coyote rounded up me and five other guys, and then he got in
contact with a guide to take us across the border. We had to go through the
hills and the desert, and we had to swim through a river. I was a little scared.
Then we come to a highway and a man was there with a van, pretending to
fix his motor. Our guide said hello, and the man jumped into the car and

we ran and jumped in, too. He began to drive down the highway fast and we knew we were safe in the United States. He took us to San Isidro that night, and the next day he took us all the way here to Watsonville. I had to pay him $250 and then, after I'd been here a month, he came back and I had to give him $50 more. He said I owed him that.

I was here for two months before I started working, and then my uncle got me a job, first in the celery fields picking celery, washing it, packing it, and later picking prunes. Then, all of a sudden, one day the Immigration showed up, and I ran and I hid in a river that was next to the orchard. The man saw me and he questioned me, and he saw I didn't have any papers. So they put me in a van and took me to Salinas, and there was some more illegals there and they put us in buses and took us all the way to Mexicali near the border. We were under guard; the driver and another one that sleeps while one drives. The seats are like hard boards. We'd get up from one side and rub, you know, that side a little bit and then sit on the other side for a while and then rub that side because it's so hard. It was a long trip.

When we arrived in Mexicali, they let us go. We caught a bus to Tijuana, and then at Tijuana, that night, we found the Coyote again and we paid him and we came back the next day. I had to pay $250 again, but this time he knew me and he let me pay $30 then and $30 each week. Because he knew me, you know. He trusted me.

We came through the mountains that time. We had to walk through a train tunnel. It all lasted maybe about three hours, through the tunnel. It was short; for me it was short. We're used to walking, you know. Over in Mexico we have to walk like ten miles to go to work or to go home or to go to school, so we're used to walking. To me it was a short distance to walk for three hours. And after we got out of the tunnel, we got into a car; and from there, from the tunnel, we came all the way into Los Angeles. That was the second time. We didn't see any border patrol either time.

The second time I was here for three months. My uncle managed to get me a job in the mushroom plant. I was working there when the Immigration came. There's this place where they blow air between the walls to make it cool and I hid there. And I was watching. The Immigration was looking around the plant everywhere. There was another illegal there, and he just kept on picking the mushrooms. He'd only been back a couple of days himself. The Immigration walked over there, and that kid turned around and looked at the Immigration and said, "What's the matter? What happened?" And the Immigration looked at him and said, "Oh, nothing," and the kid kept right on picking mushrooms. Yet he was an illegal! He knew how to act, play it cool. If you just sit tight they don't know you're illegal.

Well, the Immigration looked between the walls then and he caught me again. That was the second time. They put handcuffs on me with another guy and we were handcuffed together all the way from California to Mexicali.

Altogether I've been caught three times this year and made the trip   10
over here four times. It's cost me one thousand dollars but it's still better than
what I was making in Mexico City.

It's the money. When you come back here you get more money here
than you do over there. Right now, the most, the most that I'd be getting in
Mexico would be from 25 to 30 pesos a day, which is maybe $2.00, $2.50.
And here, with overtime, sometimes I make $150 a week. Things are ex-
pensive here, but it's expensive over there, too. And I like the way people
live here. All the—what do you call it—all the facilities that you have here,
all the things you can get and everything.

The boss at the mushroom factory doesn't ask for papers. He doesn't
say anything about it. The last time, he hired me back as soon as I got back
here, without any questions.

I learned to hide my money when the Immigration catch me. You
know, if you have a lot on you, they take you fifteen or twenty miles from
the border in Mexico. But if you have just two dollars or so, they let you go
right in Tijuana. Then it's easier to come back. You can just walk right
down the street and find the Coyote or someone like him. A man I know
was hitchhiking along the road near San Diego and someone picked him up
and it was the Immigration man who had just brought him back to Mexico!
The Immigration laughed and said, "You got back faster than I did." Of
course, he took him back to Mexico again then. But that man is back in
Watsonville now, working in the brussels sprouts. It takes a longer time for
the Immigration to catch us than it does for us to come back. [*Laughs.*]

I'd like to be able to stay here, to live here and work; but the only way
now is to find someone that'll say, "Well, I'll marry you, I'll fix your papers
for you." There's a lot of them who do that. I'd be willing to if I could find
someone that would do it for me. You pay them, you know. You don't sleep
together or even live in the same house, but they marry you. A long time
ago you could fix up papers for your nephew or brother, a friend, a cousin.
It was real easy then. But now it has to be close relations: mother, father,
wife, son, or daughter. My uncle can't do it for me. The only way I could
do it would be if I could marry an American citizen.

I'd like to learn English because it would be easier for me. There is a   15
night school here, but I don't like to go because after work I like to go out
and mess around and goof off. [*Laughs.*] Maybe I'll go later. If I could just
learn a tiny bit of English, you know, I could turn around and tell the
Immigration, "What's the matter with you? What do you want?" and I
wouldn't be recognized as an illegal.

Suggestions for Writing and Discussion
1. What is your initial reaction to the choices Miguel makes?
2. In paragraph 3, Torres describes a person called "the Coyote." What is
   the definition of the animal for which this person is named? Consider

both denotation and connotation as you explain what the name implies about the way illegal immigrants view the Coyote.

3. Reread the first paragraph of this piece. From the details and language used in these six sentences alone, what would you say Miguel's life was like before he turned fifteen?

4. What would you say are Miguel's personal strengths? What are his weaknesses? Is he someone you would probably have as a friend? Why or why not?

5. Analyze Miguel's reactions for each of the three times he is caught. Do his reactions change over the course of the year? Please explain.

6. Which life do you feel is better for Miguel—life in America with his uncle or life in Mexico City with his mother and grandmother? In a letter to Miguel, explain your point of view.

7. Make a prediction for Miguel's life ten years from the time of this interview. Where might he be living? What might he be doing? Would you see his life as better than his life at the age of fifteen?

8. Is Miguel's presence in America a hindrance or a contribution to this country? Please support your answer with examples and facts from the text itself. You may also offer any personal experiences as support. As you write, keep in mind as your audience a group of United States senators and representatives who are investigating the impact of immigrants on American life today.

Suggestions for Extended Thinking and Writing

1. Rewrite this piece from the immigration officer's point of view.
2. Write an essay in which you describe a time in your life when you felt like an outsider, a stranger in a foreign land.

LAWRENCE E. HARRISON

America and Its Immigrants

Lawrence E. Harrison is the author of Underdevelopment Is a State of Mind: The Latin American Case *(1985) and* Who Prospers? How Cultural Values Shape Economic and Political Success *(1992). In addition he has published articles in the* New York Times, *the* Wall Street Journal, *and the* Washington Post. *Harrison has been a visiting scholar at Harvard's Center for International Affairs and has directed several development programs for the United States Agency for International Development. The views he expresses in this selection reflect the growing concern among many Americans about the impact of continued immigration, both legal and illegal, of hundreds of thousands of people each year.*

Pre-Reading and Journal-Writing Suggestions

1. What do you think would be the positive and negative consequences of drastically reducing the number of immigrants admitted to the United States each year?
2. Imagine that to continue to live in America you must prove that you are a worthwhile contributor to the success of this country. How can you justify being allowed to stay here? What do you think will be the outcome of your request? Will you be able to stay, or will the authorities make you leave? Write this response in the form of a petition to an official government board that has required you to defend your right to remain here.

The United States is one of the few advanced countries in the world *1* that does not effectively control immigration. Large numbers continue to enter the United States illegally each year, most of them from Latin America, and most of those from Mexico. Conservative estimates place the number of illegal immigrants residing in the United States at three to four million. Some estimates run as high as ten million. The illegal immigrant population may be increasing by as many as three hundred thousand people each year. The Center for Immigration Studies in Washington estimates that the pool of illegal Mexican settlers alone currently may be increasing by as many as 250,000 annually.

Immigration is an important engine of growth of America's population, which has increased more rapidly since 1950 than the population of any other advanced country. Apart from the number of legal and illegal immigrants, their high fertility rates after arrival have helped drive the national fertility rate close to the 2.1 percent replacement level. Current immigration and fertility trends, if sustained, would result in a national population of five hundred million, twice that of today, by the end of the next century. The mind boggles at the implications for the quality of life—for example, the impact on the environment—not to mention the stresses of a slow pace of acculturation that threatens to transform the assimilative "melting pot" into a multicultural "salad bowl."

We are a society inspired by the words of Emma Lazarus on the Statue of Liberty: "Give me your tired, your poor, your huddled masses yearning to breathe free." When the Statue was dedicated, 105 years ago—about the time my grandparents emigrated from Eastern Europe—some sixty million people lived in the United States, less than a quarter of today's population. An open immigration policy clearly suited its needs. Today the United States, with more than 250 million people, each year accepts over half of all the persons in the world who migrate permanently across an international border. The competition of immigrants with poor citizens for jobs and social services is particularly troubling in our current economic distress. The words of Katherine Betts, in *Ideology and Immigration,* about the immigration issue in Australia are relevant to the United States: "Humanitarianism became the chief goal of immigration for some people and immigration itself came to be seen as a form of international aid . . . the relatively poor in this country pay a disproportionate share of the cost of the conscience of the rich."

Emma Lazarus notwithstanding, there is compelling evidence that most Americans are opposed to continuing high levels of immigration, legal and illegal. A 1990 Roper poll found that about three-quarters (including 74 percent of Hispanic Americans) are opposed to proposals to increase immigration, two-thirds support reducing legal immigration, and 91 percent support an all-out program to stop illegal immigration.

They are right. We should call a moratorium on immigration while   5
we forge a new policy that meshes the needs of our society with the educational and professional experience of immigrants, rather than one that emphasizes family relationships, as the current one does. We should also be moving more aggressively to deport those who are here illegally and have not qualified under the amnesty provisions of the 1986 act, and to devise an effective and humane border control system. We should not be deterred by fatuous comparisons with the Berlin Wall, whose role was to keep dissatisfied citizens in, not dissatisfied foreigners out.

Immigration—Lawful and Unlawful

The first sweeping immigration control law was passed in 1924. It attempted both to stem the flow of immigrants, principally from Europe, that totaled about thirty million in the four preceding decades, and to freeze the ethnic proportions of the United States by the use of national quotas.

While the 1924 law had some salutary effects—it let a saturated melting pot do its work and led to increased upward mobility for poor citizens, including blacks—the law was blatantly racist. "Oriental" immigrants were now totally excluded (Chinese immigration had been banned in 1882, and Japanese immigration limited "voluntarily" by the Japanese government in 1908). Hilter's rise to power generated strong pressures for liberalizing the 1924 act, but, while efforts were made during the 1930s to accommodate Jews within the German quota, it was not until the horror of the Holocaust became apparent—and when it was too late for most of its victims—that quotas were significantly relaxed. Special arrangements were made for refugees from the 1956 Hungarian Revolution, and in 1959 and thereafter for refugees from Cuba and Vietnam.

National origins quotas were eliminated in the Immigration and Naturalization Act of 1965, the principal goals of which were to reunite families and assure that immigration was consistent with manpower needs. (The reverse of "consistent with manpower needs" is, of course, the protection of American workers from an influx of competing foreign workers.) The 1965 legislation combined with the communications revolution, faster and cheaper transportation, and the revolution of rising expectations to trigger a vastly increased flow of immigrants, legal and illegal, from Latin America—above all, Mexico. The Vietnam War drove hundreds of thousands of Southeast Asians, many of them overseas Chinese, from their homelands. Large numbers of Koreans, Chinese, Filipinos, and Indians have immigrated during the past few decades. Tens of thousands of Africans, most of them young, have escaped from poverty and political turbulence to the United States. Many from the Middle East—Arabs, Iranians, Afghans—have done the same. The latest heirs to the Sephardic-German–Eastern European Jewish immigrant tradition are Jews who lived in the former Soviet Union.

With that diversity, however, has come concern that immigration is out of control. Millions of immigrants, particularly those from Latin America, are here illegally. The Immigration Reform and Control Act (IRCA) of 1986 established a formula for amnesty and regularization of illegal immigrants, imposed sanctions on employers who knowingly hired illegal immigrants, and called for a stepped-up program of border surveillance and enforcement. IRCA has had some success in reducing the flow of illegal aliens but not as much as had been hoped for by its proponents. The flow today is probably higher than it was before the act came into effect. About three million illegal aliens have applied for regularized status.

Even with the enactment of the Immigration Reform and Control Act of 1986 and the Immigration Act of 1990, the large majority of those who enter legally continue to do so under family preference provisions of the law. The 1990 law increased legal immigration by 40 percent, with the result that total immigration, legal and illegal, will probably now exceed one million annually. Nearly 70 percent of the legal nonrefugee newcomers will enter because they are related to naturalized citizens, resident aliens, and former illegal immigrants who qualified for the amnesty provisions of the 1986 immigration act. As many as three million immigrant workers will enter the United States labor force legally and illegally during the next five years.

Most will come without the skills needed to upgrade the labor force,   *10* the wage structure, and the competitiveness of our products. The availability of cheap labor skews investment decisions downward toward low-tech, low-wage, employment-intensive production. As a consequence, the skill levels of the work force, wages, and American technology do not advance as rapidly as in other advanced industrial countries, most notably Japan and Germany. As historian Otis Graham of the University of California at Santa Barbara has observed, a world-class economy "constantly moves its labor force toward higher value-added activities requiring higher skills." But George Borjas concludes that "the skill composition of the immigrant flow entering the United States has deteriorated significantly in the past two or three decades" with major implications for American global competitiveness.

High levels of immigration have not produced the positive economic results that advocates like Ben Wattenberg, the author of an article entitled "The Case for More Immigrants," and Julian Simon, author of *The Economic Consequences of Immigration,* expected. In addition to the adverse impact on productivity and wage levels in general, researchers like Rice University's Don Huddle are finding that immigrants compete for jobs with poor citizens, particularly blacks—for example, large numbers of blacks have been displaced by Hispanics, chiefly Mexican Americans, in building maintenance jobs in Los Angeles. To be sure, many immigrants pay taxes, but studies conclude that what they contribute does not cover the cost of services they receive, particularly when the costs of education are factored in (a Supreme Court ruling has assured the children of illegal aliens access to primary and secondary schools, and some states have granted residential tuition rates at public universities to illegal aliens). According to one study done in 1987, long before the recession, almost 40 percent of Haitians in Miami and Fort Lauderdale were receiving welfare assistance. A 1988 government report showed that 21 percent of California's adult welfare recipients were noncitizens. The extensive social services programs of Massachusetts have made that state a magnet for immigrants. From the 1980 census to the 1990 census, the Hispanic component of the state's population more than doubled, from 141,000 to 288,000. Almost half of the increase represents immigration. During the same period, the Asian population of Massachusetts almost tripled, from 49,000 to 143,000, with immigration accounting for the bulk of the increase. The imbalance between the state and local taxes immigrants pay and the social services they receive has contributed to the state's fiscal crisis. Recently, for example, Massachusetts officials, faced with an intensifying fiscal crisis, discovered that about 10 percent of the prison population consisted of illegal aliens. (It costs taxpayers about

$30,000 per year per prisoner.) In April of this year, New York sued the federal government to recover the $100 million the state claims it pays out annually for some four thousand illegal aliens in its prisons.

Suggestions for Writing and Discussion

1. In a sentence or two, state what you think is Harrison's basic belief in this piece.
2. Near the end of paragraph 2, Harrison uses the terms *acculturation* and *assimilative*. What do these words mean to you? Develop a definition of each word and explain how it relates to Harrison's argument.
3. Although Harrison bases most of his argument on facts and statistics, he does include one personal experience. Locate this experience and explain the effect this personal data might have on his argument as a whole.
4. In general, as you read this piece, did you find yourself agreeing with Harrison or disagreeing? What parts did you find most convincing or annoying?
5. Find one example in this piece where Harrison acknowledges the hardships of limiting immigration. What solutions can you think of that might solve—or at least address—the hardship you have identified? Write your response in the form of a letter to Harrison, asking him to consider your views when he next writes about the subject of immigration.
6. Write a response to Harrison's article in which you depend on your personal experience (your encounters in school, in the community, at work) to support his findings or refute them.

Suggestions for Extended Thinking and Writing

1. Do you think Harrison's predictions and concerns are exaggerated or realistic? Do research in the library to support your agreement or disagreement with his main points.
2. If Harrison continued the metaphor of America as a melting pot, he most likely would say that this pot is now boiling over. What experiences or events in your own life would lead you to agree with this analysis? What experiences or current events would lead you to disagree?

DAVID MORRIS

Rootlessness

David Morris is the author of The New City States *(1983) and coauthor, with Karl Hess, of* Neighborhood Power: The New Localism *(1975). Morris currently serves as codirector of the Institute for Local Self-Reliance in Washington DC, writes an editorial column for the* St. Paul Pioneer Press-Dispatch, *and contributes frequently to other magazines and journals, particularly those concerned with social issues. In an article in the March/April 1993 issue of the* Utne Reader, *Morris described America as "a nation without a sense of shared purpose, without a measure of neighborliness." He sees this lack of connection as "the most enduring legacy of the Reagan-Bush years," noting that "after more than a decade of being taught that looking out for number one is the highest social good, we now take it for granted that public is bad and private is good, that collective is bad and individual is good." In the following selection, "Rootlessness" (first published in the* Utne Reader, May/June 1990), *Morris explores and analyzes his concerns about what he sees as the pervasive lack of community throughout the United States.*

Pre-Reading and Journal-Writing Suggestions

1. What was your hometown like when you were growing up? What is it like today? Have the changes been for the better or for the worse?
2. Could you survive without a car? Write a piece in which you imagine what life would be like today if the automobile had never been invented.
3. Most Americans feel as if they know television celebrities better than their own next-door neighbors. Do you fit into this category? What explanations do you have for this phenomenon, in general?

Americans are a rootless people. Each year one in six of us changes residences; one in four changes jobs. We see nothing troubling in these statistics. For most of us, they merely reflect the restless energy that made America great. A nation of immigrants, unsurprisingly, celebrates those willing to pick up stakes and move on: the frontiersman, the cowboy, the entrepreneur, the corporate raider.

Rootedness has never been a goal of public policy in the United States. In the 1950s and 1960s local governments bulldozed hundreds of inner city neighborhoods, all in the name of urban renewal. In the 1960s and 1970s court-ordered busing forced tens of thousands of children to abandon their neighborhood schools, all in the interest of racial harmony. In the 1980s a wave of hostile takeovers shuffled hundreds of billions of dollars of corporate assets, all in the pursuit of economic efficiency.

Hundreds of thousands of informal gathering spots that once nurtured community across the country have disappeared. The soda fountain and lunch counter are gone. The branch library is an endangered species. Even the number of neighborhood taverns is declining. In the 1940s, 90 percent of beer and spirits was consumed in public places. Today only 30 percent is.

This privatization of American public life is most apparent to overseas visitors. "After four years here, I still feel more of a foreigner than in any other place in the world I have been," one well-traveled woman told Ray Oldenburg, the author of the marvelous new book about public gathering spots, *The Great Good Place* (1990, Paragon House). "There is no contact between the various households, we rarely see the neighbors and certainly do not know any of them."

The woman contrasts this with her life in Europe. "In Luxembourg, however, we would frequently stroll down to one of the local cafés in the evening and there pass a very congenial few hours in the company of the local fireman, dentist, bank employee, or whoever happened to be there at the time."

In most American cities, zoning laws prohibit mixing commerce and residence. The result is an overreliance on the car. Oldenburg cites the experience of a couple who had lived in a small house in Vienna and a large one in Los Angeles: "In Los Angeles we are hesitant to leave our sheltered home in order to visit friends or to participate in cultural or entertainment events because every such outing involves a major investment of time and nervous strain in driving long distances. In Vienna everything, opera, theaters, shops, cafés, are within easy walking distance."

Shallow roots weaken our ties in the neighborhood and workplace. The average blue-collar worker receives only seven days' notice before losing his or her job, only two days when not backed by a union. The *Whole Earth Review* unthinkingly echoes this lack of connectedness when it advises its readers to "first visit an electronics store near you and get familiar with the features—then compare price and shop mail order via [an] 800 number."

This lack of connectedness breeds a costly instability in American life. In business, when owners have no loyalty to workers, workers have no loyalty to owners. Quality of work suffers. Visiting Japanese management specialists point to our labor turnover rate as a key factor in our relative economic decline. In the pivotal electronics industry, for example, our turnover rate is four times that of Japan's.

American employers respond to declining sales and profit margins by cutting what they regard as their most expendable resource: employees. In Japan, corporate accounting systems consider labor a fixed asset. Japanese companies spend enormous amounts of money training workers. "They view that training as an investment, and they don't want to let the investment slip away," Martin K. Starr of Columbia University recently told *Business*

Week. Twenty percent of the work force, the core workers in major industrial companies, have lifetime job security in Japan.

Rootlessness in the neighborhood also costs us dearly. Neighborliness   10
saves money, a fact we often overlook because the transactions of strong, rooted neighborhoods take place outside of the money economy.

- Neighborliness reduces crime. People watch the streets where children play and know who the strangers are.
- Neighborliness saves energy. In the late 1970s Portland, Oregon, discovered it could save 5 percent of its energy consumption simply by reviving the corner grocery store. No longer would residents in need of a carton of milk or a loaf of bread have to drive to a shopping mall.
- Neighborliness lowers the cost of health care. "It is cruel and unusual punishment to send someone to a nursing home when they are not sick," says Dick Ladd, head of Oregon's Senior Services. But when we don't know our neighbors we can't rely on them. Society picks up the tab. In 1987 home-based care cost $230 a month in Oregon compared to $962 per month for nursing home care.

Psychoanalyst and author Erich Fromm saw a direct correlation between the decline in the number of neighborhood bartenders and the rise in the number of psychiatrists. "Sometimes you want to go where everybody knows your name," goes the apt refrain of the popular TV show *Cheers.* Once you poured out your troubles over a nickel beer to someone who knew you and your family. And if you got drunk, well, you could walk home. Now you drive cross town and pay $100 an hour to a stranger for emotional relief.

The breakdown of community life may explain, in part, why the three   15
best-selling drugs in America treat stress: ulcer medication (Tagamet), hypertension (Inderal), tranquilizer (Valium).

American society has evolved into a cultural environment where it is ever harder for deep roots to take hold. What can we do to change this?

- **Rebuild walking communities.** Teach urban planners that overdependence on transportation is a sign of failure in a social system. Impose the true costs of the car on its owners. Recent studies indicate that to do so would raise the cost of gasoline by as much as $2 a gallon. Recently Stockholm declared war on cars by imposing a $50 a month fee for car owners, promising to increase the fee until the city was given back to pedestrians and mass transit.
- **Equip every neighborhood with a library, a coffeehouse, a diversified shopping district, and a park.**
- **Make rootedness a goal of public policy.** In the 1970s a Vermont land use law, for example, required an economic component to environmental impact statements. In at least one case, a suburban shopping mall was denied approval because it would undermine existing city businesses. In Berkeley, citizens voted two to one to

permit commercial rent control in neighborhoods whose independently owned businesses were threatened by gentrification.

- **Reward stability and continuity.** Today, if a government seizes 20 property it pays the owner the market price. Identical homes have identical value, even if one is home to a third-generation family, while the other is occupied by a new tenant. Why not pay a premium, say 50 percent above the current market price, for every 10 years the occupant has lived there? Forty years of residence would be rewarded with compensation four times greater than the market price. The increment above the market price should go not to the owner but to the occupant, if the two are not the same. By favoring occupants over owners, this policy not only rewards neighborliness, but promotes social justice. By raising the overall costs of dislocation, it also discourages development that undermines rootedness.

- **Prohibit hostile takeovers.** Japanese, German, and Swedish corporations are among the most competitive and innovative in the world. But in these countries hostile takeovers are considered unethical business practices or are outlawed entirely.

- **Encourage local and employee ownership.** Protecting existing management is not the answer if that management is not locally rooted. Very few cities have an ongoing economic campaign to promote local ownership despite the obvious advantages to the community. Employee ownership exists in some form in more than 5,000 U.S. companies, but in only a handful is that ownership significant.

- **And above all, correct our history books.** America did not become a wealthy nation because of rootlessness, but in spite of it. A multitude of natural resources across an expansive continent and the arrival of tens of millions of skilled immigrants furnished us enormous advantages. We could overlook the high social costs of rootlessness. This is no longer true.

Instability is not the price we must pay for progress. Loyalty, in the plant and the neighborhood, does not stifle innovation. These are lessons we've ignored too long. More rooted cultures such as Japan and Germany are now outcompeting us in the marketplace, and in the neighborhood. We would do well to learn the value of community.

Suggestions for Writing and Discussion

1. Morris begins this piece by calling Americans a "rootless people." Summarize the reasons he gives for this restless condition. Can you supply any others?

2. As a result of this rootlessness, Morris sees Americans as becoming a disconnected people as well. Do you agree with him? Why or why not?

3. Do you, like Morris, believe in neighborhood and community unity? What difference does it make to the average person? Write your response as an editorial to be printed in a small newsletter, trying to convince people who live in your neighborhood or community to form an organization that will promote a sense of "rootedness."

4. According to Erich Fromm, bartenders work just as well as psychiatrists to calm people's fears and release them from their anxieties. This comparison implies that it is easy for people to pour out their troubles as long as they are talking to professionals or to friendly acquaintances rather than to close friends or family. Do you believe that it's easier to talk about problems with someone who doesn't know you well than with someone who does? Explain, using examples to illustrate your ideas.

5. Evaluate Morris's suggestions for rebuilding community closeness. Which one do you feel is most important? Are any of his ideas unrealistic? Idealistic? Explain.

6. What is Morris's main purpose in writing this piece? Who is his intended audience? What details from the article might appeal particularly to the audience you have defined? What type of reader might not be receptive to this piece? Explain your answer.

Suggestions for Extended Thinking and Writing

1. Write a descriptive piece about the neighborhood in which you presently live. In this piece, let the details you select show readers (perhaps your current classmates) how you feel about this neighborhood. In other words, try to give readers your impressions without ever coming out and stating how you feel.

2. Research the roots of your hometown or neighborhood. Find out what life was like before 1950 by conducting interviews with several of the oldest residents. Your purpose is to find out what once existed. Then in an objective essay, combine all of your primary sources and come to some conclusion about how progress and change have affected your town's sense of unity. As you write, imagine that your essay will be published in a book celebrating the anniversary of the founding of your town or city.

3. Morris doesn't mention how malls changed the downtown shopping districts in many small towns and cities. Write an essay based on one of these two suggestions:

   a. Compare the atmosphere of an older established shopping area downtown with that of a mall. Use direct observations as well as interviews for your sources.

   b. Explain why a mall can or cannot serve as a community that encourages a sense of connection and unity among those who shop and work there.

AMY TAN

Two Kinds

> *In 1952, 2½ years after her parents arrived from China and settled in Oakland, California, Amy Tan was born. During her early years, Tan yearned to escape her Asian heritage, and even as an adult she felt torn between the messages of the American culture and the values of her Chinese home culture. Tan's mother, like the mother in this selection, had great ambitions for her daughter. In fact, Tan has jokingly told interviewers that her mother wanted her to become "a neurosurgeon while being a concert pianist on the side."*
>
> *Tan, whose interest in writing began early, won a writing contest when she was eight. Later she earned both undergraduate and graduate degrees from San Francisco State University and then worked for several years as a language consultant and freelance technical writer. Inspired by the short stories of Louise Erdrich, who writes about her own Native American culture, Tan became intrigued with the possibility of writing fiction depicting the conflicts of Chinese immigrant families and their American-born children. After returning from a visit to China with her mother, she published her first book,* The Joy Luck Club *(1989), which was made into a critically acclaimed film in 1993. "Two Kinds" appears as a story in* The Joy Luck Club.

Pre-Reading and Journal-Writing Topics

1. When you were a small child, what did you imagine you'd be when you grew up? Have those dreams changed or stayed the same? Explain.
2. Write about a time you came up against something that was difficult for you to do. Perhaps some type of lessons you had to take when you were young. How did you approach this difficulty? Did anyone help you? Encourage you? Did you give up easily or after a struggle? Did you persevere? Did you learn anything about yourself from this experience?
3. In what ways is your "inner" self different from the self that your family or friends see?
4. Write about a childhood fight you had with a parent. What was this fight about? What happened? Did anybody win the fight?

My mother believed you could be anything you wanted to be in America. You could open a restaurant. You could work for the government and get good retirement. You could buy a house with almost no money down. You could become rich. You could become instantly famous.

"Of course, you can be prodigy, too," my mother told me when I was nine. "You can be best anything. What does Auntie Lindo know? Her daughter, she is only best tricky."

America was where all my mother's hopes lay. She had come to San Francisco in 1949 after losing everything in China: her mother and father, her family home, her first husband, and two daughters, twin baby girls. But she never looked back with regret. Things could get better in so many ways.

We didn't immediately pick the right kind of prodigy. At first my mother thought I could be a Chinese Shirley Temple. We'd watch Shirley's old movies on TV as though they were training films. My mother would poke my arm and say, "*Ni kan.* You watch." And I would see Shirley tapping her feet, or singing a sailor song, or pursing her lips into a very round O while saying "Oh, my goodness."

"*Ni kan,*" my mother said, as Shirley's eyes flooded with tears. "You already know how. Don't need talent for crying!"

Soon after my mother got this idea about Shirley Temple, she took me to the beauty training school in the Mission District and put me in the hands of a student who could barely hold the scissors without shaking. Instead of getting big fat curls, I emerged with an uneven mass of crinkly black fuzz. My mother dragged me off to the bathroom and tried to wet down my hair.

"You look like Negro Chinese," she lamented, as if I had done this on purpose.

The instructor of the beauty training school had to lop off these soggy clumps to make my hair even again. "Peter Pan is very popular these days," the instructor assured my mother. I now had hair the length of a boy's, with curly bangs that hung at a slant two inches above my eyebrows. I liked the haircut, and it made me actually look forward to my future fame.

In fact, in the beginning I was just as excited as my mother, maybe even more so. I pictured this prodigy part of me as many different images, and I tried each one on for size. I was a dainty ballerina girl standing by the curtain, waiting to hear the music that would send me floating on my tiptoes. I was like the Christ child lifted out of the straw manger, crying with holy indignity. I was Cinderella stepping from her pumpkin carriage with sparkly cartoon music filling the air.

In all of my imaginings I was filled with a sense that I would soon become perfect. My mother and father would adore me. I would be beyond reproach. I would never feel the need to sulk, or to clamor for anything.

But sometimes the prodigy in me became impatient. "If you don't hurry up and get me out of here, I'm disappearing for good," it warned. "And then you'll always be nothing."

Every night after dinner my mother and I would sit at the Formica-topped kitchen table. She would present new tests, taking her examples from stories of amazing children that she read in *Ripley's Believe It or Not* or *Good Housekeeping, Reader's Digest,* or any of a dozen other magazines she kept in a pile in our bathroom. My mother got these magazines from people whose houses she cleaned. And since she cleaned many houses each week, we had a great assortment. She would look through them all, searching for stories about remarkable children.

The first night she brought out a story about a three-year-old boy who knew the capitals of all the states and even of most of the European countries. A teacher was quoted as saying that the little boy could also pronounce the names of the foreign cities correctly. "What's the capital of Finland?" my mother asked me, looking at the story.

All I knew was the capital of California, because Sacramento was the name of the street we lived on in Chinatown. "Nairobi!" I guessed, saying the most foreign word I could think of. She checked to see if that might be one way to pronounce *Helsinki* before showing me the answer.

The tests got harder—multiplying numbers in my head, finding the queen of hearts in a deck of cards, trying to stand on my head without using my hands, predicting the daily temperatures in Los Angeles, New York, and London. One night I had to look at a page from the Bible for three minutes and then report everything I could remember. "Now Jehoshaphat had riches and honor in abundance and . . . that's all I remember, Ma," I said. 15

And after seeing, once again, my mother's disappointed face, something inside me began to die. I hated the tests, the raised hopes and failed expectations. Before going to bed that night I looked in the mirror above the bathroom sink, and when I saw only my face staring back—and understood that it would always be this ordinary face—I began to cry. Such a sad, ugly girl! I made high-pitched noises like a crazed animal, trying to scratch out the face in the mirror.

And then I saw what seemed to be the prodigy side of me—a face I had never seen before. I looked at my reflection, blinking so that I could see more clearly. The girl staring back at me was angry, powerful. She and I were the same. I had new thoughts, willful thoughts—or, rather, thoughts filled with lots of won'ts. I won't let her change me, I promised myself. I won't be what I'm not.

So now when my mother presented her tests, I performed listlessly, my head propped on one arm. I pretended to be bored. And I was. I got so bored that I started counting the bellows of the foghorns out on the bay while my mother drilled me in other areas. The sound was comforting and reminded me of the cow jumping over the moon. And the next day I played a game with myself, seeing if my mother would give up on me before eight bellows. After a while I usually counted only one bellow, maybe two at most. At last she was beginning to give up hope.

Two or three months went by without any mention of my being a prodigy. And then one day my mother was watching the *Ed Sullivan Show* on TV. The TV was old and the sound kept shorting out. Every time my mother got halfway up from the sofa to adjust the set, the sound would come back on and Sullivan would be talking. As soon as she sat down, Sullivan would go silent again. She got up—the TV broke into loud piano music. She sat down—silence. Up and down, back and forth, quiet and loud. It was like a stiff, embraceless dance between her and the TV set. Finally, she stood by the set with her hand on the sound dial.

She seemed entranced by the music, a frenzied little piano piece with   20
a mesmerizing quality, which alternated between quick, playful passages and teasing, lilting ones.

"*Ni kan*," my mother said, calling me over with hurried hand gestures. "Look here."

I could see why my mother was fascinated by the music. It was being pounded out by a little Chinese girl, about nine years old, with a Peter Pan haircut. The girl had the sauciness of a Shirley Temple. She was proudly modest, like a proper Chinese child. And she also did a fancy sweep of a curtsy, so that the fluffy skirt of her white dress cascaded to the floor like the petals of a large carnation.

In spite of these warning signs, I wasn't worried. Our family had no piano and we couldn't afford to buy one, let alone reams of sheet music and piano lessons. So I could be generous in my comments when my mother bad-mouthed the little girl on TV.

"Play note right, but doesn't sound good!" my mother complained. "No singing sound."

"What are you picking on her for?" I said carelessly. "She's pretty good.   25
Maybe she's not the best, but she's trying hard." I knew almost immediately that I would be sorry I had said that.

"Just like you," she said. "Not the best. Because you not trying." She gave a little huff as she let go of the sound dial and sat down on the sofa.

The little Chinese girl sat down also, to play an encore of "Anitra's Tanz," by Grieg. I remember the song, because later on I had to learn how to play it.

Three days after watching the *Ed Sullivan Show* my mother told me what my schedule would be for piano lessons and piano practice. She had talked to Mr. Chong, who lived on the first floor of our apartment building. Mr. Chong was a retired piano teacher, and my mother had traded house-cleaning services for weekly lessons and a piano for me to practice on every day, two hours a day, from four until six.

When my mother told me this, I felt as though I had been sent to hell. I whined, and then kicked my foot a little when I couldn't stand it anymore.

"Why don't you like me the way I am?" I cried. "I'm *not* a genius! I   30
can't play the piano. And even if I could, I wouldn't go on TV if you paid me a million dollars!"

My mother slapped me. "Who ask you to be genius?" she shouted. "Only ask you be your best. For you sake. You think I want you to be genius? Hnnh! What for! Who ask you!"

"So ungrateful," I heard her mutter in Chinese. "If she had as much talent as she has temper, she'd be famous now."

Mr. Chong, whom I secretly nicknamed Old Chong, was very strange, always tapping his fingers to the silent music of an invisible orchestra. He looked ancient in my eyes. He had lost most of the hair on the top of his head, and he wore thick glasses and had eyes that always looked tired. But he must have been younger than I thought, since he lived with his mother and was not yet married.

I met Old Lady Chong once, and that was enough. She had a peculiar smell, like a baby that had done something in its pants, and her fingers felt like a dead person's, like an old peach I once found in the back of the refrigerator; its skin just slid off the flesh when I picked it up.

I soon found out why Old Chong had retired from teaching piano. 35 He was deaf. "Like Beethoven!" he shouted to me. "We're both listening only in our head!" And he would start to conduct his frantic silent sonatas.

Our lessons went like this. He would open the book and point to different things, explaining their purpose: "Key! Treble! Bass! No sharps or flats! So this is C major! Listen now and play after me!"

And then he would play the C scale a few times, a simple chord, and then, as if inspired by an old unreachable itch, he would gradually add more notes and running trills and a pounding bass until the music was really something quite grand.

I would play after him, the simple scale, the simple chord, and then just play some nonsense that sounded like a cat running up and down on top of garbage cans. Old Chong would smile and applaud and say, "Very good! But now you must learn to keep time!"

So that's how I discovered that Old Chong's eyes were too slow to keep up with the wrong notes I was playing. He went through the motions in half time. To help me keep rhythm, he stood behind me and pushed down on my right shoulder for every beat. He balanced pennies on top of my wrists so that I would keep them still as I slowly played scales and arpeggios. He had me curve my hand around an apple and keep that shape when playing chords. He marched stiffly to show me how to make each finger dance up and down, staccato, like an obedient little soldier.

He taught me all these things, and that was how I also learned I could 40 be lazy and get away with mistakes, lots of mistakes. If I hit the wrong notes because I hadn't practiced enough, I never corrected myself. I just kept playing in rhythm. And Old Chong kept conducting his own private reverie.

So maybe I never really gave myself a fair chance. I did pick up the basics pretty quickly, and I might have become a good pianist at that young age. But I was so determined not to try, not to be anybody different, and I learned to play only the most ear-splitting preludes, the most discordant hymns.

Over the next year I practiced like this, dutifully in my own way. And then one day I heard my mother and her friend Lindo Jong both talking in a loud, bragging tone of voice so that others could hear. It was after church, and I was leaning against a brick wall, wearing a dress with stiff white petticoats. Auntie Lindo's daughter, Waverly, who was my age, was standing farther down the wall, about five feet away. We had grown up together and shared all the closeness of two sisters, squabbling over crayons and dolls. In other words, for the most part, we hated each other. I thought she was snotty. Waverly Jong had gained a certain amount of fame as "Chinatown's Littlest Chinese Chess Champion."

"She bring home too many trophy," Auntie Lindo lamented that Sunday. "All day she play chess. All day I have no time do nothing but dust off her winnings." She threw a scolding look at Waverly, who pretended not to see her.

"You lucky you don't have this problem," Auntie Lindo said with a sigh to my mother.

And my mother squared her shoulders and bragged: "Our problem   45 worser than yours. If we ask Jing-mei wash dish, she hear nothing but music. It's like you can't stop this natural talent."

And right then I was determined to put a stop to her foolish pride.

A few weeks later Old Chong and my mother conspired to have me play in a talent show that was to be held in the church hall. By then my parents had saved up enough to buy me a secondhand piano, a black Wurlitzer spinet with a scarred bench. It was the showpiece of our living room.

For the talent show I was to play a piece called "Pleading Child," from Schumann's *Scenes From Childhood.* It was a simple, moody piece that sounded more difficult than it was. I was supposed to memorize the whole thing. But I dawdled over it, playing a few bars and then cheating, looking up to see what notes followed. I never really listened to what I was playing. I daydreamed about being somewhere else, about being someone else.

The part I liked to practice best was the fancy curtsy: right foot out, touch the rose on the carpet with a pointed foot, sweep to the side, bend left leg, look up, and smile.

My parents invited all the couples from their social club to witness my   50 debut. Auntie Lindo and Uncle Tin were there. Waverly and her two older brothers had also come. The first two rows were filled with children either younger or older than I was. The littlest ones got to go first. They recited simple nursery rhymes, squawked out tunes on miniature violins, and twirled hula hoops in pink ballet tutus, and when they bowed or curtsied, the audience would sigh in unison, *"Awww,"* and then clap enthusiastically.

When my turn came, I was very confident. I remember my childish excitement. It was as if I knew, without a doubt, that the prodigy side of me really did exist. I had no fear whatsoever, no nervousness. I remember thinking, This is it! This is it! I looked out over the audience, at my mother's blank face, my father's yawn, Auntie Lindo's stiff-lipped smile, Waverly's sulky expression. I had on a white dress, layered with sheets of lace, and a pink bow in my Peter Pan haircut. As I sat down, I envisioned people jumping to their feet and Ed Sullivan rushing up to introduce me to everyone on TV.

And I started to play. Everything was so beautiful. I was so caught up in how lovely I looked that I wasn't worried about how I would sound. So I was surprised when I hit the first wrong note. And then I hit another, and another. A chill started at the top of my head and began to trickle down. Yet I couldn't stop playing, as though my hands were bewitched. I kept thinking my fingers would adjust themselves back, like a train switching to the right track. I played this strange jumble through to the end, the sour notes staying with me all the way.

When I stood up, I discovered my legs were shaking. Maybe I had just been nervous, and the audience, like Old Chong, had seen me go through the right motions and had not heard anything wrong at all. I swept my right foot out, went down on my knee, looked up, and smiled. The room was quiet, except for Old Chong, who was beaming and shouting, "Bravo! Bravo! Well done!" But then I saw my mother's face, her stricken face. The audience clapped weakly, and as I walked back to my chair, with my whole face quivering as I tried not to cry, I heard a little boy whisper loudly to his mother, "That was awful," and the mother whispered, "Well, she certainly tried."

And now I realized how many people were in the audience—the whole world, it seemed. I was aware of eyes burning into my back. I felt the shame of my mother and father as they sat stiffly through the rest of the show.

We could have escaped during intermission. Pride and some strange sense of honor must have anchored my parents to their chairs. And so we watched it all: The eighteen-year-old boy with a fake moustache who did a magic show and juggled flaming hoops while riding a unicycle. The breasted girl with white makeup who sang an aria from *Madame Butterfly* and got an honorable mention. And the eleven-year-old boy who won first prize playing a tricky violin song that sounded like a busy bee.

After the show the Hsus, the Jongs, and the St. Clairs, from the Joy Luck Club, came up to my mother and father.

"Lots of talented kids," Auntie Lindo said vaguely, smiling broadly.

"That was somethin' else," my father said, and I wondered if he was referring to me in a humorous way, or whether he even remembered what I had done.

Waverly looked at me and shrugged her shoulders. "You aren't a genius like me," she said matter-of-factly. And if I hadn't felt so bad, I would have pulled her braids and punched her stomach.

But my mother's expression was what devastated me: a quiet, blank look that said she had lost everything. I felt the same way, and everybody seemed now to be coming up, like gawkers at the scene of an accident, to see what parts were actually missing.

When we got on the bus to go home, my father was humming the busy-bee tune and my mother was silent. I kept thinking she wanted to wait until we got home before shouting at me. But when my father unlocked the door to our apartment, my mother walked in and went straight to the back, into the bedroom. No accusations. No blame. And in a way, I felt disappointed. I had been waiting for her to start shouting, so that I could shout back and cry and blame her for all my misery.

I had assumed that my talent-show fiasco meant that I would never have to play the piano again. But two days later, after school, my mother came out of the kitchen and saw me watching TV.

"Four clock," she reminded me, as if it were any other day. I was stunned, as though she were asking me to go through the talent-show torture again. I planted myself more squarely in front of the TV.

"Turn off TV," she called from the kitchen five minutes later.

I didn't budge. And then I decided. I didn't have to do what my mother said anymore. I wasn't her slave. This wasn't China. I had listened to her before, and look what happened. She was the stupid one.   65

She came out of the kitchen and stood in the arched entryway of the living room. "Four clock," she said once again, louder.

"I'm not going to play anymore," I said nonchalantly. "Why should I? I'm not a genius."

She stood in front of the TV. I saw that her chest was heaving up and down in an angry way.

"No!" I said, and I now felt stronger, as if my true self had finally emerged. So this was what had been inside me all along.

"No! I won't!" I screamed.   70

She snapped off the TV, yanked me by the arm and pulled me off the floor. She was frighteningly strong, half pulling, half carrying me toward the piano as I kicked the throw rugs under my feet. She lifted me up and onto the hard bench. I was sobbing by now, looking at her bitterly. Her chest was heaving even more and her mouth was open, smiling crazily as if she were pleased that I was crying.

"You want me to be someone that I'm not!" I sobbed. "I'll never be the kind of daughter you want me to be!"

"Only two kinds of daughters," she shouted in Chinese. "Those who are obedient and those who follow their own mind! Only one kind of daughter can live in this house. Obedient daughter!"

"Then I wish I weren't your daughter. I wish you weren't my mother," I shouted. As I said these things I got scared. It felt like worms and toads and slimy things crawling out of my chest, but it also felt good, that this awful side of me had surfaced, at last.

"Too late change this," my mother said shrilly.   75

And I could sense her anger rising to its breaking point. I wanted to see it spill over. And that's when I remembered the babies she had lost in

China, the ones we never talked about. "Then I wish I'd never been born!" I shouted. "I wish I were dead! Like them."

It was as if I had said magic words. Alakazam!—her face went blank, her mouth closed, her arms went slack, and she backed out of the room, stunned, as if she were blowing away like a small brown leaf, thin, brittle, lifeless.

It was not the only disappointment my mother felt in me. In the years that followed, I failed her many times, each time asserting my will, my right to fall short of expectations. I didn't get straight *A*s. I didn't become class president. I didn't get into Stanford. I dropped out of college.

Unlike my mother, I did not believe I could be anything I wanted to be. I could only be me.

And for all those years we never talked about the disaster at the recital   *80* or my terrible declarations afterward at the piano bench. Neither of us talked about it again, as if it were a betrayal that was now unspeakable. So I never found a way to ask her why she had hoped for something so large that failure was inevitable.

And even worse, I never asked her about what frightened me the most: Why had she given up hope? For after our struggle at the piano, she never mentioned my playing again. The lessons stopped. The lid to the piano was closed, shutting out the dust, my misery, and her dreams.

So she surprised me. A few years ago she offered to give me the piano, for my thirtieth birthday. I had not played in all those years. I saw the offer as a sign of forgiveness, a tremendous burden removed.

"Are you sure?" I asked shyly. "I mean, won't you and Dad miss it?"

"No, this your piano," she said firmly. "Always your piano. You only one can play."

"Well, I probably can't play anymore," I said. "It's been years."   *85*

"You pick up fast," my mother said, as if she knew this was certain. "You have natural talent. You could be genius if you want to."

"No, I couldn't."

"You just not trying," my mother said. And she was neither angry nor sad. She said it as if announcing a fact that could never be disproved. "Take it," she said.

But I didn't at first. It was enough that she had offered it to me. And after that, every time I saw it in my parents' living room, standing in front of the bay window, it made me feel proud, as if it were a shiny trophy that I had won back.

Last week I sent a tuner over to my parents' apartment and had the   *90* piano reconditioned, for purely sentimental reasons. My mother had died a few months before, and I had been getting things in order for my father, a little bit at a time. I put the jewelry in special silk pouches. The sweaters she had knitted in yellow, pink, bright orange—all the colors I hated—I put in mothproof boxes. I found some old Chinese silk dresses, the kind with little slits up the sides. I rubbed the old silk against my skin, and then wrapped them in tissue and decided to take them home with me.

After I had the piano tuned, I opened the lid and touched the keys. It sounded even richer than I remembered. Really, it was a very good piano. Inside the bench were the same exercise notes with handwritten scales, the same secondhand music books with their covers held together with yellow tape.

I opened up the Schumann book to the dark little piece I had played at the recital. It was on the left-hand page, "Pleading Child." It looked more difficult than I remembered. I played a few bars, surprised at how easily the notes came back to me.

And for the first time, or so it seemed, I noticed the piece on the right-hand side. It was called "Perfectly Contented." I tried to play this one as well. It had a lighter melody but with the same flowing rhythm and turned out to be quite easy. "Pleading Child" was shorter but slower; "Perfectly Contented" was longer but faster. And after I had played them both a few times, I realized they were two halves of the same song.

Suggestions for Writing and Discussion

1. What's your reaction to this story? Did you enjoy it? Why or why not?
2. From this story, how would you characterize Jing-mei's mother? What are her strengths? What are her weaknesses?
3. How would you characterize Jing-mei as a child? Her strengths? Weaknesses?
4. Describe the relationship between mother and daughter in the beginning of this story. When does it begin to change? Why does it change?
5. Make a list of the words, phrases, and events you responded to most strongly in this story. From this list, how would you characterize Tan's approach to telling stories?
6. Choose one quotation from this story—one that you may have noticed on your first reading. Write a brief response, explaining why this quote caught your interest.
7. In what ways does Old Chong fit into the themes in this story? What's his main contribution to this piece?
8. The conflict between mother and daughter reaches a climax when Jing-mei shouts out at her mother, "I wish I were dead! Like them!" What's your initial reaction to this confrontation? Do you think Jing-mei is being exceptionally cruel? Why or why not? In the end, who wins this battle of wills?
9. The title of this piece, "Two Kinds," can be interpreted in a number of ways. Certainly on a literal level it refers to the "two kinds" of daughters

Jing-mei's mother mentions. But what might this title refer to on a deeper, less obvious level? As you respond, consider especially the story's final paragraph.

Suggestions for Extended Thinking and Writing

1. Write about an event in your childhood where you had a disagreement (or out-and-out fight!) with a close friend or family member. Write this piece so that you show both sides of the event. Imagine that you are writing this to show the friend or family member that you have come to understand his or her side of the conflict as well as your own.

2. Try your hand at rewriting this story. Choose one scene you would want to do differently, and create your own version. After doing so, explain in a journal entry why you made this change.

3. Write an essay in which you attempt to persuade your audience of classmates that (a) Jing-mei's mother was much too demanding of her daughter; (b) Jing-mei was much too stubborn and rebellious as a daughter; (c) Jing-mei's mother was right in her perception that Jing-mei didn't try her best; (d) Jing-mei's mother didn't know her daughter—Jing-mei did try her best! Be sure to provide evidence from the story to support your ideas.

SUGGESTIONS FOR MAKING CONNECTIONS

1. Many people around the world still view the United States as the land of promise and opportunity. Despite the losses that many immigrants suffered, despite the cruel treatment many received simply because they were viewed as different, why did so many choose to remain in this country and encourage their relatives to follow? Refer to selections in this section as you write your response, using your own experience and observations as well.

2. Some argue that the concept of America as a melting pot is not entirely accurate. In a melting pot, everything blends together and unites into a new whole. In a short essay, defend this metaphor as accurate, or explain in detail a different metaphor that you believe better represents this country. Feel free to use your own experiences in this piece. In addition, refer to selections in this section that support or refute your own view of the melting-pot metaphor.

3. As Mary Antin's "The Promised Land" shows us, many immigrants came to this country with the intention of becoming part of American society. Other selections attest that many immigrants preferred to hold on to their native culture and values. Explain which approach you

would most likely adopt if you were to move to another country. Use your own experiences for support.

4. Several of the writings in this section deal with culture and how it affects the relationships formed between children and their parents or other authority figures. Analyze the inner conflicts, the discoveries, and the resolutions that occur within this framework.

5. Use at least three of the selections in this section to analyze the different processes by which we come to know who we are.

6. To what extent should one's identity, or sense of self, relate to and draw upon the past (including ethnic and religious traditions and beliefs)? In addition to several sources from this section, draw upon your own experiences and observations to answer this question.

7. Compare the differences between being rooted and being uprooted. Examine both the positive and negative aspects of each, and come to some conclusion about how each state of being contributes to what we know and who we are.

8. Analyze the effects of being caught between two identities. Besides using the sources in this section for references, rely on your own experiences and observations. What happens when we are caught in a struggle between who we know we might be and who we used to be or who someone else wants us to be?

9. Write an essay in which you show that loss of one identity is just a natural stage in the evolution of becoming a whole person.

10. Many of the writings in this section deal with the struggle to learn about oneself and one's place in the world. Examine several of these processes and come to some conclusions about the best ways to address such complex issues. What do we need to do? Where do we need to go? Who has the answers? How can we find them?

11. Review the selections in this section. Select the piece that you enjoyed the most, as well as the one that you cared for the least. Now try to analyze why you enjoyed the piece you did. Was it the topic? The theme? The style? The language? Also analyze why you didn't favor the other piece. In other words, what are the major differences between these two pieces as far as you, the reader, are concerned?

12. From all of these readings, choose the person or character you most admired and the character or person you least admired. Compare the two and explain the reasons for your evaluation.

13. List several questions and issues raised by selections in this section. Evaluate these questions and issues and explain which one is the most important to you. Write an essay in which you try to convince others that this issue is of great importance. Use contemporary examples and your own experiences as major support in this essay.

7

Parents and Children

Previews: PARENTS AND CHILDREN

Here we are materially well off, but spiritually deprived. We miss our country. Most of all we miss you. Should Buddha exist, we should keep praying to be reunited.

Dear Mother, keep up your mind. Pray to Buddha silently. We will have a future and I hope it will be soon.

We want to swim in our own pond.
Clear or stinky, still it is ours.

From: *Letter to My Mother,* TRAN THI NGA

Then I looked again at this thief, this "Loaf-of-bread gunman," as the papers had tagged him. He had taken five loaves of bread, along with twelve dollars. Suddenly I could not stay there condemning this man, my father. It seemed such a waste, this magnificently strong man sitting there, his tremendous chest barely moving, hands resting quietly, talking to me, his whole being showering torrents of words about me.

From: *I Remember Papa,* HARRY DOLAN

When I was four years old, I went to prekindergarten. . . . My heart was pounding with a force I did not know my little body had when I jumped out of the car, and I know fear was evident on my face, but Dad didn't budge. I asked, "Daddy, aren't you coming with me?" He replied, "No, Grace, you know where your class is and who your teachers are. You can go by yourself." He was teaching me to be self-sufficient at four.

From: *Chinese Puzzle,* GRACE MING-YEE WAI

Today at the beach my chubby-legged, brown-skinned daughter ran laughing into the water as fast as she could. My wife and I laughed watching her, until we heard behind us a low guttural curse and then an unpleasant voice raised in an imitation war whoop.

From: *For My Indian Daughter,* LEWIS P. JOHNSON

TRAN THI NGA

Letter to My Mother

> *Tran Thi Nga, who was born in China in 1927, was a social worker in Vietnam. In addition, she has worked as a journalist in both Asia and the United States. This letter suggests the connections she feels to her mother, as well as the differences she sees between their lives and the places they live.*

Pre-Reading and Journal-Writing Suggestions

1. Write a tribute to an older relative in your family. In this tribute, describe what you admire most about this person. What have you learned from observing and hearing about this person's life experiences and everyday values?
2. At this point in your life, what is the greatest sacrifice you have made? What is the greatest sacrifice someone else has made for you? Write a descriptive narrative responding to either of these questions.
3. If you could make one wish for one or both of your parents, what would be your wish? Explain the significance of your response.

Dear Mother,

I do not know if you are receiving my letters, but I will keep writing   *1*
to you as you are always in my mind.

We have been here three years now. I have moved from Greenwich and have a wooden shingled house in Cos Cob. We have a garden in the back where we plant vegetables, flowers in the front the way we used to when we were together. I have a pink dogwood tree that blooms in spring. It looks like the Hoa dai tree, but has no leaves, only flowers.

We worked for months to clear away the poison ivy, a plant that turns your skin red and makes you itch.

We are near a beach, a school and a shopping center. Green lawns go down to the streets and there are many cars and garages. I am even learning to drive.

When we got our new house, people from the church came and took   *5*
us to "Friendly's" for ice cream. Americans celebrate with ice cream. They have so many kinds—red like watermelon, green for pistachio, orange sherbet like Buddha's robes, mint chocolate chip. You buy it fast and take it away to eat.

Our house is small, but a place to be together and discuss our daily life. At every meal we stare at the dishes you used to fix for us and think about you. We are sorry for you and for ourselves.

If we work hard here, we have everything, but we fear you are hungry and cold and lonesome. Last week we made up a package of clothes. We all tried to figure out how thin you must be now. I do not know if you will ever receive that package wrapped with all our thoughts.

I remember the last days when you encouraged us to leave the country and refused to go yourself. You said you were too old, did not want to leave your home and would be a burden to us. We realize now that you sacrificed yourself for our well-being.

You have a new grandson born in the United States. Thanh looked beautiful at her wedding in a red velvet dress and white veil, a yellow turban in her dark hair. She carried the chrysanthemums you love.

You always loved the fall in Hanoi. You liked the cold. We don't. We   10
have just had the worst winter in a century, snow piled everywhere. I must wear a heavy coat, boots, fur gloves, and a hat. I look like a ball running to the train station. I feel that if I fell down, I could never get up.

Your grandson is three, in nursery school. He speaks English so well that we are sad. We made a rule. We must speak Vietnamese at home so that the children will not forget their mother tongue.

We have made an altar to Father. We try to keep up our traditions so that we can look forward to the day we can return to our country, although we do not know when that will be.

Here we are materially well off, but spiritually deprived. We miss our country. Most of all we miss you. Should Buddha exist, we should keep praying to be reunited.

Dear Mother, keep up your mind. Pray to Buddha silently. We will have a future and I hope it will be soon.

We want to swim in our own pond.   15
Clear or stinky, still it is ours.

Your daughter,
Nga

Suggestions for Writing and Discussion

1. How does Tran Thi Nga sound in this letter? Happy? Content? Angry? Something else? Write to a friend who has not read Tran Thi Nga's letter. As you write, refer to specific words and images she uses to explain to your friend how you think Tran Thi Nga feels about the United States and about her homeland.
2. In your own words, explain what Tran Thi Nga means when she says, "Here we are materially well off, but spiritually deprived" (paragraph 13). Pay special attention to the way you would define the words *materially* and *spiritually*.

3. In much of this letter, Nga writes about common, everyday scenes and events. She describes flowers, her neighborhood, ice cream, the clothing she wears, and even the weather. Why do you think she spends so much time explaining these simple things? How would her story be changed if she omitted these details?

4. Look again at the parts of her life Nga chooses to share with her mother. Can you speculate on parts of her life she does not mention? Why do you think this is?

5. From reading this letter, do you think Nga believes that she will see her mother someday? Do you believe she will return to her homeland? Support your response with specific evidence from the text itself.

6. In her last two lines, Nga writes, "We want to swim in our own pond/ Clear or stinky, still it is ours." Stop and think about this metaphor. What exactly is she comparing to a pond—her old way of life, her homeland, her neighborhood, her yard, or something else? What does the metaphor of the pond imply about her life now?

Suggestions for Extended Thinking and Writing

1. Assume the part of Nga's mother. Write to your daughter responding to the letter from her that you have just read.

2. Imagine that someone close to you (a family member or a good friend) has never seen your present neighborhood. Write a letter to this person in which you selectively describe what your life is like here.

3. Reflect on your response to the first journal suggestion for this piece. Revise this entry now so that you focus on one aspect of this relative: mannerisms, beliefs, appearances, most notable moment, last impression, and so on.

HARRY DOLAN

I Remember Papa

In this essay, which first appeared in From the Ashes: Voices of Watts, *edited by Budd Schulberg, Harry Dolan shows the pitfalls his parents faced as they struggled with poverty, illness, and negative racial stereotypes. By explaining his father's life, Dolan urges readers to examine their views of families like his, particularly of the choices made by the men who are the fathers of those families.*

Pre-Reading and Journal-Writing Suggestions

1. Describe the earliest memories you have of your father (or grandfather, uncle, older brother, stepfather). Try to focus on specific, vivid images: eyes, hands, gestures, facial expressions, bits of conversation.
2. If you were in charge of writing a manual that defined a "good" father, what would you include? List the top ten qualifications—in order of their importance to you—that you would believe all fathers should possess. Then reflect on the reasons for your choices and for the order in which you arranged your choices.
3. Describe a time when someone in your family embarrassed you. Explain what happened and why you responded as you did.

The other night after attending a gratifying function which had been   *1*
initiated to help the black man, specifically to help build a nursery for children of working mothers, and after seeing and hearing white people make speeches professing their understanding and desire to go to any length to help, I found myself suddenly cornered and forced to defend the fabled laziness of the black man.

What was especially surprising was the fact that I assumed this white acquaintance—since he had paid thirty dollars to attend this dinner held for the purpose of helping the black man—did, at least in part, have some sympathy with what his, the white people, had tried to accomplish.

As I stood there watching his eyes I became suspect of my own sincerity, for I stood attentively nodding my head and smiling. I lit a cigarette, raised an eyebrow, performed all of the white man's laws of etiquette, and all the while I knew if it had been others of my black brothers, they would have cursed him for his smugness and invited him outside to test his theory of black man's courage and laziness. Of course I did none of these things. I grinned as he indicated in no uncertain terms that as soon as the black man got off his lazy butt and took advantage of all the blessings that had been offered him for the last two hundred years, then he, the white man, would indeed be willing to help.

I could have answered him—and was tempted to, for he was obviously sincere. Instead, I found an excuse to slip away and let a white man fight my battle, a friend, even a close friend. I went to a far corner and blindly played a game of pool by myself as the voices of this man and my friend dissected me. I stacked the pool balls, leaned over the table, and remembered a black man I had known.

It was said of him later in his life that he had let his family down. He'd been lazy, no-account, a troublemaker. Maybe so, maybe so, but I can't help remembering nights of his pacing the squeaking floor muttering to himself, coming back across the floor, sitting down, his legs trembling as he listened to the woman plead for him not to do anything bad.

"I'll go to hell first before I'll let you and the children starve." God, how many times had I heard him say that! How many other men standing bunched in helpless stagnation have I heard vow to take a gun and get some food for their children! Yes, they were planning to commit a crime; yes, they were potential criminals. Then. They are usually black too—another crime, it seems.

I remember that man, but more I remember his woman, my mother. Curiously though, I never remember her dancing, running, playing; always lying down, the smell of disinfectant strong, the deep continuous coughing, the brown paper bag filled with the toilet paper red with bubbly spit and blood, lying half concealed under the bed.

I never remember her eating food such as bread, meat, potatoes; only apples and only Delicious apples. In those days five cents apiece. She was a small woman, barely five foot.

"Junior," she would say softly. She never spoke above a whisper. "Go to the store and get me an apple." The thin trembling hand would reverse itself and slide up and under the covers and under the pillow and then return as though of its own volition, the weight almost too much, and as I'd start out the door, she would always smile and say, "Hurry, Junior."

I'd nod, and always, always there seemed to be a need to hurry. Those trips were always made with a feeling of breathless fear. I didn't know why then, only that for some reason I must always come back as soon as possible.

I was returning with an especially large apple, walking along, tempted to bite just a tiny piece, when I turned the corner and saw the black police ambulance standing in front of my door. Suddenly I had to go to the bathroom so bad I couldn't move. I stood watching as two uniformed men came out with the stretcher, and then the sound of my mother's shrill voice hit me.

"Mama, Mama," she was screaming. I could see her twisting and swinging at the lady next door as she was held back. I stood there feeling the hot piss run down my trembling legs, feeling cold chills spatter through my body, causing frozen limbs to spasmodically begin to move. I forced myself toward the police wagon as the men opened the doors and slid the stretcher along the bare metal. I saw my mother's head bounce on the floor.

"Wait," I moaned, "don't hurt her." Then I was running, screaming, "Please don't hurt her."

I looked down at her pain-filled face, and she smiled, even then she smiled. I showed her the apple. The effort to nod seemed a terrible effort but she did, her eyes so very bright, so very shiny.

"You eat it, Junior, you and sis."   15

"What's wrong, Mama?" I asked softly. "You really, really sick now?"

She nodded.

"Your father will be home soon. Tell him I'm at the General Hospital. Tell him to—to hurry."

"I'll tell him, Mama," I promised. "I'll tell him to hurry, Mama." She nodded sadly and puckered her lips as she always did since we weren't allowed to kiss her.

That was the last time I saw my mother except at the grave. My father   20
came to the funeral with two white men who stood on each side of him all the time. There were people crying all around us. My grandmother kept squeezing me and moaning. I saw my father try to cover his face but one of the men said something and he stood up stiffly after that. I didn't cry, because my mother seemed to look happier, more rested than I had ever seen her. For some reason, I was glad she was dead. I think maybe, except for us, she was too.

I was nine, my sister five. It was not until ten years later that I saw my father again.

We sat on opposite sides of a screen and talked into telephones. I had come there to tell him that in spite of my beginning, I had made it. I was nineteen, and a radioman in the U.S. Coast Guard, ready to fight and die for my country. There had been something mysterious about his smile.

"I'm proud of you, boy," he said. "You're a real man. You know I volunteered for the front lines too, but they turned me down."

We don't want you, I thought, we're not criminals, we're honest, strong. Then I looked again at this thief, this "Loaf-of-bread gunman" as the papers had tagged him. He had taken five loaves of bread, along with twelve dollars. Suddenly I could not stay there condemning this man, my father. It seemed such a waste, this magnificently strong man sitting there, his tremendous chest barely moving, hands resting quietly, talking to me, his whole being showering torrents of words about me.

"Be careful, boy, there are so many ways to fail, the pitfall sometimes   25
seems to be the easiest way out. Beware of my future, for you must continue, you must live. You must, for in you are all the dreams of my nights, all the ambitions of my days."

A bell rang and we stood up and a man pointed me toward a heavy door. I looked back, and saw him standing easy, hands at his side, so very calm, yet my mind filled to overflowing with the many things he had not said. It was to be ten years before he walked again as a free man, that is, as a physically free man.

I remember an earlier time, an earlier chapter of my growing up. I remember the first time my mother said we were taking lunch to my father's job. We had been down to the welfare line and I had stood with her, our feet burning against the hot pavement, and slowly moved forward in the sun. Years later I stood in chow lines over half of the world, but no desert, no burning deck was as hot as that day.

At last we reached the man sitting at the desk and my mother handed him the book of stamps. She smiled, a weak almost timid smile, as he checked her name and thumbed her to the food line.

As we headed home, my wagon was loaded with cans of corned beef, powdered milk, powdered eggs, and white margarine that she would later color yellow to look like butter.

At home we made sandwiches and off we went to my father's job, to *30* take him his lunch. I pulled my sister along in my wagon, a Red Flyer.

It was to be a picnic, a celebration really, my father's new job.

I remember the wagon did not have a tongue or handle but only a rope with which I pulled it wobbling along. We were excited, my sister and I, as we left our district of dirt streets and unpaved sidewalks and began to make our way along roads called boulevards and malls we had never had occasion to travel. The streets themselves were fascinating, so different. They were twice as wide, and there were exotic trees along the sidewalks and lo and behold trees down the center of the street as far as I could see and then we turned the corner and before us stretched an overwhelming sight. An overhead highway was being built. Columns rose to staggering heights, bulldozers thrust what seemed to me mountains of dirt before them, and hundreds, no thousands of men seemed to be crawling like ants hurrying from one point to another. Cranes lifted nets of steel and laid them in rows on the crushed rock.

I stared in awe at important-looking white men in metal hats, carrying rolls of papers which they intermittently studied, then pointing into space at what to me seemed only emptiness.

And then I saw my father. He sat among fifty other black men, all surrounded by great boulders marked with red paint. They all held steel chisels with which they cut along the marked lines. They would strike a certain point and the boulder would split into smaller pieces and as we approached there was a silence around them except for the pinging of the hammer against the chisel. In all the noise it was a lonely sound, futile, lost, oppressive. My father seemed to be concentrating, his tremendous arm whipping the air. He was stripped to the waist, black muscles popping sweat, goggled eyes for the metal and stone only. We stood there, the three of us, my mother, my sister, and I, and watched my father work for us, and as he conquered the huge boulder my chest filled with pride. Each stroke shouted for all the world to hear: This is my family and I love them! No one can tell me this was the act of a lazy man.

Suddenly a white man walked up and blew a whistle and the black men all looked up and stopped working. My father glanced over at me, grinned and winked. He was glistening with sweat, the smell strong and powerful. He dropped his big hand on my shoulder and guided me to a large boulder.

"Hey, boy, you see me beat that thing to bits? This one's next," he said, indicating the one that shaded us from the sun. "I'll pound it to gravel by nightfall." It was a challenge he expected, he welcomed. That was my lazy, shiftless father.

And then one day they brought him home, his thumb, index, and middle finger gone from his left hand. They sat him in the kitchen chair and mumbled something about carelessness. He sat there for two hours before he answered our pleadings.

"Chain broke, I—I was guiding boulder. I couldn't, I just couldn't get my hand out from under in time—I, goddam it, Jean, they took my fingers off. I layed right there, my hand under the rock, and they nipped them like butchering a hog. Look at my goddam hand."

My mother held him in her arms and talked to him. She spoke softly, so softly my sister and I, standing in the corner, couldn't hear the words, only the soothing softness of her voice.

"Joe, Joe, we can." And then he began to cry like—like I sometimes did when I was hurt deep inside and couldn't do anything about it.

After that there was a change in him. My father had been a fighter. He had feared no man white or black. I remember the time we were sitting on a streetcar and a woman had forgotten her fare—or maybe she never had any in the first place. Anyway, the driver slammed the doors on her and held her squeezed between them.

My father jumped up, snatched the driver out of the seat, and let the woman out. He and the driver had words that led to battle and Pop knocked the driver down just as a patrolman arrived. The patrolman didn't listen to any of the people that tried to explain what had happened. He just began to swing his night stick at my father's head. It was a mistake. My father hit him once and even today I can see all the people laughing at the funny look on the policeman's face as he staggered back all the way across the street and up against a building, slowly sagging down.

The police wagon arrived with four other policemen and one told him they were going to beat his brains in when they got him down town.

My pop had laughed then and backed against the building.

"I guess ain't no sense me going peaceable then."

They knocked out all his upper front teeth that day, but as he said later, "Them four white boys will think of me every time they shave."

They finally overpowered him and dragged him, still struggling, to the wagon. One of them kept muttering, "He's one fighting son of a black bitch, he's a fighting son of a bitch."

All the time I hadn't said a word or cried or yelled as they stomped and kicked him. I had shut my eyes and held my lips tightly pressed together and I had done just as he'd always told me.

"You stay out of it, boy, stay real quiet, and when that wagon leaves, you run behind and keep it in sight. If they lose you, you ask someone where the closest police station is—that's where I'll be. You go home and tell your mother."

That's the way he had been before losing his left hand. Afterwards, well, it took a lot from him. He told me one day, laughing and shaking the nub as he called it, "If I'd only had the thumb, just the lousy thumb, I'd have it made."

Gradually he lost the ability to see humor in the nub. I think the whole thing came to a head the night I killed the kitten.

We hadn't had meat or potatoes for over two weeks. Even the grease drippings were gone and my mother was too sick to raise her head from the pillow. So I had gotten the skillet and put it in the open grate. We had two cups of flour so I mixed water with it and poured it into the greasy skillet. I can still recall the coldness of the room on my back and the warmth from the grate on my face as my sister and I knelt and hungrily watched the flour brown.

You know, today my wife marvels at how, no matter what she puts before me, I eat with relish. My children say that I eat very fast. I pray to God they never have to experience the causes of my obsession. But back to the story—the flour finally hardened and I broke a piece for my sister and a piece for my mother and left mine in the skillet on the table.

I took my mother's piece over to the bed and put it in her hand. She didn't move so I raised her hand to her mouth and she began to suck on it. Then I heard my sister scream, "Topsy is eating your food, Junior, Topsy's eating your food!" I turned around to see the cat tearing at my tiny piece of hard dough. I went wild. I leaped across the room and grabbed the kitten by the tail and began slamming her against the wall.

"That's my food," I kept yelling, "my food!" At last I heard my sister screaming, "She's bleeding, you're killing Topsy. Here, here, eat my bread. Please don't kill her."

I stopped, horrified, staring at the limp nothing I now held. It was two weeks later that they got me to speak and that same night my father left the house for the last time. I don't say that what he did was right. No, it most assuredly was wrong. But what I do ask is, what else could he have done? I need an answer quickly now, today, right away, for I tell you this, my children will not starve, not here, not in this time of millions to foreign countries and fountains to throw tons of water upward to the sky, and nothing to the hungry, thirsty multitudes a stone's throw away.

Suggestions for Writing and Discussion

1. After reading this piece, what's your honest reaction? Do you like it? Why or why not? Describe your response in a review that might appear in the student newspaper at your college or university. Explain to your audience of fellow students why you responded as you did to Dolan's essay.

2. Reread paragraph 6. Consider the words *stagnation* and *potential*. What do each of these words mean, and how do they relate to the situation of black men as Dolan describes it?

3. How does Dolan feel about white people? Give specific evidence from the essay to support your response. Pay special attention to his choice of words and the examples he chooses.

4. Dolan entitles this piece, "I Remember Papa." However, he writes that "I remember this man, but more I remember his woman, my mother." Why, then, doesn't he include the word *Mama* in his title?

5. Describe Dolan's mother. What type of a person was she? How does Dolan's father compare with her? Why do you think Dolan would remember her more than he remembers his father?

6. Imagine you are a rider on the bus when Dolan's father frees the woman from the bus door and then fights with four policeman. What is your response? Is he heroic? Foolish? Wise? Noble? Headstrong? Or something else? As you explain your answer, assume that your audience is the police commissioner who has asked you to write down what you saw.

7. Dolan provides close-up, detailed views of several events in which his father plays a role. Choose one event and state how Dolan might feel about his father, first when he was a child and now that he is an adult.

Suggestions for Extended Thinking and Writing

1. Reflect on a significant event in your childhood before the age of ten. Write an essay in which you make this event come alive through vivid description and apt dialogue.

2. Look back to your journal listings of the top qualities for a good father. Focus now on just one of these qualities, and describe how your own father (or another important male family member) either possessed or lacked this quality.

3. Dolan's father leaves his sick wife and two small children for the last time after his son frantically flings a kitten against the wall. Dolan says, "I don't say what he did was right. No, it was most assuredly wrong. But what I do ask is, What else could he have done?"

    Write an essay responding to Dolan's question. Did his father have any other options? What were the roadblocks in his way? Did he have anything or anyone who could have helped him out?

GRACE MING-YEE WAI

Chinese Puzzle

> *Grace Ming-Yee Wai, a first-generation Chinese American, grew up in Memphis, Tennessee. When she was ten years old, her father was shot to death during a robbery that netted the killer $26 in change. In the following essay, Wai offers a collage of episodes from her childhood as a way of describing her father and of suggesting how both his life and his death affected the values she developed.*

Pre-Reading and Journal-Writing Suggestions

1. Describe what you consider to be the ideal family. In what ways is your own family similar to or different from this ideal?
2. Write about the impact of violence as you see it in your own community. The impact may come from actual events or from the reports of these events in the media.
3. What's the greatest lesson parents can teach their children?

I am a first generation Chinese-American woman educated in both   *1* private and public American schools. I grew up in the mid-South city of Memphis, Tennessee, where there were very few other Asian families. We lived in the South, I realized after my teens, primarily for economic reasons. Although there were more Asians in cities such as New York, Los Angeles, or San Francisco, it would have been very expensive to live in those cities, and our grocery store would have had much more competition. My parents immigrated to the United States from Hong Kong before I was born, for a better life for themselves and their children. Neither had a college educa-tion, but both emphasized hard work and the importance of education. Like all parents, they hoped their children would be fortunate enough to receive a quality education that would provide future opportunity and financial security.

My sister, brother, and I have been lucky to receive an education and all of us have reached or are near our goals, but not without pain and sacrifices. When I was 10 years old, my father was shot and killed while being robbed for $26 in change. He was the favorite son of seven living children. He took in one of my cousins from Hong Kong so she could study nursing. My youngest uncle was the only one of their generation to become a professional, primarily because he was lucky enough to have the oppor-tunity to go to dental school at the University of Tennessee in Memphis.

Dad owned a small grocery store in a poor neighborhood. My parents worked more than 12 hours a day, seven days a week. We lived above the store in five rooms and one bathroom. At different times, my grandmother, three uncles, an aunt and her two sons also lived with us. My brother, sister and I had a maid who came six days a week to take care of us. I became very attached to her and cried on her day off. I still send Willie Christmas cards every year.

My father had a fierce temper. Whenever something upset him a little, he yelled a lot, so my brother, sister, and I shuddered at the thought of angering him. His bark was worse than his bite, however. He was also very fair. He loved us all very much. He and Mom worked hard for us, for the family. Family meant everything.

Since Mom and Dad worked so much, there was not much time for   5
us kids. We occasionally went to Shoney's for a hamburger. It was a big treat to pat the statue of Big Boy on the stomach upon entering and exiting the restaurant. Dad took me to the dog track once because I wanted to go with him. I think I just wanted very much to have him for myself since he was always helping other people and working in the store with Mom.

I was the first to go to school because I was the oldest child. When I was four years old, I went to prekindergarten at a small, private, Episcopal school. On my first day, Dad drove me to the door, but he would not take me to my class. I knew where my class was located because we visited earlier to meet my teachers. My heart was pounding with a force I did not know my little body had when I jumped out of the car, and I know fear was evident on my face, but Dad didn't budge. I asked, "Daddy, aren't you coming with me?" He replied, "No, Grace, you know where your class is and who your teachers are. You can go by yourself." He was teaching me to be self-sufficient at four. Still, it must have been difficult for him to watch his firstborn walk alone into a world of which he would not have a part. It was my first day of independence.

I clearly remember my sixth birthday because Dad was in the hospital with pneumonia. He was working so hard he paid very little attention to his health. As a result, he spent almost the entire summer before I entered first grade in the hospital. Mom visited him nightly. On my birthday I was allowed to see him. I have memories of sitting happily in the lobby of the hospital talking to the nurses, telling them with a big smile that I was going to see my dad because it was my birthday. I couldn't wait to see him because children under 12 were not allowed to visit patients, so I had not seen him in a long time. When I entered his hospital room, I saw tubes inserted into his nose and needles stuck in his arm. He was very, very thin. I was frightened and wanted to cry, but I was determined to have a good visit. So I stayed for a while, and he wished me a happy birthday. When it was time to go, I kissed him good-bye and waited until I left his room to cry.

In first grade, I lived with my grandparents because a public elementary school was just across the street. My father bought the house for my grandparents with plans for us three children to attend Levi Elementary School since it was close and convenient. My brother and sister stayed with my parents because Nancy was only four, and Robert was in kindergarten at my old school which was near the store. I felt very isolated and alone in that great big house away from my immediate family.

I learned from my father while in first grade one valuable lesson that still affects me now: never be afraid to ask questions. I was very self-conscious and timid in school. My grades were falling. My father asked me: "How are you going to learn if you don't ask questions?" Even then, when I was six years of age, he tried to make me realize the importance of taking initiative in school. He made me realize improving in school was up to me because he could not be with me all the time.

In those days, my grandmother took care of me. She had moved to   10
America when I was three years old to be with my youngest uncle when he came to go to college. My grandfather joined us three years later. Every morning my grandmother got me dressed and made my breakfast. While I sat at the dining room table, she combed and brushed my hair to prepare me for school. She spoke no English, so we conversed in Cantonese. Every day after school, I called the store to talk to my mother. I really missed being with my parents, brother, and sister and looked forward to their weekly visits. Of course, only one parent visited at a time because someone had to be at the store. I was very jealous that Robert and Nancy were able to stay with my parents.

After school, my grandfather liked to see what I learned that day. It was always a treat to show him the new words I was taught to write in school. Every night I rewrote all the new words for him. He always smiled with approval. Sometimes he helped me with my mathematics. My grandfather played with numbers a lot and actually had an abacus on his desk, which he used daily.

My grandmother did not read or write English. I was learning material she would never understand. She was my caretaker. She cooked and cleaned the house. She fed and bathed me. Neither of my grandparents worked. At that time, they were in their mid-sixties. They had no desire to learn the culture of the new land. Their livelihood depended upon my father, and they were happy merely to be near their children's families.

In the summer, my sister and brother joined me at our grandparents' house. We played a lot more since we had a yard. At the store, we stayed upstairs mostly. When summer was over, I was alone with my grandparents again. That year, in second grade, I was often chased around by Albert, a little black boy in my class. He would try to kiss me. Other children were fascinated by my straight black hair, and would constantly try to touch it. I was jeered at by other children for being Chinese, for having squinty eyes and a flat nose. I was almost ashamed of being Chinese, and being so young I did not understand it at all. I had grown up around other blacks who had frequented our store. Many were my friends, but in school I was having trouble—with black and white children. There were no other Chinese children in my school.

I refrained from telling my parents about Albert because earlier in the school year, I had been hit on the head during recess by a classmate with a baseball bat and had to have stitches. My father told me I should not have been playing so recklessly in school. But one day, in my attempt to hide from Albert, I fell and scraped both knees badly. The principal found me and told me that I should tell my teacher if he did it again. After the next episode, I told my teacher, but made the mistake of embarrassing myself by telling in front of the class. What hurt even more was the fact that my teacher did not do anything about it. Finally, I decided I must tell my parents. I think I feared they would think I had done something wrong, that it was my fault—that perhaps I provoked the boy. I also feared my father's temper.

First I told my mother, and she encouraged me to tell my dad about it. He would make the final decision. I sighed and then proceeded to creep upstairs where he was taking a nap and sat outside their bedroom. When my father awoke, fearfully, I told him about what was happening to me in school. Dad was so understanding. To my relief, he was calm and collected, not angry. He asked me what I wanted to do. He asked if I would like to go to the private school my brother and sister attended. Would I! I was so happy. Yes! I wanted to go back to school with Robert and Nancy! That meant, also, that I would be moving back to the store to live with my parents.

I realize now that Dad was very angry. Not at me, but angry with the teachers and the principal of my elementary school for ignoring my distress. He took me out of Levi in the middle of the year. I feel for the people Dad dealt with to get me out of school. I imagine he probably went there red-faced and smoking with anger to fill out the necessary paperwork. It is funny, though, how Dad let me feel I made the decision to leave Levi.

My father was a loving and devoted son to my grandparents. He made sure they were happy and comfortable. He wanted them with us so he was assured of their well-being. My grandfather had fallen ill when I was around seven years old. The doctors thought he had cancer. Twenty years ago, that meant certain death. The night the diagnosis was given, I was alone with my parents after the store was closed. Dad was crying. I was frightened because I had never before seen him cry. Taking off his glasses and looking at me with red, teary eyes and unmistakable pain, he asked me, "Do you love your Ye-Ye?" It was difficult to speak to him when he seemed so vulnerable, but with all the courage I could muster and tears welling up in my eyes, I answered, "Yes." Mom was behind Dad comforting him. At seven years of age, I was learning what it is to love your parents, and I was learning even Dads cry. Thankfully, my grandfather's cancer went into remission after treatment.

When Dad caught wind of the fact that I was doing poorly on my multiplication tables in third grade, he drilled me nightly in the back of the store where he stood behind the meat counter. I remember sweating and

15

feeling extremely apprehensive and fearful of his wrath if I answered incorrectly. I quickly learned my multiplication tables inside out.

On the day he died, Dad came to my grandparents' house where my brother, sister, and I were staying for Thanksgiving weekend. He planned to go car-shopping with his older brother. I went along with them. We had lunch at Shoney's afterward, at my suggestion, of course. I did not care about car-shopping. I just wanted to spend time with Dad, even if we were with my uncle. I chattered away while we had lunch. When we returned to my grandparents' house, he took a nap in my bedroom before going back to work at the store. I was to wake him in an hour. Upon leaving, he picked me up for a big hug and kiss good-bye. I had my arms around his neck and my head on his shoulder. He told me to be good before putting me down. I did not know it would be the last time I would see him alive.

Later, in the afternoon, I heard my grandfather making dozens of phone calls, saying with grief and shock: "Ah, Davey say joh loh, Davey say joh loh!" meaning, "Davey's dead, Davey's dead!" I couldn't believe his words and rushed to tell my sister and brother, who responded with disbelief and dismay. They thought I was lying to them, playing a cruel trick on them. Later, when we had heard the grown-ups talking and were in fact sure Dad was killed, the three of us went up to our favorite spot in the attic where we cried and cried and hugged one another. We were in the way of the adults. They did not know how to talk to us, nor would they answer our questions. We only had each other for comfort.

My aunts and uncles from various parts of the country left their families to rush to Memphis the day Dad was shot. We had a full house of people who came by to bring food, to pay respects. It was very late in the evening before all but family were left in our house. It seemed peaceful once again. My best friend brought a plant the next day. We were both at a loss for words—we did not need them. It was enough just to see her.

The next day, there was an article in the newspaper about what happened. My aunt said it did not do my father justice. The robber was never caught by the police. In fact, the police later found the bag of change lying in an alley nearby. My mom's reaction was calm as she told me, "Even if they find him, it won't bring your daddy back, Grace."

The day of my father's funeral was rainy and cold. There was a long procession of cars on the way to the cemetery. My father was well respected by others in the community and had many friends. My grandmother did not attend the funeral. As long as I knew her, she never once set foot in a hospital, nor did she go to funerals. My grandfather also elected not to attend, but as the hearse passed by their house, he ran out, down the long walkway to the gate with a black raincoat held above his head. He wished to open the coffin to see his son one more time, but it was nailed shut. It was only possible for him to touch the casket.

All my teachers and the principal of our school attended Dad's funeral. Willie was there too. We were all crying when they came to see us. Later, my best friend told me the teachers didn't think we would be returning to school for a while. They were surprised to find us in class the following day. My friends did not know how to react to me, and in homeroom, my teacher asked, in front of everyone, if I was okay. I was not okay. I was in pain, but what could I do? I lost my father. He was never coming back. I tried to be strong, and looking down at my desk, I said, "Yes, I'm okay."

We were so young: Robert eight, and Nancy seven. Now we are grown adults. I wonder what it would have been like if Dad were living during our developing years. I suspect I would be a very different person. I am very much a feminist and a professional now. I don't think he would have allowed me to move 1,000 miles from home to live on my own after college. I probably would not have been allowed to participate in many things such as dating, parties, and school activities if he were alive during my adolescence, for he was extremely strict.

We visited his gravesite every year on his birthday, on the anniversary of his death, and on holidays such as New Year's and Christmas. Following my grandmother's Asian traditions, we brought incense to burn at the gravesite, and food: a bowl of rice, fruit, a main dish for his spirit to eat. We also burned special paper, which my grandmother stated represented money for Dad to spend in the afterlife. We did these things for her since she would not go to the cemetery. Following American tradition, we also brought flowers. When the incense was lit, the money burning, and the food set out with chopsticks along with tea and sometimes scotch (he had to have something to drink as well as utensils!), we took turns paying our respects by bowing to the headstone three times and silently told his spirit whatever we wanted to tell him, whatever was on our minds. When done, we bowed again three times to bid farewell until the next time.

I write this now because it is more than 14 years since my father's death. I think about how fast those 14 years have gone by and all the changes and growing that have taken place. I wonder if he is proud of me now. I wonder what I would be like today if he were alive. Even though I only had him in the first 10 years of my life, I know there is much of him in me. I have his temperament, his strictness, and his self-righteous nature. I have his sense of fairness, generosity, and loyalty. He taught me much in those first 10 years. There are also scars from his death because my family did not talk about our loss. We took the blow and went on with life.

In the last four years, I have also lost both grandparents. They are buried with my father. One day, my mother and uncles will join them. Whenever I return to Memphis to visit family and friends, I also go to the cemetery to visit my father and grandparents. I don't follow all the traditions my grandmother so treasured, but I do carry incense and flowers with me. I still bow and have my talk with each. Those are always peaceful and contemplative moments. Sometimes I drive by the old store, the old house, and the private elementary school to relive some of my past.

Death does not get easier. The people I love will not be with me forever. That hurts. Death, however, is a part of life we all face at some point. Nevertheless, it is a comfort to me to believe that after death, those I love go somewhere nice and comfortable. My grandmother always wished to return as a bird—to fly over the earth—soaring and free. I hope she made it.

Suggestions for Writing and Discussion

1. Describe the relationship between Ming-Yee Wai and her father. Were they close? Distant? Comfortable with one another? Something else?
2. Reread paragraph 17. What does Ming-Yee Wai mean when she says her father was "vulnerable"? Why did her view of him as vulnerable make it difficult for her to speak to him?
3. Compare the values held by Ming-Yee Wai's Chinese family with the values held by what you consider a typical American family today. How do you account for any differences?
4. Why might Ming-Yee Wai have had trouble with some of the children in school, but not with the same children in her neighborhood? Use your response to this topic to write a brief article intended for parents whose children face some of the same problems with peers that Ming-Yee Wai describes.
5. In paragraph 17, Ming-Yee Wai writes that she "was learning what it meant to love your parents." What does she mean by this statement?
6. What do the events surrounding the father's funeral signify about the relationship between her family and the surrounding community?
7. In paragraph 27, Ming-Yee Wai muses, "I wonder if he is proud of me now." What do you think? Based on his expectations for his young daughter, would he be proud of this grown one? Please explain.

Suggestions for Extended Thinking and Writing

1. Interview two people, one from outside the mainstream American culture and one whom you would consider part of mainstream America. Choose people who for some reason (marriage, work, school) have had experience with blending cultures. Ask their responses to this experience. Then write an essay explaining what you have learned from these interviews.
2. Write a descriptive narrative in which you focus on one event in your past that explains what your relationship was like with one of your parents. Try not to "tell" what this relationship was like; rather, become a storyteller of this event and let the readers "see" for themselves what it was like.
3. Compare the family relationships and circumstances described in this piece with the relationships and circumstances described in Harry Dolan's essay (p. 122).

LEWIS P. JOHNSON

For My Indian Daughter

> *Born in 1935, Lewis Johnson grew up in Harbor Springs, Michigan, where his great-grandfather lived out his final days as the last recognized chief of the Potawatomi Ottawas. During the 1600s, these Native Americans lived in present-day Michigan, Wisconsin, Indiana, and Illinois. But during the 1800s, as white settlers moved west, government agents implemented a federal policy that forced the Potawatomi nation to leave the land they occupied and split into many groups. Some fled to Canada or Mexico, while others were removed to reservations in Washington, Iowa, Kansas, and Oklahoma. Groups called the Forest or "Stray" Potawatomi later fled Kansas for the wooded areas of Wisconsin, Michigan, and Ontario.*
>
> *A surveyor by profession, Johnson has done extensive research on Indian approaches to interpretive dreams and has written many essays like "For My Indian Daughter" that suggest the complexities raised by the modern juxtaposition of Native American and European culture and values.*

Pre-Reading and Journal-Writing Suggestions

1. Choose from your family's past one story in which you take a great deal of pride. After describing the incident, explain what you think it reveals about your family's values.
2. Write about a time someone ridiculed or belittled you. How did you react? How do you evaluate the episode now that you can look back at it?
3. In three minutes, list all the words, phrases, and images that come to your mind when you hear the word *Indian.*

    Read your list and reflect on what you have written. What is first on your list? What words did you end with? Can you see any groups of words or phrases that go together?

My little girl is singing herself to sleep upstairs, her voice mingling with the sounds of the birds outside in the old maple trees. She is two and I am nearly 50, and I am very taken with her. She came along late in my life, unexpected and unbidden, a startling gift.

Today at the beach my chubby-legged, brown-skinned daughter ran laughing into the water as fast as she could. My wife and I laughed watching her, until we heard behind us a low guttural curse and then an unpleasant voice raised in an imitation war whoop.

I turned to see a fat man in a bathing suit, white and soft as a grub, as he covered his mouth and prepared to make the Indian war cry again. He was middle-aged, younger than I, and had three little children lined up next to him, grinning foolishly. My wife suggested we leave the beach, and I agreed.

I knew the man was not unusual in his feelings against Indians. His beach behavior might have been socially unacceptable to more civilized whites, but his basic view of Indians is expressed daily in our small town, frequently on the editorial pages of the county newspaper, as white people speak out against Indian fishing rights and land rights, saying in essence, "Those Indians are taking our fish, our land." It doesn't matter to them that we were here first, that the U.S. Supreme Court has ruled in our favor. It matters to them that we have something they want, and they hate us for it. Backlash is the common explanation of the attacks on Indians, the bumper stickers that say, "Spear an Indian, Save a Fish," but I know better. The hatred of Indians goes back to the beginning when white people came to this country. For me it goes back to my childhood in Harbor Springs, Michigan.

Theft

Harbor Springs is now a summer resort for the very affluent, but a   *5* hundred years ago it was the Indian village of my Ottawa ancestors. My grandmother, Anna Showanessy, and other Indians like her, had their land there taken by treaty, by fraud, by violence, by theft. They remembered how whites had burned down the village at Burt Lake in 1900 and pushed the Indians out. These were the stories in my family.

When I was a boy my mother told me to walk down the alleys in Harbor Springs and not to wear my orange football sweater out of the house. This way I would not stand out, not be noticed, and not be a target.

I wore my orange sweater anyway and deliberately avoided the alleys. I was the biggest person I knew and wasn't really afraid. But I met my comeuppance when I enlisted in the U.S. Army. One night all the men in my barracks gathered together and, gang-fashion, pulled me into the shower and scrubbed me down with rough brushes used for floors, saying, "We won't have any dirty Indians in our outfit." It is a point of irony that I was cleaner than any of them. Later in Korea I learned how to kill, how to bully, how to hate Koreans. I came out of the war tougher than ever and, strangely, white.

I went to college, got married, lived in La Porte, Indiana, worked as a surveyor and raised three boys. I headed Boy Scout groups, never thinking it odd when the Scouts did imitation Indian dances, imitation Indian lore.

One day when I was 35 or thereabouts I heard about an Indian pow-wow. My father used to attend them and so with great curiosity and a strange joy at discovering a part of my heritage, I decided the thing to do to get ready for this big event was to have my friend make me a spear in his forge. The steel was fine and blue and iridescent. The feathers on the shaft were bright and proud.

In a dusty state fairground in southern Indiana, I found white people   10 dressed as Indians. I learned they were "hobbyists," that is, it was their hobby and leisure pastime to masquerade as Indians on weekends. I felt ridiculous with my spear, and I left.

It was years before I could tell anyone of the embarrassment of this weekend and see any humor in it. But in a way it was that weekend, for all its silliness, that was my awakening. I realized I didn't know who I was. I didn't have an Indian name. I didn't speak the Indian language. I didn't know the Indian customs. Dimly I remembered the Ottawa word for dog, but it was a baby word, *kahgee*, not the full word, *muhkahgee,* which I was later to learn. Even more hazily I remembered a naming ceremony (my own). I remembered legs dancing around me, dust. Where had that been? Who had I been? "Suwaukquat," my mother told me when I asked, "where the tree begins to grow."

That was 1968, and I was not the only Indian in the country who was feeling the need to remember who he or she was. There were others. They had powwows, real ones, and eventually I found them. Together we researched our past, a search that for me culminated in the Longest Walk, a march on Washington in 1978. Maybe because I now know what it means to be Indian, it surprises me that others don't. Of course there aren't very many of us left. The chances of an average person knowing an average Indian in an average lifetime are pretty slim.

Circle

Still, I was amused one day when my small, four-year-old neighbor looked at me as I was hoeing in my garden and said, "You aren't a real Indian, are you?" Scotty is little, talkative, likable. Finally I said, "I'm a real Indian." He looked at me for a moment and then said, squinting into the sun, "Then where's your horse and feathers?" The child was simply a smaller, whiter version of my own ignorant self years before. We'd both seen too much TV, that's all. He was not to be blamed. And so, in a way, the moronic man on the beach today is blameless. We come full circle to realize other people are like ourselves, as discomfiting as that may be sometimes.

As I sit in my old chair on my porch, in a light that is fading so the leaves are barely distinguishable against the sky, I can picture my girl asleep upstairs. I would like to prepare her for what's to come, take her each step of the way saying, there's a place to avoid, here's what I know about this, but much of what's before her she must go through alone. She must pass through pain and joy and solitude and community to discover her own inner self that is unlike any other and come through that passage to the place where she sees all people are one, and in so seeing may live her life in a brighter future.

Suggestions for Writing and Discussion

1. Why do you think Johnson wrote this piece? Who might his intended audience be? Primarily his daughter? Other Indians? Non-Indians? All Americans? Himself?
2. How do you think Johnson feels about the middle-aged man on the beach? Explain.
3. Do you think people today would react to Indians the way the man on the beach did? Write your response as a speech you have been asked to give to a class of eight-year-old students.
4. Describe and evaluate Johnson's feelings and reactions when he attends the powwow.
5. In paragraph 12, Johnson says that his search for the past "culminated in the Longest Walk, a march on Washington in 1978." What does he mean by this? Pay special attention to the definition of the word *culminated* as well as to the history of forced marches Native Americans were required to make as they were driven from the lands on which they had always lived.

Suggestions for Extended Thinking and Writing

1. Write an essay in which you describe some ritual that explains your family's culture.
2. Write an essay in which you answer the question "Who are you?" in five different ways.
3. If you wrote in response to journal-writing suggestion 2, look back at your entry and revise it so that you are objectively describing the event.

SUE HORTON

Mothers, Sons, and the Gangs

> *Sue Horton teaches journalism at the University of Southern California.
> She also publishes widely in a variety of newspapers and magazines, including
> the* Los Angeles Times Magazine, *where this investigative report first ap-
> peared in the October 16, 1988, issue. In her report, Horton focuses on the
> conflicts and hardships faced by women trying to raise sons in communities
> where gangs are an everyday fact of life.*

Pre-Reading and Journal-Writing Suggestions

1. Write a general description of your neighborhood and the people who
   live there.
2. Can any parent control how a teenager acts? Explain why or why not.
3. What's your general reaction to or impression of teenagers who join
   gangs and break the law? Why do you think certain young people join
   these gangs?

On the side of a market in East Los Angeles is a roughly done mural,   *1*
painted by gang members from the Lil' Valley Barrio. The untrained artists
did the wall to honor homeboys who met violent deaths on the streets. Two
blocks away, the same gang painted another mural, this one depicting the
mothers of slain gang members. But, when earthquake repairs were made
on the small store that held the mural, the painting was covered over. The
mothers are forgotten.

To many mothers of gang members, all across Southern California,
the obliterated mural could be taken as an appropriate symbol of their lives.
They are, they feel, almost invisible, ignored by many of the law-enforcement agencies and institutions set up to deal with their sons. These women
feel isolated, frustrated and angry. "I am tired of people assuming I must be
a bad person because my son is a Crip," says a mother who lives in South-
Central L.A. "I love my son and have cared for him just like any other
mother. Maybe I wasn't perfect, but what mother is?"

Lately, however, some of the officials most involved in dealing with
local street gangs have come to realize that to blame a gang member's family
and upbringing is to grossly oversimplify the problem. "There is no typical
profile of a gang parent," says Jim Galipeau, a Los Angeles County probation
officer who works exclusively with gang kids and their families in South-
Central Los Angeles. "I have one mother who owns a 12-unit complex, and

on the other end of the spectrum is a mom who's a cocaine addict and a prostitute. Mostly it's a one-parent family with the mom making the money, but there are working families with nice homes and gardeners. These parents just happen to live where the gangs are a way of life and their kids become involved."

In many parts of Southern California where street gangs flourish, drop-out rates from neighborhood high schools are as high as 35%. A significant proportion of the families in South-Central and East L.A. are living below the poverty level. Drug use and violent crime are rampant. And opportunities for jobs, education and recreation are limited. It's a setting, authorities say, that causes youths to turn to gangs regardless of their upbringing. "For a lot of these kids," says one LAPD officer, "the gang is about the only happening thing in the neighborhood."

Gangs and gang violence have become subjects of great interest and   5
concern for all of Southern California. Law-enforcement agencies are expending enormous resources in their fight against gang-related crime. But, for the mothers of the targets of this law-enforcement effort, the problem is far more immediate than newspaper headlines and stories on TV news. The problem is family.

And now, some police departments are beginning to realize that mothers, instead of being viewed as part of the problem, should be enlisted to help search for solutions.

Capt. Jack Blair of the Pomona Police Department leads weekly gang-truce meetings attended by parents, gang members and local clergy. In the course of his yearlong involvement with the Pomona program, he has become convinced that "parents are the key to [solving] the whole problem." At his meetings, and at other meetings of parents around the county, Blair believes that parents have begun to make a difference. "Once the parents unite and form groups, talking to each other and sharing information, that is threatening to the gang members. They want anonymity. They don't want their tactics or activities talked about with parents of rival gangs. When the moms are saying, 'Hey, don't go over to this neighborhood,' or 'I know that you went over to that neighborhood,' there is a certain amount of sport removed."

"Ours is not a program to turn your kid in. We don't ask parents to be informants on their child. But the moms realize what an effect they can have on the kids," Blair says. "The kids may go out gang-banging at night, but eventually they have to go back home and eat the dinner their mom's prepared. Even though they might exhibit some of the machismo characteristics, there is still concern on how they are impacting their family."

"Just because you shoot someone," Galipeau adds, "it doesn't mean that you don't love your mother."

Still, even as outsiders begin to recognize the contributions they can   10
make, mothers of gang members face constant fear and worry. They feel

overwhelming guilt, asking themselves again and again where they've failed as parents. And they have to deal with the scorn of a society that holds them in some measure responsible for the actions of their sons.

Although these mothers of gang members live in divergent parts of the city and come from a variety of cultures, they share similar pains. These are some of their stories.

TERESA RODRIGUEZ
Fear: Her Son Lived and the Family Became the Target

Teresa Rodriguez spends her Friday nights cowering in a back bedroom of the tiny stucco house she shares with her husband and eight children in a west Pomona barrio. The living room, she knows from experience, is simply not safe.

During the past two years, most often on Fridays, Rodriguez's home has been shot up half a dozen times, and one night recently when her husband came home late from work, someone shot at him. The family's car and house still bear bullet holes.

The problems all started two years ago, when Rodriguez's youngest son was 13. Unbeknown to his mother, he had become a member of a small Pomona gang, Sur 13. One day when he and several other Sur 13 members were out walking, a car full of rival gang members passed by. "Which barrio are you from?" the other gang demanded to know. Most of the Sur 13 boys didn't answer; Rodriguez's son did. Upon hearing the hated neighborhood name spoken aloud, one of the boys in the car leaned out the window with a gun and pulled the trigger.

Rodriguez didn't know for several hours that her son had been shot. 15 "His friends took him to the hospital and left him there. They couldn't find the courage to tell me," she said recently through an interpreter. Finally, one of the neighborhood kids came to the door and told Rodriguez what had happened. She was stunned. Having come to the United States from Mexico in 1973, she was still timid and uncertain about the culture here. "I had no idea any of my sons was in a gang until that day," she said.

The bullet had lodged near the 13-year-old's heart but hadn't damaged any internal organs. "The doctor told me we were very, very lucky," Rodriguez recalls. Her son recovered, but Rodriguez's life was irreversibly changed.

Because the boy claimed his neighborhood with so much bravado on the day he was shot, he has become a target for the rival gang, which now sees the boy as Sur 13's most visible member. "Whenever there is a problem, they come after him," his mother says. "The problem is no longer just on him; it is on the house."

Immediately after the shooting, Rodriguez was too grateful that her son was alive to reprimand him. But events soon prompted her to take action. Shortly after the boy returned to school, Rodriguez was summoned by the principal. Four members of the rival gang had been circling the campus all day waiting for her son. The school couldn't take that sort of disruption, so officials were asking the boy to leave and attend continuation school. "My older son told me that if I didn't get [his brother] away from here, he'd be killed," Rodriguez says. He is looked on as a particular enemy now."

Rodriguez says she knew she would have to talk to the boy, as her husband had always left rearing the children to her. But getting her son to listen proved difficult. "I said to him, 'You're going to get killed,' but he just said, 'I don't care.' He is very rebellious."

This year he is enrolled in a Pomona program for gang members who   *20* are at risk in other schools. He continues to dress like and act the part of a Sur 13, although he no longer hangs out on the street. "I finally told him that if he went out, I would send him to live in Mexico," Rodriguez says. "He doesn't want that, so he stays inside."

The shooting, says Rodriguez, has had some positive effects. For one thing, she acknowledged that all three of her older sons were in the gang. "Looking back now, I remember that when they were 9 years old they started wearing khakis and white T-shirts. They started coming home later and later," Rodriguez says. One son had a size 32 waist, but he had his mother buy him size 42 pants. "I didn't know these were gang clothes. Now I do.

"My 16-year-old threw away his *cholo* clothes right when he heard about his brother," she says. "He hasn't been with the gang since then. The two older boys are very repentant, but it is hard to step away from their pasts."

Rodriguez has begun attending meetings of the Pomona chapter of Concerned Parents, a group working to stop gang violence, and is hopeful for the first time that something can be done to prevent recurrences of the kind of gang activity that nearly killed her son. "Communication between parents, police and the church is very important. Together we can solve the problem. We can't do it alone."

Still, Rodriguez dreads Friday nights. On her front door, where a thick board has replaced a window shot out by a gang, she has posted a small picture of Jesus on the cross. "The only thing I can do about the shooting is put it in his hands," she says, gesturing toward the picture. "He's the only one who can take care of me."

MAGGIE GARCIA
Acceptance: Mean Streets, But the Neighborhood Is Still Everything

A few blocks from the Rodriguez house, in another Pomona barrio,   *25* Maggie Garcia doesn't really see her youngest son as a gang member. He is just, she says, very loyal to his friends and his neighborhood.

Loyalty to the Cherryville barrio in Pomona where she lives is something Garcia understands completely: "I was raised in the house next door to the one in which I raised my kids. Two of my sisters and one of my brothers live in the neighborhood, too." Maggie Garcia's whole life, she says, is wrapped up in the few blocks radiating from her house. "Here in the neighborhood, it is family."

Garcia realizes that her youngest son has taken his feelings for his barrio a little far on occasion. Last September, when the boy had just turned 14, he got into a fight at school. "He claimed his neighborhood, and the other boy claimed his neighborhood, and all of a sudden they are fighting for two gangs."

After the fight, he was expelled and sent to a local continuation school. "The principal at his old school was upset because my son said, 'I'd die for my neighborhood.' If he'd said, 'I'd die for my country,' the principal probably would have given him a medal."

Garcia worried about her son at the continuation school. Because it drew students from the whole Pomona school district, her son was in constant contact with boys from rival gangs. "One day, two boys from Twelfth Street [another Pomona gang] laid in wait for my son. He came home all bloody and with bruises," Garcia recalls. "I told him you're not going back to school. You could be killed."

Garcia knew that inter-neighborhood conflicts could be deadly in the   30
Pomona barrios: Three nephews and three of her nieces' boyfriends had been killed by rival gang members. She told her son that if he was out late with his cousins, he wasn't to walk home on the streets but should instead cut through neighbors' back yards. When he goes out the door, Garcia blesses him in hopes that God will protect him out on the streets. But there is only so much, she feels, that she can do. "I've tried to talk to him," she says. "Some people think I should forbid him from being with his friends, but that would be like his telling me, 'Mom, I don't want you hanging out with your best friends in this neighborhood.' It's such a small neighborhood, there are only a few boys my son has here. If he didn't hang out with them, he wouldn't have any friends."

"I see it this way," she says. "Nowadays you have to protect yourself as much as possible, and the friends help protect. The Bible says when you are slapped you turn the other cheek, but you don't do that around here because they will shoot you if you're not looking. Children in any neighborhood have to be aware and have eyes in the back of their heads or they will be dead. They are streetwise. I've taught them to be that way. I feel that when a child is running with three or four of his friends it's better than being alone."

So instead of forbidding her son to associate with the gang, Garcia says, she has taken a more moderate line. "I tell him you can live in the fire, but you don't have to let yourself get burned. You've got to learn to live outside, but when you see something about to go down, you have to get out of there."

In early August, it became apparent that Garcia's youngest son hadn't absorbed the lessons his mother was trying to teach him. After coming home late one night, the boy went back out into the neighborhood. What happened next is in dispute, but in the end he was arrested and charged with an armed robbery that took place a few blocks from his house. Garcia insists that her son was simply in the wrong place at the wrong time. After being held at Los Padrinos Juvenile Hall in Downey, he was released into this mother's custody and is attending school through a Pomona program for gang members who are at risk in other schools. His case will be reviewed by a judge in December.

"My older son has gotten very angry at my younger son," Garcia says. "He tells [his brother], 'You know, if they kill you, your friends will go to your Rosary and they'll go to your funeral. Then they'll have a party and forget you.' But my younger son doesn't see it that way. He sort of says, 'Here today, gone tomorrow—so what?'"

GAYLE THOMAS KARY
Death: Just When She Thought She'd Beaten the Odds

Fifteen-year-old Jamee Kary hadn't been active in the Five Deuce Broadway Crips in recent months. But that didn't matter to a car full of the rival Blood gang members who spotted the boy crossing West 27th Street on the night of Sept. 10. The Bloods called the boy to their car. Words were exchanged. The Bloods began to drive off, but then stopped and got out of their car. Jamee tried to run, but he was shot in the face before he could reach cover. He died within minutes.

Gayle Thomas Kary had worried frantically about Jamee, her middle son, for more than two years before his death. His problems, she feels, started four years ago when tight finances forced her to move from Long Beach to a family-owned house in South-Central Los Angeles half a block from the Harbor Freeway. In the old neighborhood, there had been so much for an adolescent boy to do. There were youth centers and year-round organized sports. In the new neighborhood, there was only the gang.

Because Jamee had a slight learning disability, school had always been difficult for him, but he had always had friends. A charming boy with a quick smile and easy affability, Jamee fit right into the new neighborhood. By the time he was 13, he had fit right into the gang.

Kary could tell from her son's style of dress and friends that he had become a gang member. And she was very worried. A data-entry operator with a full-time job and a steady life style, Kary had always believed that if she set a good example and enforced limits, her sons would turn out well. Her oldest son, now 20, had always met his mother's expectations. But Jamee seemed torn. At home he was respectful and loving, but out on the streets, he seemed like a different boy. "He knew that he was loved at home," Kary says, sitting in the immaculate California bungalow she shares with her sons. "But he somehow felt the need to be out there with those boys and not be considered a wimp."

One day during the summer of 1986, when Jamee was 13, his mother found him cutting up soap to look like cocaine. Kary was horrified that the boy found the drug culture so appealing. Within weeks, she sent Jamee off to stay with his father, a Louisiana minister, hoping that a change of environment would divert Jamee from trouble. Three weeks later, his father sent him back, saying he couldn't control the boy.

Later that summer, Jamee stole his mother's car one evening. He was 40 stopped by police for driving the wrong way on a one-way street. But the police just gave the boy a traffic citation and told him to lock up the car and go home. When Kary heard about the incident, she was outraged. She bundled Jamee into the car, drove to the police station, and asked the police there to arrest her son. "I needed help in dealing with my son, but they just said, 'There's nothing we can do,'" Kary says, a bitter sorrow apparent in her voice.

In the months that followed, Jamee was increasingly out of control. Kary had always expected her sons to abide by certain household rules if they wanted to live under her roof. Jamee was required to attend school and do his homework, to keep his room clean, to wash his clothes, to wash dishes on alternate days and to feed the dogs. It was not too much to ask, Kary felt.

Jamee, by the fall of his 14th year, felt differently. "Jamee started seeing these guys out there who were wearing expensive clothes and they didn't have to go to school or do chores or ask their parents for money," Kary recalls. Unwilling to meet his mother's demands, Jamee began running away from home for short periods of time to live with members of the Five Deuce Broadway Crips. By this time, his mother knew from other kids in the neighborhood, her son was also selling drugs.

During his times away from home, Kary tried to keep tabs on him. "I always knew where he was and that he was safe," Kary says. "He'd sneak over and try to get his brothers to get him a clean set of clothes." Eventually, Jamee would tire of life on the streets and return home. "He'd always promise to toe the line," Kary says. "He'd say he had changed. He knew my rules were the same."

When her son was at home, Kary tried to reason with him. "I told him that kind of life could lead to no good," Kary says with tears in her eyes. "I told him that a fast life goes fast." She warned him, she says, that he could be arrested or killed. "He would just tell me he wouldn't get busted because he could run faster than the police. He told me nobody would kill him because he didn't do any bad drug deals."

In the spring of 1987, Jamee was arrested for possession of cocaine 45 with intent to sell. The arrest was a relief for his mother, who hoped that at last her son would be in the hands of people who could help him. But when the time came for Jamee's sentencing, Kary was once again disappointed.

"They wanted to give him probation. The conditions were things like he had to be in by 10 and stop associating with gang members. I told them I'd been trying to get him to do those things and he wouldn't. There was no way he was going to do them now, either. I said I wouldn't take him," Kary recalls.

Instead, the court sentenced Jamee to juvenile hall and later to a youth camp. After five months, Jamee returned home. At first he seemed to be less involved with the gang, but he soon returned to his old ways. There was just one difference now: Jamee had been assigned to probation officer Jim Galipeau, who seemed to really care about the boy. Galipeau also listened to Kary's concerns.

"I called Mr. Galipeau and said Jamee was in trouble again. He told me to keep a record of what he was doing and when," Kary recalls. Thankful for something to do, Kary kept detailed notes on her son's transgressions, hoping to build a case for revoking Jamee's probation. But before she could do that, Galipeau had a heart-to-heart talk with her son. "Jamee told Mr. Galipeau he was tired of life on the streets," Kary says. "He got tired of the police swooping up the street and having to run and not knowing where he was going to sleep." At his probation officer's suggestion, Jamee agreed to request placement in a county-run youth facility to get away from his life in Los Angeles.

By last summer, Jamee was doing beautifully. "I knew I still had to take it one day at a time," his mother says, "but he really seemed to have changed. It was like he was the child I used to know. He wouldn't even go up to Broadway [where the gang liked to hang out]. The friends he associated with were not gang members."

Jamee arrived home for his last weekend furlough on Friday, Sept. 9. On Saturday evening, he asked his mother if he could go with a friend to pick up another fellow and get something to eat. She readily agreed. An hour and a half later, a neighbor came to the door with the news that Jamee had been shot on 27th Street.

Kary raced to the scene, where she saw police had cordoned off a large *50* area. "I saw that yellow police rope, and I knew right then my son was dead," Kary recalls. But police at the scene refused to let her see whether the victim was her son, and after pleading to no avail for information, Kary was finally persuaded to go home and wait. Several hours later, the police called and asked Kary's oldest son to go and identify photographs. Kary finally knew for sure. Her 15-year-old son was dead.

After Jamee's killing, Kary continued to learn what it was like to have a gang member for a son. She wanted to have the funeral service at her own church, but neighbors dissuaded her. "They told me there was a rival gang over there. They said, 'You can't have it there or there'll be troubles,'" Kary says. She also realized with shock that colors, particularly Crip blue, had taken on a new meaning in her life. "All those years that blue stood for boys, and I couldn't let my boy wear blue at his funeral or have the programs printed in blue," Kary says. She had originally planned to wear her nicest dress to the services, but then she realized that it, too, was blue. "A friend told me, 'You can't wear that or you'll be sitting there looking the queen Crip mother,'" Kary says.

Kary worried about how the Five Deuce Broadways would behave at her son's funeral. But that, she says, turned out to be a pleasant surprise. Several days after Jamee's death, some 20 of the gang's members came to Kary's house. While Jamee was alive, she had never allowed gang members in her house, but this once she decided to make an exception.

The young men who gathered in her living room were, she says, very respectful. "They said that even though Jamee wasn't actively involved with them at the time, he was still a member of their family, and they wanted to offer financial support," Kary recalls. The boys contributed about $400 toward funeral costs.

"After they spoke," Kary says, "I said to them, 'I don't like what you do out there on the streets, but I want to tell you something from my heart. You say Jamee was a member of your family. That makes you a member of my family, too, because Jamee was my son. I'm asking you a favor as family members. I don't want any colors at the funeral. I don't want rags, and I don't want trouble.'" To a person, Kary says, the young men honored her requests, and since the funeral they have been eager to help in any way they can.

In the aftermath of Jamee's death, Kary feels lost. Her youngest son, 11-year-old Lewis, had decided just before his brother's death to go live with his father in Louisiana. "He did not want to be involved on the streets with the gangs and the colors and the drugs. He was scared. He didn't want to go to junior high school here," Kary recalls. While Kary supports Lewis' decision, she is lonely. "I feel so empty inside," she says. "I can't remember when I last felt my heart beat inside my chest. The only thing I can feel in my whole body is my head because it hurts all the time."

In her lowest moments, Kary takes some solace in a poem Jamee wrote for her while he was incarcerated after his cocaine arrest. She included the poem, which Jamee had entitled "If You Only Knew," in the program for Jamee's funeral.

55

I sit here on my bunk
And don't know what to do
My life just caught up in a mess
Because I was a fool
I sometimes wonder to myself
With my heart just full of pain
Boy when I get out of this place
My life won't be the same
I'm sorry for all the pain I caused
For you as well as them

I promise you, and I'll try my best
To not do wrong again ·
Every night and every day
I always think of you
I just sit here thinking but
If you only knew

Dedicated to my Mom
I love you

_____

Suggestions for Writing and Discussion

1. Select two or three points that Horton makes or two or three examples that she uses to which you have a strong response. Write a letter to the author explaining your response. Try to convince her that she should consider the points you are making if she writes another article on this topic.
2. In paragraph 8, Horton suggests a relationship between gangs and the concept of machismo. How would you define the term *machismo?* What is the dictionary definition? Do you agree that there is a causal connection between gang activity and machismo? Explain.
3. Without going back to this selection, which one event, character, or phrase stands out in your mind?
4. To what extent, if at all, are parents responsible for how their children turn out? Explain your answer with evidence from the text and from your own life experiences and observations.
5. Comment on the father's role in the three scenarios within this reading.
6. Being an "in" member of one culture often automatically excludes a person from some other cultures. From what cultures are these gang members excluded? To what extent do they choose to be excluded? To what extent is the exclusion forced on them?
7. What do the three gang members described in this selection have in common? In what ways are they different?

_____

Suggestions for Extended Thinking and Writing

1. Write an essay in which you describe the culture to which you belonged as a teenager.
2. Write an essay in which you narrate the outcome of heeding or not heeding your parents' advice.
3. Imagine you have been assigned to counsel one of the parents or one of the gang members from this piece. Write an essay in which you give this person advice both for the present and for the future.

_____

CATHY SONG

The Youngest Daughter

> *Born in 1955, Cathy Song grew up in Honolulu, Hawaii, with her Chinese mother and Korean father. She attended Wellesley College and received an M.A. in Creative Writing from Boston University in 1981. Her first book of poems,* Picture Bride, *won the Yale Series of Younger Poets award in 1983. The poems in this book exemplify Song's interest in the intersections and connections of the generations that comprise families. While critic Steven Sumida points out that Song has been "steeped in the great tradition of English and American literature" and that it would be misleading to evaluate her work "by any sort of supposed East Asian cultural or literary notions" (*Contact *11 Winter/Spring 1986:55), "The Youngest Daughter" shows a balance between Song's sense of her Asian heritage and her commitment to the growth of her Asian American self.*

Pre-Reading and Journal-Writing Suggestions

1. What is your place in the birth order of your family (oldest, middle, youngest, only child)? How do you think this order has affected the role you play in the family and the way you look at and think about yourself?
2. What do you think your life will be like when you grow old? How do you envision yourself at 65, 70, or older? Where do you think you will live? Who will be the important people in your life? What will you be doing?

The sky has been dark   1
for many years.
My skin has become as damp
and pale as rice paper
and feels the way   5
mother's used to before the drying sun
parched it out there in the fields.

　　Lately, when I touch my eyelids,
my hands react as if
I had just touched something   10
hot enough to burn.
My skin, aspirin colored,
tingles with migraine. Mother
has been massaging the left side of my face

especially in the evenings   15
when the pain flares up.

This morning
her breathing was graveled,
her voice gruff with affection
when I wheeled her into the bath.   20
She was in a good humor,
making jokes about her great breasts,
floating in the milky water
like two walruses,
flaccid and whiskered around the nipples.   25
I scrubbed them with a sour taste
in my mouth, thinking:
six children and an old man
have sucked from these brown nipples.

I was almost tender   30
when I came to the blue bruises
that freckle her body,
places where she has been injecting insulin
for thirty years. I soaped her slowly,
she sighed deeply, her eyes closed.   35
It seems it has always
been like this: the two of us
in this sunless room,
the splashing of the bathwater.

In the afternoons   40
when she has rested,
she prepares our ritual of tea and rice,
garnished with a shred of gingered fish,
a slice of pickled turnip,
a token for my white body.   45
We eat in the familiar silence.
She knows I am not to be trusted,
even now planning my escape.
As I toast to her health
with the tea she has poured,   50
a thousand cranes curtain the window,
fly up in a sudden breeze.

Suggestions for Writing and Discussion

1. Many of the images in this poem could be described as hard and painful. List several of these images and discuss what connection they have to the author's underlying message or theme.

2. Speculate on what the author means by her opening lines, "The sky has been dark/for many years."

3. Describe your first reaction to the speaker's description of her mother in the bath.

4. What does the mother do for the daughter? What is the daughter's reaction to her mother's care?

5. In line 46, the speaker says, "We eat in the familiar silence." Sometimes silence can be more powerful than words. In this poem, what is the silence "saying"? During the next few days, notice silences in your own life. How do you interpret those silences?

Suggestions for Extended Thinking and Writing

1. Interview several people whose birth order is the same as yours, asking them what effect they believe their position in the family has had on their character and personality. Compare their observations with your own.

2. Should children be morally and legally obliged to care for their aging parents? Explain clearly the reasons for your beliefs.

SUGGESTIONS FOR MAKING CONNECTIONS

1. Write an essay in which you explain a conflict in your own childhood. Refer to at least three of the selections in this section as you describe the conflict, explaining how your own experiences, challenges, and choices were the same as or different from those described in the readings.

2. What do children contribute to their parents' lives? Refer to at least three selections in this section as you respond to this question.

3. Are parents to blame for the way children turn out? Write an essay that takes a stand on this issue. For support, use your own experience and several selections from this section.

4. Write an essay in which you describe to an "outsider" how it feels to be a member of your main "culture." (Example: As a college student, you write to a parent of a prospective college student or to a high school student who is considering applying to your college. Describe the special aspects of this culture. Further examples: As an art student, you write to a friend of yours in business; as a parent, you write to a friend of yours who does not have children).

5. Imagine that you are one of the people described in any selection in this section. Write a letter to the editor of your local paper in which you explain your point of view on any controversial issue.
6. Compare the challenges faced by any three of the families described in these selections. Explain why you do or do not consider these challenges typical of those faced by many families in our society today.

8
Ways of Learning

Previews: WAYS OF LEARNING

It was on these rockers that my mother, her sisters, and my grandmother sat on these afternoons of my childhood to tell their stories, teaching each other, and my cousin and me, what it was like to be a woman, more specifically, a Puerto Rican woman. They talked about life on the island, and life in *Los Nueva Yores,* their way of referring to the United States from New York City to California: the other place, not home, all the same.

From: Casa: *A Partial Remembrance of a Puerto Rican Childhood,* JUDITH ORTIZ COFER

It went without saying that all girls could iron and wash, but the finer touches around the home, like setting a table with real silver, baking roasts and cooking vegetables without meat, had to be learned elsewhere. Usually at the source of those habits. During my tenth year, a white woman's kitchen became my finishing school.

From: *Finishing School,* MAYA ANGELOU

I developed further into a mediocre student and a somnambulant problem solver, and that affected the subjects I did have the wherewithal to handle: I detested Shakespeare; I got bored with history. My attention flitted here and there. I fooled around in class and read my books indifferently—the intellectual equivalent of playing with your food. I did what I had to do to get by, and I did it with half a mind.

From: *"I Just Wanna Be Average,"* MIKE ROSE

In our isolated Greek village, my mother had bribed a cousin to teach her to read, for girls were not supposed to attend school beyond a certain age. She had always dreamed of her children receiving an education. She couldn't be there when I graduated from Boston University, but the person who came with my father and shared our joy was my former teacher, Marjorie Hurd. We celebrated not only my bachelor's degree but also the scholarships that paid my way to Columbia's Graduate School of Journalism. There, I met the woman who would eventually become my wife. At our wedding and at the baptisms of our three children, Marjorie Hurd was always there, dancing alongside the Greeks.

From: *The Teacher Who Changed My Life,* NICHOLAS GAGE

JUDITH ORTIZ COFER

Casa: *A Partial Remembrance of a Puerto Rican Childhood*

Born in Puerto Rico in 1952, Judith Ortiz Cofer spent her early years moving from place to place within Puerto Rico and the mainland United States in accordance with the orders received by her career Navy father. Because of these moves she attended school in many different cultural environments, eventually earning an M.A. in English from the University of Florida and pursuing further graduate work at Oxford University in England. In Casa, Ortiz Cofer focuses not on formal schooling but on the lessons she learned during afternoons spent at her grandmother's house, visiting and talking with her mother, her aunts, and her grandmother.

Pre-Reading and Journal-Writing Suggestions

1. What tales has your family handed down from generation to generation? Pick your favorite scandal or heroic episode and tell it as you have heard it from your relatives.
2. Describe the room in your house where you feel most comfortable sitting and talking.

At three or four o'clock in the afternoon, the hour of *café con leche,* the women of my family gathered in Mamá's living room to speak of important things and retell familiar stories meant to be overheard by us young girls, their daughters. In Mamá's house (everyone called my grandmother Mamá) was a large parlor built by my grandfather to his wife's exact specifications so that it was always cool, facing away from the sun. The doorway was on the side of the house so no one could walk directly into her living room. First they had to take a little stroll through and around her beautiful garden where prize-winning orchids grew in the trunk of an ancient tree she had hollowed out for that purpose. This room was furnished with several mahogany rocking chairs, acquired at the births of her children, and one intricately carved rocker that had passed down to Mamá at the death of her own mother.

It was on these rockers that my mother, her sisters, and my grandmother sat on these afternoons of my childhood to tell their stories, teaching each other, and my cousin and me, what it was like to be a woman, more specifically, a Puerto Rican woman. They talked about life on the island, and life in *Los Nueva Yores,* their way of referring to the United States from New York City to California: the other place, not home, all the same. They told real-life stories though, as I later learned, always embellishing them

with a little or a lot of dramatic detail. And they told *cuentos,* the morality
and cautionary tales told by the women in our family for generations: stories
that became a part of my subconscious as I grew up in two worlds, the
tropical island and the cold city, and that would later surface in my dreams
and in my poetry.

One of these tales was about the woman who was left at the altar.
Mamá liked to tell that one with histrionic intensity. I remember the rise
and fall of her voice, the sighs, and her constantly gesturing hands, like two
birds swooping through her words. This particular story usually would come
up in a conversation as a result of someone mentioning a forthcoming
engagement or wedding. The first time I remember hearing it, I was sitting
on the floor at Mamá's feet, pretending to read a comic book. I may have
been eleven or twelve years old, at that difficult age when a girl was no
longer a child who could be ordered to leave the room if the women wanted
freedom to take their talk into forbidden zones, nor really old enough to be
considered a part of their conclave. I could only sit quietly, pretending to be
in another world, while absorbing it all in a sort of unspoken agreement of
my status as silent auditor. On this day, Mamá had taken my long, tangled
mane of hair into her ever-busy hands. Without looking down at me and
with no interruption of her flow of words, she began braiding my hair,
working at it with the quickness and determination that characterized all
her actions. My mother was watching us impassively from her rocker across
the room. On her lips played a little ironic smile. I would never sit still for
her ministrations, but even then, I instinctively knew that she did not possess
Mamá's matriarchal power to command and keep everyone's attention. This
was never more evident than in the spell she cast when telling a story.

"It is not like it used to be when I was a girl," Mamá announced.
"Then, a man could leave a girl standing at the church altar with a bouquet
of fresh flowers in her hands and disappear off the face of the earth. No way
to track him down if he was from another town. He could be a married
man, with maybe even two or three families all over the island. There was
no way to know. And there were men who did this. Hombres with the devil
in their flesh who would come to a pueblo, like this one, take a job at one
of the haciendas, never meaning to stay, only to have a good time and to
seduce the women."

The whole time she was speaking, Mamá would be weaving my hair   5
into a flat plait that required pulling apart the two sections of hair with little
jerks that made my eyes water; but knowing how grandmother detested
whining and *boba* (sissy) tears, as she called them, I just sat up as straight and
stiff as I did at La Escuela San Jose, where the nuns enforced good posture
with a flexible plastic ruler they bounced off of slumped shoulders and
heads. As Mamá's story progressed, I noticed how my young Aunt Laura
lowered her eyes, refusing to meet Mamá's meaningful gaze. Laura was
seventeen, in her last year of high school, and already engaged to a boy from
another town who had staked his claim with a tiny diamond ring, then left

for Los Nueva Yores to make his fortune. They were planning to get married in a year. Mamá had expressed serious doubts that the wedding would ever take place. In Mamá's eyes, a man set free without a legal contract was a man lost. She believed that marriage was not something men desired, but simply the price they had to pay for the privilege of children and, of course, for what no decent (synonymous with "smart") woman would give away for free.

"María La Loca was only seventeen when *it* happened to her." I listened closely at the mention of this name. María was a town character, a fat middle-aged woman who lived with her old mother on the outskirts of town. She was to be seen around the pueblo delivering the meat pies the two women made for a living. The most peculiar thing about María, in my eyes, was that she walked and moved like a little girl though she had the thick body and wrinkled face of an old woman. She would swing her hips in an exaggerated, clownish way, and sometimes even hop and skip up to someone's house. She spoke to no one. Even if you asked her a question, she would just look at you and smile, showing her yellow teeth. But I had heard that if you got close enough, you could hear her humming a tune without words. The kids yelled out nasty things at her, calling her *La Loca*, and the men who hung out at the bodega playing dominoes sometimes whistled mockingly as she passed by with her funny, outlandish walk. But María seemed impervious to it all, carrying her basket of *pasteles* like a grotesque Little Red Riding Hood through the forest.

María La Loca interested me, as did all the eccentrics and crazies of our pueblo. Their weirdness was a measuring stick I used in my serious quest for a definition of normal. As a Navy brat shuttling between New Jersey and the pueblo, I was constantly made to feel like an oddball by my peers, who made fun of my two-way accent: a Spanish accent when I spoke English, and when I spoke Spanish I was told that I sounded like a *Gringa*. Being the outsider had already turned my brother and me into cultural chameleons. We developed early on the ability to blend into a crowd, to sit and read quietly in a fifth story apartment building for days and days when it was too bitterly cold to play outside, or, set free, to run wild in Mamá's realm, where she took charge of our lives, releasing Mother for a while from the intense fear for our safety that our father's absences instilled in her. In order to keep us from harm when Father was away, Mother kept us under strict surveillance. She even walked us to and from Public School No. 11, which we attended during the months we lived in Paterson, New Jersey, our home base in the states. Mamá freed all three of us like pigeons from a cage. I saw her as my liberator and my model. Her stories were parables from which to glean the *Truth*.

"María La Loca was once a beautiful girl. Everyone thought she would marry the Méndez boy." As everyone knew, Rogelio Méndez was the richest man in town. "But," Mamá continued, knitting my hair with the same intensity she was putting into her story, "this *macho* made a fool out of her and ruined her life." She paused for the effect of her use of the word "macho," which at that time had not yet become a popular epithet for an unliberated man. This word had for us the crude and comical connotation of "male of the species," stud; a *macho* was what you put in a pen to increase your stock.

I peeked over my comic book at my mother. She too was under Mamá's spell, smiling conspiratorially at this little swipe at men. She was safe from Mamá's contempt in this area. Married at an early age, an unspotted lamb, she had been accepted by a good family of strict Spaniards whose name was old and respected, though their fortune had been lost long before my birth. In a rocker Papá had painted sky blue sat Mamá's oldest child, Aunt Nena. Mother of three children, stepmother of two more, she was a quiet woman who liked books but had married an ignorant and abusive widower whose main interest in life was accumulating wealth. He too was in the mainland working on his dream of returning home rich and triumphant to buy the *finca* of his dreams. She was waiting for him to send for her. She would leave her children with Mamá for several years while the two of them slaved away in factories. He would one day be a rich man, and she a sadder woman. Even now her life-light was dimming. She spoke little, an aberration in Mamá's house, and she read avidly, as if storing up spiritual food for the long winters that awaited her in Los Nueva Yores without her family. But even Aunt Nena came alive to Mamá's words, rocking gently, her hands over a thick book in her lap.

Her daughter, my cousin Sara, played jacks by herself on the tile porch outside the room where we sat. She was a year older than I. We shared a bed and all our family's secrets. Collaborators in search of answers, Sara and I discussed everything we heard the women say, trying to fit it all together like a puzzle that, once assembled, would reveal life's mysteries to us. Though she and I still enjoyed taking part in boys' games—chase, volleyball, and even *vaqueros,* the island version of cowboys and Indians involving cap-gun battles and violent shoot-outs under the mango tree in Mamá's backyard—we loved best the quiet hours in the afternoon when the men were still at work, and the boys had gone to play serious baseball at the park. Then Mamá's house belonged only to us women. The aroma of coffee perking in the kitchen, the mesmerizing creaks and groans of the rockers, and the women telling their lives in *cuentos* are forever woven into the fabric of my imagination, braided like my hair that day I felt my grandmother's hands teaching me about strength, her voice convincing me of the power of storytelling.

That day Mamá told how the beautiful María had fallen prey to a man whose name was never the same in subsequent versions of the story; it was Juan one time, José, Rafael, Diego, another. We understood that neither the name nor any of the *facts* were important, only that a woman had allowed love to defeat her. Mamá put each of us in María's place by describing her wedding dress in loving detail: how she looked like a princess in her lace as she waited at the altar. Then, as Mamá approached the tragic denouement of her story, I was distracted by the sound of my Aunt Laura's violent rocking. She seemed on the verge of tears. She knew the fable was intended for her. That week she was going to have her wedding gown fitted, though no firm date had been set for the marriage. Mamá ignored Laura's obvious discomfort, digging out a ribbon from the sewing basket she kept by her rocker while describing María's long illness, "a fever that would not break for days." She spoke of a mother's despair: "that woman climbed the church steps on her knees every morning, wore only black as a *promesa* to the Holy Virgin in exchange for her daughter's health." By the time María returned from her honeymoon with death, she was ravished, no longer young or sane. "As you can see, she is almost as old as her mother already," Mamá lamented while tying the ribbon to the ends of my hair, pulling it back with such force that I just knew I would never be able to close my eyes completely again.

"That María's getting crazier every day." Mamá's voice would take a lighter tone now, expressing satisfaction, either for the perfection of my braid, or for a story well told—it was hard to tell. "You know that tune María is always humming?" Carried away by her enthusiasm, I tried to nod, but Mamá still had me pinned between her knees.

"Well, that's the wedding march." Surprising us all, Mamá sang out, "Da, da, dara . . . da, da, dara." Then lifting me off the floor by my skinny shoulders, she would lead me around the room in an impromptu waltz—another session ending with the laughter of women, all of us caught up in the infectious joke of our lives.

Suggestions for Writing and Discussion

1. From the stories these women tell, what was life like for them? Do you think women from other times and cultures could relate to these stories? Explain.

2. After reading this essay, return to paragraph 2 where Cofer describes the stories her relatives told as "morality and cautionary tales." Now that you have read some of these tales, how would you define the words *morality* and *cautionary* as Cofer uses them here?

3. The tales the older women tell all have a moral. What is the moral of the story about María La Loca? Do you see this moral as important to young women today? Explain.

4. In what ways is María La Loca like Little Red Riding Hood? Explain these similarities in an essay intended for people who work with young children. You are trying to convince them of the importance of seeing similarities as well as differences between the stories told by various cultures.

5. What do these women think about men? Do you think they are being fair? Are men generally like the men in the stories the women tell?

6. Cofer recalls the family secrets she shared with her cousin Sara. If you had a confidante while you were growing up (a family member or best friend), describe this person and explain what you gained from the time you spent together and from the conversations you shared.
7. What is your reaction to the ending of this piece where Mamá reveals that María, the crazy woman, has been humming the wedding march for years on end? Why do you think the women laugh at this revelation?

Suggestions for Extended Thinking and Writing
1. The women in Cofer's family had a special talent for creating parables (brief stories that convey a moral or message). Try your own hand at writing a parable designed to carry a lesson you believe to be important for an audience of your choice (young people, parents, children, young men, young women).
2. What memories do you have of the women or men in your family? Write your own "partial remembrance," using Cofer's format as a model.

MAYA ANGELOU

Finishing School

> *Originally named Marguerita Johnson, Maya Angelou was born in St. Louis in 1928. From the age of three until she was eight, Angelou and her brother grew up in Stamps, Arkansas, under the watchful, loving eye of the grandmother they called "Momma." Unfortunately her grandmother's boundless energy and affection could not protect Angelou from the pain of poverty, segregated schools, and violence at the hands of both whites and blacks. At age eight, she went to stay with her mother and was raped by her mother's lover; subsequently Angelou refused to talk for more than a year. Shortly after the rape, she returned to her grandmother's home where she began to read voraciously, memorizing extensive passages from writers varying from Shakespeare to the poets of the Harlem Renaissance. The cadences and rhythms of her early love affair with poetry weave throughout her works. In addition to being a disciplined writer who works each day from 6 a.m. until noon, Angelou is a gifted actress, dancer, and musician. She has starred in the European and African road production of* Porgy and Bess *and has written scores and lyrics for screenplays. In 1973 and again in 1977 she received Tony award nominations, while in 1972 her book of poems,* Just Give Me a Cool Drink of Water 'fore I Diiie, *was nominated for a Pulitzer Prize. In 1993, as poet laureate of the United States, she wrote and read a poem for the inauguration of President Clinton.*
>
> *A champion of the narrative as complex, serious art, Angelou sees her work as "stemming from the slave narrative and developing into a new American literary form." In this selection, a chapter from Angelou's highly praised autobiography* I Know Why the Caged Bird Sings *(1969), she tells the story of a painful lesson she learned in a white woman's kitchen that she ironically calls her "finishing school."*

Pre-Reading and Journal-Writing Suggestions

1. How do you feel about your name? In other words, if someone calls you something slightly different from your name ("Cathy" instead of "Kate," for instance), does it bother you? How important is your name to you?
2. Write about a significant educational experience you have had *outside* the classroom.

Recently a white woman from Texas, who would quickly describe   *1*
herself as a liberal, asked me about my hometown. When I told her that in
Stamps my grandmother had owned the only Negro general merchandise

store since the turn of the century, she exclaimed, "Why, you were a debu-tante." Ridiculous and even ludicrous. But Negro girls in small Southern towns, whether poverty-stricken or just munching along on a few of life's necessities, were given as extensive and irrelevant preparations for adulthood as rich white girls shown in magazines. Admittedly the training was not the same. While white girls learned to waltz and sit gracefully with a tea cup balanced on their knees, we were lagging behind, learning the mid-Victorian values with very little money to indulge them. . . .

We were required to embroider and I had trunkfuls of colorful dish-towels, pillowcases, runners and handkerchiefs to my credit. I mastered the art of crocheting and tatting, and there was a life-time's supply of dainty doilies that would never be used in sacheted dresser drawers. It went without saying that all girls could iron and wash, but the finer touches around the home, like setting a table with real silver, baking roasts and cooking vegeta-bles without meat, had to be learned elsewhere. Usually at the source of those habits. During my tenth year, a white woman's kitchen became my finishing school.

Mrs. Viola Cullinan was a plump woman who lived in a three-bed-room house somewhere behind the post office. She was singularly unattrac-tive until she smiled, and then the lines around her eyes and mouth which made her look perpetually dirty disappeared, and her face looked like the mask of an impish elf. She usually rested her smile until late afternoon when her women friends dropped in and Miss Glory, the cook, served them cold drinks on the closed-in porch.

The exactness of her house was inhuman. This glass went here and only here. That cup had its place and it was an act of impudent rebellion to place it anywhere else. At twelve o'clock the table was set. At 12:15 Mrs. Cullinan sat down to dinner (whether her husband had arrived or not). At 12:16 Miss Glory brought out the food.

It took me a week to learn the difference between a salad plate, a bread plate and a dessert plate.

Mrs. Cullinan kept up the tradition of her wealthy parents. She was from Virginia. Miss Glory, who was a descendant of slaves that had worked for the Cullinans, told me her history. She had married beneath her (accord-ing to Miss Glory). Her husband's family hadn't had their money very long and what they had "didn't 'mount to much."

As ugly as she was, I thought privately, she was lucky to get a husband above or beneath her station. But Miss Glory wouldn't let me say a thing against her mistress. She was very patient with me, however, over the house-work. She explained the dishware, silverware and servants' bells. The large round bowl in which soup was served wasn't a soup bowl, it was a tureen. There were goblets, sherbet glasses, ice-cream glasses, wine glasses, green glass coffee cups with matching saucers, and water glasses. I had a glass to drink from, and it sat with Miss Glory's on a separate shelf from the others.

Soup spoons, gravy boat, butter knives, salad forks and carving platter were additions to my vocabulary and in fact almost represented a new language. I was fascinated with the novelty, with the fluttering Mrs. Cullinan and her Alice-in-Wonderland house.

Her husband remains, in my memory, undefined. I lumped him with all the other white men that I had ever seen and tried not to see.

On our way home one evening, Miss Glory told me that Mrs. Cullinan couldn't have children. She said that she was too delicate-boned. It was hard to imagine bones at all under those layers of fat. Miss Glory went on to say that the doctor had taken out all her lady organs. I reasoned that a pig's organs included the lungs, heart and liver, so if Mrs. Cullinan was walking around without those essentials, it explained why she drank alcohol out of unmarked bottles. She was keeping herself embalmed.

When I spoke to Bailey about it, he agreed that I was right, but he 10 also informed me that Mr. Cullinan had two daughters by a colored lady and that I knew them very well. He added that the girls were the spitting image of their father. I was unable to remember what he looked like, although I had just left him a few hours before, but I thought of the Coleman girls. They were very light-skinned and certainly didn't look very much like their mother (no one ever mentioned Mr. Coleman).

My pity for Mrs. Cullinan preceded me the next morning like the Cheshire cat's smile. Those girls, who could have been her daughters, were beautiful. They didn't have to straighten their hair. Even when they were caught in the rain, their braids still hung down straight like tamed snakes. Their mouths were pouty little cupid's bows. Mrs. Cullinan didn't know what she missed. Or maybe she did. Poor Mrs. Cullinan.

For weeks after, I arrived early, left late and tried very hard to make up for her barrenness. If she had her own children, she wouldn't have had to ask me to run a thousand errands from her back door to the back door of her friends. Poor old Mrs. Cullinan.

Then one evening Miss Glory told me to serve the ladies on the porch. After I set the tray down and turned toward the kitchen, one of the women asked, "What's your name, girl?" It was the speckled-faced one. Mrs. Cullinan said, "She doesn't talk much. Her name's Margaret."

"Is she dumb?"

"No. As I understand it, she can talk when she wants to but she's 15 usually quiet as a little mouse. Aren't you, Margaret?"

I smiled at her. Poor thing. No organs and couldn't even pronounce my name correctly.

"She's a sweet little thing, though."

"Well, that may be, but the name's too long. I'd never bother myself. I'd call her Mary if I was you."

I fumed into the kitchen. That horrible woman would never have the chance to call me Mary because if I was starving I'd never work for her. . . .

That evening I decided to write a poem on being white, fat, old and   20
without children. It was going to be a tragic ballad. I would have to watch
her carefully to capture the essence of her loneliness and pain.

The very next day, she called me by the wrong name. Miss Glory and
I were washing up the lunch dishes when Mrs. Cullinan came to the doorway. "Mary?"

Miss Glory asked, "Who?"

Mrs. Cullinan, sagging a little, knew and I knew. "I want Mary to go
down to Mrs. Randall's and take her some soup. She's not been feeling well
for a few days."

Miss Glory's face was a wonder to see. "You mean Margaret, ma'am.
Her name's Margaret."

"That's too long. She's Mary from now on. Heat that soup from last   25
night and put it in the china tureen and, Mary, I want you to carry it
carefully."

Every person I knew had a hellish horror of being "called out of his
name." It was a dangerous practice to call a Negro anything that could be
loosely construed as insulting because of the centuries of their having been
called niggers, jigs, dinges, blackbirds, crows, boots and spooks.

Miss Glory had a fleeting second of feeling sorry for me. Then as she
handed me the hot tureen she said, "Don't mind, don't pay that no mind.
Sticks and stones may break your bones, but words . . . You know, I been
working for her for twenty years."

She held the back door open for me. "Twenty years. I wasn't much
older than you. My name used to be Hallelujah. That's what Ma named me,
but my mistress give me 'Glory,' and it stuck. I likes it better too."

I was in the little path that ran behind the houses when Miss Glory
shouted, "It's shorter too."

For a few seconds it was a tossup over whether I would laugh (imagine   30
being named Hallelujah) or cry (imagine letting some white woman rename
you for her convenience). My anger saved me from either outburst. I had to
quit the job, but the problem was going to be how to do it. Momma
wouldn't allow me to quit for just any reason.

"She's a peach. That woman is a real peach." Mrs. Randall's maid was
talking as she took the soup from me, and I wondered what her name used
to be and what she answered to now.

For a week I looked into Mrs. Cullinan's face as she called me Mary.
She ignored my coming late and leaving early. Miss Glory was a little annoyed because I had begun to leave egg yolk on the dishes and wasn't putting
much heart in polishing the silver. I hoped that she would complain to our
boss, but she didn't.

Then Bailey solved my dilemma. He had me describe the contents of
the cupboard and the particular plates she liked best. Her favorite piece was
a casserole shaped like a fish and the green glass coffee cups. I kept his
instructions in mind, so on the next day when Miss Glory was hanging out

clothes and I had again been told to serve the old biddies on the porch, I dropped the empty serving tray. When I heard Mrs. Cullinan scream, "Mary!" I picked up the casserole and two of the green glass cups in readiness. As she rounded the kitchen door I let them fall on the tiled floor.

I could never absolutely describe to Bailey what happened next, because each time I got to the part where she fell on the floor and screwed up her ugly face to cry, we burst out laughing. She actually wobbled around on the floor and picked up shards of the cups and cried, "Oh, Momma. Oh, dear Gawd. It's Momma's china from Virginia. Oh, Momma, I'm sorry."

Miss Glory came running in from the yard and the women from the *35* porch crowded around. Miss Glory was almost as broken up as her mistress. "You mean to say she broke our Virginia dishes? What we gone do?"

Mrs. Cullinan cried louder, "That clumsy nigger. Clumsy little black nigger."

Old speckled-faced leaned down and asked, "Who did it, Viola? Was it Mary? Who did it?"

Everything was happening so fast I can't remember whether her action preceded her words, but I know that Mrs. Cullinan said, "Her name's Margaret, goddamn it, her name's Margaret." And she threw a wedge of broken plate at me. It could have been the hysteria which put her aim off, but the flying crockery caught Miss Glory right over her ear and she started screaming.

I left the front door wide open so all the neighbors could hear.

Mrs. Cullinan was right about one thing. My name wasn't Mary. *40*

Suggestions for Writing and Discussion

1. Write your immediate reaction to this story.
2. In paragraph 13, Angelou speaks of Mrs. Cullinan's *barrenness.* What is the literal meaning of this word? What are its connotations? Cite details from this piece to explain the ways in which Mrs. Cullinan (and her life) can be seen as barren.
3. Why do Miss Glory's cup and Margaret's cup sit on a separate shelf? Can you think of similar distinctions you have seen or experienced? (Example: children eating at tables apart from adults)
4. Angelou writes that she felt sorry for Mrs. Cullinan, so she tried to make up for it by working extra hard. What does this tell you about Angelou's personality and character? When and why does her attitude change toward Mrs. Cullinan?
5. What do you think of Miss Glory? In what ways is she like Margaret? In what ways do they differ? Why do you think Miss Glory has stayed with Mrs. Cullinan for so many years? What do their different decisions suggest about their values? With whom do you more closely identify? Why?
6. Angelou makes several references to *Alice in Wonderland* in this piece. Identify as many references as you can and explain how the *Alice* images

connect to the central idea Angelou conveys. As you write your response, consider as your audience a friend who remains, even as an adult, devoted to the *Alice* stories. You are trying to convince this friend to read Angelou's piece.

7. Mrs. Cullinan says that the name Margaret is too long, so she shortens it to Mary. She also does this to Glory's name. Apart from being a convenience, why else does she do this?

8. What do you think of Bailey's solution to Margaret's dilemma? Could she have solved her problem any other way? Explain.

Suggestions for Extended Thinking and Writing

1. Are you a rebel, like Margaret, or a conformist, like Glory? Write an essay in which you explain the causes and effects of an event in your life that shows your approach to challenge and conflict.

2. Margaret says that to really capture someone, you have to watch very carefully. Practice the art of observation yourself. Watch someone very carefully, making notes about what the person does and says. Then write a brief analysis of the person's actions, based on your notes.

3. Time for revenge (and fun). Using precise, vivid description, write an essay highlighting the nastiest, meanest person you've ever met.

MIKE ROSE

"I Just Wanna Be Average"

Born to immigrant Italian parents in 1944, Mike Rose grew up in South Los Angeles. After beginning school tracked as a "slow learner," Rose went on to graduate from Loyola University of Los Angeles and to earn master's degrees from the University of Southern California and UCLA. He later earned a doctorate in educational psychology from UCLA, where he currently directs the writing program.

Rose is an outstanding scholar and teacher, known especially for his autobiographical book Lives on the Boundary *(1989), which explains the school experiences of America's students who grow up without privilege or power over their education. "I Just Wanna Be Average," a chapter from that book, shows the terrifying ways students can slip through the cracks in the educational system. Rose also shows, however, that there is hope for the individual lucky enough to encounter a caring teacher and find the motivation to pursue learning both in and out of school.*

Pre-Reading and Journal-Writing Suggestions

1. Do you see yourself (or perhaps a close friend or sibling) as having had a label during your school years? For instance, did your teachers or classmates see you (or your friend or sibling) as the class clown, the brain, or the quiet one? In what ways was this label fitting? What might a teacher (or classmates) have missed because of this label?
2. Describe your attitude toward school during your high school years. What interested you? What did school mean to you? What were your best moments? Your worst?
3. If you could go back and change anything about your past educational experiences, what would you change? How? Why?

It took two buses to get to Our Lady of Mercy. The first started deep in South Los Angeles and caught me at midpoint. The second drifted through neighborhoods with trees, parks, big lawns, and lots of flowers. The rides were long but were livened up by a group of South L.A. veterans whose parents also thought that Hope had set up shop in the west end of the country. There was Christy Biggars, who, at sixteen, was dealing and was, according to rumor, a pimp as well. There were Bill Cobb and Johnny Gonzales, grease-pencil artists extraordinaire, who left Nembutal-enhanced swirls of "Cobb" and "Johnny" on the corrugated walls of the bus. And then there was Tyrrell Wilson. Tyrrell was the coolest kid I knew. He ran the dozens like a metric halfback, laid down a rap that outrhymed and out-pointed Cobb, whose rap was good but not great—the curse of a moder-ately soulful kid trapped in white skin. But it was Cobb who would sneak a radio onto the bus, and thus underwrote his patter with Little Richard, Fats Domino, Chuck Berry, the Coasters, and Ernie K. Doe's mother-in-law, an awful woman who was "sent from down below." And so it was that Christy and Cobb and Johnny G. and Tyrrell and I and assorted others picked up along the way passed our days in the back of the bus, a funny mix brought together by geography and parental desire.

Entrance to school brings with it forms and releases and assessments. Mercy relied on a series of tests, mostly the Stanford-Binet, for placement, and somehow the results of my tests got confused with those of another student named Rose. The other Rose apparently didn't do very well, for I was placed in the vocational track, a euphemism for the bottom level. Nei-ther I nor my parents realized what this meant. We had no sense that Busi-ness Math, Typing, and English-Level D were dead ends. The current spate of reports on the schools criticizes parents for not involving themselves in the education of their children. But how would someone like Tommy Rose, with his two years of Italian schooling, know what to ask? And what sort of pressure could an exhausted waitress apply? The error went undetected, and I remained in the vocational track for two years. What a place.

My homeroom was supervised by Brother Dill, a troubled and unsta-ble man who also taught freshman English. When his class drifted away from him, which was often, his voice would rise in paranoid accusations, and occasionally he would lose control and shake or smack us. I hadn't been there two months when one of his brisk, face-turning slaps had my glasses sliding down the aisle. Physical education was also pretty harsh. Our teacher was a stubby ex-lineman who had played old-time pro ball in the Midwest. He routinely had us grabbing our ankles to receive his stinging paddle across our butts. He did that, he said, to make men of us. "Rose," he bellowed on our first encounter; me standing geeky in line in my baggy shorts. "'Rose'? What the hell kind of name is that?"

"Italian, sir," I squeaked.

"Italian! Ho. Rose, do you know the sound a bag of shit makes when   5 it hits the wall?"

"No, sir."

"Wop!"

Sophomore English was taught by Mr. Mitropetros. He was a large, bejeweled man who managed the parking lot at the Shrine Auditorium. He would crow and preen and list for us the stars he'd brushed against. We'd ask questions and glance knowingly and snicker, and all that fueled the poor guy to brag some more. Parking cars was his night job. He had little training in English, so his lesson plan for his day work had us reading the district's required text, *Julius Caesar,* aloud for the semester. We'd finish the play way before the twenty weeks was up, so he'd have us switch parts again and again and start again: Dave Snyder, the fastest guy at Mercy, muscling through Caesar to the breathless squeals of Calpurnia, as interpreted by Steve Fusco, a surfer who owned the school's most envied paneled wagon. Week ten and Dave and Steve would take on new roles, as would we all, and render a water-logged Cassius and a Brutus that are beyond my powers of description.

Spanish I—taken in the second year—fell into the hands of a new recruit. Mr. Montez was a tiny man, slight, five foot six at the most, soft-spoken and delicate. Spanish was a particularly rowdy class, and Mr. Montez was as prepared for it as a doily maker at a hammer throw. He would tap his pencil to a room in which Steve Fusco was propelling spitballs from his heavy lips, in which Mike Dweetz was taunting Billy Hawk, a half-Indian, half-Spanish, reed-thin, quietly explosive boy. The vocational track at Our Lady of Mercy mixed kids traveling in from South L.A. with South Bay surfers and a few Slavs and Chicanos from the harbors of San Pedro. This was a dangerous miscellany: surfers and hodads and South-Central blacks all ablaze to the metronomic tapping of Hector Montez's pencil.

One day Billy lost it. Out of the corner of my eye I saw him strike out   *10* with his right arm and catch Dweetz across the neck. Quick as a spasm, Dweetz was out of his seat, scattering desks, cracking Billy on the side of the head, right behind the eye. Snyder and Fusco and others broke it up, but the room felt hot and close and naked. Mr. Montez's tenuous authority was finally ripped to shreds, and I think everyone felt a little strange about that. The charade was over, and when it came down to it, I don't think any of the kids really wanted it to end this way. They had pushed and pushed and bullied their way into a freedom that both scared and embarrassed them.

Students will float to the mark you set. I and the others in the vocational classes were bobbing in pretty shallow water. Vocational education has aimed at increasing the economic opportunities of students who do not do well in our schools. Some serious programs succeed in doing that, and through exceptional teachers—like Mr. Gross in *Horace's Compromise*—students learn to develop hypotheses and troubleshoot, reason through a problem, and communicate effectively—the true job skills. The vocational track, however, is most often a place for those who are just not making it, a dumping ground for the disaffected. There were a few teachers who worked hard at education; young Brother Slattery, for example, combined a stern voice with weekly quizzes to try to pass along to us a skeletal outline of world history. But mostly the teachers had no idea of how to engage the imaginations of us kids who were scuttling along at the bottom of the pond.

And the teachers would have needed some inventiveness, for none of us was groomed for the classroom. It wasn't just that I didn't know things—didn't know how to simplify algebraic fractions, couldn't identify different kinds of clauses, bungled Spanish translations—but that I had developed various faulty and inadequate ways of doing algebra and making sense of Spanish. Worse yet, the years of defensive tuning out in elementary school had given me a way to escape quickly while seeming at least half alert. During my time in Voc. Ed., I developed further into a mediocre student and a somnambulant problem solver, and that affected the subjects I did have the wherewithal to handle: I detested Shakespeare; I got bored with history. My attention flitted here and there. I fooled around in class and read my books indifferently—the intellectual equivalent of playing with your food. I did what I had to do to get by, and I did it with half a mind.

But I did learn things about people and eventually came into my own socially. I liked the guys in Voc. Ed. Growing up where I did, I understood and admired physical prowess, and there was an abundance of muscle here. There was Dave Snyder, a sprinter and halfback of true quality. Dave's ability and his quick wit gave him a natural appeal, and he was welcome in any clique, though he always kept a little independent. He enjoyed acting the fool and could care less about studies, but he possessed a certain maturity and never caused the faculty much trouble. It was a testament to his independence that he included me among his friends—I eventually went out for track, but I was no jock. Owing to the Latin alphabet and a dearth of *R*s and *S*s, Snyder sat behind Rose, and we started exchanging one-liners and became friends.

There was Ted Richard, a much-touted Little League pitcher. He was chunky and had a baby face and came to Our Lady of Mercy as a seasoned street fighter. Ted was quick to laugh and he had a loud, jolly laugh, but when he got angry he'd smile a little smile, the kind that simply raises the corner of the mouth a quarter of an inch. For those who knew, it was an eerie signal. Those who didn't found themselves in big trouble, for Ted was very quick. He loved to carry on what we would come to call philosophical discussions: What is courage? Does God exist? He also loved words, enjoyed picking up big ones like *salubrious* and *equivocal* and using them in our conversations—laughing at himself as the word hit a chuckhole rolling off his tongue. Ted didn't do all that well in school—baseball and parties and testing the courage he'd speculated about took up his time. His textbooks were *Argosy* and *Field and Stream,* whatever newspapers he'd find on the bus stop—from the *Daily Worker* to pornography—conversations with uncles or hobos or businessmen he'd meet in a coffee shop, *The Old Man and the Sea.* With hindsight, I can see that Ted was developing into one of those rough-hewn intellectuals whose sources are a mix of the learned and the apocryphal, whose discussions are both assured and sad.

And then there was Ken Harvey. Ken was good-looking in a puffy way and had a full and oily ducktail and was a car enthusiast . . . a hodad. One day in religion class, he said the sentence that turned out to be one of the most memorable of the hundreds of thousands I heard in those Voc. Ed. years. We were talking about the parable of the talents, about achievement, working hard, doing the best you can do, blah-blah-blah, when the teacher called on the restive Ken Harvey for an opinion. Ken thought about it, but just for a second, and said (with studied, minimal affect), "I just wanna be   15 average." That woke me up. Average? Who wants to be average? Then the athletes chimed in with the clichés that make you want to laryngectomize them, and the exchange became a platitudinous melee. At the time, I thought Ken's assertion was stupid, and I wrote him off. But his sentence has stayed with me all these years, and I think I am finally coming to understand it.

Ken Harvey was gasping for air. School can be a tremendously disorienting place. No matter how bad the school, you're going to encounter notions that don't fit with the assumptions and beliefs that you grew up with—maybe you'll hear these dissonant notions from teachers, maybe from the other students, and maybe you'll read them. You'll also be thrown in with all kinds of kids from all kinds of backgrounds, and that can be unsettling—this is especially true in places of rich ethnic and linguistic mix, like the L.A. basin. You'll see a handful of students far excel you in courses that sound exotic and that are only in the curriculum of the elite: French, physics, trigonometry. And all this is happening while you're trying to shape an identity, your body is changing, and your emotions are running wild. If you're a working-class kid in the vocational track, the options you'll have to deal with this will be constrained in certain ways: you're defined by your school as "slow"; you're placed in a curriculum that isn't designed to liberate you but to occupy you, or, if you're lucky, train you, though the training is for work the society does not esteem; other students are picking up the cues from your school and your curriculum and interacting with you in particular ways. If you're a kid like Ted Richard, you turn your back on all this and let your mind roam where it may. But youngsters like Ted are rare. What Ken and so many others do is protect themselves from such suffocating madness by taking on with a vengeance the identity implied in the vocational track. Reject the confusion and frustration by openly defining yourself as the Common Joe. Champion the average. Rely on your own good sense. Fuck this bullshit. Bullshit, of course, is everything you—and the others—fear is beyond you: books, essays, tests, academic scrambling, complexity, scientific reasoning, philosophical inquiry.

The tragedy is that you have to twist the knife in your own gray matter to make this defense work. You'll have to shut down, have to reject intellectual stimuli or diffuse them with sarcasm, have to cultivate stupidity, have to convert boredom from a malady into a way of confronting the world. Keep your vocabulary simple, act stoned when you're not or act more stoned than you are, flaunt ignorance, materialize your dreams. It is a powerful and effective defense—it neutralizes the insult and the frustration of being a vocational kid and, when perfected, it drives teachers up the wall, a delightful secondary effect. But like all strong magic, it exacts a price.

My own deliverance from the Voc. Ed. world began with sophomore biology. Every student, college prep to vocational, had to take biology, and unlike the other courses, the same person taught all sections. When teaching the vocational group, Brother Clint probably slowed down a bit or omitted a little of the fundamental biochemistry, but he used the same book and more or less the same syllabus across the board. If one class got tough, he could get tougher. He was young and powerful and very handsome, and looks and physical strength were high currency. No one gave him any trouble.

I was pretty bad at the dissecting table, but the lectures and the textbook were interesting: plastic overlays that, with each turned page, peeled away skin, then veins and muscle, then organs, down to the very bones that Brother Clint, pointer in hand, would tap out on our hanging skeleton. Dave Snyder was in big trouble, for the study of life—versus the living of it—was sticking in his craw. We worked out a code for our multiple-choice exams. He'd poke me in the back: once for the answer under *A,* twice for *B,* and so on; and when he'd hit the right one, I'd look up to the ceiling as though I were lost in thought. Poke: cytoplasm. Poke, poke: methane. Poke, poke, poke: William Harvey. Poke, poke, poke, poke: islets of Langerhans. This didn't work out perfectly, but Dave passed the course, and I mastered the dreamy look of a guy on a record jacket. And something else happened. Brother Clint puzzled over this Voc. Ed. kid who was racking up 98s and 99s on his tests. He checked the school's records and discovered the error. He recommended that I begin my junior year in the College Prep program. According to all I've read since, such a shift, as one report put it, is virtually impossible. Kids at that level rarely cross tracks. The telling thing is how chancy both my placement into and exit from Voc. Ed. was; neither I nor my parents had anything to do with it. I lived in one world during spring semester, and when I came back to school in the fall, I was living in another.

Switching to College Prep was a mixed blessing. I was an erratic student. I was undisciplined. And I hadn't caught onto the rules of the game: why work hard in a class that didn't grab my fancy? I was also hopelessly behind in math. Chemistry was hard; toying with my chemistry set years before hadn't prepared me for the chemist's equations. Fortunately, the priest who taught both chemistry and second-year algebra was also the school's athletic director. Membership on the track team covered me; I knew I wouldn't get lower than a *C.* U.S. history was taught pretty well, and I did okay. But civics was taken over by a football coach who had trouble reading the textbook aloud—and reading aloud was the centerpiece of his pedagogy. College Prep at Mercy was certainly an improvement over the vocational program—at least it carried some status—but the social science curriculum was weak, and the mathematics and physical sciences were simply beyond me. I had a miserable quantitative background and ended up copying some assignments and finessing the rest as best I could. Let me try to explain how it feels to see again and again material you should once have learned but didn't.

You are given a problem. It requires you to simplify algebraic fractions or to multiply expressions containing square roots. You know this is pretty basic material because you've seen it for years. Once a teacher took some

20

time with you, and you learned how to carry out these operations. Simple versions, anyway. But that was a year or two or more in the past, and these are more complex versions, and now you're not sure. And this, you keep telling yourself, is ninth- or even eighth-grade stuff.

Next it's a word problem. This is also old hat. The basic elements are as familiar as story characters: trains speeding so many miles per hour or shadows of buildings angling so many degrees. Maybe you know enough, have sat through enough explanations, to be able to begin setting up the problem: "If one train is going this fast . . ." or "This shadow is really one line of a triangle . . ." Then: "Let's see . . ." "How did Jones do this?" "Hmmmm." "No." "No, that won't work." Your attention wavers. You wonder about other things: a football game, a dance, that cute new checker at the market. You try to focus on the problem again. You scribble on paper for a while, but the tension wins out and your attention flits elsewhere. You crumple the paper and begin daydreaming to ease the frustration.

The particulars will vary, but in essence this is what a number of students go through, especially those in so-called remedial classes. They open their textbooks and see once again the familiar and impenetrable formulas and diagrams and terms that have stumped them for years. There is no excitement here. *No* excitement. Regardless of what the teacher says, this is not a new challenge. There is, rather, embarrassment and frustration and, not surprisingly, some anger in being reminded once again of long-standing inadequacies. No wonder so many students finally attribute their difficulties to something inborn, organic: "That part of my brain just doesn't work." Given the troubling histories many of these students have, it's miraculous that any of them can lift the shroud of hopelessness sufficiently to make deliverance from these classes possible.

Through this entire period, my father's health was deteriorating with cruel momentum. His arteriosclerosis progressed to the point where a simple nick on his shin wouldn't heal. Eventually it ulcerated and widened. Lou Minton would come by daily to change the dressing. We tried renting an oscillating bed—which we placed in the front room—to force blood through the constricted arteries in my father's legs. The bed hummed through the night, moving in place to ward off the inevitable. The ulcer continued to spread, and the doctors finally had to amputate. My grandfather had lost his leg in a stockyard accident. Now my father too was crippled. His convalescence was slow but steady, and the doctors placed him in the Santa Monica Rehabilitation Center, a sun-bleached building that opened out onto the warm spray of the Pacific. The place gave him some strength and some color and some training in walking with an artificial leg. He did pretty well for a year or so until he slipped and broke his hip. He was confined to a wheelchair after that, and the confinement contributed to the diminishing of his body and spirit.

I am holding a picture of him. He is sitting in his wheelchair and   25
smiling at the camera. The smile appears forced, unsteady, seems to quaver,

though it is frozen in silver nitrate. He is in his mid–sixties and looks eighty. Late in my junior year, he had a stroke and never came out of the resulting coma. After that, I would see him only in dreams, and to this day that is how I join him. Sometimes the dreams are sad and grisly and primal: my father lying in a bed soaked with his suppuration, holding me, rocking me. But sometimes the dreams bring him back to me healthy: him talking to me on an empty street, or buying some pictures to decorate our old house, or transformed somehow into someone strong and adept with tools and the physical.

Jack MacFarland couldn't have come into my life at a better time. My father was dead, and I had logged up too many years of scholastic indifference. Mr. MacFarland had a master's degree from Columbia and decided, at twenty-six, to find a little school and teach his heart out. He never took any credentialing courses, couldn't bear to, he said, so he had to find employment in a private system. He ended up at Our Lady of Mercy teaching five sections of senior English. He was a beatnik who was born too late. His teeth were stained, he tucked his sorry tie in between the third and fourth buttons of his shirt, and his pants were chronically wrinkled. At first, we couldn't believe this guy, thought he slept in his car. But within no time, he had us so startled with work that we didn't much worry about where he slept or if he slept at all. We wrote three or four essays a month. We read a book every two to three weeks, starting with the *Iliad* and ending up with Hemingway. He gave us a quiz on the reading every other day. He brought a prep school curriculum to Mercy High.

MacFarland's lectures were crafted, and as he delivered them he would pace the room jiggling a piece of chalk in his cupped hand, using it to scribble on the board the names of all the writers and philosophers and plays and novels he was weaving into his discussion. He asked questions often, raised everything from Zeno's paradox to the repeated last line of Frost's "Stopping by Woods on a Snowy Evening." He slowly and carefully built up our knowledge of Western intellectual history—with facts, with connections, with speculations. We learned about Greek philosophy, about Dante, the Elizabethan world view, the Age of Reason, existentialism. He analyzed poems with us, had us reading sections from John Ciardi's *How Does a Poem Mean?,* making a potentially difficult book accessible with his own explanations. We gave oral reports on poems Ciardi didn't cover. We imitated the styles of Conrad, Hemingway, and *Time* magazine. We wrote and talked, wrote and talked. The man immersed us in language.

Even MacFarland's barbs were literary. If Jim Fitzsimmons, hung over and irritable, tried to smart-ass him, he'd rejoin with a flourish that would spark the indomitable Skip Madison—who'd lost his front teeth in a hapless tackle—to flick his tongue through the gap and opine, "good chop," drawing out the single "o" in stinging indictment. Jack MacFarland, this tobacco-stained intellectual, brandished linguistic weapons of a kind I hadn't encountered before. Here was this *egghead,* for God's sake, keeping some pretty difficult people in line. And from what I heard, Mike Dweetz and Steve Fusco and all the notorious Voc. Ed. crowd settled down as well when MacFarland took the podium. Though a lot of guys groused in the school-yard, it just seemed that giving trouble to this particular teacher was a silly thing to do. Tomfoolery, not to mention assault, had no place in the world he was trying to create for us, and instinctively everyone knew that. If nothing else, we all recognized MacFarland's considerable intelligence and respected the hours he put into his work. It came to this: the troublemaker would look foolish rather than daring. Even Jim Fitzsimmons was reading *On the Road* and turning his incipient alcoholism to literary ends.

There were some lives that were already beyond Jack MacFarland's ministrations, but mine was not. I started reading again as I hadn't since elementary school. I would go into our gloomy little bedroom or sit at the dinner table while, on the television, Danny McShane was paralyzing Mr. Moto with the atomic drop, and work slowly back through *Heart of Darkness,* trying to catch the words in Conrad's sentences. I certainly was not MacFarland's best student; most of the other guys in College Prep, even my fellow slackers, had better backgrounds than I did. But I worked very hard, for MacFarland had hooked me. He tapped my old interest in reading and creating stories. He gave me a way to feel special by using my mind. And he provided a role model that wasn't shaped on physical prowess alone, and something inside me that I wasn't quite aware of responded to that. Jack MacFarland established a literacy club, to borrow a phrase of Frank Smith's, and invited me—invited all of us—to join.

There's been a good deal of research and speculation suggesting that   *30* the acknowledgement of school performance with extrinsic rewards—smiling faces, stars, numbers, grades—diminishes the intrinsic satisfaction children experience by engaging in reading or writing or problem solving. While it's certainly true that we've created an educational system that encourages our best and brightest to become cynical grade collectors and, in general, have developed an obsession with evaluation and assessment, I must tell you that venal though it may have been, I loved getting good grades from MacFarland. I now know how subjective grades can be, but then they came tucked in the back of essays like bits of scientific data, some sort of spectroscopic readout that said, objectively and publicly, that I had made something of value. I suppose I'd been mediocre for too long and enjoyed a public redefinition. And I suppose the workings of my mind, such as they were, had been private for too long. My linguistic play moved into the world; . . . these papers with their circled, red B-pluses and A-minuses linked my mind to something outside it. I carried them around like a club emblem.

One day in the December of my senior year, Mr. MacFarland asked me where I was going to go to college. I hadn't thought much about it. Many of the students I teach today spent their last year in high school with a physics text in one hand and the Stanford catalog in the other, but I wasn't even aware of what "entrance requirements" were. My folks would say that they wanted me to go to college and be a doctor, but I don't know how seriously I ever took that; it seemed a sweet thing to say, a bit of supportive family chatter, like telling a gangly daughter she's graceful. The reality of higher education wasn't in my scheme of things: no one in the family had gone to college; only two of my uncles had completed high school. I figured I'd get a night job and go to the local junior college because I knew that Snyder and Company were going there to play ball. But I hadn't even prepared for that. When I finally said, "I don't know," MacFarland looked down at me—I was seated in his office—and said, "Listen, you can write."

My grades stank. I had A's in biology and a handful of B's in a few English and social science classes. All the rest were C's—or worse. Mac-Farland said I would do well in his class and laid down the law about doing well in the others. Still, the record for my first three years wouldn't have been acceptable to any four-year school. To nobody's surprise, I was turned down flat by USC and UCLA. But Jack MacFarland was on the case. He had received his bachelor's degree from Loyola University, so he made calls to old professors and talked to somebody in admissions and wrote me a strong letter. Loyola finally accepted me as a probationary student. I would be on trial for the first year, and if I did okay, I would be granted regular status. MacFarland also intervened to get me a loan, for I could never have afforded a private college without it. Four more years of religion classes and four more years of boys at one school, girls at another. But at least I was going to college. Amazing.

In my last semester of high school, I elected a special English course fashioned by Mr. MacFarland, and it was through this elective that there arose at Mercy a fledgling literati. Art Mitz, the editor of the school newspaper and a very smart guy, was the kingpin. He was joined by me and by Mark Dever, a quiet boy who wrote beautifully and who would die before he was forty. MacFarland occasionally invited us to his apartment, and those visits became the high point of our apprenticeship: we'd clamp on our training wheels and drive to his salon.

He lived in a cramped and cluttered place near the airport, tucked away in the kind of building that architectural critic Reyner Banham calls a *dingbat*. Books were all over: stacked, piled, tossed, and crated, underlined and dog eared, well worn and new. Cigarette ashes crusted with coffee in saucers or spilled over the sides of motel ashtrays. The little bedroom had, along two of its walls, bricks and boards loaded with notes, magazines, and oversized books. The kitchen joined the living room, and there was a stack of German newspapers under the sink. I had never seen anything like it: a great flophouse of language furnished by City Lights and Café le Metro. I read every title. I flipped through paperbacks and scanned jackets and memorized names: Gogol, *Finnegans Wake*, Djuna Barnes, Jackson Pollock, *A Coney Island of the Mind*, F. O. Matthiessen's *American Renaissance*, all sorts of Freud, *Troubled Sleep*, Man Ray, *The Education of Henry Adams*, Richard

Wright, *Film as Art,* William Butler Yeats, Marguerite Duras, *Redburn, A Season in Hell, Kapital.* On the cover of Alain-Fournier's *The Wanderer* was an Edward Gorey drawing of a young man on a road winding into dark trees. By the hotplate sat a strange Kafka novel called *Amerika,* in which an adolescent hero crosses the Atlantic to find the Nature Theater of Oklahoma. Art and Mark would be talking about a movie or the school newspaper, and I would be consuming my English teacher's library. It was heady stuff. I felt like a Pop Warner athlete on steroids.

Art, Mark, and I would buy stogies and triangulate from MacFarland's   35 apartment to the Cinema, which now shows X-rated films but was then L.A.'s premier art theater, and then to the musty Cherokee Bookstore in Hollywood to hobnob with beatnik homosexuals—smoking, drinking bourbon and coffee, and trying out awkward phrases we'd gleaned from our mentor's bookshelves. I was happy and precocious and a little scared as well, for Hollywood Boulevard was thick with a kind of decadence that was foreign to the South Side. After the Cherokee, we would head back to the security of MacFarland's apartment, slaphappy with hipness.

Let me be the first to admit that there was a good deal of adolescent passion in this embrace of the avant-garde: self-absorption, sexually charged pedantry, an elevation of the odd and abandoned. Still it was a time during which I absorbed an awful lot of information: long lists of titles, images from expressionist paintings, new wave shibboleths, snippets of philosophy, and names that read like Steve Fusco's misspellings—Goethe, Nietzsche, Kierkegaard. Now this is hardly the stuff of deep understanding. But it was an introduction, a phrase book, a Baedeker to a vocabulary of ideas, and it felt good at the time to know all these words. With hindsight I realize how layered and important that knowledge was.

It enabled me to do things in the world. I could browse bohemian bookstores in far-off, mysterious Hollywood; I could go to the Cinema and see events through the lenses of European directors; and, most of all, I could share an evening, talk that talk, with Jack MacFarland, the man I most admired at the time. Knowledge was becoming a bonding agent. Within a year or two, the persona of the disaffected hipster would prove too cynical, too alienated to last. But for a time it was new and exciting: it provided a critical perspective on society, and it allowed me to act as though I were living beyond the limiting boundaries of South Vermont.

Suggestions for Writing and Discussion

1. Respond to this piece. Did you enjoy it? Identify with it? Find it difficult? Boring? Something else? Explain.
2. In paragraph 2, Rose refers to the Stanford-Binet test. From what he says in the rest of the paragraph, what kind of test do you think this is? How can you infer the definition of this test from the details that Rose provides?

3. Rose's experience was based on what is known in education as tracking or homogeneous grouping. Did the schools you attended use this system of grouping? How did grouping (or nongrouping) work out for you?

    Based on your own experiences, what do you see as the advantages and disadvantages of tracking? Write your response in the form of a report you might send to the school committee, the principal, or the guidance counselors of the secondary school you attended.

4. Rose gives five examples of different teachers in his high school. What are the general characteristics of each teacher?

5. After Brother Clint discovered that Rose was misplaced in his classes, Rose says he hadn't quite "caught onto the rules of the game: why work hard in a class that didn't catch my fancy?" What are the "rules of the game" in education today? What advice would you give to a student who finds a particular (required) class boring?

6. Rose's most influential teacher, Jack MacFarland, "immersed" his class in language. What subjects—if any—have you been immersed in during your educational experience? What subjects were taught to you on a surface, cursory level? What effect did each approach have on you?

Suggestions for Extended Thinking and Writing

1. Write an imaginary letter to your school district's school board in which you describe the positive, as well as the negative, experiences you had during your high school years.

2. Write an essay in which you compare your attitude to learning with Mike Rose's. Use specific episodes from your school experiences and show how they contributed to making your attitude similar to or different from Rose's.

NICHOLAS GAGE

The Teacher Who Changed My Life

Born in Greece in 1940, Nicholas Gage has written movingly of the murder in 1948 of his mother, Eleni Gatzoyiannis. During the Greek Civil war, when Gage was nine years old, Communist guerrillas arrested, tortured, and executed his mother because she arranged the escape of her five children from their occupied mountain village. Gage grew up and was educated in the United States. As an adult, he became an investigative reporter and, haunted by his mother's death, returned to Greece to track down the story of her final weeks of life. In his best-selling book Eleni, *he describes the events of this traumatic, terrifying, and astonishingly heroic time.*

Following the publication of Eleni, *Gage wrote another book,* A Place for Us, *from which the following essay is taken. In this autobiography, Gage describes the difficult adjustment he and his sisters faced after arriving in the United States and pays tribute to the teacher he sees as the inspiration and motivating force behind his later success as a writer.*

Pre-Reading and Journal-Writing Suggestions

1. Write about someone you see as your mentor, your inspiration.
2. Describe your past experiences with writing, especially in a school environment. How did you learn to write? How do you feel about writing? How would you assess your writing ability at this point in your life?
3. What three characteristics are most important for a good teacher to possess? Explain your answer by describing your own specific experiences with good teachers.

The person who set the course of my life in the new land I entered as   *1*
a young war refugee—who, in fact, nearly dragged me onto the path that would bring all the blessings I've received in America—was a salty-tongued, no-nonsense schoolteacher named Marjorie Hurd. When I entered her classroom in 1953, I had been to six schools in five years, starting in the Greek village where I was born in 1939.

When I stepped off a ship in New York Harbor on a gray March day in 1949, I was an undersized 9-year-old in short pants who had lost his mother and was coming to live with the father he didn't know. My mother, Eleni Gatzoyiannis, had been imprisoned, tortured and shot by Communist guerrillas for sending me and three of my four sisters to freedom. She died so that her children could go to their father in the United States.

The portly, bald, well-dressed man who met me and my sisters seemed a foreign, authoritarian figure. I secretly resented him for not getting the whole family out of Greece early enough to save my mother. Ultimately, I would grow to love him and appreciate how he dealt with becoming a single parent at the age of 56, but at first our relationship was prickly, full of hostility.

As Father drove us to our new home—a tenement in Worcester, Mass.—and pointed out the huge brick building that would be our first school in America, I clutched my Greek notebooks from the refugee camp, hoping that my few years of schooling would impress my teachers in this cold, crowded country. They didn't. When my father led me and my 11-year-old sister to Greendale Elementary School, the grim-faced Yankee principal put the two of us in a class for the mentally retarded. There was no facility in those days for non-English-speaking children.

By the time I met Marjorie Hurd four years later, I had learned English, been placed in a normal, graded class and had even been chosen for the college preparatory track in the Worcester public school system. I was 13 years old when our father moved us yet again, and I entered Chandler Junior High shortly after the beginning of seventh grade. I found myself surrounded by richer, smarter and better-dressed classmates who looked askance at my strange clothes and heavy accent. Shortly after I arrived, we were told to select a hobby to pursue during "club hour" on Fridays. The idea of hobbies and clubs made no sense to my immigrant ears, but I decided to follow the prettiest girl in my class—the blue-eyed daughter of the local Lutheran minister. She led me through the door marked "Newspaper Club" and into the presence of Miss Hurd, the newspaper adviser and English teacher who would become my mentor and my muse.

A formidable, solidly built woman with salt-and-pepper hair, a steely eye and a flat Boston accent, Miss Hurd had no patience with layabouts. "What are all you goof-offs doing here?" she bellowed at the would-be journalists. "This is the Newspaper Club! We're going to put out a *newspaper.* So if there's anybody in this room who doesn't like work, I suggest you go across to the Glee Club now, because you're going to work your tails off here!"

I was soon under Miss Hurd's spell. She did indeed teach us to put out a newspaper, skills I honed during my next 25 years as a journalist. Soon I asked the principal to transfer me to her English class as well. There, she drilled us on grammar until I finally began to understand the logic and structure of the English language. She assigned stories for us to read and discuss; not tales of heroes, like the Greek myths I knew, but stories of underdogs—poor people, even immigrants, who seemed ordinary until a crisis drove them to do something extraordinary. She also introduced us to the literary wealth of Greece—giving me a new perspective on my war-ravaged, impoverished homeland. I began to be proud of my origins.

One day, after discussing how writers should write about what they know, she assigned us to compose an essay from our own experience. Fixing

5

me with a stern look, she added, "Nick, I want you to write about what happened to your family in Greece." I had been trying to put those painful memories behind me and left the assignment until the last moment. Then, on a warm spring afternoon, I sat in my room with a yellow pad and pencil and stared out the window at the buds on the trees. I wrote that the coming of spring always reminded me of the last time I said goodbye to my mother on a green and gold day in 1948.

I kept writing, one line after another, telling how the Communist guerrillas occupied our village, took our home and food, how my mother started planning our escape when she learned that the children were to be sent to re-education camps behind the Iron Curtain and how, at the last moment, she couldn't escape with us because the guerrillas sent her with a group of women to thresh wheat in a distant village. She promised she would try to get away on her own, she told me to be brave and hung a silver cross around my neck, and then she kissed me. I watched the line of women being led down into the ravine and up the other side, until they disappeared around the bend—my mother a tiny brown figure at the end who stopped for an instant to raise her hand in one last farewell.

I wrote about our nighttime escape down the mountain, across the minefields and into the lines of the Nationalist soldiers, who sent us to a refugee camp. It was there that we learned of our mother's execution. I felt very lucky to have come to America, I concluded, but every year, the coming of spring made me feel sad because it reminded me of the last time I saw my mother. 10

I handed in the essay, hoping never to see it again, but Miss Hurd had it published in the school paper. This mortified me at first, until I saw that my classmates reacted with sympathy and tact to my family's story. Without telling me, Miss Hurd also submitted the essay to a contest sponsored by the Freedoms Foundation at Valley Forge, Pa., and it won a medal. The Worcester paper wrote about the award and quoted my essay at length. My father, by then a "five-and-dime-store chef," as the paper described him, was ecstatic with pride, and the Worcester Greek community celebrated the honor to one of its own.

For the first time I began to understand the power of the written word. A secret ambition took root in me. One day, I vowed, I would go back to Greece, find out the details of my mother's death and write about her life, so her grandchildren would know of her courage. Perhaps I would even track down the men who killed her and write of their crimes. Fulfilling that ambition would take me 30 years.

Meanwhile, I followed the literary path that Miss Hurd had so forcefully set me on. After junior high, I became the editor of my school paper at Classical High School and got a part-time job at the Worcester *Telegram and Gazette*. Although my father could only give me $50 and encouragement toward a college education, I managed to finance four years at Boston University with scholarships and part-time jobs in journalism. During my last year of college, an article I wrote about a friend who had died in the

Philippines—the first person to lose his life working for the Peace Corps— led to my winning the Hearst Award for College Journalism. And the plaque was given to me in the White House by President John F. Kennedy.

For a refugee who had never seen a motorized vehicle or indoor plumbing until he was 9, this was an unimaginable honor. When the Worcester paper ran a picture of me standing next to President Kennedy, my father rushed out to buy a new suit in order to be properly dressed to receive the congratulations of the Worcester Greeks. He clipped out the photograph, had it laminated in plastic and carried it in his breast pocket for the rest of his life to show everyone he met. I found the much-worn photo in his pocket on the day he died 20 years later.

In our isolated Greek village, my mother had bribed a cousin to teach   15 her to read, for girls were not supposed to attend school beyond a certain age. She had always dreamed of her children receiving an education. She couldn't be there when I graduated from Boston University, but the person who came with my father and shared our joy was my former teacher, Marjorie Hurd. We celebrated not only my bachelor's degree but also the scholarships that paid my way to Columbia's Graduate School of Journalism. There, I met the woman who would eventually become my wife. At our wedding and at the baptisms of our three children, Marjorie Hurd was always there, dancing alongside the Greeks.

By then, she was Mrs. Rabidou, for she had married a widower when she was in her early 40s. That didn't distract her from her vocation of introducing young minds to English literature, however. She taught for a total of 41 years and continually would make a "project" of some balky student in whom she spied a spark of potential. Often these were students from the most troubled homes, yet she would alternately bully and charm each one with her own special brand of tough love until the spark caught fire. She retired in 1981 at the age of 62 but still avidly follows the lives and careers of former students while overseeing her adult stepchildren and driving her husband on camping trips to New Hampshire.

Miss Hurd was one of the first to call me on Dec. 10, 1987, when President Reagan, in his television address after the summit meeting with Gorbachev, told the nation that Eleni Gatzoyiannis' dying cry, "My children!" had helped inspire him to seek an arms agreement "for all the children of the world."

"I can't imagine a better monument for your mother," Miss Hurd said with an uncharacteristic catch in her voice.

Although a bad hip makes it impossible for her to join in the Greek dancing, Marjorie Hurd Rabidou is still an honored and enthusiastic guest at all family celebrations, including my 50th birthday picnic last summer, where the shish kebab was cooked on spits, clarinets and *bouzoukis* wailed, and costumed dancers led the guests in a serpentine line around our Colonial farmhouse, only 20 minutes from my first home in Worcester.

My sisters and I felt an aching void because my father was not there to   *20*
lead the line, balancing a glass of wine on his head while he danced, the way
he did at every celebration during his 92 years. But Miss Hurd was there,
surveying the scene with quiet satisfaction. Although my parents are gone,
her presence was a consolation, because I owe her so much.

This is truly the land of opportunity, and I would have enjoyed its
bounty even if I hadn't walked into Miss Hurd's classroom in 1953. But she
was the one who directed my grief and pain into writing, and if it weren't
for her I wouldn't have become an investigative reporter and foreign corre-
spondent, recorded the story of my mother's life and death in *Eleni* and now
my father's story in *A Place for Us,* which is also a testament to the country
that took us in. She was the catalyst that sent me into journalism and indi-
rectly caused all the good things that came after. But Miss Hurd would
probably deny this emphatically.

A few years ago, I answered the telephone and heard my former teacher's voice telling me, in that won't-take-no-for-an-answer tone of hers, that
she had decided I was to write and deliver the eulogy at her funeral. I agreed
(she didn't leave me any choice), but that's one assignment I never want to
do. I hope, Miss Hurd, that you'll accept this remembrance instead.

Suggestions for Writing and Discussion

1. Gage attributes his success in America to his seventh-grade English
   teacher. After reading this piece, summarize the other factors you see
   that may have contributed to Gage's success in writing.

2. In paragraph 3, Gage describes his father as "authoritarian." Explain what
   this means and what it tells the reader about Gage's view of his father.

3. Miss Hurd opens up a new world for Gage, and at the same time she
   makes him proud of his origins. Think back to your own school days.
   Did you ever have a teacher who made you feel proud? Describe this
   teacher as best you can, as well as the incident(s) that encouraged your
   pride. As you write, imagine that your audience will be other students
   who have also been in this teacher's class. Your purpose for writing is to
   convince your fellow students to join you in planning a celebration on
   the occasion of this teacher's twenty-fifth year of teaching.

4. What do you think about Miss Hurd's advice—to compose an essay
   based on one's own experience? Do you think this type of assignment
   might be particularly effective for seventh graders, or do you think it
   would be very difficult for most of them? Explain.

5. Gage writes poignantly about how the spring makes him remember the
   last time he saw his mother. Do you, too, associate a particular season
   with a powerful memory (either sad or joyful)? If so, write about the
   season and describe specifically what you see, hear, and smell that triggers
   thoughts of the past.

6. Miss Hurd succeeded in finding the potential in her students. Have you ever had a teacher who sparked your potential? If so, describe this person and explain what talent or ability this person helped you develop. Explain the process and the effects of discovering this ability.
7. Gage describes Miss Hurd as a catalyst in his life. What does he mean by this metaphor? List other metaphors to describe the good teachers in your own life. Then explain why you chose these metaphors.

Suggestions for Extended Thinking and Writing

1. When Gage's piece was published, he realized how powerful language can be. Consider trying to publish something yourself. Start writing about something that deeply concerns you—perhaps an issue in your school or community. Rewrite this piece as a letter to the editor and send it out to your local or school newspaper.
2. Write an essay that publicly thanks a teacher, that is, a person either in or out of the school system, who has taught you something important. Explain the difference that he or she has made in your life. Consider your audience as you write. You are not addressing only the teacher; you are also trying to convey to others who have never met him or her the profound effect this person has had on you.

JACQUES D'AMBOISE
I Show a Child What Is Possible

Born in 1935, Jacques d'Amboise grew up in the inner city of New York. On the streets, he was surrounded every day by the threat of drugs, zip guns, and gangs. At home, on the other hand, his French Canadian mother read to him about the elegant court life of Versailles, telling tales of nobility and chivalry. Following her dream of beauty and culture, d'Amboise's mother arranged for her daughter to take classical ballet lessons and insisted that her son accompany his sister, hoping that at least for those few hours he would be safe from the dangers and temptations of every neighborhood street corner. After being encouraged by his sister's teacher to join the ballet class, d'Amboise discovered his talent and love for dancing. At the age of fifteen, he joined George Balanchine's New York City Ballet and went on to become one of the finest classical dancers of our time.

Because of his own childhood experiences, d'Amboise developed a strong commitment to bringing dance to other young people whose circumstances were similar to his own. In 1976 he founded the National Dance Institute (NDI), which today has programs in more than thirty public schools in the New York City area. Most NDI dancers come from neighborhoods similar to the one d'Amboise grew up in. Most (80 percent) are black, Hispanic, or Asian. Some are homeless or have handicaps such as visual impairment or hearing loss. To each child, d'Amboise brings his joy of dance and his belief that energy and commitment to dance can bring meaning to all our lives.

Pre-Reading and Journal-Writing Suggestions

1. Everyone is an expert at something. Choose one thing you can do well, and write about it.

2. Fill in the following blanks, and write about this completed statement in your journal.

    "If only someone had taught me to _____ , I could be a great _____ right now."

3. Spend the next ten minutes jotting down your immediate response to these questions: Who was the teacher who has most affected your life? Why and how did this teacher affect your life? Do not worry about organizing your thoughts; just write without stopping. If you get stuck, copy the previous sentence until your ideas start flowing again. The point here is to spend ten full minutes actually writing so that you move responses from your mind to the paper in front of you.

When I was 7 years old, I was forced to watch my sister's ballet classes. *1* This was to keep me off the street and away from my pals, who ran with gangs like the ones in *West Side Story*. The class was taught by Madame Seda, a Georgian-Armenian who had a school at 181st Street and St. Nicholas Avenue in New York City. As she taught the little girls, I would sit, fidget and diabolically try to disrupt the class by making irritating little noises.

But she was very wise, Madame Seda. She let me get away with it, ignoring me until the end of the class, when everybody did the big jumps, a series of leaps in place, called *changements.*

At that point, Madame Seda turned and, stabbing a finger at me, said, "All right, little brother, if you've got so much energy, get up and do these jumps. See if you can jump as high as the girls." So I jumped. And loved it. I felt like I was flying. And she said, "Oh, that was wonderful! From now on, if you are quiet during the class, I'll let you join in the *changements.*"

After that, I'd sit quietly in the class and wait for the jumps. A few classes later, she said, "You've got to learn how to jump and not make any noise when you come down. You should learn to do the *pliés* [graceful knee bends] that come at the beginning of the class." So I would do *pliés,* then wait respectfully for the end of class to do the jumps.

Finally she said, "You jump high, and you are landing beautifully, but *5* you look awful in the air, flaying your arms about. You've got to take the rest of the class and learn how to do beautiful hands and arms."

I was hooked.

An exceptional teacher got a bored little kid, me, interested in ballet. How? She challenged me to a test, complimented me on my effort and then immediately gave me a new challenge. She set up an environment for the achievement of excellence and cared enough to invite me to be part of it. And, without realizing it fully at the time, I made an important discovery.

Dance is the most immediate and accessible of the arts because it involves your own body. When you learn to move your body on a note of music, it's exciting. You have taken control of your body and, by learning to do that, you discover that you can take control of your life.

I took classes with Madame Seda for six months, once a week, but at the end of spring, in June 1942, she called over my mother, my sister and me and did an unbelievably modest and generous thing. She said, "You and your sister are very talented. You should go to a better teacher." She sent us to George Balanchine's school—the School of American Ballet.

Within a few years, I was performing children's roles. At 15, I became *10* part of a classical ballet company. What an extraordinary thing for a street boy from Washington Heights, with friends in gangs. Half grew up to become policemen and the other half gangsters—and I became a ballet dancer!

I had dreamed of being a doctor or an archaeologist or a priest. But by the time I was 17, I was a principal dancer performing major roles in the ballets, and by the time I was 21, I was doing movies, Broadway shows and choreography. I then married a ballerina from New York City Ballet, Carolyn George, and we were (and still are) blessed with two boys and twin daughters.

It was a joyful career that lasted four decades. That's a long time to be dancing and, inevitably, a time came when I realized that there were not many years left for me as a performer. I wasn't sure what to do next, but then I thought about how I had become a dancer, and the teachers who had graced my life. Perhaps I could engage young children, especially boys, in the magic of the arts—in dance in particular. Not necessarily to prepare them to be professional performers, but to create an awareness by giving them a chance to experience the arts. So I started National Dance Institute.

That was 13 years ago. Since then, with the help of fellow teachers and staff at NDI, I have taught dance to thousands of inner-city children. And in each class, I rediscover why teaching dance to children is so important.

Each time I can use dance to help a child discover that he can control the way he moves, I am filled with joy. At a class I recently taught at P.S. 59 in Brooklyn, there was one boy who couldn't get from his right foot to his left. He was terrified. Everyone was watching. And what he had to do was so simple: take a step with his left foot on a note of music. All his classmates could do it, but he couldn't.

He kept trying, but he kept doing it wrong until finally he was frozen,   *15* unable to move at all. I put my arm around him and said, "Let's do it together. We'll do it in slow motion." We did it. I stepped back and said, "Now do it alone, and fast." With his face twisted in concentration, he slammed his left foot down correctly on the note. He did it!

The whole class applauded. He was so excited. But I think I was even happier, because I knew what had taken place. He had discovered he could take control of his body, and from that he can learn to take control of his life. If I can open the door to show a child that that is possible, it is wonderful.

Dance is the art to express time and space. That is what our universe is about. We can hardly make a sentence without signifying some expression of distance, place or time: "See you later." "Meet you at the corner in five minutes."

Dance is the art that human beings have developed to express that we live, right now, in a world of movement and varying tempos.

Dance, as an art, has to be taught. However, when teaching, it's important to set up an environment where both the student and teacher can discover together. Never teach something you don't love and believe in. But how to set up that environment?

When I have a new group of young students and I'm starting a class, I   *20* use Madame Seda's technique. I say, "Can you do this test? I'm going to give all 100 of you exactly 10 seconds to get off your seats and be standing and spread out all over the stage floor. And do it silently. Go!" And I start a countdown. Naturally, they run, yelling and screaming, and somehow arrive with several seconds to spare. I say, "Freeze. You all failed. You made noise, and you got there too soon. I said 'exactly 10 seconds'—not 6 or 8 or 11. Go back to your seats, and we'll do it again. And if you don't get it, we'll go back and do it again until you do. And if, at the end of the hour, you still haven't gotten it, I'm not going to teach you."

They usually get it the second time. Never have I had to do it more than three.

Demand precision, be clear and absolutely truthful. When they respond—and they will—congratulate them on the extraordinary control they have just exhibited. Why is that important? Because it's the beginning of knowing yourself, knowing that you can manage yourself if you want. And it's the beginning of dance. Once the children see that we are having a class of precision, order and respect, they are relieved, and we have a great class.

I've taught dance to Russian children, Australian children, Indian children, Chinese children, fat children, skinny children, handicapped children, groups of Australian triathletes, New York City police, senior citizens and 3-year-olds. The technique is the same everywhere, although there are cultural differences.

For example, when I was in China, I would say to the children, "I want everybody to come close and watch what I am going to do." But in China they have had to deal with following a teacher when there are masses of them. And they discovered that the way to see what the teacher does is not to move close but to move away. So 100 people moved back to watch the one—me.

I realized they were right. How did they learn that? Thousands of years of masses of people having to follow one teacher.   *25*

There are cultural differences and there are differences among people. In any group of dancers, there are some who are ready and excel more than others. There are many reasons—genetic, environment, the teachers they had. People blossom at different times.

But whatever the differences, someone admiring you, encouraging you, works so much better than the reverse. "You can do it, you are wonderful," works so much better than, "You're no good, the others are better than you, you've got to try harder." That never works.

I don't think there are any untalented children. But I think there are those whose talents never get the chance to flower. Perhaps they were never encouraged. Perhaps no one took the time to find out how to teach them. That is a tragedy.

However, the single most terrible thing we are doing to our children, I believe, is polluting them. I don't mean just with smog and crack, but by not teaching them the civilizing things we have taken millions of years to develop. But you cannot have a dance class without having good manners, without having respect. Dance can teach those things.

I think of each person as a trunk that's up in the attic. What are you going to put in the trunk? Are you going to put in machine guns, loud   *30* noises, foul language, dirty books and ignorance? Because, if you do, that's what is going to be left after you, that's what your children are going to have, and that will determine the world of the future. Or are you going to fill that trunk with music, dance, poetry, literature, good manners and loving friends?

I say, fill your trunk with the best that is available to you from the wealth of human culture. Those things will nourish you and your children. You can clean up your own environment and pass it on to the next generation. That's why I teach dance.

Suggestions for Writing and Discussion

1. What aspects of your own life were you thinking about as you read this piece?
2. In paragraph 1, d'Amboise describes himself as "diabolically" trying to disrupt his sister's dance class. How would you define the word *diabolically?* After writing your own definition, based on the context of the sentence in which it appears, look it up in the dictionary. Pay particular attention to the origin of this word. How does understanding the word's origin add to your understanding of the image d'Amboise seeks to convey?
3. What qualities did Madame Seda possess that made her a good teacher? What qualities did the author possess that made him a good pupil? Using the examples of Madame Seda and Jacques d'Amboise, write an extended definition of an ideal teacher-student relationship. As you write, assume that your audience will be college students who are currently training to be teachers.
4. Have you ever had a teacher like Madame Seda or Jacques d'Amboise? Explain.
5. If you were a teacher, what qualities would you like to pass on to the next generation? Explain.
6. In paragraph 22, the author says a teacher should "[d]emand precision, be clear and absolutely truthful." What else should a great teacher do?

Suggestions for Extended Thinking and Writing

1. Write an essay in which you describe a process you went through to learn something new.
2. D'Amboise writes that he thinks of each person "as a trunk that's up in the attic." Write an essay in which you not only explain what this comparison implies, but take it a step further: Devise your own metaphor for the way you see each new person you meet. Explain your reasons for using this metaphor.

GRACE PALEY

The Loudest Voice

Born into a family of socialist Russian Jews in 1922, Grace Paley spent hours listening to the tales of her parents, uncles, and aunts. Although she earned poor grades in high school (because, she claimed, she was "writing poetry and thinking about boys"), the stories her relatives told, alternately in Russian, English, and Yiddish, inspired Paley to become a writer. Long before Paley was born, these tales originated in the ghettos of eastern Europe as overloaded wagons and crowded trains moved toward the great port cities transporting hundreds of immigrants to steerage compartments in the ships that would carry them to the United States. As she explained in an interview with Shenandoah *magazine (1981), when she first began writing, Paley found herself too focused on "me—me—me." To get beyond this point, she started listening carefully to "other people's voices" and integrating them into her work by "writing with an accent." In "The Loudest Voice," she offers a fictional picture of a young Jewish girl who learns to listen to the voices around her and to value them all, yet to recognize that her own voice is especially important.*

Pre-Reading and Journal-Writing Suggestions

1. What is one ability that makes you feel proud of yourself—something you can do better than most others?
2. If you could play a starring role in any play or film you've seen, which would you choose? Explain.

There is a certain place where dumbwaiters boom, doors slam, dishes crash; every window is a mother's mouth bidding the street shut up, go skate somewhere else, come home. My voice is the loudest.

There, my own mother is still as full of breathing as me and the grocer stands up to speak to her. "Mrs. Abramowitz," he says, "people should not be afraid of their children."

"Ah, Mr. Bialik," my mother replies, "if you say to her or her father 'Ssh,' they say, 'In the grave it will be quiet.'"

"From Coney Island to the cemetery," says my papa. "It's the same subway; it's the same fare."

I am right next to the pickle barrel. My pinky is making tiny whirl-pools in the brine. I stop a moment to announce: "Campbell's Tomato Soup. Campbell's Vegetable Beef Soup. Campbell's S-c-otch Broth . . ."

"Be quiet," the grocer says, "the labels are coming off."

"Please, Shirley, be a little quiet," my mother begs me.

In that place the whole street groans: Be quiet! Be quiet! but steals from the happy chorus of my inside self not a tittle or a jot.

There, too, but just around the corner, is a red brick building that has been old for many years. Every morning the children stand before it in double lines which must be straight. They are not insulted. They are waiting anyway.

I am usually among them. I am, in fact, the first, since I begin with "A."

One cold morning the monitor tapped me on the shoulder. "Go to Room 409, Shirley Abramowitz," he said. I did as I was told. I went in a hurry up a down staircase to Room 409, which contained sixth-graders. I had to wait at the desk without wiggling until Mr. Hilton, their teacher, had time to speak.

After five minutes he said, "Shirley?"

"What?" I whispered.

He said, "My! My! Shirley Abramowitz! They told me you had a particularly loud, clear voice and read with lots of expression. Could that be true?"

"Oh, yes," I whispered.

"In that case, don't be silly; I might very well be your teacher someday. Speak up, speak up."

"Yes," I shouted.

"More like it," he said. "Now, Shirley, can you put a ribbon in your hair or a bobby pin? It's too messy."

"Yes!" I bawled.

"Now, now, calm down." He turned to the class. "Children, not a sound. Open at page 39. Read till 52. When you finish, start again." He looked me over once more. "Now, Shirley, you know, I suppose, that Christmas is coming. We are preparing a beautiful play. Most of the parts have been given out. But I still need a child with a strong voice, lots of stamina. Do you know what stamina is? You do? Smart kid. You know, I heard you read 'The Lord is my shepherd' in Assembly yesterday. I was very impressed. Wonderful delivery. Mrs. Jordan, your teacher, speaks highly of you. Now listen to me, Shirley Abramowitz, if you want to take the part and be in the play, repeat after me, 'I swear to work harder than I ever did before.'"

I looked to heaven and said at once, "Oh, I swear." I kissed my pinky and looked at God.

"That is an actor's life, my dear," he explained. "Like a soldier's, never tardy or disobedient to his general, the director. Everything," he said, "absolutely everything will depend on you."

That afternoon, all over the building, children scraped and scrubbed the turkeys and the sheaves of corn off the schoolroom windows. Goodbye Thanksgiving. The next morning a monitor brought red paper and green paper from the office. We made new shapes and hung them on the walls and glued them to the doors.

The teachers became happier and happier. Their heads were ringing like the bells of childhood. My best friend Evie was prone to evil, but she did not get a single demerit for whispering. We learned "Holy Night" without an error. "How wonderful!" said Miss Glacé, the student teacher. "To think that some of you don't even speak the language!" We learned "Deck the Halls" and "Hark! The Herald Angels." . . . They weren't ashamed and we weren't embarrassed.

Oh, but when my mother heard about it all, she said to my father: "Misha, you don't know what's going on there. Cramer is the head of the Tickets Committee." 25

"Who?" asked my father. "Cramer? Oh yes, an active woman."

"Active? Active has to have a reason. Listen," she said sadly, "I'm surprised to see my neighbors making tra-la-la for Christmas."

My father couldn't think of what to say to that. Then he decided: "You're in America! Clara, you wanted to come here. In Palestine the Arabs would be eating you alive. Europe you had pogroms. Argentina is full of Indians. Here you got Christmas. . . . Some joke, ha?"

"Very funny, Misha. What is becoming of you? If we came to a new country a long time ago to run away from tyrants, and instead we fall into a creeping pogrom, that our children learn a lot of lies, so what's the joke? Ach, Misha, your idealism is going away."

"So is your sense of humor." 30

"That I never had, but idealism you had a lot of."

"I'm the same Misha Abramovitch, I didn't change an iota. Ask anyone."

"Only ask me," says my mama, may she rest in peace. "I got the answer."

Meanwhile the neighbors had to think of what to say too.

Marty's father said: "You know, he has a very important part, my boy." 35

"Mine also," said Mr. Sauerfeld.

"Not my boy!" said Mrs. Klieg. "I said to him no. The answer is no. When I say no! I mean no!"

The rabbi's wife said, "It's disgusting!" But no one listened to her. Under the narrow sky of God's great wisdom she wore a strawberry-blond wig.

Every day was noisy and full of experience. I was Right-hand Man. Mr. Hilton said: "How could I get along without you, Shirley?"

He said: "Your mother and father ought to get down on their knees 40 every night and thank God for giving them a child like you."

He also said: "You're absolutely a pleasure to work with, my dear, dear child."

Sometimes he said: "For God's sakes, what did I do with the script? Shirley! Shirley! Find it."

Then I answered quietly: "Here it is, Mr. Hilton."

Once in a while, when he was very tired, he would cry out: "Shirley, I'm just tired of screaming at those kids. Will you tell Ira Pushkov not to come in till Lester points to that star the second time?"

Then I roared: "Ira Pushkov, what's the matter with you? Dope!   *45* Mr. Hilton told you five times already, don't come in till Lester points to that star the second time."

"Ach, Clara," my father asked, "what does she do there till six o'clock she can't even put the plates on the table?"

"Christmas," said my mother coldly.

"Ho! Ho!" my father said. "Christmas. What's the harm? After all, history teaches everyone. We learn from reading this is a holiday from pagan times also, candles, lights, even Chanukah. So we learn it's not altogether Christian. So if they think it's a private holiday, they're only ignorant, not patriotic. What belongs to history, belongs to all men. You want to go back to the Middle Ages? Is it better to shave your head with a secondhand razor? Does it hurt Shirley to learn to speak up? It does not. So maybe someday she won't live between the kitchen and the shop. She's not a fool."

I thank you, Papa, for your kindness. It is true about me to this day. I am foolish but I am not a fool.

That night my father kissed me and said with great interest in my   *50* career, "Shirley, tomorrow's your big day. Congrats."

"Save it," my mother said. Then she shut all the windows in order to prevent tonsillitis.

In the morning it snowed. On the street corner a tree had been decorated for us by a kind city administration. In order to miss its chilly shadow our neighbors walked three blocks east to buy a loaf of bread. The butcher pulled down black window shades to keep the colored lights from shining on his chickens. Oh, not me. On the way to school, with both my hands I tossed it a kiss of tolerance. Poor thing, it was a stranger in Egypt.

I walked straight into the auditorium past the staring children. "Go ahead, Shirley!" said the monitors. Four boys, big for their age, had already started work as propmen and stagehands.

Mr. Hilton was very nervous. He was not even happy. Whatever he started to say ended in a sideward look of sadness. He sat slumped in the middle of the first row and asked me to help Miss Glacé. I did this, although she thought my voice too resonant and said, "Show-off!"

Parents began to arrive long before we were ready. They wanted to   *55* make a good impression. From among the yards of drapes I peeked out at the audience. I saw my embarrassed mother.

Ira, Lester, and Meyer were pasted to their beards by Miss Glacé. She almost forgot to thread the star on its wire, but I reminded her. I coughed a few times to clear my throat. Miss Glacé looked around and saw that everyone was in costume and on line waiting to play his part. She whispered, "All right . . ." Then:

Jackie Sauerfeld, the prettiest boy in first grade, parted the curtains with his skinny elbow and in a high voice sang out:

"Parents dear
We are here
To make a Christmas play in time.
It we give
In narrative
And illustrate with pantomime."

He disappeared.

My voice burst immediately from the wings to the great shock of Ira, Lester, and Meyer, who were waiting for it but were surprised all the same.

"I remember, I remember, the house where I was born . . ."   60

Miss Glacé yanked the curtain open and there it was, the house—an old hayloft, where Celia Kornbluh lay in the straw with Cindy Lou, her favorite doll. Ira, Lester, and Meyer moved slowly from the wings toward her, sometimes pointing to a moving star and sometimes ahead to Cindy Lou.

It was a long story and it was a sad story. I carefully pronounced all the words about my lonesome childhood, while little Eddie Braunstein wandered upstage and down with his shepherd's stick, looking for sheep. I brought up lonesomeness again, and not being understood at all except by some women everybody hated. Eddie was too small for that and Marty Groff took his place, wearing his father's prayer shawl. I announced twelve friends, and half the boys in the fourth grade gathered round Marty, who stood on an orange crate while my voice harangued. Sorrowful and loud, I declaimed about love and God and Man, but because of the terrible deceit of Abie Stock we came suddenly to a famous moment. Marty, whose remembering tongue I was, waited at the foot of the cross. He stared desperately at the audience. I groaned, "My God, my God, why hast thou forsaken me?" The soldiers who were shieks grabbed poor Marty to pin him up to die, but he wrenched free, turned again to the audience, and spread his arms aloft to show despair and the end. I murmured at the top of my voice, "The rest is silence, but as everyone in this room, in this city—in this world—now knows, I shall have life eternal."

That night Mrs. Kornbluh visited our kitchen for a glass of tea.

"How's the virgin?" asked my father with a look of concern.

"For a man with a daughter, you got a fresh mouth, Abramovitch."   65

"Here," said my father kindly, "have some lemon, it'll sweeten your disposition."

They debated a little in Yiddish, then fell in a puddle of Russian and Polish. What I understood next was my father, who said, "Still and all, it was certainly a beautiful affair, you have to admit, introducing us to the beliefs of a different culture."

"Well, yes," said Mrs. Kornbluh. "The only thing . . . you know Charlie Turner—that cute boy in Celia's class—a couple others? They got very small parts or no part at all. In very bad taste, it seemed to me. After all, it's their religion."

"Ach," explained my mother, "what could Mr. Hilton do? They got very small voices; after all, why should they holler? The English language they know from the beginning by heart. They're blond like angels. You think it's so important they should get in the play? Christmas . . . the whole piece of goods . . . they own it."

I listened and listened until I couldn't listen any more. Too sleepy, I *70* climbed out of bed and kneeled. I made a little church of my hands and said, "Hear, O Israel . . ." Then I called out in Yiddish, "Please, good night, good night. Ssh." My father said, "Ssh yourself," and slammed the kitchen door.

I was happy. I fell asleep at once. I had prayed for everybody: my talking family, cousins far away, passersby, and all the lonesome Christians. I expected to be heard. My voice was certainly the loudest.

Suggestions for Writing and Discussion

1. What kind of person is Shirley Abramowitz? If you were in sixth grade with her, do you think you two would be friends? Explain.

2. How do you define the words *conformist* and *nonconformist?* Who would you categorize as a conformist in this story? As a nonconformist? Explain your reasons.

3. Shirley has a reputation for a "loud, clear voice." When you were in sixth grade, were you known for any outstanding characteristic? Explain by telling a story that illustrates this characteristic.

4. Mr. Hilton tells Shirley that an actor's life is much like a soldier's: She cannot be late and she must always listen to the general (the director). Create an analogy that explains what your life as a student is like. Develop and explain the comparison you make.

5. Although both are practicing Jews, Shirley's parents find themselves divided on the issue of letting her participate in the Christmas program. Describe each parent's reactions. Do you sympathize equally with each position, or do you find yourself favoring one or the other?

    As you write, assume that your audience is a community where the question of celebrating December holidays in public schools has been hotly debated. Your purpose is to argue for the point of view you have developed after reading and thinking about this story.

6. Only Mrs. Klieg won't allow her son to be in the Christmas play. In your opinion, when most parents are under pressure related to a controversial issue, do they give in to please their children? To please the schools? Explain your answer.

7. What does the Christmas tree on the corner symbolize to the Jewish residents who live nearby?

8. Shirley's mother comes to the performance even though she is embarrassed and against her daughter's performing. Why, then, does she come? What does her action say about her?

9. What point does Shirley's mother make when she expresses her concern with the children who got such small parts in the play? How does her view of the selection of the cast differ from Mr. Hilton's? What are his primary concerns as he casts the play?

10. Why, in the end, does Shirley see the Christians as "lonesome"? What is your response to this observation?

_____

Suggestions for Extended Thinking and Writing

1. This story is told from Shirley's point of view. Rewrite any episode in the story through the eyes of another character.

2. If you (or one of your children) were asked to take part in a religious celebration that was contrary to your own religious beliefs, would you do it? Would you allow your child to do it? Why or why not?

3. Describe and explain, to someone outside of your culture, one special observance in which you participate.

_____

SUGGESTIONS FOR MAKING CONNECTIONS

1. Use at least two sources from this section and consider your own educational experiences as you plan and write an essay on this question: What are the most important factors to consider when planning a child's education?

2. Write an essay proposing an ideal grade school. Base your description on your personal educational philosophies and experiences.

3. Define what it means to be an educated person. As you write this definition, use examples from at least three of the selections in this section to illustrate the points you are making.

4. Write an essay exploring one of the following two alternatives to public schooling: private schools and home schooling.

5. Compare the learning experiences of two people whose stories appear in this section. Come to some conclusions about why and how these individuals learn or fail to learn.

6. Write an essay agreeing or disagreeing with the following statement: The trouble with education in the United States today is that it is a guaranteed right, whether or not a student wants to learn. To be effective, education must be a privilege, not a right.

7. Reflecting on your own educational experiences, who or what was most influential as far as your success, or lack of success, was concerned? Refer

to at least two of the selections in this section when you explore your own educational experiences.

8. Write an essay in which you categorize three types of teachers. (You may use any teachers in this section as well as those in your past as examples within these categories.)

9

American Dreams and Creations

Previews: AMERICAN DREAMS AND CREATIONS

Yet, if "Dances With Wolves" had been about *people* who happen to be Indians, rather than about *Indians* (uniformly stoic, brave, nasty to their enemies, nice to their friends), it might have stood a better chance of acting as a bridge between societies that have for too long woodenly characterized each other.

From: *Indians in Aspic,* MICHAEL DORRIS

"Everyone seemed to have some communal knowledge which I did not have—and then I realized that the metaphor of *house* was totally wrong for me. Suddenly I was homeless. There were no attics and cellars and crannies. I had no such house in my memories. As a child I had read of such things in books, and my family had promised such a house, but the best they could do was offer the miserable bungalow I was embarrassed with all my life."

From: *Sandra Cisneros: Sneaking Past the Guards,* JIM SAGEL

The Civil Rights Movement changed my view of music. It was after my first march. I began to sing a song and in the course of singing changed the song so that it made sense for that particular moment. Although I was not consciously aware of it, this was one of my earliest experiences with how my music was supposed to *function*. This music was to be integrative of and consistent with everything I was doing at that time; it was to be tied to activities that went beyond artistic affairs such as concerts, dances, and church meetings.

From: *Black Music in Our Hands,* BERNICE REAGON

He talks of his own dreams. He hopes to finish his associate's degree—the same one he has been working on between hospitalizations for almost eight years now. . . .

Time stands still. This could be last year, or the year before, or the year before that. I'm within range of becoming a physician, of realizing something I've been working toward for almost five years, while my brother still dreams of having a small job, living in his own apartment and of being well.

From: *A Brother's Dreams,* PAUL ARONOWITZ

MICHAEL DORRIS

Indians in Aspic

After his father was killed in World War II, Michael Dorris, who is of Modoc, Irish, and French descent, lived for a while with his mother on a reservation in eastern Montana. Most of his early years, however, were spent in Louisville, Kentucky, where he was raised jointly by his mother, his aunt, and his grandmother. Later he earned degrees from Georgetown and Yale. As a single adult, Dorris adopted three Native American children, one of whom, Abel, suffered severely from the effects of fetal exposure to alcohol. It is Abel's story that Dorris movingly depicts in his best-selling book The Broken Cord *(1989). During the 1970s, while teaching at Dartmouth, Dorris met Louise Erdrich who would later become his wife. Erdrich has written several novels and short stories about her own mixed Native American background. In addition, she and Dorris have collaborated on a novel,* The Crown of Columbus. *Dorris contributes frequently to the* New York Times, *where this essay first appeared in February 1991. Currently Dorris is adjunct full professor of anthropology and Native American studies at Dartmouth, where he founded the Native American Studies program in 1972. In 1985 he received the Indian Achievement Award for his work in education.*

Pre-Reading and Journal-Writing Suggestions

1. Think back on your earliest impressions of American Indians. What did you think Indians were like? Where did you get this impression? From a book, a story you heard, a television show, a movie, or something else? Try to remember the specific source that shaped your views on Indians. Did this source present you with what you would now consider a fair picture? Explain.
2. Use your imagination: You get the chance to star in a Hollywood movie hit. You can be either a member of a group of early settlers or a member of an Indian tribe. Which do you choose to be and why?

The Sioux and Lieut. John Dunbar, the character enthusiastically   *1*
played by Kevin Costner in "Dances With Wolves," meet auspiciously: He's naked, and that so disconcerts a group of mounted warriors that the naïve young soldier lives to tell the tale, a sort of Boy Scout Order of the Arrow ritual carried to the nth power.

Dunbar, renamed Dances With Wolves, quickly earns merit badges in Pawnee-bashing and animal telepathy, and marries Stands With a Fist (Mary McDonnell), a passionate young widow who just happens to be a white captive cum Campfire Girl of impressive cross-cultural accomplishments. Eventually the "With" family strikes out on their own—the nucleus of a handsome new Anglo tribe—sadder, wiser and certainly more sensitive as a result of their native American immersion.

Mr. Costner follows in a long tradition of literary and cinematic heroes who have discovered Indians. Robinson Crusoe did it off the coast of Brazil, Natty Bumppo did it in New York State and everyone from Debra Paget ("Broken Arrow," 1950) and Natalie Wood ("The Searchers," 1956) to Dustin Hoffman ("Little Big Man," 1970) and Richard Harris ("A Man Called Horse," 1970) has done it in Hollywood.

Usually these visits do not bode well for the aboriginal hosts—just ask the Mohicans. Appreciative white folks always seem to show up shortly before the cavalry (who are often looking for them) or Manifest Destiny, and record the final days of peace before the tribe is annihilated. Readers and viewers of such sagas are left with a predominant emotion of regret for a golden age now but a faint memory. In the imaginary mass media world of neat beginnings, middles and ends, American Indian society, whatever its virtues and fascinations as an arena for Euro-American consciousness-raising, is definitely past tense.

Thematically virtually all of these works share a subtle or not so subtle 5 message: Indians may be poor, they may at first seem strange or forbidding or primitive, but by golly once you get to know them they have a thing or two to teach us about The Meaning of Life.

The tradition goes back a long way. Europeans like Jean-Jacques Rousseau and Karl May (the turn-of-this-century novelist whose books, a mixture of Louis L'Amour and the Hardy Boys, have been a rite of passage for generations of German youth) laid out a single range for Indians to inhabit: savage-savage to noble-savage. Indians embody the concept of "the other"—a foreign, exotic, even cartoonish panorama against which "modern" (that is, white) men can measure and test themselves, and eventually, having proved their mettle in battle, be dubbed as natural leaders by their hosts.

Placed within the genre, "Dances With Wolves" shows some signs of evolution. Kevin Costner obviously spared no expense to achieve a sense of authenticity in his production. He filmed on the Pine Ridge reservation in South Dakota and defied conventional Hollywood wisdom to assemble a large and talented native American supporting cast. Great attention was paid to ethnographically correct costumes, and if the streets in the native camp seem a tad too spotless to be believed, at least the tepees are museum quality.

Impressively, large segments of the film are spoken in Lakota, the language of the western Sioux, and though the subtitles are stilted—Indians in the movies seem incapable of using contractions—they at least convey the impression that native Americans had an intellectual life.

When I saw "Dances With Wolves" at an advance screening, I predicted that it would be less than a box-office smash. Though spectacular to look at, it struck me as too long, too predictable, too didactic to attract a large audience. Twelve Academy Award nominations and $100 million in revenue later, was I ever wrong. In fact, the movie probably sells tickets precisely *because* it delivers the old-fashioned Indians that the ticket-buying audience expects to find. Dunbar is our national myth's everyman—handsome, sensitive, flexible, right-thinking. He passes the test of the frontier, out-Indians the Indians, achieves a pure soul by encountering and surmounting the wilderness.

Yet, if "Dances With Wolves" had been about *people* who happen to   10
be Indians, rather than about *Indians* (uniformly stoic, brave, nasty to their enemies, nice to their friends), it might have stood a better chance of acting as a bridge between societies that have for too long woodenly characterized each other.

With such tremendous popularity, the film is sure to generate a bubble of sympathy for the Sioux, but hard questions remain: Will this sentiment be practical, translating into public support for native American religious freedom cases before the Supreme Court, for restoration of Lakota sacred lands (the Black Hills) or water rights, for tribal sovereignty, for providing the money desperately needed by reservation health clinics? Pine Ridge is the most economically impoverished corner of America today, the Census Bureau says, but will its modern Indian advocates in business suits, men and women with lap-top computers and perfect English, be the recipients of a tidal wave of good will?

Or will it turn out, once again, that the only good Indians—the only Indians whose causes and needs we can embrace—are lodged safely in the past, wrapped neatly in the blankets of history, magnets for our sympathy because they require nothing of us but tears in a dark theater?

Suggestions for Writing and Discussion
1. Think about the title of this piece: What exactly *is* aspic? How might it connect to the author's point in this piece? As you write, keep in mind that your purpose is to explain this connection to a person who does not know the meaning of the word *aspic* and who has not seen the film *Dances with Wolves.*
2. From the first two paragraphs, what clues can you find to suggest the author's tone (his attitude toward his subject and toward his readers)? What might be Dorris's purpose for using this tone? As a reader, does this tone appeal to you? Why or why not?
3. Why, in paragraph 5, does Dorris capitalize The Meaning of Life? Does this technique add to or detract from his critique? Explain your answer.
4. In what ways does Dorris believe *Dances with Wolves* is different from most films about Indians? In what ways is it typical? From your own television- and film-viewing experiences, do you agree or disagree with his evaluation? Explain.

5. What is Dorris's main point in this piece? To whom is he addressing this message—Hollywood film makers or those of us in the audience? Does he seem to be suggesting changes he would like to see or simply explaining problems? Explain your answer.

6. Should a movie or a television show aim for realism and truth? Explain the reasons for your response by referring to specific films or programs that you have found either highly praiseworthy or extremely lacking in those qualities you admire.

Suggestions for Extended Thinking and Writing

1. If you have seen *Dances with Wolves,* write your own critique of this film and the issues it deals with. Refer to several points that Dorris makes in his essay—do you agree or disagree with him on these points? Support your opinion with specific examples from the movie itself and other films related to the early American West.

2. Search for several other reviews of *Dances with Wolves* as well as written interviews with Kevin Costner regarding this film. (You might try the *New York Times Index* as a place to begin looking for such reviews.) Write an analysis in which you synthesize these reviews and interviews as well as the Dorris essay.

3. Argue that general audiences should or should not trust the evaluation of a film to a movie critic, such as Siskel or Ebert (or Dorris!). Use as your support at least two other specific movies you have seen and subsequent reviews of these films. As your audience, imagine readers of *People* magazine.

JIM SAGEL

Sandra Cisneros: Sneaking Past the Guards

> *Jim Sagel writes poems in both English and Spanish. He is the winner of the Casa de las Americas literary award. In this essay, which first appeared in* Publisher's Weekly, March 1991, *he analyzes the challenges faced by writers such as Sandra Cisneros, who come from a culture different from mainstream America and whose works strive to "startle the jaded reader" and "poetically unravel stereotypes."*

Pre-Reading and Journal-Writing Suggestions

1. Each one of us has at least one book within us. What is your great book about? List the events, people, and conflicts that you could write about. What would be your purpose for writing this book?
2. List all of the different cultures represented by any writers you have read. Are any Hispanic American authors on this list? If so, who are they? If not, why do you think you've never read anything by a Hispanic American author?

Taped to her word processor is a prayer card to San Judas, a gift from a   *1*
Mexico City cabdriver. Her two indispensable literary sources are mail order catalogues and the San Antonio (Tex.) phone book. She lights candles and reads the *Popul Vuh* before sitting down to write long into the night, becoming so immersed in her characters that she dreams their dialogue: once she awoke momentarily convinced she was Inés, bride of the Mexican revolutionary Emiliano Zapata.

Such identification with her characters and her culture is altogether natural for Sandra Cisneros, a writer who has always found her literary voice in the real voices of her people, her immediate family and the extended *famiulis* of Latino society.

"I'm trying to write the stories that haven't been written. I feel like a cartographer; I'm determined to fill a literary void," Cisneros says. With the Random House publication of her new collection of stories, *Woman Hollering Creek* (Fiction Forecasts, Feb. 15), and the simultaneous reissuing of her earlier collection of short fiction, *The House on Mango Street,* in a Vintage edition, Cisneros finds herself in a position to chart those barrio ditches and borderland arroyos that have not appeared on most copies of the American literary map but which, nonetheless, also flow into the "mainstream."

The 36-year-old daughter of a Mexican father and a Chicana mother, Cisneros is well aware of the additional pressure to succeed with this pair of books that represent the opportunity for a wider readership, not only for herself but for scores of other Latina and Latino writers right behind the door that she is cracking open.

"One of the most frightening pressures I faced as I wrote this book was the fear that I would blow it," Cisneros says, sweeping a lock of her closely cropped black hair from her forehead as she sips a midmorning cup of coffee. "I kept asking myself, What have I taken on here? That's why I was so obsessed with getting everybody's stories out. I didn't have the luxury of doing my own."

Coupled with that "responsibility to do a collective good job," is Cisneros's anxiety about how her work will be perceived by the general reading public. Universal as her themes are, Cisneros knows her characters live in an America very different from that of her potential readers. From her friend Lucy, "who smells like corn," to Salvador, whose essence resides "inside that wrinkled shirt, inside the throat that must clear itself and apologize each time it speaks," Cisneros's literary landscape teems with characters who live, love and laugh in the flowing cadences of the Spanish language.

Yet, unlike her character Salvador, Cisneros offers no apologies when she speaks. Energetic and abounding with *gusto*—only the Spanish word will do to describe her engaging humor—Cisneros relishes the opportunity to startle the jaded reader and poetically unravel stereotypes, especially those that relate to Latinas.

"I'm the mouse who puts a thorn in the lion's paw," she says, with an arch smile reminiscent of the red-lipped *sonrisa* on the cover of *My Wicked Wicked Ways* (Third Woman Press, 1987), a collection of poetry celebrating the "bad girl" with her "lopsided symmetry of sin / and virtue."

"An unlucky fate is mine / to be born woman in a family of men," Cisneros writes in one of her "wicked" poems, yet it is that very "fate" that laid the groundwork for the literary career of this writer, whose name derives from the Spanish word for "swan."

Born in Chicago in 1954, Cisneros grew up in a family of six brothers and a father, or "seven fathers," as she puts it. She recalls spending much of her early childhood moving from place to place. Because her paternal grandmother was so attached to her favorite son, the Cisneros family returned to Mexico City "like the tides."

"The moving back and forth, the new schools, were very upsetting to me as a child. They caused me to be very introverted and shy. I do not remember making friends easily, and I was terribly self-conscious due to the cruelty of the nuns, who were majestic at making one feel little. Because we moved so much, and always in neighborhoods that appeared like France after World War II—empty lots and burned-out buildings—I retreated inside myself."

It was that "retreat" that transformed Cisneros into an observer, a role she feels she still plays today. "When I'm washing sheets at the laundromat, people still see me as just a girl. I take advantage of that idea. The little voice I used to hate I now see as an asset. It helps me get past the guards."

Among the first "guards" that Cisneros sneaked past were the literary sentinels at the University of Iowa's Writer's Workshop, which she attended in the late '70s. Her "breakthrough" occurred during a seminar discussion of archetypal memories in Bachelard's *Poetics of Space*. As her classmates spoke about the house of the imagination, the attics, stairways and cellars of childhood, Cisneros felt foreign and out of place.

"Everyone seemed to have some communal knowledge which I did not have—and then I realized that the metaphor of *house* was totally wrong for me. Suddenly I was homeless. There were no attics and cellars and crannies. I had no such house in my memories. As a child I had read of such things in books, and my family had promised such a house, but the best they could do was offer the miserable bungalow I was embarrassed with all my life. This caused me to question myself, to become defensive. What did I, Sandra Cisneros, know? What *could* I know? My classmates were from the best schools in the country. They had been bred as fine hothouse flowers. I was a yellow weed among the city's cracks.

"It was not until this moment when I separated myself, when I consid- 15 ered myself truly distinct, that my writing acquired a voice. I knew I was a Mexican woman, but I didn't think it had anything to do with why I felt so much imbalance in my life, whereas it had everything to do with it! My race, my gender, my class! That's when I decided I would write about something my classmates couldn't write about."

Thus it was that *The House on Mango Street* was born and Cisneros discovered what she terms her "first love," a fascination with speech and voices. Writing in the voice of the adolescent Esperanza, Cisneros created a series of interlocking stories, alternately classified as a novel and as a collection of prose poems because of the vivid and poignant nature of the language. Since its first publication in 1984 by Arte Público Press, *Mango Street* has sold some 30,000 copies. The book is used in classes from junior high school through graduate school in subjects ranging from Chicano studies to psychology to culture, ideas and values at Stanford University, where it has been adopted as part of the "new curriculum."

Mango Street was also the catalyst that drew Cisneros to her literary agent or, to be more accurate, that led Susan Bergholz to Cisneros. Bergholz was so moved after reading the book that she did something she had never done before: she set out to track down the writer. "It was a delightful chase," Bergholz recalls, in spite of the fact that it took some three to four years to accomplish.

Ironically, even while Bergholz was enlisting the aid of Richard Bray of Guild Books to contact Cisneros, the writer was going through what she calls the worst year of her life, 1987. She had spent the previous year in Texas through the auspices of a Dobie-Paisano fellowship. Though the experience had convinced her to make Texas her permanent home, the writer found herself unable to make a living once the fellowship expired.

While her boyfriend waited tables, Cisneros handed out fliers in local supermarkets and laundromats, trying to scrape together enough students to teach a private writing workshop. At last, she was forced to leave her newly adopted home, her confidence shaken and her outlook on life darkened.

The depression she sank into followed her to California, where she accepted a guest lectureship at California State University in Chico. "I thought I couldn't teach. I found myself becoming suicidal. Richard Bray had told me Susan was looking for me, but I was drowning, beyond help. I had the number for months, but I didn't call. It was frightening because it was such a calm depression."

An NEA fellowship in fiction revitalized Cisneros and helped her get on her feet again, both financially and spiritually. Finally calling that Manhattan phone number stuffed in her pocket, Cisneros sent Bergholz a small group of new stories. With only 39 pages in hand, Bergholz sold *Woman Hollering Creek* to Joni Evans and Erroll McDonald at Random House/Vintage; Julie Grau became the book's enthusiastic editor.

Then, of course, the real work began for Cisneros, whose previous output had been about one story every six months. "There's nothing like a deadline to teach you discipline, especially when you've already spent your advance. *Susto* helps," Cisneros says, explaining that fear motivated her to put in eight-to-12 hour days. Though exhausting, the experience was genuinely empowering.

"Before, I'd be scratching my *nalgas,* waiting for inspiration. Now I know I can work this hard. I know I did the best I could."

That's not to say Cisneros believes she's done the best work of her career. "I'm looking forward to the books I'll write when I'm 60," she observes. She's also looking forward to the contributions other Latina and Latino writers will be making in the future. "There's a lot of good writing in the mainstream press that has nothing to say. Chicano writers have a lot to say. The influence of our two languages is profound. The Spanish language is going to contribute something very rich to American literature."

Meanwhile, this self-described "migrant professor" plans to continue her personal and literary search for the "home in the heart," as Elenita the Witch Woman describes it in *Mango Street*. As "nobody's mother and nobody's wife," Cisneros most resembles Inés Alfaro, the powerful central character in "Eyes of Zapata," the story Cisneros considers her finest achievement.

Small, but "bigger" than the general himself, Inés is the woman warrior, the *Soldadera* who understands what the men will never comprehend, that "the wars begin here, in our hearts and in our beds." She is the *bruja,* the *nagual* who flies through the night, the fierce and tender lover who risks all, the eater of black things that make her hard and strong.

She is, in short, a symbol of the Latina herself, the Mexican woman whose story is at last being told, a story of life and blood and grief and "all the flower colors of joy." It is a story at once intimate and universal, guaranteed to shove a bittersweet thorn into the paws of literary lions everywhere.

Suggestions for Writing and Discussion

1. Summarize the main points Sagel makes about Cisneros and her writing.
2. Cisneros admits to being concerned about how a general audience might respond to the characters she creates. As she says, her characters "live in an America very different from that of her potential readers." As a reader, do you think Cisneros's concern is justified? Do most readers shy away from books in which main characters are of different nationalities or ethnic backgrounds? Explain by referring to your own experience as a reader.

    (If you do not read many novels, consider the films you see. Do you prefer to watch movies where the characters are culturally similar to you? Culturally different? Or does culture make no difference when you chose which film to see? Explain, making references to specific movies. Write your response with Cisneros in mind as your audience. Try to convince her that she should consider the point of view you express when she gives future interviews.)
3. What aspects of Cisneros's early childhood might have contributed to her eventual life as a writer? What aspects of her education may also have contributed to this career?
4. Explain the levels of meaning found in Cisneros's metaphor comparing herself and her classmates: "They had been bred as fine hothouse flowers. I was a yellow weed among the city's cracks." Create a metaphor to compare yourself to your classmates in elementary or high school. Will your metaphor reflect similarity or difference to your colleagues? Explain.
5. Cisneros admits that she wrote 8 to 12 hours a day, not because she was inspired by a higher muse, but out of fear of her impending deadlines. What is your own response to deadlines? Do you think you write (or study or work in general) more productively when you are under pressure or when you are able to set your own deadlines? Explain.
6. Analyze Sagel's closing comment on Cisneros's work: "It is a story at once intimate and universal, guaranteed to shove a bittersweet thorn into the paws of literary lions everywhere." What do you think he means by *literary lions?* Why would Cisneros's story shove a thorn in their paws? Can you think of other works you have read or films you have seen that would fit this description? Explain.

Suggestions for Extended Thinking and Writing

1. Practice using a writer's greatest tool—being a good observer. Recall a significant person or place in your life and write a descriptive narrative as if you were seeing this person or place for the last time.

2. Write an extended metaphor that explains your cultural experiences compared to those of the majority of students in the classes you are currently taking.

3. Read Cisneros's *The House on Mango Street* and write a review that addresses the characters' values. Consider the conflicts they face and the way they resolve, or fail to resolve, these conflicts.

BERNICE REAGON
Black Music in Our Hands

> *Bernice Reagon, who grew up in Albany, Georgia, demonstrated her com-*
> *mitment to civil rights when she was a student at Albany State College. She*
> *joined the Student Nonviolent Coordinating Committee and was expelled*
> *because of her activism with this group. She then transferred to Spelman Col-*
> *lege, earning a degree in black history and music; in 1975 she received a Ph.D.*
> *in these fields from Howard University. Currently Reagon serves as curator in*
> *the Division of Community Life at the Smithsonian Institution's National*
> *Museum of American History, where she is a specialist in African-American*
> *oral, performance, and protest traditions. In addition, Reagon founded and now*
> *serves as artistic director of Sweet Honey in the Rock, an internationally*
> *acclaimed African-American women's a cappella quintet, whose repertoire spe-*
> *cialty is African-American song and singing traditions. Reagon's most recent*
> *research includes documentation of early twentieth century gospel repertoire and*
> *performance traditions and of nineteenth-century worship traditions as practiced*
> *in churches in Southwest Georgia and in prayer bands formed in the Baltimore-*
> *Washington area after their members migrated from South Carolina in the*
> *1930s and 1940s.*
>
> *Reagon was featured in the 1992 Emmy-nominated "The Songs Are Free:*
> *Bernice Johnson Reagon with Bill Moyers," a 60-minute production of Public*
> *Affairs Television. She has served as music consultant, composer, and performer*
> *for several film and video projects, including the award-winning "Eyes on the*
> *Prize (I)" series; the Emmy-winning "We Shall Overcome," and "Roots of*
> *Resistance: A Story of the Underground Railroad."*

Pre-Reading and Journal-Writing Suggestions

1. Think about a hobby you enjoy: reading, singing, jogging, playing an instrument, dancing, drawing. Write about your experience when you do this hobby alone. Now write about how this experience changes (or might change) when you share it with another person. For example, what's the difference between playing a flute alone in your room and playing with another person? A small group? A large orchestra? What are the benefits of being alone? Of being a part of a group?

2. What songs, composers, or specific types of music move your spirit? Think back to an early memory that involves one of your specific choices. How important were the events surrounding this memory to your love of this type of music or selection today?

3. Would the world be any different if people went through life, day after day, without any music, any singing, any melodies, any whistling, any harmony whatsoever? Write about a world in which music has yet to be discovered or a world in which music is banned on the basis that it is a powerful, dangerous force.

In the early 1960's, I was in college at Albany State. My major interests   *1*
were music and biology. In music I was a contralto soloist with the choir,
studying Italian arias and German lieder. The Black music I sang was of
three types:

1) Spirituals sung by the college choir. These were arranged by such
people as Nathaniel Dett and William Dawson and had major injections of
European musical harmony and composition. 2) Rhythm'n'Blues, music
done by and for Blacks in social settings. This included the music of bands
at proms, juke boxes, and football game songs. 3) Church music; gospel was
a major part of Black church music by the time I was in college. I was a
soloist with the gospel choir.

Prior to the gospel choir, introduced in my church when I was twelve,
was many years' experience with unaccompanied music—Black choral singing, hymns, lined out by strong song leaders with full, powerful, richly
ornate congregational responses. These hymns were offset by upbeat, clap-
ping call-and-response songs.

I saw people in church sing and pray until they shouted. I knew *that*
music as a part of a cultural expression that was powerful enough to take
people from their conscious selves to a place where the physical and intellectual being worked in harmony with the spirit. I enjoyed and needed that
experience. The music of the church was an integral part of the cultural
world into which I was born.

Outside of church, I saw music as good, powerful sounds you made   *5*
or listened to. Rhythm and blues—you danced to; music of the college
choir—you clapped after the number was finished.

The Civil Rights Movement changed my view of music. It was after
my first march. I began to sing a song and in the course of singing changed
the song so that it made sense for that particular moment. Although I was
not consciously aware of it, this was one of my earliest experiences with
how my music was supposed to *function*. This music was to be integrative of
and consistent with everything I was doing at that time; it was to be tied to
activities that went beyond artistic affairs such as concerts, dances, and
church meetings.

The next level of awareness came while in jail. I had grown up in a
rural area outside the city limits, riding a bus to public school or driving to
college. My life had been a pretty consistent, balanced blend of church,
school, and proper upbringing. I was aware of a Black educated class that
taught me in high school and college, of taxi cabs I never rode in, and of
people who used buses I never boarded. I went to school with their children.

In jail with me were all these people. All ages. In my section were
women from about thirteen to eighty years old. Ministers' wives and teachers and teachers' wives who had only nodded at me or clapped at a concert
or spoken to my mother. A few people from my classes. A large number of

people who rode segregated city buses. One or two women who had been drinking along the two-block stretch of Little Harlem as the march went by. Very quickly, clashes arose: around age, who would have authority, what was proper behavior?

The Albany Movement was already a singing movement, and we took the songs to jail. There the songs I had sung because they made me feel good or because they said what I thought about a specific issue did something. I would start a song and everybody would join in. After the song, the differences among us would not be as great. Somehow, making a song required an expression of that which was common to us all. The songs did not feel like the same songs I had sung in college. This music was like an instrument, like holding a tool in your hand.

I found that although I was younger than many of the women in my   *10* section of the jail, I was asked to take on leadership roles. First as a song leader and then in most other matters concerning the group, especially in discussions, or when speaking with prison officials.

I fell in love with that kind of music. I saw that to define music as something you listen to, something that pleases you, is very different from defining it as an instrument with which you can drive a point. In both instances, you can have the same song. But using it as an instrument makes it a different kind of music.

The next level of awareness occurred during the first mass meeting after my release from jail. I was asked to lead the song that I had changed after the first march. When I opened my mouth and began to sing, there was a force and power within myself I had never heard before. Somehow this music—music I could use as an instrument to do things with, music that was mine to shape and change so that it made the statement I needed to make—released a kind of power and required a level of concentrated energy I did not know I had. I liked the feeling.

For several years, I worked with the Movement eventually doing Civil Rights songs with the Freedom Singers. The Freedom Singers used the songs, interspersed with narrative, to convey the story of the Civil Rights Movement's struggles. The songs were more powerful than spoken conversation. They became a major way of making people who were not on the scene feel the intensity of what was happening in the south. Hopefully, they would move the people to take a stand, to organize support groups or participate in various projects.

The Georgia Sea Island Singers, whom I first heard at the Newport Festival, were a major link. Bessie Jones, coming from within twenty miles of Albany, Georgia, had a repertoire and song-leading style I recognized from the churches I had grown up in. She, along with John Davis, would talk about songs that Black people had sung as slaves and what those songs meant in terms of their struggle to be free. The songs did not sound like the spirituals I had sung in college choirs; they sounded like the songs I had grown up with in church. There I had been told the songs had to do with worship of Jesus Christ.

The next few years I spent focusing on three components: 1) The music I had found in the Civil Rights Movement. 2) Songs of the Georgia Sea Island Singers and other traditional groups, and the ways in which those songs were linked to the struggles of Black peoples at earlier times. 3) Songs of the church that now sounded like those traditional songs and came close to having, for many people, the same kind of freeing power.

There was another experience that helped to shape my present-day use of music. After getting out of jail, the mother of the church my father pastored was at the mass meeting. She prayed, a prayer I had heard hundreds of times. I had focused on its sound, tune, rhythm, chant, whether the moans came at the proper pace and intensity. That morning I heard every word that she said. She did not have to change one word of prayer she had been praying for much of her Christian life for me to know she was addressing the issues we were facing at that moment. More than her personal prayer, it felt like an analysis of the Albany, Georgia, Black community.

My collection, study, and creation of Black music has been, to a large extent, about freeing the sounds and the words and the messages from casings in which they have been put, about hearing clearly what the music has to say about Black people and their struggle.

When I first began to search, I looked for what was then being called folk music, rather than for other Black forms, such as jazz, rhythm and blues, or gospel. It slowly dawned on me that during the Movement we had used all those forms. When we were relaxing in the office, we made up songs using popular rhythm and blues tunes; songs based in rhythm and blues also came out of jails, especially from the sit-in movement and the march to Selma, Alabama. "Oh Wallace, You Never Can Jail Us All" is an example from Selma. "You Better Leave Segregation Alone" came out of the Nashville Freedom Rides and was based on a bit by Little Willie John, "You Better Leave My Kitten Alone." Gospel choirs became the major musical vehicle in the urban center of Birmingham, with the choir led by Carlton Reese. There was also a gospel choir in the Chicago work, as well as an instrumental ensemble led by Ben Branch.

Jazz had not been a strong part of my musical life. I began to hear it as I traveled north. Thelonious Monk and Charlie Mingus played on the first SNCC benefit at Carnegie Hall. I heard of and then heard Coltrane. Then I began to pick up the pieces that had been laid by Charlie Parker and Coleman Hawkins and whole lifetimes of music. This music had no words. But, it had power, intensity, and movement under various degrees of pressure; it had vocal texture and color. I could feel that the music knew how it felt to be Black and Angry, Black and Down, Black and Loved, Black and Fighting.

I now believe that Black music exists in every place where Black people run, every corner where they live, every level on which they struggle. We have been here a long while, in many situations. It takes all that we have created to sing our song. I believe that Black musicians/artists have a responsibility to be conscious of their world and to let their consciousness be heard in their songs.

And we need it all—blues, gospel, ballads, children's games, dance, rhythms, jazz, lovesongs, topical songs—doing what it has always done. We need Black music that functions in relation to the people and community who provide the nurturing compost that makes its creation and continuation possible.

Suggestions for Writing and Discussion

1. Summarize the different roles that music has played in Reagon's life. Then explain what these roles suggest about her character and her values.
2. In paragraph 9, Reagon writes that "the music was like an instrument, like holding a tool in your hand." She repeats this comparison throughout the essay. Find several other references to music as an instrument and analyze what this comparison implies about music as well as the musician.
3. Why, in paragraph 10, do the women in jail ask Reagon to take on the role of leader, even though she was one of the youngest women there? Do you think she has strong leadership qualities? Explain. As you write, consider that your audience is a group of young women (ages sixteen to eighteen) who have been chosen to attend a statewide leadership conference. Your purpose is to give them ideas for thinking about leadership to read before they attend the conference.
4. According to Reagon, music is a powerful, moving force within the black community. How does Reagon define black music? Do you agree with her definition? According to her definition, how is black music different from, or similar to, other types of music, such as country and western, classical, pop-rock, and Muzak?
5. As Reagon implies, music can be used for several purposes. After you identify some of these purposes, consider another artistic expression that shares these same levels of purpose.
6. What might be Reagon's purpose in writing this piece? For what specific audience, if any, is this essay intended? Explain your answers.

Suggestions for Extended Thinking and Writing

1. Research the historical roots of a specific type of black music, such as gospel, jazz, spirituals, or rap. Applying Reagon's theme that music is a powerful, moving force, what specific issues or values within the historical context are being "moved"? In other words, what part does music play in the problems, conflicts, issues, and conquests of the times?
2. Research the life, times, influences, and artistic achievements of a specific black musician, living or dead. Besides taking a strict library approach to

this topic, list and respond to several works by this artist. In addition, conduct several interviews or survey a number of your fellow students, friends, and relatives to discover their responses to this musician and his or her music. Explain what you have discovered through your research.

3. John Ciardi, a noted poet and teacher, believed that if students wanted to understand poetry, they only had to know one great poem well. Applying this same principle to music, choose one musical selection that represents the kind of music you love best. Learn this piece well inside and out. Your learning process may involve playing an instrument, or you might choose simply to listen to the music on tape or CD. In an oral presentation (or a brief paper accompanied by a tape) teach an appreciation of this song to your peers and your instructor, and explain why you chose this selection.

NORA EPHRON

People *Magazine*

Born in New York in 1941 and transplanted to Beverly Hills at the age of three, Nora Ephron grew up in the Hollywood world of her screenwriter parents, Phoebe and Henry Ephron, whose credits include Carousel, There's No Business Like Show Business, *and* What Price Glory? *After earning degrees at Wellesley and Briarcliffe, she pursued a career as a journalist and novelist and is perhaps best known for* Heartburn, *a fictionalized account of her marriage to, and divorce from,* Washington Post *writer Carl Bernstein. Ephron began her career as a writer by working as a reporter for the* New York Post. *She later joined the staff of* Esquire *magazine, where she wrote the "Women" column from 1972 through 1973. She has published two collections of essays, as well as a nonfiction book,* Scribble, Scribble: Notes on the Media. *In addition, she coauthored (with Alice Arden) the screenplay for* Silkwood *and in 1989 wrote the much-praised script for* When Harry Met Sally; *both were nominated for Academy Awards. Most recently Ephron has gained acclaim as director of* Sleepless in Seattle.

Pre-Reading and Journal-Writing Suggestions

1. Explain your favorite magazine to someone who has never seen it. In your explanation, consider telling who the target audience is, what most of the articles are about, why you buy the magazine, and so on. Your purpose is to convince this person to buy a copy of the magazine.
2. Imagine you have the choice of reading a magazine of your choice or a classic novel in class. Which choice do you make, and why?

The people over at *People* get all riled up if anyone suggests that *People*   *1*
is a direct descendant of anything at all. You do not even have to suggest that it is; the first words anyone over there says, *insists*, really, is that *People* is *not* a spin-off of the *Time* "People" section (which they are right about), and that it is *not* a reincarnation of *Life* (which they are, at least in part, wrong about). *People,* they tell you, is an original thing. Distinctive. Different. Unto itself. They make it sound a lot like a cigarette.

People was introduced by Time Inc. a year ago, and at last reports it was selling 1,250,000 copies a week, all of them on newsstands. It is the first national weekly that has been launched since *Sports Illustrated* in 1954, and it will probably lose some three million dollars in its first year, a sum that fazes no one at Time Inc., since it is right on target. *Sports Illustrated* lost twenty-six million in the ten years before it turned the corner, and *People* is expected to lose considerably less and turn the corner considerably quicker. There is probably something to be said for all this—something about how healthy it is for the magazine business that a thing like this is happening, a new magazine with good prospects and no nudity that interests over a million readers a week—but I'm not sure that I am the person who is going to say it. *People* makes me grouchy, and I have been trying for months to figure out why. I do read it. I read it in the exact way its editors intend me to—straight through without stopping. I buy it in airline terminals, and I find that if I start reading it at the moment I am seated on the Eastern shuttle, it lasts until shortly before takeoff. This means that its time span is approximately five minutes longer than the *New York Post* on a day with a good Rose Franzblau column, and five minutes less than *Rona Barrett's Gossip,* which in any case is not available at the Eastern shuttle terminal in La Guardia Airport.

My problem with the magazine is not that I think it is harmful or dangerous or anything of the sort. It's almost not worth getting upset about. It's a potato chip. A snack. Empty calories. Which would be fine, really—I like potato chips. But they make you feel lousy afterward too.

People is a product of something called the Magazine Development Group at Time Inc., which has been laboring for several years to come up with new magazines and has brought forth *Money* and two rejected dummy magazines, one on photography, the other on show business. The approach this group takes is a unique one in today's magazine business: Most magazines tend to be about a sensibility rather than a subject, and tend to be dominated not by a group but by one editor and his or her concept of what that sensibility is. In any event, the idea for *People*—which was a simple, five-word idea: let's-call-a-magazine-*People*—started kicking around the halls of Time Inc. a couple of years ago. Some people, mainly Clare Boothe Luce, think it originated with Clare Boothe Luce; others seem to lean toward a great-idea-whose-time-has-come theory, not unlike the Big Bang, and they say that if anyone thought of it at all (which they are not sure of), it was Andrew Heiskell, Time Inc.'s chairman of the board. But the credit probably belongs, in some transcendental way, to Kierkegaard, who in 1846 said that in time, all anyone would be interested in was gossip.

From the beginning, *People* was conceived as an inexpensive maga-   5
zine—cheap to produce and cheap to buy. There would be a small staff. Low overhead. Stringers. No color photographs except for the cover. It was intended to be sold only on newsstands—thus eliminating the escalating cost of mailing the magazine to subscribers and mailing the subscribers reminders to renew their subscriptions. It was clear that the magazine would have to have a very strong appeal for women; an increasing proportion of newsstands in this country are in supermarkets. Its direct competitor for rack space at the check-out counter was the *National Enquirer.* A pilot issue of the magazine, with Richard Burton and Elizabeth Taylor on the cover, was produced in August, 1973, and test-marketed in seven cities, and it is the

pride of the Time Inc. marketing department that this was done in the exact way Procter & Gamble introduces a new toilet paper. When Malcolm B. Ochs, marketing director of the Magazine Development Group at Time Inc., speaks about *People,* he talks about selling "packaged goods" and "one million units a week" and "perishable products." This sort of talk is not really surprising—I have spent enough time around magazine salesmen to know they would all be more comfortable selling tomatoes—but it is nonetheless a depressing development.

The second major decision that was arrived at early on was to keep the stories short. "We always want to leave people wishing for more," says Richard B. Stolley, *People*'s managing editor. This is a perfectly valid editorial slogan, but what Stolley does not seem willing to admit is the reason for it, which is that *People* is essentially a magazine for people who don't like to read. The people at *People* seem to believe that people who read *People* have the shortest attention spans in the world. *Time* and *Life* started out this way too, but both of them managed to rise above their original intentions.

The incarnation of *Life* that *People* most resembles is not the early era, where photographs dominated, nor even the middle-to-late period, when the photography and journalism struck a nice balance, but the last desperate days, when Ralph Graves was trying to save the magazine from what turned out to be its inevitable death. This is not the time to go into Graves's most serious and abhorrent editorial decision, which was to eliminate the *Life* Great Dinners series; what I want to talk about instead is his decision to shorten the articles. There are people over at the Time-Life Building, defenders of Graves, who insist he did this for reasons of economy—there was no room for long pieces in a magazine that was losing advertising and therefore editorial pages—but Graves himself refuses to be so defended. He claims he shortened the articles because he believes in short articles. And the result, in the case of *Life,* was a magazine that did nothing terribly well.

People has this exact quality—and I'm not exactly sure why. I have nothing against short articles, and no desire to read more than 1500 words or so on most of the personalities *People* profiles. In fact, in the case of a number of those personalities—and here the name of Telly Savalas springs instantly to mind—a caption would suffice. I have no quarrel with the writing in the magazine, which is slick and perfectly competent. I wouldn't mind if *People* were just a picture magazine, if I could at least see the pictures; there is an indefinable something in its art direction that makes the magazine look remarkably like the centerfold of the *Daily News.* And I wouldn't even mind if it were a fan magazine for grownups—if it delivered the goods. But the real problem is that when I finish reading *People,* I always feel that I have just spent four days in Los Angeles. *Women's Wear Daily* at least makes me feel dirty; *People* makes me feel that I haven't read or learned or seen anything at all. I don't think this is what Richard Stolley means when he says he wants to leave his readers wanting more: I tend to be left feeling that I haven't gotten anything in the first place. And even this feeling is hard to pinpoint; I am looking at a recent issue of *People,* with Hugh Hefner on the cover, and I can't really say I didn't learn anything in it: On page 6 it says that Hefner told his unauthorized biographer that he once had a homosexual experience. I didn't actually know that before reading *People,* but somehow it doesn't surprise me.

Worst of all—yes, there is a worst of all—I end up feeling glutted with celebrity. I stopped reading movie magazines in the beauty parlor a couple of years ago because I could not accommodate any more information about something called the Lennon Sisters. I had got to the point where I thought I knew what celebrity was—celebrity was anyone I would stand up in a restaurant and stare at. I had whittled the list down to Marlon Brando, Mary Tyler Moore and Angelo "Gyp" DeCarlo, and I was fairly happy. Now I am confronted with *People,* and the plain fact is that a celebrity is anyone *People* writes about; I know the magazine is filling some nameless, bottomless pit of need for gossip and names, but I haven't got room in my life for so many lights.

People's only serious financial difficulty at this point is in attracting advertisers, and one of the reasons the people at *People* think they are having trouble doing so is that their advertisers don't know who the *People* reader is. Time Inc. has issued a demographic survey which shows that *People*'s readers are upscale, whatever that means, and that 48 percent of them have been to college. I never believe these surveys—*Playboy* and *Penthouse* have them, and theirs show that their readers are mainly interested in the fine fiction; in any case, I suspect that *People*'s real problem with advertisers is not that they don't know exactly who's reading the magazine, but that they know exactly who's reading it. In one recent issue there are three liquor ads—for Seagram's Seven Crown, Jim Beam and a bottled cocktail called the Brass Monkey, all of them brands bought predominantly by the blue-collar middle class. It's logical that these brands would buy space in *People*—liquor companies can't advertise on television. But any product that could would probably do better to reach nonreaders through the mass-market women's magazines, which at least sit around all month, or on television itself.

"The human element really is being neglected in national reporting," says Richard Stolley. "The better newspapers and magazines deal more and more with events and issues and debates. The human beings caught up in them simply get squelched. If we can bring a human being out of a massive event, then we've done what I want to do." I don't really object to this philosophy—I'm not sure that I agree with it, but I don't object to it. But it seems a shame that so much of the reporting of the so-called human element in *People* is aimed at the lowest common denominator of the also-so-called human element, that all this coverage of humanity has to be at the expense of the issues and events and ideas involved. It seems even sadder that there seems to be no stopping it. *People* is the future, and it works, and that makes me grouchiest of all.

Suggestions for Writing and Discussion

1. In your own words, summarize Nora Ephron's objections to *People* magazine. Write this summary by showing how you think Nora Ephron would complete the sentence "For me, the trouble with *People* magazine is . . . ."

2. As you were reading this piece, did you get the impression that Ephron was writing in a fair, unbiased manner? Support your impression with a few examples from the text.

3. In general, why do you think *People* is such a success in America? Do you think it would have the same appeal in another country, such as Japan or China? Please explain.

4. Ephron writes that Americans are obsessed with celebrities and famous people. Do you agree with her viewpoint? Please explain your answer with specific, personal observations.

5. Read an article in *People* magazine about a topic that has also been covered in news magazines such as *Time* and *Newsweek*. Compare the article in *People* with an article on the same subject in a news magazine. Write an essay explaining the differences you observed and commenting on what you learned from observing these differences. As you write, imagine that you will be sending a copy of your essay to *People* as well as to *Time* or *Newsweek*. Your purpose is to convince the editors to consider your point of view as they plan their coverage of current events.

Suggestions for Extended Thinking and Writing

1. After reading Ephron's article, examine your own favorite magazine. Then write an essay in which you evaluate the significance of the articles in this magazine. Are they substantial or are they, as Ephron might say, merely "snack food"?

2. Conduct a survey among different groups on your college campus to discover who today's heroes are. After collecting your data, write an essay in which you come to some conclusions about what types of people students hold in esteem.

PAUL ARONOWITZ

A Brother's Dreams

> *While he was a medical student at Case Western Reserve University, Paul Aronowitz wrote this moving essay, showing the different worlds he and his schizophrenic brother inhabit and describing his own growing understanding of his brother's situation. "A Brother's Dreams" was first published in the* New York Times Magazine's *weekly "About Men" column.*

Pre-Reading and Journal-Writing Suggestions

1. A journal is a place for big dreams. Write about your wildest dreams, your greatest desires.
2. Write about a time you felt uncomfortable or even ashamed to be around someone you knew: a friend, perhaps, or a family member. Or write about a time someone you knew felt ashamed or uncomfortable to be around you.
3. Which handicap do you think you would have a harder time handling: a mental handicap or a physical one? Please explain.

Each time I go home to see my parents at their house near Pough-   1
keepsie, N.Y., my brother, a schizophrenic for almost nine years now, comes to visit from the halfway house where he lives nearby. He owns a car that my parents help him to maintain, and his food and washing are taken care of by the halfway house. Somewhere, somehow along the way, with the support of a good physician, a social worker and my ever-resilient parents, he has managed to carve a niche for himself, to bite off some independence and, with it, elusive dreams that, to any healthy person, might seem trivial.

My brother sits in a chair across from me, chain-smoking cigarettes, trying to take the edge off the medications he'll be on for the rest of his life. Sometimes his tongue hangs loosely from his mouth when he's listening or pops out of his mouth as he speaks—a sign of tardive dyskinesia, an often-irreversible side effect of his medication.

He draws deeply on his cigarette and tells me he can feel his mind healing—cells being replaced, tissue being restored, thought processes returning. He knows this is happening because he dreams of snakes, and hot, acrid places in which he suffocates if he moves too fast. When he wakes, the birds are singing in the trees outside his bedroom window. They imitate people in his halfway house, mocking them and calling their names. The birds are so smart, he tells me, so much smarter than we are.

His face, still handsome despite its puffiness (another side effect of the medications that allow him to function outside the hospital), and warm brown eyes are serious. When I look into his eyes I imagine I can see some of the suffering he has been through. I think of crossed wires, of receptors and neurotransmitters, deficits and surpluses, progress and relapse, and I wonder, once again, what has happened to my brother.

My compassion for him is recent. For many years, holidays, once *5* happy occasions for our family of seven to gather together, were emotional torture sessions. My brother would pace back and forth in the dining room, lecturing us, his voice loud, dominating, crushing all sound but his own, about the end of the world, the depravity of our existences. His speeches were salted with paranoid delusions: our house was bugged by the F.B.I.; my father was Josef Mengele; my mother was selling government secrets to the Russians.

His life was decaying before my eyes, and I couldn't stand to listen to him. My resentment of him grew as his behavior became more disruptive and aggressive. I saw him as being ultimately responsible for his behavior. As my anger increased, I withdrew from him, avoiding him when I came home to visit from college, refusing to discuss the bizarre ideas he brought up over the dinner table. When I talked with my sister or other two brothers about him, our voices always shadowed in whispers, I talked of him as of a young man who had chosen to spend six months of every year in a pleasant, private hospital on the banks of the Hudson River, chosen to alienate his family with threats, chosen to withdraw from the stresses of the world. I hated what he had become. In all those years, I never asked what his diagnosis was.

Around the fifth year of his illness, things finally changed. One hot summer night, he attacked my father. When I came to my father's aid, my brother broke three of my ribs and nearly strangled me. The State Police came and took him away. My father's insurance coverage had run out on my brother, so this time he was taken to a locked ward at the state hospital where heavily sedated patients wandered aimlessly in stockinged feet up and down long hallways. Like awakening from a bad dream, we gradually began talking about his illness. Slowly and painfully, I realized that he wasn't responsible for his disease any more than a cancer patient is for his pain.

As much as I've learned to confront my brother's illness, it frightens me to think that one day, my parents gone from the scene, my siblings and I will be responsible for portions of my brother's emotional and financial support. This element of the future is one we still avoid discussing, much the way we avoided thinking about the nature of his disease and his prognosis. I'm still not capable of thinking about it.

Now I come home and listen to him, trying not to react, trying not to show disapproval. His delusions are harmless and he is, at the very least, communicating. When he asks me about medical school, I answer with a sentence or two—no elaboration, no revelations about the dreams I cradle in my heart.

He talks of his own dreams. He hopes to finish his associate's degree— *10* the same one he has been working on between hospitalizations for almost eight years now—at the local community college. Next spring, with luck, he'll get a job. His boss will be understanding, he tells me, cutting him a little slack when he has his "bad days," letting him have a day off here or there when things aren't going well. He puts out his cigarette and lights another one.

Time stands still. This could be last year, or the year before, or the year before that. I'm within range of becoming a physician, of realizing something I've been working toward for almost five years, while my brother still dreams of having a small job, living in his own apartment and of being well. As the smoke flows from his nose and mouth, I recall an evening some time ago when I drove upstate from Manhattan to tell my parents and my brother that I was getting married (an engagement later severed). My brother's eyes lit up at the news, and then a darkness fell over them.

"What's wrong?" I asked him.

"It's funny," he answered matter-of-factly, "You're getting married, and I've never even had a girlfriend." My mother's eyes filled with tears, and she turned away. She was trying her best to be happy for me, for the dreams I had—for the dreams so many of us take for granted.

"You still have us," I stammered, reaching toward him and touching his arm. All of a sudden my dreams meant nothing; I didn't deserve them and they weren't worth talking about. My brother shrugged his shoulders, smiled and shook my hand, his large, tobacco-stained fingers wrapping around my hand, dwarfing my hand.

Suggestions for Writing and Discussion

1. After reading this piece, what's your initial reaction to the author? What kind of person do you think he is? If you met him, would you like him? Why or why not?

2. Aronowitz writes that during one point in his life, he was resentful of his brother's behavior. What is your response to this reaction? Please explain.

3. After reading this piece, how would you characterize a person who has schizophrenia? As you explain what you have learned, imagine that the members of your audience have heard of schizophrenia but know very little about it. Your purpose is to help them understand the complex issues surrounding this mental illness.

4. What, if anything, did you learn or discover as you read this piece?

5. Go back to Aronowitz's piece and select the one paragraph that you enjoyed the most. Then go back and choose the one line that moved you the most. Briefly explain why you chose these two specific parts of this writing.

6. Paul's brother's schizophrenic behavior set him apart from others who were not suffering from this illness. In varying extremes, we all suffer from moments of feeling different, either because of our life experiences or for some other reason. Write a personal narrative about a time you felt different or misunderstood.

Suggestions for Extended Thinking and Writing

1. Why do some people reach their dreams while others only flounder? Contrast any other selection in this section with Paul's brother's experience as you explore this question.
2. Compare Paul's relationship with his brother with any other family relationship from the Parents and Children section (pp. 117–153).

TOSHIO MORI

Abalone, Abalone, Abalone

> *Born in California, Toshio Mori began his career as an author in his late teens. Drawing on his Japanese-American heritage, he has written several books, including* Yokohama, California *(1949),* The Chauvinist and Other Stories *(1979), and* The Woman from Hiroshima *(1979). He has published essays and short stories in such magazines as* New Directions *and* Writer's Forum.

Pre-Reading and Journal-Writing Suggestions

1. Freewrite about someone who has shared a hobby or an interest with you. This could be a grandmother teaching you to knit or make cookies or a friend who shared a baseball card collection with you. Whatever it is, keep writing for twenty minutes on this person and this hobby.
2. Write about a special family tradition that is rooted in your family's heritage.
3. At one time or another, most people make a hobby of collecting something. If you've had this experience, write about it now. Explain how you got started and what this collection means to you. If you have not had this experience, write about what you would collect if you had the chance.

Before Mr. Abe went away I used to see him quite often at his nursery. 1
He was a carnation grower just as I am one today. At noontime I used to go to his front porch and look at his collection of abalone shells.

They were lined up side by side against the side of his house on the front porch. I was curious as to why he bothered to collect them. It was a lot of bother polishing them. I had often seen him sit for hours on Sundays and noon hours polishing each one of the shells with the greatest of care. Of course I knew these abalone shells were pretty. When the sun strikes the insides of these shells it is something beautiful to behold. But I could not understand why he continued collecting them when the front porch was practically full.

He used to watch for me every noon hour. When I appeared he would look out of his room and bellow, "Hello, young man!"

"Hello, Abe-*san*," I said. "I came to see the abalone shells."

Then he came out of the house and we sat on the front porch. But he 5
did not tell me why he collected these shells. I think I have asked him dozens of times but each time he closed his mouth and refused to answer.

"Are you going to pass this collection of abalone shells on to your children?" I said.

"No," he said. "I want my children to collect for themselves. I wouldn't give it to them."

"Why?" I said. "When you die?"

Mr. Abe shook his head. "No. Not even when I die," he said. "I couldn't give the children what I see in these shells. The children must go out for themselves and find their own shells."

"Why, I thought this collecting hobby of abalone shells was a simple   *10* affair," I said.

"It is simple. Very simple," he said. But he would not tell me further.

For several years I went steadily to his front porch and looked at the beautiful shells. His collection was getting larger and larger. Mr. Abe sat and talked to me and on each occasion his hands were busy polishing shells.

"So you are still curious?" he said.

"Yes," I said.

One day while I was hauling the old soil from the benches and replac-   *15* ing it with new soil I found an abalone shell half buried in the dust between the benches. So I stopped working. I dropped my wheelbarrow and went to the faucet and washed the abalone shell with soap and water. I had a hard time taking the grime off the surface.

After forty minutes of cleaning and polishing the old shell it became interesting. I began polishing both the outside and the inside of the shell. I found after many minutes of polishing I could not do very much with the exterior side. It had scabs of the sea which would not come off by scrubbing and the surface itself was rough and hard. And in the crevices the grime stuck so that even with a needle it did not become clean.

But on the other side, the inside of the shell, the more I polished the more lustre I found. It had me going. There were colors which I had not seen in the abalone shells before or anywhere else. The different hues, running berserk in all directions, coming together in harmony. I guess I could say they were not unlike a rainbow which men once symbolized. As soon as I thought of this I thought of Mr. Abe.

I remember running to his place, looking for him. "Abe-*san!*" I said when I found him. "I know why you are collecting the abalone shells!"

He was watering the carnation plants in the greenhouse. He stopped watering and came over to where I stood. He looked me over closely for awhile and then his face beamed.

"All right," he said. "Do not say anything. Nothing, mind you. When   *20* you have found the reason why you must collect and preserve them, you do not have to say anything more."

"I want you to see it, Abe-*san*," I said.

"All right. Tonight," he said. "Where did you find it?"

"In my old greenhouse, half buried in the dust," I said.

He chuckled. "That is pretty far from the ocean," he said, "but pretty close to you."

At each noon hour I carried my abalone shell and went over to   25
Mr. Abe's front porch. While I waited for his appearance I kept myself busy
polishing the inside of the shell with a rag.

One day I said, "Abe-*san,* now I have three shells."

"Good!" he said. "Keep it up!"

"I have to keep them all," I said. "They are very much alike and very
much different."

"Well! Well!" he said and smiled.

That was the last I saw of Abe-*san.* Before the month was over he sold   30
his nursery and went back to Japan. He brought his collection along and
thereafter I had no one to talk to at the noon hour. This was before I
discovered the fourth abalone shell, and I should like to see Abe-*san* someday
and watch his eyes roll as he studies me whose face is now akin to the
collectors of shells or otherwise.

Suggestions for Writing and Discussion

1. What's your overall reaction to this selection? Would you consider it one
   of your favorites? Why or why not?
2. In your own words, how would you describe Mr. Abe? How would you
   describe the young boy? How would you describe their relationship?
3. Mr. Abe really has two collections or hobbies: his abalone shells and his
   carnations. What might these flowers and shells tell us about Mr. Abe's
   values?
4. Do you think the young boy finds his first shell purely by chance? Please
   explain.
5. Mr. Abe tells the young boy that even when he dies, he will not give his
   collection away. Do you think this is a selfish reaction on his part? Why
   or why not?
6. After reading this piece, why, would you say, do Mr. Abe and the boy
   collect these shells? Can you identify with this passion they both have for
   collecting shells? Please explain.
7. Look back to the pre-reading exercise about someone who shared his or
   her love of something with you. Write a narrative, based on your notes,
   describing a time when you two were together. As Mori does in his
   story, aim to incorporate dialogue into your essay, aim to describe the
   process of the hobby, as well as the people involved.

Suggestions for Extended Thinking and Writing

1. Write an essay in which you compare your commitment to a hobby or
   activity with that of the young boy in this selection.
2. Conduct an interview with someone you know who has a special hobby
   or interest, and write an essay in which you explain the reasons why this

person became involved with this activity as well as how the person sees
him- or herself as having been changed by commitment to the hobby or
interest.

SUGGESTIONS FOR MAKING CONNECTIONS

1. Analyze the various ways in which art can be conceived, delivered, and
    nourished within various cultures. As you respond, consider "Black
    Music in Our Hands," "Sandra Cisneros: Sneaking Past the Guards,"
    and "Indians in Aspic."
2. Compare the dreams of the brother in Paul Aronowitz's essay with the
    dreams implied by the readers of *People* magazine as it is evaluated by
    Nora Ephron.
3. What do you think it means when someone says that a piece of music,
    a film, a painting, or a book has "artistic truth"? Referring to any of the
    selections here, as well as to your own experiences with music, films,
    art, or literature, develop a definition of *artistic truth*.
4. Compare the artistic processes from at least three of the essays in this
    section.
5. Referring to several selections from this section, as well as to your own
    experiences, analyze art's contribution to people's daily lives.
6. Analyze the importance of a mentor in the process of realizing one's
    dreams. Refer to selections in this section as you write.
7. Where do we get creative ideas? Where do our dreams come from?
    Analyze several of the essays in this section to discover a variety of
    possibilities for the beginnings of an artistic idea.
8. Compare the values and beliefs inherent in three different cultures rep-
    resented in this section.
9. Argue that someone born outside a culture can or cannot come to a
    deeper understanding of the values and beliefs within a certain culture
    by observing its popular works of art.
10. Considering selections in this section, as well as your own observations,
    which do you believe is greater: culture's influence on art and the artist,
    or the artist's influence on the culture?

10
Men and Women

Previews: MEN AND WOMEN

The definitions of woman's roles are as diverse as tribal cultures in the Americas. In some she is devalued, in others she wields considerable power. In some she is a familial/clan adjunct, in some she is as close to autonomous as her economic circumstances and psychological traits permit. But in no tribal definitions is she perceived in the same way as are women in western industrial and postindustrial cultures.

From: *Where I Come from Is Like This,* PAULA GUNN ALLEN

Just so, I recall the points at which some of my boyhood friends were finally seduced by the perception of themselves as tough guys. When a mark cowered and surrendered his money without resistance, myth and reality merged—and paid off. It is, after all, only manly to embrace the power to frighten and intimidate. We, as men, are not supposed to give an inch of our lane on the highway; we are to seize the fighter's edge in work and in play and even in love; we are to be valiant in the face of hostile forces.

From: *Just Walk on By: A Black Man Ponders His Power to Alter Public Space,* BRENT STAPLES

The first thing you do if you want to destroy somebody is rob him of his humanity. If you can persuade yourself that someone is a gook and therefore not a real person, you can kill him rather more easily, burn down his home, separate him from his family. If you can persuade yourself that someone is not really a person but a spade, a Wasp, a kike, a wop, a mick, a fag, a dike, and therefore not a real man or woman, you can more easily hate and hurt him.

From: *"Real" Men and Women,* CHARLES OSGOOD

The new svelte Betty Crocker looks as if she's never tasted an angel food cake, much less a double fudge brownie, and the Campbell kids have lost a lot of their baby-fat bounce. And when was the last time you saw a size 12 model smiling from the pages of a magazine?

If the media message is thin, thin, thin, and if the ordinary person is exposed to 400 to 1,500 advertising messages per day, is it coincidence that medical specialists estimate—conservatively—that 12 percent of college-age females have serious eating disorders?

From: *A Thinly Disguised Message,* DEBORAH MARQUARDT

PAULA GUNN ALLEN

Where I Come from Is Like This

> *Born in Albuquerque, New Mexico, and raised on a Spanish Land Grant, Paula Gunn Allen comes from roots that include both the Laguna Pueblo, Sioux, and Lebanese-Jewish cultures. An acclaimed essayist, poet, and fiction writer, Allen's best-known novel is* The Woman Who Owned the Shadows *(1983). She has taught Native American and ethnic studies at the University of California, Berkeley.*
>
> *In* The Sacred Hoop *(1986), her book-length study of the feminine aspect of Native American traditions, Allen explains the power of language in a culture in which women were revered as teachers and storytellers:*
>
> > *The tribes seek through song, ceremony, legend, sacred stories (myths), and tales to embody, articulate, and share reality, to bring the isolated self into harmony and balance with this reality, to verbalize the sense of the majesty and the reverent mystery of all things, and to actualize, in language, those truths of being and experience that give humanity its greatest significance and dignity.*
>
> *As Allen notes in this essay, many Native American tribes accorded women special respect, as reflected in their creation myths. The Judeo-Christian idea that woman was made from man is not found in most Native American religions; instead, their creation stories suggest that male and female came into being simultaneously. Each was accorded particular powers and characteristics. Neither held supreme power; they were interdependent.*

Pre-Reading and Journal-Writing Suggestions

1. In your journal, freewrite for twenty minutes by completing the statement "Where I come from is like . . . ."
2. Set a timer for three minutes and look at yourself in a mirror until the timer rings. Next sit down and describe who you saw in that mirror and what you thought about as you studied your physical image.

I

Modern American Indian women, like their non-Indian sisters, are   *1*
deeply engaged in the struggle to redefine themselves. In their struggle they must reconcile traditional tribal definitions of women with industrial and postindustrial non-Indian definitions. Yet while these definitions seem to be more or less mutually exclusive, Indian women must somehow harmonize and integrate both in their own lives.

An American Indian woman is primarily defined by her tribal identity. In her eyes, her destiny is necessarily that of her people, and her sense of herself as a woman is first and foremost prescribed by her tribe. The definitions of woman's roles are as diverse as tribal cultures in the Americas. In some she is devalued, in others she wields considerable power. In some she is a familial/clan adjunct, in some she is as close to autonomous as her economic circumstances and psychological traits permit. But in no tribal definitions is she perceived in the same way as are women in western industrial and postindustrial cultures.

In the west, few images of women form part of the cultural mythos, and these are largely sexually charged. Among Christians, the madonna is the female prototype, and she is portrayed as essentially passive: her contribution is simply that of birthing. Little else is attributed to her and she certainly possesses few of the characteristics that are attributed to mythic figures among Indian tribes. This image is countered (rather than balanced) by the witch-goddess/whore characteristics designed to reinforce cultural beliefs about women, as well as western adversarial and dualistic perceptions of reality.

The tribes see women variously, but they do not question the power of femininity. Sometimes they see women as fearful, sometimes peaceful, sometimes omnipotent and omniscient, but they never portray women as mindless, helpless, simple, or oppressed. And while the women in a given tribe, clan, or band may be all these things, the individual woman is provided with a variety of images of women from the interconnected supernatural, natural, and social worlds she lives in.

As a half-breed American Indian woman, I cast about in my mind for negative images of Indian women, and I find none that are directed to Indian women alone. The negative images I do have are of Indians in general and in fact are more often of males than of females. All these images come to me from non-Indian sources, and they are always balanced by a positive image. My ideas of womanhood, passed on largely by my mother and grandmothers, Laguna Pueblo women, are about practicality, strength, reasonableness, intelligence, wit, and competence. I also remember vividly the women who came to my father's store, the women who held me and sang to me, the women at Feast Day, at Grab Days, the women in the kitchen of my Cubero home, the women I grew up with; none of them appeared weak or helpless, none of them presented herself tentatively. I remember a certain reserve on those lovely brown faces; I remember the direct gaze of eyes framed by bright-colored shawls draped over their heads and cascading down their backs. I remember the clean cotton dresses and carefully pressed hand-embroidered aprons they always wore; I remember laughter and good food, especially the sweet bread and the oven bread they gave us. Nowhere in my mind is there a foolish woman, a dumb woman, a vain woman, or a plastic woman, though the Indian women I have known have shown a wide range of personal style and demeanor.

My memory includes the Navajo woman who was badly beaten by her Sioux husband; but I also remember that my grandmother abandoned her Sioux husband long ago. I recall the stories about the Laguna woman beaten regularly by her husband in the presence of her children so that the children would not believe in the strength and power of femininity. And I remember the women who drank, who got into fights with other women and with the men, and who often won those battles. I have memories of tired women, partying women, stubborn women, sullen women, amicable women, selfish women, shy women, and aggressive women. Most of all I remember the women who laugh and scold and sit uncomplaining in the long sun on feast days and who cook wonderful food on wood stoves, in beehive mud ovens, and over open fires outdoors.

Among the images of women that come to me from various tribes as well as my own are White Buffalo Woman, who came to the Lakota long ago and brought them the religion of the Sacred Pipe which they still practice; Tinotzin the goddess who came to Juan Diego to remind him that she still walked the hills of her people and sent him with her message, her demand and her proof to the Catholic bishop in the city nearby. And from Laguna I take the images of Yellow Woman, Coyote Woman, Grandmother Spider (Spider Old Woman), who brought the light, who gave us weaving and medicine, who gave us life. Among the Keres she is known as Thought Woman who created us all and who keeps us in creation even now. I remember Iyatiku, Earth Woman, Corn Woman, who guides and counsels the people to peace and who welcomes us home when we cast off this coil of flesh as huskers cast off the leaves that wrap the corn. I remember Iyatiku's sister, Sun Woman, who held metals and cattle, pigs and sheep, highways and engines and so many things in her bundle, who went away to the east saying that one day she would return.

II

Since the coming of the Anglo-Europeans beginning in the fifteenth century, the fragile web of identity that long held tribal people secure has gradually been weakened and torn. But the oral tradition has prevented the complete destruction of the web, the ultimate disruption of tribal ways. The oral tradition is vital; it heals itself and the tribal web by adapting to the flow of the present while never relinquishing its connection to the past. Its adaptability has always been required, as many generations have experienced. Certainly the modern American Indian woman bears slight resemblance to her forebears—at least on superficial examination—but she is still a tribal woman in her deepest being. Her tribal sense of relationship to all that is continues to flourish. And though she is at times beset by her knowledge of the enormous gap between the life she lives and the life she was raised to live, and while she adapts her mind and being to the circumstances of her present life, she does so in tribal ways, mending the tears in the web of being from which she takes her existence as she goes.

My mother told me stories all the time, though I often did not recognize them as that. My mother told me stories about cooking and childbearing; she told me stories about menstruation and pregnancy; she told me stories about gods and heroes, about fairies and elves, about goddesses and spirits; she told me stories about the land and the sky, about cats and dogs, about snakes and spiders; she told me stories about climbing trees and exploring the mesas; she told me stories about going to dances and getting married; she told me stories about dressing and undressing, about sleeping and waking; she told me stories about herself, about her mother, about her grandmother. She told me stories about grieving and laughing, about thinking and doing; she told me stories about school and about people; about darning and mending; she told me stories about turquoise and about gold; she told me European stories and Laguna stories; she told me Catholic stories and Presbyterian stories; she told me city stories and country stories; she told me political stories and religious stories. She told me stories about living and stories about dying. And in all of those stories she told me who I was, who I was supposed to be, whom I came from, and who would follow me. In this way she taught me the meaning of the words she said, that all life is a circle and everything has a place within it. That's what she said and what she showed me in the things she did and the way she lives.

Of course, through my formal, white, Christian education, I discov- *10* ered that other people had stories of their own—about women, about Indians, about fact, about reality—and I was amazed by a number of startling suppositions that others made about tribal customs and beliefs. According to the un-Indian, non-Indian view, for instance, Indians barred menstruating women from ceremonies and indeed segregated them from the rest of the people, consigning them to some space specially designed for them. This showed that Indians considered menstruating women unclean and not fit to enjoy the company of decent (nonmenstruating) people, that is, men. I was surprised and confused to hear this because my mother had taught me that white people had strange attitudes toward menstruation: they thought something was bad about it, that it meant you were sick, cursed, sinful, and weak and that you had to be very careful during that time. She taught me that menstruation was a normal occurrence, that I could go swimming or hiking or whatever else I wanted to do during my period. She actively scorned women who took to their beds, who were incapacitated by cramps, who "got the blues."

As I struggled to reconcile these very contradictory interpretations of American Indians' traditional beliefs concerning menstruation, I realized that the menstrual taboos were about power, not about sin or filth. My conclusion was later borne out by some tribes' own explanations, which, as you may well imagine, came as quite a relief to me.

The truth of the matter as many Indians see it is that women who are at the peak of their fecundity are believed to possess power that throws male power totally out of kilter. They emit such force that, in their presence, any male-owned or -dominated ritual or sacred object cannot do its usual task. For instance, the Lakota say that a menstruating woman anywhere near a yuwipi man, who is a special sort of psychic, spirit-empowered healer, for a day or so before he is to do his ceremony will effectively disempower him. Conversely, among many, if not most, tribes, important ceremonies cannot be held without the presence of women. Sometimes the ritual woman who empowers the ceremony must be unmarried and virginal so that the power she channels is unalloyed, unweakened by sexual arousal and penetration by a male. Other ceremonies require tumescent women, others the presence of mature women who have borne children, and still others depend for empowerment on postmenopausal women. Women may be segregated from the company of the whole band or village on certain occasions, but on certain occasions men are also segregated. In short, each ritual depends on a certain balance of power, and the positions of women within the phases of womanhood are used by tribal people to empower certain rites. This does not derive from a male-dominant view; it is not a ritual observance imposed on women by men. It derives from a tribal view of reality that distinguishes tribal people from feudal and industrial people.

Among the tribes, the occult power of women, inextricably bound to our hormonal life, is thought to be very great; many hold that we possess innately the blood-given power to kill—with a glance, with a step, or with a judicious mixing of menstrual blood into somebody's soup. Medicine women among the Pomo of California cannot practice until they are sufficiently mature; when they are immature, their power is diffuse and is likely to interfere with their practice until time and experience have it under control. So women of the tribes are not especially inclined to see themselves as poor helpless victims of male domination. Even in those tribes where something akin to male domination was present, women are perceived as powerful, socially, physically, and metaphysically. In times past, as in times present, women carried enormous burdens with aplomb. We were far indeed from the "weaker sex," the designation that white aristocratic sisters unhappily earned for us all.

I remember my mother moving furniture all over the house when she wanted it changed. She didn't wait for my father to come home and help— she just went ahead and moved the piano, a huge upright from the old days, the couch, the refrigerator. Nobody had told her she was too weak to do such things. In imitation of her, I would delight in loading trucks at my father's store with cases of pop or fifty-pound sacks of flour. Even when I was quite small I could do it, and it gave me a belief in my own physical strength that advancing middle age can't quite erase. My mother used to tell me about the Acoma Pueblo women she had seen as a child carrying huge ollas (water pots) on their heads as they wound their way up the tortuous stairwell carved into the face of the "Sky City" mesa, a feat I tried to imitate with books and tin buckets. ("Sky City" is the term used by the Chamber of Commerce for the mother village of Acoma, which is situated atop a high sandstone table mountain.) I was never very successful, but even the attempt reminded me that I was supposed to be strong and balanced to be a proper girl.

Of course, my mother's Laguna people are Keres Indian, reputed to be   15 the last extreme mother-right people on earth. So it is no wonder that I got notably nonwhite notions about the natural strength and prowess of women. Indeed, it is only when I am trying to get non-Indian approval, recognition, or acknowledgment that my "weak sister" emotional and intellectual ploys get the better of my tribal woman's good sense. At such times I forget that I just moved the piano or just wrote a competent paper or just completed a financial transaction satisfactorily or have supported myself and my children for most of my adult life.

Nor is my contradictory behavior atypical. Most Indian women I know are in the same bicultural bind: we vacillate between being dependent and strong, self-reliant and powerless, strongly motivated and hopelessly insecure. We resolve the dilemma in various ways: some of us party all the time; some of us drink to excess; some of us travel and move around a lot; some of us land good jobs and then quit them; some of us engage in violent exchanges; some of us blow our brains out. We act in these destructive ways because we suffer from the societal conflicts caused by having to identify with two hopelessly opposed cultural definitions of women. Through this destructive dissonance we are unhappy prey to the self-disparagement common to, indeed demanded of, Indians living in the United States today. Our situation is caused by the exigencies of a history of invasion, conquest, and colonization whose searing marks are probably ineradicable. A popular bumper sticker on many Indian cars proclaims: "If You're Indian You're In," to which I always find myself adding under my breath, "Trouble."

III

No Indian can grow to any age without being informed that her people were "savages" who interfered with the march of progress pursued by respectable, loving, civilized white people. We are the villains of the scenario when we are mentioned at all. We are absent from much of white history except when we are calmly, rationally, succinctly, and systematically dehumanized. On the few occasions we are noticed in any way other than as howling, bloodthirsty beings, we are acclaimed for our noble quaintness. In this definition, we are exotic curios. Our ancient arts and customs are used to draw tourist money to state coffers, into the pocketbooks and bank accounts of scholars, and into support of the American-in-Disneyland promoters' dream.

As a Roman Catholic child I was treated to bloody tales of how the savage Indians martyred the hapless priests and missionaries who went among them in an attempt to lead them to the one true path. By the time I was through high school I had the idea that Indians were people who had benefited mightily from the advanced knowledge and superior morality of the Anglo-Europeans. At least I had, perforce, that idea to lay beside the other one that derived from my daily experience of Indian life, an idea less dehumanizing and more accurate because it came from my mother and the other Indian people who raised me. That idea was that Indians are a people who don't tell lies, who care for their children and their old people. You never see an Indian orphan, they said. You always know when you're old that someone will take care of you—one of your children will. Then they'd list the old folks who were being taken care of by this child or that. No child is ever considered illegitimate among the Indians, they said. If a girl gets pregnant, the baby is still part of the family, and the mother is too. That's what they said, and they showed me real people who lived according to those principles.

Of course the ravages of colonization have taken their toll; there are orphans in Indian country now, and abandoned, brutalized old folks; there are even illegitimate children, though the very concept still strikes me as absurd. There are battered children and neglected children, and there are battered wives and women who have been raped by Indian men. Proximity to the "civilizing" effects of white Christians has not improved the moral quality of life in Indian country, though each group, Indian and white, explains the situation differently. Nor is there much yet in the oral tradition that can enable us to adapt to these inhuman changes. But a force is growing in that direction, and it is helping Indian women reclaim their lives. Their power, their sense of direction and of self will soon be visible. It is the force of the women who speak and work and write, and it is formidable.

Through all the centuries of war and death and cultural and psychic destruction have endured the women who raise the children and tend the fires, who pass along the tales and the traditions, who weep and bury the dead, who are the dead, and who never forget. There are always the women, who make pots and weave baskets, who fashion clothes and cheer their children on at powwow, who make fry bread and piki bread, and corn soup and chili stew, who dance and sing and remember and hold within their hearts the dream of their ancient peoples—that one day the woman who thinks will speak to us again, and everywhere there will be peace. Meanwhile we tell the stories and write the books and trade tales of anger and woe and stories of fun and scandal and laugh over all manner of things that happen every day. We watch and we wait.

My great-grandmother told my mother: Never forget you are Indian. And my mother told me the same thing. This, then, is how I have gone about remembering, so that my children will remember too.

Suggestions for Writing and Discussion

1. Allen believes that Indian women, like other women, must strive for harmony between traditional roles and those of modern society. What part of the traditional Indian role does Allen want to embrace? What new characteristics does she think the Indian women's role should incorporate?

2. In paragraph 5, Allen writes that she formed her ideas of womanhood from her female relatives. Although each woman was unique, Allen writes that they all had one thing in common: "none of them presented herself tentatively." What do you think Allen means by this phrase? You will need to define the word *tentatively* to complete your response.

   After you define Allen's phrase, write a phrase that describes what your female or male relatives had in common. Use your phrase to develop an essay that explains male-female relationships where you "come from."

3. Allen goes on to write that in her past, she remembers no woman who was "foolish," "dumb," "vain," or "plastic." Looking back on your own past, can you make the same claim? Can you make this claim about the men you know? Explain your responses.

4. Look closely at the topics that Allen's mother dealt with in her stories (paragraph 9). Make a list of these topics. After thinking about the list, explain what skills, knowledge, emotions, and values seem to be important to Allen's mother.

5. According to Allen, how does a Native American woman view her "hormonal life" compared with her white, middle-class counterpart? What cultural values does each view reflect?

6. Allen writes that women in her community wish for their daughters to become "strong and balanced." What two goals do you think the mothers in your own cultural community wish for their daughters today? Are these goals different from those they wish for their sons? Explain.

7. Allen lists various ways in which Native American women deal with the conflicts related to womanhood (paragraph 16). Compare her list with the ways you believe women in your community deal with conflicts in their own lives. Do you see these ways as different from those of the men in your community? Explain.

8. The values of a culture are often reflected by how it treats its young and its aged. Describe Allen's view of the way her Native American community cares for these groups of people. How do people in your community today care for these same groups? What is your response to these comparisons? As you write, imagine that you will be submitting your essay to a magazine published primarily for people who are retired and are past the age of sixty.

9. Allen's great-grandmother gave her the following advice: "Never forget you are Indian." If you had one last piece of advice to give to your

children, how would you complete this sentence? "Never forget . . . ."
Why would you choose this advice for your children?

Suggestions for Extended Thinking and Writing

1. Choose a popular television show or movie today in which women assume the key roles. What role do these media characters portray, and in what ways does a woman's real-life role differ from the television version?

2. Research the roles of women in another American Indian tribe: for example, Hopi, Sioux, Iroquois, Algonquin. Compare the rituals, roles, and values of these Indian women to those of the Laguna Pueblo women.

BRENT STAPLES

*Just Walk on By: A Black Man Ponders
His Power to Alter Public Space*

Educated at Widener University and the University of Chicago, where he earned a Ph.D. in psychology in 1982, Brent Staples has served on the editorial board of the New York Times *since 1990. Staples has also been an editor of the* New York Times Book Review *and an assistant metropolitan editor. A prolific writer, he has been published in such magazines and journals as* Down Beat, Harper's, New York Woman, *and the* New York Times Magazine. "Just Walk on By" *was first published in* Ms. *magazine in 1986. Most recently Staples has written a memoir,* Parallel Time *(Pantheon Books, 1994), which examines the contrast between his current life as a highly acclaimed writer and that of his blue-collar family in Chester, Pennsylvania.*

In describing his own growing consciousness of what it means to be a black writer and scholar in America today, Staples recounts an episode that happened when he was a graduate student at the University of Chicago. A professor told him he had been admitted to a seminar only because, "We've been so mean to black people, we've got to make it up." Staples notes that he felt profoundly humiliated by the professor's condescension: "My grades were absolutely at the top of my class. I knew then I was going to be judged as black no matter what" (GQ, March 1992).

Pre-Reading and Journal-Writing Suggestions

1. To people who don't know you, in what ways is your personal appearance misleading about the person deep inside, the person you really are?
2. Write about a time in which your initial impression of someone else was wrong. On what facts did you make your initial judgment? What caused you to change your mind? What, if anything, did you learn from this event?
3. If you are walking all alone at night and a black man in jeans and a beard is following close behind you, what thought might go through your head? If you are alone at night and a black man in a conservative suit is walking behind you, do you have the same thoughts? What if each of these men were white? What if each were a black woman (minus the beard, of course)? A white woman? Explain the differences and similarities in the responses you describe.

My first victim was a woman—white, well dressed, probably in her *1*
early twenties. I came upon her late one evening on a deserted street in

Hyde Park, a relatively affluent neighborhood in an otherwise mean, impoverished section of Chicago. As I swung onto the avenue behind her, there seemed to be a discreet, uninflammatory distance between us. Not so. She cast back a worried glance. To her, the youngish black man—a broad six feet two inches with a beard and billowing hair, both hands shoved into the pockets of a bulky military jacket—seemed menacingly close. After a few more quick glimpses, she picked up her pace and was soon running in earnest. Within seconds she disappeared into a cross street.

That was more than a decade ago. I was twenty-two years old, a graduate student newly arrived at the University of Chicago. It was in the echo of that terrified woman's footfalls that I first began to know the unwieldy inheritance I'd come into—the ability to alter public space in ugly ways. It was clear that she thought herself the quarry of a mugger, a rapist, or worse. Suffering a bout of insomnia, however, I was stalking sleep, not defenseless wayfarers. As a softy who is scarcely able to take a knife to a raw chicken—let alone hold it to a person's throat—I was surprised, embarrassed, and dismayed all at once. Her flight made me feel like an accomplice in tyranny. It also made it clear that I was indistinguishable from the muggers who occasionally seeped into the area from the surrounding ghetto. That first encounter, and those that followed, signified that a vast, unnerving gulf lay between nighttime pedestrians—particularly women—and me. And I soon gathered that being perceived as dangerous is a hazard in itself. I only needed to turn a corner into a dicey situation, or crowd some frightened, armed person in a foyer somewhere, or make an errant move after being pulled over by a policeman. Where fear and weapons meet—and they often do in urban America—there is always the possibility of death.

In that first year, my first away from my hometown, I was to become thoroughly familiar with the language of fear. At dark, shadowy intersections in Chicago, I could cross in front of a car stopped at a traffic light and elicit the *thunk, thunk, thunk, thunk* of the driver—black, white, male, or female—hammering down the door locks. On less traveled streets after dark, I grew accustomed to but never comfortable with people who crossed to the other side of the street rather than pass me. Then there were the standard unpleasantries with police, doormen, bouncers, cabdrivers, and others whose business is to screen out troublesome individuals *before* there is any nastiness.

I moved to New York nearly two years ago and I have remained an avid night walker. In central Manhattan, the near-constant crowd cover minimizes tense one-on-one street encounters. Elsewhere—visiting friends in SoHo, where sidewalks are narrow and tightly spaced buildings shut out the sky—things can get very taut indeed.

Black men have a firm place in New York mugging literature. Norman Podhoretz in his famed (or infamous) 1963 essay, "My Negro Problem—And Ours," recalls growing up in terror of black males; they "were tougher than we were, more ruthless," he writes—and as an adult on the

5

Upper West Side of Manhattan, he continues, he cannot constrain his nervousness when he meets black men on certain streets. Similarly, a decade later, the essayist and novelist Edward Hoagland extols a New York where once "Negro bitterness bore down mainly on other Negroes." Where some see mere panhandlers, Hoagland sees "a mugger who is clearly screwing up his nerve to do more than just *ask* for money." But Hoagland has "the New Yorker's quick-hunch posture for broken-field maneuvering," and the bad guy swerves away.

I often witness that "hunch posture," from women after dark on the warrenlike streets of Brooklyn where I live. They seem to set their faces on neutral and, with their purse straps strung across their chests bandolier style, they forge ahead as though bracing themselves against being tackled. I understand, of course, that the danger they perceive is not a hallucination. Women are particularly vulnerable to street violence, and young black males are drastically overrepresented among the perpetrators of that violence. Yet these truths are no solace against the kind of alienation that comes of being ever the suspect, against being set apart, a fearsome entity with whom pedestrians avoid making eye contact.

It is not altogether clear to me how I reached the ripe old age of twenty-two without being conscious of the lethality nighttime pedestrians attributed to me. Perhaps it was because in Chester, Pennsylvania, the small, angry industrial town where I came of age in the 1960s, I was scarcely noticeable against a backdrop of gang warfare, street knifings, and murders. I grew up one of the good boys, had perhaps a half-dozen fistfights. In retrospect, my shyness of combat has clear sources.

Many things go into the making of a young thug. One of those things is the consummation of the male romance with the power to intimidate. An infant discovers that random flailings send the baby bottle flying out of the crib and crashing to the floor. Delighted, the joyful babe repeats those motions again and again, seeking to duplicate the feat. Just so, I recall the points at which some of my boyhood friends were finally seduced by the perception of themselves as tough guys. When a mark cowered and surrendered his money without resistance, myth and reality merged—and paid off. It is, after all, only manly to embrace the power to frighten and intimidate. We, as men, are not supposed to give an inch of our lane on the highway; we are to seize the fighter's edge in work and in play and even in love; we are to be valiant in the face of hostile forces.

Unfortunately, poor and powerless young men seem to take all this nonsense literally. As a boy, I saw countless tough guys locked away; I have since buried several, too. They were babies, really—a teenage cousin, a brother of twenty-two, a childhood friend in his midtwenties—all gone down in episodes of bravado played out in the streets. I came to doubt the virtues of intimidation early on. I chose, perhaps even unconsciously, to remain a shadow—timid, but a survivor.

The fearsomeness mistakenly attributed to me in public places often   *10* has a perilous flavor. The most frightening of these confusions occurred in the late 1970s and early 1980s when I worked as a journalist in Chicago. One day, rushing into the office of a magazine I was writing for with a deadline story in hand, I was mistaken for a burglar. The office manager called security and, with an ad hoc posse, pursued me through the labyrinthine halls, nearly to my editor's door. I had no way of proving who I was. I could only move briskly toward the company of someone who knew me.

Another time I was on assignment for a local paper and killing time before an interview. I entered a jewelry store on the city's affluent Near North Side. The proprietor excused herself and returned with an enormous red Doberman pinscher straining at the end of a leash. She stood, the dog extended toward me, silent to my questions, her eyes bulging nearly out of her head. I took a cursory look around, nodded, and bade her good night. Relatively speaking, however, I never fared as badly as another black male journalist. He went to nearby Waukegan, Illinois, a couple of summers ago to work on a story about a murderer who was born there. Mistaking the reporter for the killer, police hauled him from his car at gunpoint and but for his press credentials would probably have tried to book him. Such episodes are not uncommon. Black men trade tales like this all the time.

In "My Negro Problem—And Ours," Podhoretz writes that the hatred he feels for blacks makes itself known to him through a variety of avenues—one being his discomfort with that "special brand of paranoid touchiness" to which he says blacks are prone. No doubt he is speaking here of black men. In time, I learned to smother the rage I felt at so often being taken for a criminal. Not to do so would surely have led to madness—via that special "paranoid touchiness" that so annoyed Podhoretz at the time he wrote the essay.

I began to take precautions to make myself less threatening. I move about with care, particularly late in the evening. I give a wide berth to nervous people on subway platforms during the wee hours, particularly when I have exchanged business clothes for jeans. If I happen to be entering a building behind some people who appear skittish, I may walk by, letting them clear the lobby before I return, so as not to seem to be following them. I have been calm and extremely congenial on those rare occasions when I've been pulled over by the police.

And on late-evening constitutionals along streets less traveled by, I employ what has proved to be an excellent tension-reducing measure: I whistle melodies from Beethoven and Vivaldi and the more popular classical composers. Even steely New Yorkers hunching toward nighttime destinations seem to relax, and occasionally they even join in the tune. Virtually everybody seems to sense that a mugger wouldn't be warbling bright, sunny selections from Vivaldi's *Four Seasons*. It is my equivalent of the cowbell that hikers wear when they know they are in bear country.

Suggestions for Writing and Discussion

1. In his opening paragraph, Staples describes a woman who was so nervous because a black man was walking behind her that she began running. Do you think her reaction is a common one? Is it justified? Explain your answers.

2. Why, at the age of twenty-two, is Staples, a black man, surprised at the reaction that people have toward him on his nightly walks? Besides the reaction of surprise, what other feelings might he have when people avoid him or hurry away from him, simply because he is a black man?

3. In paragraph 5, Staples cites two pieces of literature that convey the image of black man as mugger. When people fear someone because he is a black male, does this fear usually occur because, like Norman Podhoretz, they have been mugged by a black man? If not, where does their concept of "black as dangerous" come from?

4. Staples admits that women are "particularly vulnerable to street violence and young black males are overly represented among perpetrators of that violence." So what is his point in this essay? Does he seek to place blame or analyze causes? Something else?

5. According to Staples, in what ways do the concepts of being male and having power connect? Do you agree with his point that men are supposed to be tough? Write this piece for an audience that is (a) all male or (b) all female. When you finish your final draft, on a separate piece of paper write a paragraph describing briefly what you think you might have done differently if you were writing for an audience other than the one you chose.

6. Briefly summarize Staples's solution to avoid frightening others while he takes walks. Explain why this tactic apparently works to ease a stranger's fear. What is your response to his solution?

Suggestions for Extended Thinking and Writing

1. Watch prime-time television for several weeks. Notice how many shows and commercials include black male characters, and note the types of roles these characters play. Based on your observations, what categories do these characters fall into? Are any of the roles stereotypes? Are any of the characters "real" people? Come to some conclusion about how black men are portrayed on television.

2. Staples explains why he did not get pulled into the life of a street mugger. Drawing on your own experiences with peer pressure as well as on your reading or viewing of television documentaries, explain why you think young people are attracted to gangs or to other negative behaviors. In addition, explain how you think young people can be convinced not to be influenced by negative peer pressure. Use specific examples to illustrate your points.

BERNARD R. GOLDBERG

Television Insults Men, Too

>   *Born in 1945 in New York City, Bernard R. Goldberg is a journalist and CBS news correspondent. Immediately following his graduation from Rutgers University, he began work at the Associated Press office in New York City. Since 1972 he has worked for CBS, as a correspondent for both the CBS Evening News and the news magazine programs "48 Hours" and "Eye to Eye." "Television Insults Men, Too" first appeared on the op-ed page of the New York Times in March 1989.*

Pre-Reading and Journal-Writing Suggestions

1. Make a list of the shows you usually watch on television. After making this list, consider how you think these shows generally portray men? How about the women? Does any particular show come to mind that degrades either men or women? Please explain.
2. In your opinion, what are the benefits of being an American female? An American male? In your opinion, is it more beneficial to be male or female in America?
3. What do you imagine your life would be like right now if you were a member of the opposite sex? You might try to write this explanation by imagining a typical day.

It was front page news and it made the TV networks. A mother from   *1*
Michigan single-handedly convinces some of America's biggest advertisers to cancel their sponsorship of the Fox Broadcasting Company's "Married . . . With Children" because, as she put it, the show blatantly exploits women and the family.

The program is about a blue collar family in which the husband is a chauvinist pig and his wife is—excuse the expression—a bimbo.

These are the late 1980's, and making fun of people because of their gender—on TV no less, in front of millions of people—is déclassé. Unless, of course, the gender we're ridiculing is the male gender. Then it's O.K.

Take "Roseanne." (Please!) It's the season's biggest new hit show, which happens to be about another blue collar family. In this one, the wife calls her husband and kids names.

"Roseanne" is Roseanne Barr who has made a career saying such cute   *5*
things as: "You may marry the man of your dreams, ladies, but 15 years later you are married to a reclining chair that burps." Or to her TV show son: "You're not stupid. You're just clumsy like your daddy."

The producer of "Roseanne" does not mince words either: "Men are slime. They say they're going to do 50 percent of the work around the house, but they never do."

I will tell you that the producer is a man, which does not lessen the ugliness of the remark. But because his target is men, it becomes acceptable. No one, to my knowledge, is pulling commercials from "Roseanne."

In matters of gender discrimination, it has become part of the accepted orthodoxy—of many feminists and a lot of the media anyway—that only women have the right to complain. Men have no such right. Which helps explain why there have been so many commercials ridiculing men—and getting away with it.

In the past year or so, I have seen a breakfast cereal commercial showing a husband and wife playing tennis. She is perky and he is jerky.

She is a regular Martina Navratilova of the suburbs and he is virtually 10 dead (because he wasn't smart enough to eat the right cereal).

She doesn't miss a shot. He lets the ball hit him in the head. If he were black, his name would be Stepin Fetchitt.

I have seen a commercial for razor blades that shows a woman in an evening gown smacking a man in a tuxedo across the face, suggesting, I suppose, that the male face takes enough punishment to deserve a nice, smooth shave. If he hit her (an absolutely inconceivable notion, if a sponsor is trying to sell a woman something) he would be a batterer.

I have seen an airline commercial showing two reporters from competing newspapers. She's strong and smart. He's a nerd. He says to her: I read your story this morning; you scooped me again. She replies to him: I didn't know you could read.

I have seen a magazine ad for perfume showing a business woman patting a businessman's behind as they walk down the street. *Ms* magazine, the Journal of American feminism, ran the ad. The publisher told me there was nothing sexist about it.

A colleague who writes about advertising and the media says advertis- 15 ers are afraid to fool around with women's roles. They know, as she puts it, they'll "set off the feminist emergency broadcast system" if they do. So, she concludes, men are fair game.

In 1987, Fred Hayward, who is one of the pioneers of the men's rights movement (yes, there is a men's rights movement), studied thousands of TV and print ads and concluded: "If there's a sleazy character in an ad, 100 percent of the ones that we found were male. If there's an incompetent character, 100 percent of them in the ads are male."

I once interviewed Garrett Epps, a scholar who has written on these matters, who told me: "The female executive who is driven, who is strong, who lives for her work, that's a very positive symbol in our culture now. The male who has the same traits—that guy is a disaster: He harms everybody around him; he's cold; he's unfeeling; he's hurtful."

The crusading mother from Michigan hit on a legitimate issue. No more cheap shots, she seems to have said. And the advertisers listened. No more cheap shots is what a lot of men are saying also. Too bad nobody is listening to *them*.

Suggestions for Writing and Discussion

1. After reading this selection once, write a brief summary. Then reread the essay and return to your summary. Make any changes (additions, deletions, revisions) that you now believe are necessary.
2. Throughout this essay, the author relies on slang terms such as *bimbo* (paragraph 2), *jerky* (paragraph 9), and *nerd* (paragraph 13). How do these terms affect your response to what you are reading?
3. In paragraph 5, Goldberg cites two examples of what the character Roseanne says about her husband. If you had to put these jokes under one of these categories—funny or offensive—which would you choose and why?
4. Look over the examples Goldberg uses to support his contention that men are degraded on television, too. Which *one* example do you find the most convincing? Which *one* example do you find weakest? Explain your choices.
5. After reading this piece, what do you think? Do you agree or disagree with the author? (You can, of course, be in partial agreement or disagreement.) Consider watching a variety of television commercials as you work to draw your own conclusions. How are men portrayed? How are women portrayed? As you respond, imagine that you are writing an article that will appear in *TV Guide*.

Suggestions for Extended Thinking and Writing

1. Take on Roseanne Barr's character and write a response to Goldberg regarding your show's purpose as well as your main character.
2. In this section, both Goldberg and Brent Staples (p. 244) offer a male perspective. After reading both of these selections, write an essay explaining which selection you found more convincing. Give specific reasons and examples to support your explanation.

CHARLES OSGOOD

"Real" Men and Women

Noted CBS television commentator Charles Osgood began his career as a radio journalist. Currently he writes and anchors "The Osgood File" over the CBS radio network and on "CBS This Morning." He also coanchors the "CBS Morning News" and "Sunday Morning." He has repeatedly been named "Best in the Business" by the Washington Journalism Review, *and in 1990 he was inducted into the National Association of Broadcasters' Broadcasting Hall of Fame.*

His lively wit and telling insights have won him a large following of viewers who look forward to his commentaries, which are often delivered as humorous poems, filled with word play and ironic inferences. " 'Real' Men and Women" first appeared in his 1979 collection of writings, Nothing Could Be Finer Than a Crisis That Is Minor in the Morning.

Pre-Reading and Journal-Writing Suggestions

1. Imagine you have been assigned to write about either one of these topics: What is a real man? What is a real woman? First of all, consider your reaction to this assignment. What difficulties might you encounter? How would you approach this writing assignment?
2. Freewrite for ten minutes on the word *man.* Now do the same for the word *woman.* Looking over your two entries, what conclusions can you draw?

Helene, a young friend of mine, has been assigned a theme in English   *1*
composition class. She can take her choice: "What is a *real* man?" or if she wishes, "What is a *real* woman?" Seems the instructor has some strong ideas on these subjects. Helene says she doesn't know which choice to make. "I could go the women's-lib route," she says, "but I don't think he'd like that. I started in on that one once in a class, and it didn't go over too well." So, what is a real man and what is a real woman?

"As opposed to what?" I asked.

"I don't know, as opposed to unreal men and women, I suppose. Got any ideas?"

Yes, it just so happens I do. Let's start with the assumption that reality is that which is, as opposed to that which somebody would like, or something that is imagined or idealized. Let's assume that all human beings who are alive, therefore, are real human beings, who can be divided into two categories: real men and real women. A man who exists is a real man. His reality is in no way lessened by his race, his nationality, political affiliation, financial status, religious persuasion, or personal proclivities. All men are real men. All women are real women.

The first thing you do if you want to destroy somebody is rob him of his humanity. If you can persuade yourself that someone is a gook and therefore not a real person, you can kill him rather more easily, burn down his home, separate him from his family. If you can persuade yourself that someone is not really a person but a spade, a Wasp, a kike, a wop, a mick, a fag, a dike, and therefore not a real man or woman, you can more easily hate and hurt him.

People who go around making rules, setting standards that other people are supposed to meet in order to qualify as real, are real pains in the neck—and worse, they are real threats to the rest of us. They use their own definitions of real and unreal to filter out unpleasant facts. To them, things like crime, drugs, decay, pollution, slums, et cetera, are not the real America. In the same way, they can look at a man and say he is not a real man because he doesn't give a hang about pro football and would rather chase butterflies than a golfball; or they can look at a woman and say she is not a real woman because she drives a cab or would rather change the world than change diapers.

To say that someone is not a real man or woman is to say that they are something less than, and therefore not entitled to the same consideration as, real people. Therefore, Helene, contained within the questions "What is a real man?" and "What is a real woman?" are the seeds of discrimination and of murders, big and little. Each of us has his own reality, and nobody has the right to limit or qualify that—not even English composition instructors.

Suggestions for Writing and Discussion

1. In this piece, the author says he has an idea for approaching this assignment. In your own words, summarize the advice he would give to someone who is approaching the same assignment.
2. What is the author's interpretation of the word *real?* What other interpretations can you think of for this word?
3. In paragraph 5, the author lists terms that degrade different nationalities and groups. Why do you think he uses these specific terms? What effect does his choosing to use these words have on you as a reader?
4. Consider your own definitions of *real man* and *real woman.* How do your views compare to the stereotypes Osgood describes in paragraph 6?
5. What is your response to Osgood's last line? What is he saying? Do you agree with him? Please explain.
6. The newspaper in your university or college community has asked you to write a paper describing the "real" college man or the "real" college woman of the 1990s. What is your response?

Suggestions for Extended Thinking and Writing

1. Try this assignment out on several of your acquaintances (fellow students, co-workers, family, friends). Ask both men and women the question "What is a real man?" Then ask the same people, "What is a real woman?" After collecting your data, write a paper in which you discuss your findings.

2. Select several advertisements from the same magazine and write an essay in which you analyze these ads and infer what they suggest about "real" men and women.

DEBORAH MARQUARDT

A Thinly Disguised Message

In "A Thinly Disguised Message," first published in Ms. *in May 1987, Deborah Marquardt examines the way women respond to the "ideal" female images projected in advertising. A widely published freelance writer, Marquardt's essays have appeared in many national publications, including* Business Magazine, McCall's, *and the* New York Times.

Pre-Reading and Journal-Writing Suggestions

1. You've got the choice of having one of these body types: overweight, underweight, or average. Which do you choose and why?
2. Write about the first time in your life that you began to be dissatisfied with what you looked like. What do you think was the source of this dissatisfaction? (If you have never been dissatisfied with your looks or never wanted to change anything about your physical self, then write about what has made you satisfied with how you look.)
3. Finish one of the following statements with your first thoughts and then briefly explain why you completed the sentence the way you did:
   "Teenage girls usually feel good about themselves when . . . ."
   "Teenage boys usually feel good about themselves when . . . ."

The new svelte Betty Crocker looks as if she's never tasted an angel   *1*
food cake, much less a double fudge brownie, and the Campbell Kids have
lost a lot of their baby-fat bounce. And when was the last time you saw a
size 12 model smiling from the pages of a magazine?

If the media message is thin, thin, thin, and if the ordinary person is
exposed to 400 to 1,500 advertising messages per day, is it coincidence that
medical specialists estimate—conservatively—that 12 percent of college-age
females have serious eating disorders?

Two media researchers, armed with separate studies, think not. They
believe that many young women are literally dying to achieve the pervasive,
incredibly thin image spawned by the advertising industry because women
perceive these images as "standard" and "acceptable."

Linda Lazier-Smith, Ph.D., currently teaching advertising at the Ohio
State University in Columbus, and Alice Gagnard, Ph.D., at Southern
Methodist University in Dallas, both became interested in the advertise-
ments/anorexic link through encounters with students. "I was teaching
at Marquette University in Milwaukee when one of my students missed
four weeks of school because she was hospitalized with anorexia," recalls

Gagnard. "She described her rehabilitation program in which she had to 'unlearn' how to look at the media."

Lazier-Smith had similar experiences at Indiana University in Bloom-   5
ington when she began lecturing students on media and societal expectations. Many young women in the room said, "I'm trying to be like those
women."

Although the researchers approached their studies differently, the conclusions were startlingly similar. Gagnard, in "From Feast to Famine: Depic-
tion of Ideal Body Type in Magazine Advertising, 1950–1984," reviewed
961 half page or larger ads in *Ladies' Home Journal, Woman's Day,* and *McCall's*
in the years 1950, 1960, 1970, and 1984. Her findings weren't surprising:
most models were young, white, and female. The use of thin models increased each decade since 1950, reaching 46 percent in the 1980s, while the
use of overweight and obese models decreased from 12 percent in 1950 to
3 percent in 1984. (Overweight male models were far more common in all
decades.)

The models were also rated by trained researchers, and although the
thin models were judged to be more attractive and successful, the overweight and obese models were considered the happiest, revealing, Gagnard
notes, the age-old "fat and jolly" stereotype. But she concludes that the
advertising studied shows "a reflection of our perpetuation of America's
preoccupation with slimness."

Lazier-Smith asked three groups of young women to complete ques-
tionnaires to elicit attitudes on physical attractiveness, such as the existence
of an "ideal body shape," and media influences in promoting it. Thirty high-
school students, a group of college-age anorexics, and a group of Indiana
University women students were asked to evaluate the successfulness and
happiness of women models in print ads and to match models—who were
extremely thin (anorexic shape), normal (size 12 to 14), or full-figured—
with various occupations and roles in commercials.

Most of the women surveyed agreed that there is an "ideal body shape
in American society to which women are expected to conform." Both the
high schoolers (the high-risk age for anorexia) and anorexics selected body
size and shape as the most important features in women, and the "ideal"
woman for all three groups was a size seven and a half.

On the success scale, the thin models were overwhelmingly voted most   10
successful and the heavier models least. And when asked to match the models in the pictures with occupations or commercials, no one picked "average" size women. This startled Lazier-Smith above all. "Average is invisible.
You have to be either extreme to be noticed."

In presentations to national professional organizations, both educators
have detected an interest in the findings, although they admit most people
still aren't sensitive to eating disorders. "We would like to see more realism
in ads," said Lazier-Smith. "That doesn't have to mean fat and ugly. We got
away from asses and boobs and superwoman because women complained.

We'd like an awareness in the ad community that the constant use of over-thin models is totally unrealistic, that it's not necessary to sell products, and that it might be injuring young minds."

Suggestions for Writing and Discussion

1. In your own words and in one sentence, summarize Marquardt's message. Do you agree with this thought? Explain briefly.
2. Although Marquardt's main concern has to be with advertising and teenage girls, expand on the media's influence by writing how young men might be affected by today's advertising.
3. What sources does Marquardt use as her primary support? How effective are these sources? What other sources could she use to support her argument?
4. How would you describe the overall tone of this piece? Is it emotional? Angry? Cynical? Detached? How does it compare to the essay by Charles Osgood (p. 252) or the essay by Bernard Goldberg (p. 249)? Which of these pieces do you like the best? Explain.
5. Look at a popular magazine whose main audience is composed of young women (*Seventeen, Teen, Glamour, Mademoiselle, Sassy*). In general, how would you characterize the models in the ads? Can you find any exceptions to Marquardt's contention that models are "thin, thin, thin"? Write your response in the form of a speech you will give at the secondary school from which you graduated to an audience of males and females between the ages of thirteen and nineteen.

Suggestions for Extended Thinking and Writing

1. If you feel strongly about the media's influence on young women's eating habits, write a letter to any one of the advertisers in any one of the magazines mentioned in topic 5. Tell them how their advertising affects you. Before writing this letter, decide on the tone you want to adopt in your writing, as well as your purpose: Do you want to just let off steam or do you want a real change?
2. Write an essay in which you evaluate solutions that have been proposed to help young women who have problems with their self-image. Explain why you believe these solutions are or are not effective. Then make your own proposal to address problems you have seen in other solutions.

JOANNA RUSS

When It Changed

> *Born and raised in New York City, Joanna Russ earned degrees from Cornell University and from the Yale School of Drama. She has taught English at several universities. In addition to criticism and reviews, she has written plays, essays, novels, and short stories, many in the fantasy–science fiction genre and most related to gender issues. Russ is noted for her resistance to the stereotyped, male-dominated plots and characterizations of much science fiction. By creating strong female characters and dealing with thoughtful, carefully conceived feminist themes, Russ successfully challenges science fiction traditions and clichés. Her best known novels include* The Female Man *(1975) and* The Two of Them *(1978). In addition, she is the author of a book of feminist criticism, whose title—*How to Suppress Women's Writing—*suggests the witty, ironic tone characteristic of all her writing.*

Pre-Reading and Journal-Writing Suggestion

Imagine a world in which the species is either all men or all women, and reproduction is possible due to innovative scientific discoveries. First of all, which group would have the easiest time surviving, men or women? Secondly, what might this single-sex group be able to achieve that they couldn't in a mixed-sex situation? Lastly, what might be the greatest problems this group would have to deal with?

Katy drives like a maniac; we must have been doing over 120 kilometers per hour on those turns. She's good, though, extremely good, and I've seen her take the whole car apart and put it together again in a day. My birthplace on Whileaway was largely given to farm machinery and I refuse to wrestle with a five-gear shift at unholy speeds, not having been brought up to it, but even on those turns in the middle of the night, on a country road as bad as only our district can make them, Katy's driving didn't scare me. The funny thing about my wife, though: she will not handle guns. She has even gone hiking in the forests above the forty-eighth parallel without firearms, for days at a time. And that *does* scare me.

Katy and I have three children between us, one of hers and two of mine. Yuriko, my eldest, was asleep in the back seat, dreaming twelve-year-old dreams of love and war: running away to sea, hunting in the North, dreams of strangely beautiful people in strangely beautiful places, all the wonderful guff you think up when you're turning twelve and the glands start going. Some day soon, like all of them, she will disappear for weeks on

1

end to come back grimy and proud, having knifed her first cougar or shot her first bear, dragging some abominably dangerous dead beastie behind her, which I will never forgive for what it might have done to my daughter. Yuriko says Katy's driving puts her to sleep.

For someone who has fought three duels, I am afraid of far, far too much. I'm getting old. I told this to my wife.

"You're thirty-four," she said. Laconic to the point of silence, that one. She flipped the lights on, on the dash—three kilometers to go and the road getting worse all the time. Far out in the country. Electric-green trees rushed into our headlights and around the car. I reached down next to me where we bolt the carrier panel to the door and eased my rifle into my lap. Yuriko stirred in the back. My height but Katy's eyes, Katy's face. The car engine is so quiet, Katy says, that you can hear breathing in the back seat. Yuki had been alone in the car when the message came, enthusiastically decoding her dot-dashes (silly to mount a wide-frequency transceiver near an I.C. engine, but most of Whileaway is on steam). She had thrown herself out of the car, my gangly and gaudy offspring, shouting at the top of her lungs, so of course she had had to come along. We've been intellectually prepared for this ever since the Colony was founded, ever since it was abandoned, but this is different. This is awful.

"Men!" Yuki had screamed, leaping over the car door. "They've come back! Real Earth men!"   5

We met them in the kitchen of the farmhouse near the place where they had landed; the windows were open, the night air very mild. We had passed all sorts of transportation when we parked outside—steam tractors, trucks, an I.C. flatbed, even a bicycle. Lydia, the district biologist, had come out of her Northern taciturnity long enough to take blood and urine samples and was sitting in a corner of the kitchen shaking her head in astonishment over the results; she even forced herself (very big, very fair, very shy, always painfully blushing) to dig up the old language manuals—though I can talk the old tongues in my sleep. And do. Lydia is uneasy with us; we're Southerners and too flamboyant. I counted twenty people in that kitchen, all the brains of North Continent. Phyllis Spet, I think, had come in by glider. Yuki was the only child there.

Then I saw the four of them.

They are bigger than we are. They are bigger and broader. Two were taller than I, and I am extremely tall, one meter eighty centimeters in my bare feet. They are obviously of our species but *off,* indescribably off, and as my eyes could not and still cannot quite comprehend the lines of those alien bodies, I could not, then, bring myself to touch them, though the one who spoke Russian—what voices they have—wanted to "shake hands," a custom from the past, I imagine. I can only say they were apes with human faces. He seemed to mean well, but I found myself shuddering back almost the length of the kitchen—and then I laughed apologetically—and then to set a good example (*interstellar amity,* I thought) did "shake hands" finally. A hard,

hard hand. They are heavy as draft horses. Blurred, deep voices. Yuriko had sneaked in between the adults and was gazing at *the men* with her mouth open.

He turned *his* head—those words have not been in our language for six hundred years—and said, in bad Russian:

"Who's that?"

"My daughter," I said, and added (with that irrational attention to good manners we sometimes employ in moments of insanity), "My daughter, Yuriko Janeston. We use the patronymic. You would say matronymic."

He laughed, involuntarily. Yuki exclaimed, "I thought they would be *good-looking!*" greatly disappointed at this reception of herself. Phyllis Helgason Spet, whom someday I shall kill, gave me across the room a cold, level venomous look, as if to say: *Watch what you say. You know what I can do.* It's true that I have little formal status, but Madam President will get herself in serious trouble with both me and her own staff if she continues to consider industrial espionage good clean fun. Wars and rumors of wars, as it says in one of our ancestors' books. I translated Yuki's words into *the man's* dog-Russian, once our *lingua franca,* and *the man* laughed again.

"Where are all your people?" he said conversationally.

I translated again and watched the faces around the room; Lydia embarrassed (as usual), Spet narrowing her eyes with some damned scheme, Katy very pale.

"This is Whileaway," I said.

He continued to look unenlightened.

"Whileaway," I said. "Do you remember? Do you have records? There was a plague on Whileaway."

He looked moderately interested. Heads turned in the back of the room, and I caught a glimpse of the local professions-parliament delegate; by morning every town meeting, every district caucus, would be in full session.

"Plague?" he said. "That's most unfortunate."

"Yes," I said. "Most unfortunate. We lost half our population in one generation."

He looked properly impressed.

"Whileaway was lucky," I said. "We had a big initial gene pool, we had been chosen for extreme intelligence, we had a high technology and a large remaining population in which every adult was two-or-three experts in one. The soil is good. The climate is blessedly easy. There are thirty millions of us now. Things are beginning to snowball in industry—do you understand?—give us seventy years and we'll have more than one real city, more than a few industrial centers, full-time professions, full-time radio operators, full-time machinists, give us seventy years and not everyone will have to spend three-quarters of a lifetime on the farm." And I tried to explain how hard it is when artists can practice full-time only in old age, when there are so few, so very few who can be free, like Katy and myself. I tried also to outline our government, the two houses, the one by professions and the geographic one; I told him the district caucuses handled problems too big for the individual towns. And that population control was not a political issue, not yet, though give us time and it would be. This was a delicate point in our history; give us time. There was no need to sacrifice the quality of life for an insane rush into industrialization. Let us go our own pace. Give us time.

"Where are all the people?" said that monomaniac.

I realized then that he did not mean people, he meant *men,* and he was giving the word the meaning it had not had on Whileaway for six centuries.

"They died," I said. "Thirty generations ago."   25

I thought we had poleaxed him. He caught his breath. He made as if to get out of the chair he was sitting in; he put his hand to his chest; he looked around at us with the strangest blend of awe and sentimental tenderness. Then he said, solemnly and earnestly:

"A great tragedy."

I waited, not quite understanding.

"Yes," he said, catching his breath again with that queer smile, that adult-to-child smile that tells you something is being hidden and will be presently produced with cries of encouragement and joy, "a great tragedy. But it's over." And again he looked around at all of us with the strangest deference. As if we were invalids.

"You've adapted amazingly," he said.   30

"To what?" I said. He looked embarrassed. He looked inane. Finally he said, "Where I come from, the women don't dress so plainly."

"Like you?" I said. "Like a bride?" for the men were wearing silver from head to foot. I had never seen anything so gaudy. He made as if to answer and then apparently thought better of it; he laughed at me again. With an odd exhilaration—as if we were something childish and something wonderful, as if he were doing us an enormous favor—he took one shaky breath and said, "Well, we're here."

I looked at Spet, Spet looked at Lydia, Lydia looked at Amalia, who is the head of the local town meeting, Amalia looked at I don't know whom. My throat was raw. I cannot stand local beer, which the farmers swill as if their stomachs had iridium linings but I took it anyway, from Amalia (it was her bicycle we had seen outside as we parked), and swallowed it all. This was going to take a long time. I said, "Yes, here you are," and smiled (feeling like a fool), and wondered seriously if male-Earth-people's minds worked so very differently from female-Earth-people's minds, but that couldn't be so or the race would have died out long ago. The radio network had got the news around planet by now and we had another Russian speaker, flown in from Varna; I decided to cut out when *the man* passed around pictures of his wife, who looked like the priestess of some arcane cult. He proposed to question Yuki, so I barreled her into a back room in spite of her furious protests, and went out on the front porch. As I left, Lydia was explaining the

difference between parthenogenesis (which is so easy that anyone can practice it) and what we do, which is the merging of ova. That is why Katy's
baby looks like me. Lydia went on to the Ansky Process and Katy Ansky,
our one full-polymath genius and the great-great- I don't know how many
times great-grandmother of my own Katharina.

A dot-dash transmitter in one of the outbuildings chattered faintly to
itself: operators flirting and passing jokes down the line.

There was a man on the porch. The other tall man. I watched him for 35
a few minutes—I can move very quietly when I want to—and when I
allowed him to see me, he stopped talking into the little machine hung
around his neck. Then he said calmly, in excellent Russian, "Did you know
that sexual equality has been reestablished on Earth?"

"You're the real one," I said, "aren't you? The other one's for show." It
was a great relief to get things cleared up. He nodded affably.

"As a people, we are not very bright," he said. "There's been too much
genetic damage in the last few centuries. Radiation. Drugs. We can use
Whileaway's genes, Janet." Strangers do not call strangers by the first name.

"You can have cells enough to drown in," I said. "Breed your own."

He smiled. "That's not the way we want to do it." Behind him I saw
Katy come into the square of light that was the screened-in door. He went
on, low and urbane, not mocking me, I think, but with the self-confidence
of someone who has always had money and strength to spare, who doesn't
know what it is to be second-class or provincial. Which is very odd, because
the day before, I would have said that was an exact description of me.

"I'm talking to you, Janet," he said, "because I suspect you have more 40
popular influence than anyone else here. You know as well as I do that
parthenogenetic culture has all sorts of inherent defects, and we do not—if
we can help it—mean to use you for anything of the sort. Pardon me; I
should not have said 'use.' But surely you can see that this kind of society is
unnatural."

"Humanity is unnatural," said Katy. She had my rifle under her left
arm. The top of that silky head does not quite come up to my collarbone,
but she is as tough as steel; he began to move, again with that queer smiling
deference (which his fellow had showed to me but he had not), and the gun
slid into Katy's grip as if she had shot with it all her life.

"I agree," said the man. "Humanity is unnatural. I should know. I have
metal in my teeth and metal pins here." He touched his shoulder. "Seals are
harem animals," he added, "and so are men; apes are promiscuous and so are
men; doves are monogamous and so are men; there are even celibate men
and homosexual men. There are homosexual cows, I believe. But Whileaway is still missing something." He gave a dry chuckle. I will give him the
credit of believing that it had something to do with nerves.

"I miss nothing," said Katy, "except that life isn't endless."

"You are—?" said the man, nodding from me to her.

"Wives," said Katy. "We're married." Again the dry chuckle. 45

"A good economic arrangement," he said, "for working and taking care of the children. And as good an arrangement as any for randomizing heredity, if your reproduction is made to follow the same pattern. But think, Katharina Michaelason, if there isn't something better that you might secure for your daughters. I believe in instincts, even in Man, and I can't think that the two of you—a machinist, are you? and I gather you are some sort of chief of police—don't feel somehow what even you must miss. You know it intellectually, of course. There is only half a species here. Men must come back to Whileaway."

Katy said nothing.

"I should think, Katharina Michaelason," said the man gently, "that you, of all people, would benefit most from such a change," and he walked past Katy's rifle into the square of light coming from the door. I think it was then that he noticed my scar, which really does not show unless the light is from the side: a fine line that runs from temple to chin. Most people don't even know about it.

"Where did you get that?" he said, and I answered with an involuntary grin. "In my last duel." We stood there bristling at each other for several seconds (this is absurd but true) until he went inside and shut the screen door behind him. Katy said in a brittle voice, "You damned fool, don't you know when we've been insulted?" and swung up the rifle to shoot him through the screen, but I got to her before she could fire and knocked the rifle out of aim; it burned a hole through the porch floor. Katy was shaking. She kept whispering over and over, "That's why I never touched it, because I knew I'd kill someone. I knew I'd kill someone." The first man—the one I'd spoken with first—was still talking inside the house, something about the grand movement to recolonize and rediscover all that Earth had lost. He stressed the advantages to Whileaway: trade, exchange of ideas, education. He, too, said that sexual equality had been reestablished on Earth.

Katy was right, of course; we should have burned them down where they stood. Men are coming to Whileaway. When one culture has the big guns and the other has none, there is a certain predictability about the outcome. Maybe men would have come eventually in any case, I like to think that a hundred years from now my great-grandchildren could have stood them off or fought them to a standstill, but even that's no odds; I will remember all my life those four people I first met who were muscled like bulls and who made me—if only for a moment—feel small. A neurotic reaction, Katy says. I remember everything that happened that night; I remember Yuki's excitement in the car, I remember Katy's sobbing when we got home as if her heart would break, I remember her lovemaking, a little peremptory as always, but wonderfully soothing and comforting. I remember prowling restlessly around the house after Katy fell asleep with one bare arm flung into a patch of light from the hall. The muscles of her forearms are like metal bars from all that driving and testing of her machines. Sometimes I dream about Katy's arms. I remember wandering into the

50

nursery and picking up my wife's baby, dozing for a while with the poignant, amazing warmth of an infant in my lap, and finally returning to the
kitchen to find Yuriko fixing herself a late snack. My daughter eats like a
Great Dane.

"Yuki," I said, "do you think you could fall in love with a man?" and
she whooped derisively. "With a ten-foot toad!" said my tactful child.

But men are coming to Whileaway. Lately I sit up nights and worry
about the men who will come to this planet, about my two daughters and
Betta Katharinason, about what will happen to Katy, to me, to my life. Our
ancestors' journals are one long cry of pain and I suppose I ought to be glad
now, but one can't throw away six centuries, or even (as I have lately discovered) thirty-four years. Sometimes I laugh at the question those four men
hedged about all evening and never quite dared to ask, looking at the lot of
us, hicks in overalls, farmers in canvas pants and plain shirts: *Which of you
plays the role of the man?* As if we had to produce a carbon copy of their
mistakes! I doubt very much that sexual equality has been reestablished on
Earth. I do not like to think of myself mocked, of Katy deferred to as if she
were weak, of Yuki made to feel unimportant or silly, of my other children
cheated of their full humanity or turned into strangers. And I'm afraid that
my own achievements will dwindle from what they were—or what I
thought they were—to the not-very-interesting curiosa of the human race,
the oddities you read about in the back of the book, things to laugh at
sometimes because they are so exotic, quaint but not impressive, charming
but not useful. I find this more painful than I can say. You will agree that for
a woman who has fought three duels, all of them kills, indulging in such
fears is ludicrous. But what's around the corner now is a duel so big that I
don't think I have the guts for it; in Faust's words: *Verweile doch, du bist so
schoen!* Keep it as it is. Don't change.

Sometimes at night I remember the original name of this planet,
changed by the first generation of our ancestors, those curious women for
whom, I suppose, the real name was too painful a reminder after the men
died. I find it amusing, in a grim way, to see it all so completely turned
around. This, too, shall pass. All good things must come to an end.

Take my life but don't take away the meaning of my life.

For-A-While.   *55*

Suggestions for Writing and Discussion
1. What could be the different meanings of *it* in the title of this piece?
2. Compare the relationship that Katy and the speaker, Janet, have with a
   typical man-woman marriage relationship with which you are familiar.
3. Examine the various reactions that the women have to the appearance of
   the four men. Which of these reactions do you feel are similar to those
   women might have today if men they do not know should unexpectedly
   arrive at an all-female meeting? Which reactions do you see as different?

4. Examine the reactions of the main man to the women in Whileaway. What do you think motivates his responses? Explain.

5. When the women try to explain how self-sufficient their lives are, the alien man says, "Whileaway is still missing something." Besides the actual presence of men, what—if anything—is Whileaway missing? Explain your response.

Suggestions for Extended Thinking and Writing

1. Review a movie, book, or television show in which women assume the heroic, central role. How realistic are these roles, and what are the central messages in this piece? As your audience for this review, imagine your readers to be subscribers to *Ms.* magazine.

2. Choose one of the following creative approaches to this story:
   - Assume that this short story is really only the first chapter in Russ's book. Write the final chapter.
   - Rewrite this story from the four men's point of view.
   - Write your own version of this story, showing a Whileaway that has been occupied for 600 years by men only, and where the aliens who appear are four women.

SUGGESTIONS FOR MAKING CONNECTIONS

1. Watch a few popular sitcoms on television today, noting especially the roles that men and women play. After several observations, compare these media roles to those mentioned in any two essays in this section. Do the media portrayals support the conflicts mentioned in either one of the essays? As far as your own experience is concerned, which portrayal is most true?

2. Write an essay in which you analyze the relationships between men and women according to several sources in this section. Feel free to include your own personal knowledge about this topic as well.

3. Which sex really has the upper hand in America today? Write an essay in which you argue effectively for either the men or the women. Refer to selections in this section as you respond.

4. In what ways does a black man's life differ from a white man's life? Write an essay in which you compare these two groups and draw some conclusions about what traits these men share, as well as what, if anything, keeps them distinct and apart.

5. In what ways do you see white women's lives in the United States as different from the lives of minority women? Write an essay in which you analyze these two groups to find the similarities and the differences among women, according to their culture.

6. "Am I really my brother's or sister's keeper?" Write an essay in which you explore whether each human has a moral responsibility to aid fellow humans. Here, you will explore your own philosophy on this question as well as referring to several sources in this section.

7. Working as a group with several other students in your class, design a questionnaire that raises questions about how men view women on your college campus or how women view men. Distribute the questionnaire among faculty, staff, and students. After studying the data you gather, write an essay in which you draw conclusions based on the information you received and on the discussions with your group about these data. Do your conclusions coincide with or contradict any of the writers in this section?

8. Compare the power that men have with the power that women possess. Are these two groups equally "strong," or does one group have an advantage over the other? Document your findings with sources from this section as well as any outside sources you care to consult.

9. You have the choice of being born a white male, a black male, a white woman, a black woman, or a Native American man or woman. Based on the opinions and facts offered in this section, make a decision. Support your answer not from a personal standpoint, but from the standpoint that you are "unborn" and have only these sources to guide you.

10. Working with a group of your fellow students, interview professional women to discover how the feminist movement has affected their careers, their roles, and the quality of their lives. Interview professional men for the same purpose. Write a report explaining and evaluating your findings. Do these findings contradict or confirm any author's beliefs in this section? Do they contradict or confirm your own?

11

Rights and Responsibilities

Previews: RIGHTS AND RESPONSIBILITIES

I will remove myself as an obstacle in the path that your children, against all odds, are making toward the light. I will not assassinate them for dreaming dreams and offering new visions of how to live. I will cease trying to lead your children, for I can see I have never understood where I was going. I will agree to sit quietly for a century or so, and meditate on this.

That is what the white man can say to the black woman.

We are listening.

From: *The Right to Life: What Can the White Man Say to the Black Woman?* ALICE WALKER

Blacks must no longer keep silent on this issue. We cannot permit the public to continue to imagine that we are obediently following our national leaders in endorsing abortion on demand and we must resist the forces that drive black women to seek abortion. . . . We are already besieged by homicide, drugs, AIDS, and an alarmingly high infant mortality rate. We do not need to reenact the sterilization programs of the 1930s and 1940s.

From: *Abortion Is Not a Civil Right,* GREG KEATH

[F]ive minutes into [the interview], I could feel the atmosphere chill. The interviewer gave me general information instead of trying to find out if I was right for the job. I've been there before. Then the session closed with a handshake, and those same old words: "We'll let you know." They said I should be so proud of myself for doing what I am doing. That's what they always say. I'm tired of hearing how courageous I am. So are other disabled people. We need jobs, and we want to work like anyone else.

From: *Give Us Jobs, Not Admiration,* ERIC BIGLER

This brings us to the fundamental truth about the military's policies toward homosexuals. The point is not to eject all gays, but to allow the military to say it does not accept homo-sexuals. This preserves its image as the upholder of traditional notions of masculinity, the one institution in the nation that claims to take boys and turn them into men.

From: *What's Fair in Love and War,* RANDY SHILTS

ALICE WALKER

The Right to Life: What Can the White Man Say to the Black Woman?

Born in 1944 in Eatonton, Georgia, the youngest of the eight children of sharecroppers Minnie and Willie Lee Walker, Alice Walker was shaped by a number of contradictory forces. On the one hand, she suffered from economic deprivation and the hardships imposed by segregation. On the other hand, she grew strong within her close-knit family and the extended black church congregation and community. She credits her mother with passing on creativity as expressed through the flower gardens she nurtured and the stories she told. Walker describes the pivotal role her mother played in her life in the moving essay "In Search of Our Mothers' Gardens," which traces the roots of current black women writers to the artistry of their mothers and grandmothers, which often came to light through handwork such as quilting or, as in her own mother's case, through growing flowers to provide beauty and sustenance for the spirits of their families.

Walker began her college education at Spelman in Atlanta, and later transferred to Sarah Lawrence in New York. Her first publications came shortly after her graduation in 1965. She has been widely acclaimed for her novel The Color Purple, *which was awarded both the Pulitzer Prize and the American Book Award in 1983 and was later made into a highly acclaimed film. Since then, she has published two more novels,* The Temple of My Familiar *(1989) and* Possessing the Secret of Joy *(1992). In addition to her novels, Walker has written many short stories, essays, and poems. She is also the author of biographical and critical works on writers such as Langston Hughes and Zora Neale Hurston. Walker has worked diligently to win recognition for Hurston, a writer from the period of the Harlem Renaissance who died penniless in a Florida welfare hotel. Through Walker's efforts, Hurston's novel* Their Eyes Were Watching God *has been republished and has finally gained well-deserved attention and critical respect.*

Best known for her works of fiction, Alice Walker has also been active for many years in the civil rights movement. During her time at Spelman College, she worked for voter registration, and later she became involved in welfare rights issues in Mississippi and New York.

This selection appears in Walker's anthology Her Blue Body Everything We Know; *it originated as a speech she made at a pro-choice rally in Washington, D.C., on April 8, 1989.*

Pre-Reading and Journal-Writing Suggestions

1. Write about a significant event during which you felt you had little or no control. How did you react in this situation? Were you completely helpless? Were you alone or with someone else? What happened in the end?

2. A sense of injustice is fine fuel for journal writing. Write about a time in your life when you were either a witness to or a victim of injustice.

_____

What is of use in these words I offer in memory and recognition of our common   *1*
mother. And to my daughter.

What can the white man say to the black woman?

For four hundred years he ruled over the black woman's womb.

Let us be clear. In the barracoons and along the slave shipping coasts of Africa, for more than twenty generations, it was he who dashed our babies' brains out against the rocks.

What can the white man say to the black woman?   *5*

For four hundred years he determined which black woman's children would live or die.

Let it be remembered. It was he who placed our children on the auction block in cities all across the Eastern half of what is now the United States, and listened to and watched them beg for their mothers' arms, before being sold to the highest bidder and dragged away.

What can the white man say to the black woman?

We remember that Fannie Lou Hamer, a poor sharecropper on a Mississippi plantation, was one of twenty-one children; and that on plantations across the South black women often had twelve, fifteen, twenty children. Like their enslaved mothers and grandmothers before them, these black women were sacrificed to the profit the white man could make from harnessing their bodies and their children's bodies to the cotton gin.

What can the white man say to the black woman?   *10*

We see him lined up, on Saturday nights, century after century, to make the black mother, who must sell her body to feed her children, go down on her knees to him.

Let us take note:

He has not cared for a single one of the dark children in his midst, over hundreds of years.

Where are the children of the Cherokee, my great-grandmother's people?
Gone.   *15*
Where are the children of the Blackfoot?
Gone.
Where are the children of the Lakota?
Gone.

Of the Cheyenne?   *20*
Of the Chippewa?
Of the Iroquois?
Of the Sioux?
Of the Akan?
Of the Ibo?   *25*
Of the Ashanti?
Of the Maori and the Aborigine?[1]

Where are the children of "the slave coast" and Wounded Knee?

We do not forget the forced sterilizations and forced starvations on the reservations, here as in South Africa. Nor do we forget the smallpox-infested blankets Indian children were given by the Great White Fathers of the United States Government.

What has the white man to say to the black woman?   *30*

When we have children you do everything in your power to make them feel unwanted from the moment they are born. You send them to fight and kill other dark mothers' children around the world. You shove them onto public highways into the path of oncoming cars. You shove their heads through plate glass windows. You string them up and you string them out.

What has the white man to say to the black woman?

From the beginning, you have treated all dark children with absolute hatred.

30,000,000 African children died on the way to the Americas, where nothing awaited them but endless toil and the crack of a bullwhip. They

[1]Tribal, indigenous children destroyed during the white "settlement" of the West.

died of a lack of food, of lack of movement in the holds of ships. Of lack of friends and relatives. They died of depression, bewilderment and fear.

What has the white man to say to the black woman?   35

Let us look around us: Let us look at the world the white man has made for the black woman and her children.

It is a world in which the black woman is still forced to provide cheap labor, in the form of children, for the factory farms and on the assembly lines of the white man.

It is a world into which the white man dumps every foul, person-annulling drug he smuggles into Creation.

It is a world where many of our babies die at birth, or later of malnu-trition, and where many more grow up to live lives of such misery they are forced to choose death by their own hands.

What has the white man to say to the black woman, and to all women   40
and children everywhere?

Let us consider the depletion of the ozone; let us consider homeless-ness and the nuclear peril; let us consider the destruction of the rainforests—in the name of the almighty hamburger. Let us consider the poisoned apples and the poisoned water and the poisoned air, and the poisoned earth.

And that all of our children, because of the white man's assault on the planet, have a possibility of death by cancer in their almost immediate future.

What has the white male lawgiver to say to any of us? Those of us who love life too much to willingly bring more children into a world satu-rated with death.

Abortion, for many women, is more than an experience of suffering beyond anything most men will ever know, it is an act of mercy, and an act of self-defense.

To make abortion illegal, again, is to sentence millions of women and   45
children to miserable lives and even more miserable deaths.

Given his history, in relation to us, I think the white man should be ashamed to attempt to speak for the unborn children of the black woman. To force us to have children for him to ridicule, drug, turn into killers and homeless wanderers is a testament to his hypocrisy.

What can the white man say to the black woman?

Only one thing that the black woman might hear.

Yes, indeed, the white man can say, your children have the right to life. Therefore I will call back from the dead those 30,000,000 who were tossed overboard during the centuries of the slave trade. And the other millions who died in my cotton fields and hanging from my trees.

I will recall all those who died of broken hearts and broken spirits, *50* under the insult of segregation.

I will raise up all the mothers who died exhausted after birthing twenty-one children to work sunup to sundown on my plantation. I will restore to full health all those who perished for lack of food, shelter, sunlight, and love; and from my inability to recognize them as human beings.

But I will go even further:

I will tell you, black woman, that I wish to be forgiven the sins I commit daily against you and your children. For I know that until I treat your children with love, I can never be trusted by my own. Nor can I respect myself.

And I will free your children from insultingly high infant mortality rates, short life spans, horrible housing, lack of food, rampant ill health. I will liberate them from the ghetto. I will open wide the doors of all the schools and the hospitals and businesses of society to your children. I will look at your children and see, not a threat, but a joy.

I will remove myself as an obstacle in the path that your children, *55* against all odds, are making toward the light. I will not assassinate them for dreaming dreams and offering new visions of how to live. I will cease trying to lead your children, for I can see I have never understood where I was going. I will agree to sit quietly for a century or so, and meditate on this.

That is what the white man can say to the black woman.

We are listening.

Suggestions for Writing and Discussion
1. Read this piece all the way through, marking the passages and images that strike you most strongly (obviously, individual responses to these images will differ widely and may include affirmation, horror, anger, inspiration, and so on). What images have you chosen on this initial

reading? What is your reaction to these images and to this piece in general?

2. After considering your response to Walker's images, summarize the message of this poetic essay.

3. Define the word *sterilization*. Then read paragraph 29 and explain the definition as Walker uses the word.

4. This piece originated as a speech at a pro-choice rally in Washington, D.C., in April 1989. Given the meeting, the location, and the date of events, what effect do you think this speech might have had on the audience? Explain your answer with specific reasons.

5. What, if anything, surprised you as you were reading this piece?

6. Consider Walker's choice of language and the way she organizes her information. What might be the advantages of adopting this repetitive format of raising the same question and then moving on to specific images? What might be the disadvantages?

7. This piece focuses primarily on white men and black women, yet many in Walker's audience saw these two groups as representative of many groups of people. What other specific groups could you place under the category "white men"? Under the category "black women"?

8. One line in this piece goes as follows: "From the beginning, you have treated all dark children with absolute hatred." Is this statement fair? Is it true? Why would the author choose such strong words here?

    Write three different one-page responses to this topic. For each topic, imagine a different audience:
    - Members of the black students' caucus on a university campus
    - Members of a reactionary group called White Is Right
    - Members of a group with mixed cultural background who support a lecture, art, and music forum aimed at improving communications among people from different ethnic groups.

9. Comment on the effectiveness of the ending of this piece. How did you react to Walker's final words?

Suggestions for Extended Thinking and Writing

1. Write a speech that you intend to give at either a pro-choice rally or a pro-life rally or at a rally dedicated to some other controversial issue. Model the organization of this piece by choosing one central question to ask throughout your speech.

2. Make a list of the historic wrongs Walker mentions as she moves from the capture of African slaves to the present treatment of minorities. Based on what you know from your own experiences, from your reading in other classes or on your own, and from viewing television news programs and documentaries, explain how you see any of the events Walker cites as related to race-related conflicts in today's society.

GREG KEATH

Abortion Is Not a Civil Right

Founder and president of the Black Alliance for Family, Greg Keath writes and speaks frequently on black family issues. This argument first appeared in the Wall Street Journal *on September 27, 1989.*

Pre-Reading and Journal-Writing Suggestions

1. List the reasons a woman might choose to have an abortion.
2. Explain your response to each of these reasons.

The battle around the abortion issue has raged for years with the understanding that the major combatants involved are either white liberals, white evangelical Protestants, or white Catholics. Meanwhile, black America—which is affected more profoundly by abortion than is any other group in society—has experienced its own sharp internal division. While most black leaders have favored abortion rights, opinion surveys have found mainstream blacks to be among those most strongly opposed to abortion on demand.

Where does black America really stand on the issue? Statistics from the Department of Health and Human Services suggest that black women are more than twice as likely to abort their children as white women. For every three black babies born, two are aborted. Forty-three percent of all abortions in the United States are performed on black women. From figures supplied by the federal government and the Alan Guttmacher Institute, Richard D. Glasow of National Right to Life has estimated that some 400,000 black pregnancies are aborted each year. At the same time, according to a 1988 poll taken by the National Opinion Research Center, 62 percent of blacks said abortion should be illegal under all circumstances.

How can blacks consistently tell pollsters they oppose abortion while we exercise that right proportionately more than any other group in America? In part, black abortion rates reflect the pressure of social service and private welfare agencies in our communities. A black teenager told me she had asked Planned Parenthood in Detroit for help in carrying her baby to term and putting it up for adoption. But because the baby's father was white, a clinician advised her to abort the baby because, "No one wants to adopt a zebra." Better-educated black women are pushed toward abortion by different forces: the threat to educational hopes or aspirations to economic independence.

As these women struggle with their profound moral choices, many national black leaders have ceased to look at abortion as a moral problem with moral consequences, and have come to see it instead as an opportunity for forging political alliances. At the March for Life rally in 1977 Jesse Jackson said, "The solution to a [crisis pregnancy] is not to kill the innocent baby but to deal with [the mother's] values and her attitudes toward life." Twelve years later, he spoke to the enormous April 1989 abortion rights march in Washington.

The black leadership has succumbed to the temptation to present abortion as a civil-rights issue. By this reasoning, abortion is to women in the 1980s what desegregation was to blacks in the 1960s. Any erosion of abortion rights would accelerate the "move to the right" that black leaders say threatens black progress. At a news conference earlier this year sponsored by Planned Parenthood, Jesse Jackson, Andrew Young, and Julian Bond issued a statement denouncing Operation Rescue, comparing those who participate in abortion clinic sit-ins to "the segregationists who fought desperately to block black Americans from access to their rights."

But many blacks wonder whether black civil rights and abortion fit so neatly together. Black pregnancies have historically been the target of social engineers such as Margaret Sanger, founder of Planned Parenthood. Sanger was convinced that blacks, Jews, Eastern Europeans, and other non-Aryan groups were detracting from the creative intellectual and social potential of America, and she wanted those groups' numbers reduced. In her first book, *Pivot of Civilization,* she warned of free maternity care for the poor: "Instead of decreasing and aiming to eliminate the stocks that are most detrimental to the future of the race and the world it tends to render them to a menacing degree dominant."

In the late 1930s Sanger instituted the Negro Project, a program to gain the backing of black ministers, physicians, and political leaders for birth control and sterilization in the black community. Sanger wrote, "The most successful education approach to the Negro is through a religious appeal. We do not want word to go out that we want to exterminate the Negro population, and the minister is the man who can straighten out that idea if it ever occurs to any of their more rebellious members."

There are disturbing indications that this state of mind has not vanished. Even now, 70 percent of the clinics operated by Planned Parenthood—the operator of the largest chain of abortion facilities in the nation—are in black and Hispanic neighborhoods. The schools in which their school-based clinics are located are substantially nonwhite. In a March 1939 letter, Sanger explained why clinics had to be located where the "dysgenic" races lived: "The birth control clinics all over the country are doing their utmost to reach the lower strata of our population . . . but we must realize that there are hundreds of thousands of women who never leave their own vicinity."

Blacks must no longer keep silent on this issue. We cannot permit the public to continue to imagine that we are obediently following our national leaders in endorsing abortion on demand and we must resist the forces that drive black women to seek abortion. The black community in cities such as Baltimore, Chicago, Detroit, and Washington, D.C., has started crisis pregnancy centers to help these women. We are already besieged by homicide, drugs, AIDS, and an alarmingly high infant mortality rate. We do not need to reenact the sterilization programs of the 1930s and 1940s.

Suggestions for Writing and Discussion

1. Summarize Greg Keath's main point in this article. What may have prompted him to write this piece in the first place?
2. What is a "segregationist" (paragraph 5)? Is your response to this word positive or negative? How does Keath use this term?
3. What does Keath believe are the causes for the black abortion rate in this country? What other causes might you add to this list?
4. If Jesse Jackson were running for president, do you think Keath would campaign for or against him? Explain your answer with inferences drawn from the text. Imagine that you are writing an article for a pro-life newsletter comparing Keath's views to Jackson's.
5. Keath writes that "black pregnancies have historically been the target of social engineers such as Margaret Sanger, founder of Planned Parenthood." What does he believe was Sanger's main purpose for targeting the black community? What evidence does he offer to support his idea that Sanger was mainly concerned with the black community?
6. What does Keath gain or lose by using Sanger as the sole example for one-third of this article? What might his purpose be in doing this?
7. Keath gives possible reasons why blacks have so many abortions, but he does not give reasons why they should not. How can you tell what his position is on this issue? In your opinion, why doesn't Keath give positive reasons for black women to avoid abortions?

Suggestions for Extended Thinking and Writing

1. Do your own research on Margaret Sanger. According to your findings, what was her personal philosophy about women's rights, the poor, and minorities? Do your findings support or contradict the charges that Keath has made in this article?
2. Read speeches made by black leaders today. What is the primary message that they seem to be giving to the black American community?

ERIC BIGLER

Give Us Jobs, Not Admiration

> *Born in Ohio in 1958, Eric Bigler was paralyzed from the chest down by a high school diving accident. He later attended Wright State University in Dayton, Ohio, earning degrees in social work and business and industrial counseling management. Bigler's primary commitment is to developing computer programs for those with disabilities.*

Pre-Reading and Journal-Writing Suggestions

1. Write about the first time you applied for a job. What were your hopes and fears as you went through the application process? What was the outcome?
2. What are your personal career goals? Can you foresee any factors that might prevent you from attaining these goals?
3. Write two portraits of yourself, one from your own point of view and the other from an outsider's viewpoint. After writing these two pieces, explain to the outsider what he or she cannot possibly know just by looking at you.

Tuesday I have another job interview. Like most I have had so far, it will probably end with the all-too-familiar words, "We'll let you know of our decision in a few days." *1*

Many college graduates searching for their first career job might simply accept that response as, "Sorry, we're not interested in you," and blame the rejection on inexperience or bad chemistry. For myself and other disabled people, however, this response often seems to indicate something more worrisome: a reluctance to hire the handicapped even when they're qualified. I have been confined to a wheelchair since 1974, when a high-school diving accident left me paralyzed from the chest down. But that didn't prevent me from earning a bachelor's in social work in 1983, and I am now finishing up a master's degree in business and industrial management, specializing in employee relations and human-resource development.

Our government spends a great deal of money to help the handicapped, but it does not necessarily spend it all wisely. For example, in 1985 Ohio's Bureau of Vocational Rehabilitation (BVR) spent more than $4 million in tuition and other expenses so that disabled students could obtain a college education. BVR's philosophy is that the amount of money spent educating students will be repaid in disabled employees' taxes. The agency assists graduates by offering workshops on résumé writing and interviewing techniques, skills many already learned in college. BVR also maintains files of résumés that are matched with help-wanted notices from local companies and employs placement specialists to work directly with graduates during their job search.

Even with all this assistance, however, graduates still have trouble getting hired. Such programs might do better if they concentrated on the perceptions of employers as well as the skills of applicants. More important, improving contacts with prospective employers might encourage them to actively recruit the disabled.

Often, projects that *do* show promise don't get the chance to thrive. I   *5* was both a client and an informal consultant to one program, Careers for the Disabled in Dayton, which asked local executives to make a commitment to hire disabled applicants whenever possible. I found this strategy to be on target, since support for a project is more likely when it is ordered from the top. The program also offered free training seminars to corporations on how they can work effectively with the disabled candidate. In April of 1986—less than a year after it was started and after only three disabled people were placed—the program was discontinued because, according to the director, they had "no luck at getting [enough] corporations to join the program."

Corporations need to take a more independent and active part in hiring qualified handicapped persons. Today's companies try to show a willingness to innovate, and hiring people like myself would enhance that image. Madison Avenue has finally recognized that the disabled are also consumers; more and more often, commercials include them. But advertisers could break down even more stereotypes. I would like to see one of those Hewlett-Packard commercials, for instance, show an employee racing down the sidewalk in his wheelchair, pulling alongside a pay phone and calling a colleague to ask "What if . . . ?"

Corporate recruiters also need to be better prepared for meeting with disabled applicants. They should be ready to answer queries about any barriers that their building's design may pose, and they should be forthright about asking their own questions. It's understandable that employers are afraid to mention matters that are highly personal and may prove embarrassing—or, even worse, discriminatory. There's nothing wrong, however, with an employer reassuring him or herself about whether an applicant will be able to reach files, operate computers or even get into the bathroom. Until interviewers change their style, disabled applicants need to initiate discussion of disability-related issues.

Government has tried to improve hiring for the disabled through Affirmative Action programs. The Rehabilitation Act of 1973 says institutions or programs receiving substantial amounts of federal money can't discriminate on the basis of handicap. Yet I was saddened and surprised to discover how many companies spend much time and money writing great affirmative-action and equal-opportunity guidelines but little time following them. Then there are the cosmetic acts, such as the annual National Employ the Handicapped Week every October. If President Reagan (or anyone else) wants to help the disabled with proclamations, more media exposure is necessary. I found out about the last occasion in 1985 from a brief article on the back of a campus newspaper—a week after it had happened.

As if other problems were not enough, the disabled who search unsuccessfully for employment often face a loss of self-esteem and worth. In college, many disabled people I have talked to worked hard toward a degree so they would be prepared for jobs after graduation. Now they look back on their four or more years as wasted time. For these individuals, the days of earning good grades and accomplishing tough tasks fade away, leaving only frustrating memories. Today's job market is competitive enough without prejudice adding more "handicaps."

About that interview . . . five minutes into it, I could feel the atmo- 10 sphere chill. The interviewer gave me general information instead of trying to find out if I was right for the job. I've been there before. Then the session closed with a handshake, and those same old words: "We'll let you know." They said I should be so proud of myself for doing what I am doing. That's what they always say. I'm tired of hearing how courageous I am. So are other disabled people. We need jobs, and we want to work like anyone else.

But still, I remain an optimist. I know someday soon a company will be smart enough to realize how much I have to offer them in both my head and my heart.

Maybe then I'll hear the words so many of us really want to hear: "You're hired."

Suggestions for Writing and Discussion

1. In paragraph 1, Bigler mentions a job interview. He concludes with the outcome of the interview. Summarize the events of the interview and explain how he uses this interview to express his main idea.
2. In paragraph 3, Bigler refers to "Vocational Rehabilitation." Explain the meaning of this phrase.
3. What's your initial reaction to the author after reading this piece? Do you feel sorry for him? Indifferent toward him? Angry? Something else? Please explain.
4. After reading this piece, how would you characterize the author? Does he sound intelligent? Angry? Lazy? Sincere? Honest? Point to three places in this writing that support your response.
5. Why do you think some employers might be reluctant to hire a handicapped worker? For every reason you give, try to provide a counterargument. Imagine that you are writing a proposal for an organization of business and industry executives who are in the process of developing a policy for hiring (or not hiring) handicapped workers. Your purpose is to provide them with many possible ways of looking at this issue.

6. What do you see as Bigler's main purpose in writing this piece? What might he hope to accomplish?
7. Reflect on the career goals you wrote about in your journal before reading this piece. Imagine, now, that you still have these same goals but that you are confined to a wheelchair. Write a letter to an employer who has just refused you this job, despite your qualifications.

Suggestions for Extended Thinking and Writing

1. Using this essay, as well as any two other sources from this text, write an extended definition paper in which you expand on the meaning of the word *right* or the word *responsibility*. Feel free to use your own experiences as illustrations as you develop this definition.
2. Write an essay in which you explain the differences between a right and a privilege. Refer to examples from this selection, as well as from your own experiences, as you explain the distinction.

RANDY SHILTS

What's Fair in Love and War

> *Randy Shilts was born in Aurora, Illinois. After graduating from the University of Oregon School of Journalism, he became a staff writer for* The Advocate, *a national gay newsmagazine. In 1977 he was hired by San Francisco public television station KQED's award-winning "Newsroom" program as a correspondent. He also served as San Francisco city hall correspondent for KTVU-TV's award-winning "Ten O'Clock News" program. While holding these positions, Shilts worked closely with the San Francisco gay and lesbian population and was one of the first news correspondents in the nation to report the earliest cases of AIDS.*
>
> *Following the epidemic across thirty nations and four continents, including equatorial Africa, Shilts was widely regarded as the nation's primary reporter on AIDS until his death from the disease in February 1994. In addition to newspaper and magazine articles, gay rights activist Shilts wrote the book* And the Band Played On, *which won critical acclaim for its hard-hitting look at the early years of the AIDS crisis.*
>
> *This essay is based on information gathered for his book* Conduct Unbecoming: Gays and Lesbians in the U.S. Military *(1993), for which he conducted interviews with more than 1,100 gay U.S. military men and women.* Conduct Unbecoming *grew out of Shilts's desire to make it possible for heterosexuals to understand what it is like to be gay in America. He chose to write about the military because of his belief that it reflects American societal prejudice to an exaggerated degree. The book traces the history of homosexuals in the military from the 1950s through U.S. involvement in Vietnam up to the Persian Gulf conflict.*

Pre-Reading and Journal-Writing Suggestions

1. What's your initial reaction to gays serving in the American military? Freewrite on this topic for ten minutes.
2. What qualifications do you think a person needs to serve in the U.S. military? Do you think that most people in the military today measure up to your list of qualifications? Please explain.

On the first night of the Scud missile attacks on American troops in   1
the Persian Gulf, an army specialist fourth class with the 27th Field Artillery found himself cramped in a foxhole with three other men. Like many young enlisted men, the specialist (who asked that his name not be used) had previously confided to the other men, his friends, that he was gay.

During that night in the foxhole, they huddled together in their suffocating suits meant to protect them from chemical and biological warfare agents. They could not see one another, but to reassure themselves that they were still there, still alive, each man kept one hand on the other. Nobody seemed to mind that one reassuring hand belonged to a homosexual, the soldier recalls—there were more important things to think about.

Defense Department policy contends that the purpose of excluding gays from the armed forces is to preserve the "good order, discipline and morale" of the military, because no heterosexual soldier would want to serve with, take orders from or share a foxhole with a homosexual. America's experience in its past three wars suggests otherwise. The behavior of military officials in accepting gays during these wars also suggests that the generals themselves know their arguments are fallacious. At no time is good order, discipline and morale more crucial for a fighting unit than in time of combat; at no time have the military's regulations against gays been more roundly ignored than in periods when troops were sent out to fight.

President Clinton's intention of integrating acknowledged lesbians and gay men into the armed forces has raised a great cry from opponents of reform, most of whom question how soldiers will respond to sharing a foxhole with a gay soldier. These arguments belie the fact that gay soldiers have served in U.S. military foxholes since the days of Valley Forge, some openly.

From the first days of the Defense Department's anti-gay regulations in the early 1940s, the government was willing to waive the for-heterosexuals-only requirement for military service if barring gays interfered with manpower exigencies. In 1945, just two years after the regulation was adopted, and during the height of the final European offensive against the Third Reich, Secretary of War Henry Stimson ordered a review of all gay discharges in the previous two years, with an eye toward reinducting gay men who had not committed any in-service homosexual acts. At the same time, orders went out to "salvage" homosexuals for the service whenever possible.

The Korean War saw a dramatic plunge in gay-related discharges. In the late 1940s, the navy meted out 1,100 undesirable discharges a year to gay sailors. In 1950, at the height of the Korean War, that number was down to 483. But in 1953, when the armistice was signed at Panmunjom, the navy cracked down again with vigor, distributing 1,353 gay-related undesirable discharges in that year alone.

The Vietnam War provides some of the most striking examples of the military's tacit acceptance of homosexuality in times of war. When Air Force Sgt. Roberto Reyes-Colon was seen leaving his base near the demilitarized zone with his Marine Corps boyfriend, military police brought him before his commanding officer the next day. The commander listened to the MPs complain that they had seen Reyes-Colon kiss the Marine, but once they left the room, the commanding officer ripped up the report they had written on the incident. Reyes-Colon's defense was that "there's a war going on," and the officer agreed.

Marine Corps Lt. Ben Dillingham, assigned to lead a reconnaissance platoon in Vietnam in 1970, was surprised to discover that two of his enlisted men were lovers, inseparable, patrolling together, even sleeping together under the same blanket. All the other soldiers in the tightly knit platoon were aware of the relationship, and no one cared. It seemed to Dillingham that with a war going on, and everyone's life depending on the others, no one had time to quibble about gay soldiers.

Discharges for homosexuality still occurred, but Pentagon statistics themselves bear out that the armed forces became strangely uninterested in enforcing their regulations against homosexuals during this period. Between 1963 and 1966, the navy, which at the time was the only branch of the military to keep detailed statistics of gay discharges, "separated" between 1,600 and 1,700 enlisted members a year for homosexuality. From 1966 to 1967, as the Vietnam buildup began in earnest, the number of gay discharges dropped from 1,708 to 1,094. In 1969, at the peak of the escalation, gay discharges dropped to 643. A year later, only 461 sailors were relieved of duty for being gay.

These dramatic reductions occurred during a period of some of the service's highest membership since World War II. It was not that there were any fewer gays in the navy; by all appearances there were many more. But the navy had effectively stopped enforcing regulations against homosexuality. Draftees who announced themselves to be homosexual at their induction centers frequently were told by army doctors that they were welcome in the army just the same. In at least three circumstances in the early 1970s, gay activists had to go to federal court to force the government to observe its own policies regarding the exclusion of gays.

History repeated itself two years ago during Operation Desert Storm when numerous military personnel, most serving in the reserves, tried to escape mobilization by telling their reserve commanders they were gay—and many reserve commanders responded that gay soldiers could serve anyway. When a lesbian officer in a Western medical-support group told her commander that she was a lesbian, he replied, "That's all right. We wouldn't have a medical service without gays." When army reservist Donna Lynn Jackson told her commander she was a lesbian, she says he told her bluntly that she would go to Saudi Arabia, and be discharged for homosexuality at the end of the war. Jackson went to the newspapers, and an embarrassed Pentagon discharged her quickly, insisting that such cases were aberrations and that the Defense Department had an ironclad ban on gays in the military.

Despite the public pronouncements, military commanders made it as difficult as possible to separate gay personnel for the duration of the conflict. Decade-old Defense Department regulations demanded that anyone who even intimated that he or she was gay—or had the "intent" to commit gay sexual acts in the future—must be discharged, with no exceptions allowed. In the days before the ground war in the gulf started, however, the staff judge advocate's office of the Marine Corps Reserve Support Center instructed a lesbian who had acknowledged her homosexuality that "claimed sexual preferences do not constitute an exemption from the mobilization process."

At the 40th Aeromedical Evacuation Squadron at McChord Air Force Base in Washington, another gay reservist seeking to avoid mobilization by announcing she was gay was told that she would not be certified as a homosexual by the air force unless she produced a marriage license listing another woman as a spouse. No jurisdiction in the United States allows gays to marry. Demanding that the woman produce a marriage license was like insisting she produce a piece of Mars.

Once stationed in the gulf, many of the gay military personnel found a remarkably accepting environment. When officers supervising a navy corpsman stationed with a Marine Corps unit on the front lines of Kuwait became concerned that his Marines all knew he was gay, the corpsman was transferred to another unit. The Marines in the new unit soon heard the rumors that he was gay, but befriended him anyway, and even jokingly nicknamed him "Precious," after the miniature poodle in the movie "The Silence of the Lambs."

The acceptance of gays in some quarters does not mean that lesbians and gay men will be easily integrated into every fighting unit. As with African-Americans and with women, the ability of the tradition-bound institution to accommodate gay members will take years, if not decades. The travails of gays in the military will not stop with a new president's executive order—they will just begin.

Still, animosity toward gays in the armed forces is not nearly so ingrained as opponents of the change would have us believe. For the past several years, some navy ship commanders have been privately candid with their crews about no longer having any intention of enforcing the ban on homosexuals. In 1990, the reluctance of ship commanders to pursue lesbians led Vice Adm. Joseph Donnell, commander of the U.S. Atlantic fleet, to order all his commanding officers to enforce regulations more aggressively against lesbians. The memorandum acknowledged why many commanders were reluctant to do this: because, Donnell wrote, "the stereotypical female homosexual" was "hardworking, career-oriented, willing to put in long hours on the job and among the command's top professionals."

Tens of thousands of gay military personnel, particularly those in the enlisted ranks, serve with some degree of openness in the military today, informing their co-workers, though not the press or their officers, that they are gay. Over the past five years, many more officers have served openly as well, though they do not tempt fate by allowing their names to be released publicly. Typical of stories from the new military is the tale I heard of an air force major serving in Florida whose colleagues threw him a 40th birthday party, and enlisted the major's lover to organize it.

This brings us to the fundamental truth about the military's policies toward homosexuals. The point is not to eject all gays, but to allow the military to say it does not accept homosexuals. This preserves its image as the upholder of traditional notions of masculinity, the one institution in the nation that claims to take boys and turn them into men. In harsh economic times, this raises the question as to whether the taxpayers grant the Defense Department nearly $300 billion a year to provide the most cost-effective defense for the nation, or whether it is an investment in preserving a club where heterosexual men can assure themselves of their masculinity.

The argument that gays will unalterably subvert discipline and good order in the armed forces is also hard to justify within the context of the history of the U.S. military. History tells us that the man who first instilled discipline in the ragtag Continental Army at Valley Forge was the Prussian Baron Frederick William von Steuben. It was he who took what were essentially 13 different colonial militias and molded them into one army.

Von Steuben at first had declined Benjamin Franklin's offer of the job,   20 because the Continental Congress could not pay him. But when von Steuben learned that ecclesiastical authorities were planning to try him for homosexuality, he renegotiated with Franklin and was appointed a major general to the Continental Army. When he came to Valley Forge to begin his drills, he appeared with a 17-year-old French interpreter, who must have had other talents useful to the general, because it soon became clear that he had no linguistic skills.

Nevertheless, von Steuben, the army's first inspector general, came to have an incalculable impact on the U.S. military, writing the drill books that would be used for the next 35 years by the fledgling U.S. Army. His plans for a military academy became embodied in West Point. Some military historians have judged von Steuben as one of only two men whose contributions were "indispensable" toward winning the Revolutionary War; the other was George Washington.

It is a crowning irony that anti-gay policies are defended in the name of preserving the good order and discipline of the U.S. military, when that very order and discipline was the creation of a gay man.

Suggestions for Writing and Discussion
1. Summarize what Shilts calls "the fundamental truth about the military's policies toward homosexuals" (paragraph 18).
2. In paragraph 3, what does Shilts mean when he calls the arguments of military officers "fallacious"? Do not simply say "wrong"; explain the full denotation and connotation of the word.
3. Obviously Shilts wrote this piece to present his stance on gays in the military. How do you think *Newsweek* readers reacted to his views? Write a letter to the editor of *Newsweek* to explain your response to Shilts's ideas.
4. Reflect on your response to the first journal suggestion. After reading Shilts's piece, have you changed your views in any way? Please explain.

5. Imagine you have been assigned to debate Shilts on this issue. What counterarguments can you come up with?
6. What specific parts of this essay do you find most interesting or effective? Are there any parts that you find boring or repetitive? Please explain.
7. What do you think Shilts might say about U.S. women being able to serve in active combat? What arguments does he make about gays in the military that might also apply to women in combat? What arguments might work against the argument for women in combat?
8. Interview three friends about the question of gays in the military. Take notes on their answers as well as their reactions and responses to your questions. Perhaps work with other class members to write a report on your findings.

Suggestions for Extended Thinking and Writing

1. Interview at least three acquaintances about the question of gays in the military. Take notes on their responses to the questions you ask. Then write a paper explaining what you learned about this controversy, both from the interviews you conducted and from the information provided in Shilts's essay.
2. Write an essay in which you compare the dilemma of gays in the military with any other form of discrimination.

KATHERINE BARRETT

Old Before Her Time

> Katherine Barrett is a contributing editor to the Ladies' Home Journal. She also writes a regular column for Finance World. This biographical essay reflecting Barrett's commitment to human interest stories first appeared in the August 1983 issue of the Ladies Home Journal.

Pre-Reading and Journal-Writing Suggestions

1. Imagine you are eighty years old. Describe what a typical day might be like for you.
2. If you could stay one age forever, what age would you choose to be and why?
3. Write about the oldest person you've ever known. Besides describing this person, also focus on this person's attitude, character, and activities.

This is the story of an extraordinary voyage in time, and of a young   *1*
woman who devoted three years to a singular experiment. In 1979, Patty Moore—then aged twenty-six—transformed herself for the first of many times into an eighty-five-year-old woman. Her object was to discover first-hand the problems, joys and frustrations of the elderly. She wanted to know for herself what it's like to live in a culture of youth and beauty when your hair is gray, your skin is wrinkled and no men turn their heads as you pass.

Her time machine was a makeup kit. Barbara Kelly, a friend and professional makeup artist, helped Patty pick out a wardrobe and showed her how to use latex to create wrinkles, and wrap Ace bandages to give the impression of stiff joints. "It was peculiar," Patty recalls, as she relaxes in her New York City apartment. "Even the first few times I went out I realized that I wouldn't have to *act* that much. The more I was perceived as elderly by others, the more 'elderly' I actually became . . . I imagine that's just what happens to people who really are old."

What motivated Patty to make her strange journey? Partly her career—as an industrial designer, Patty often focuses on the needs of the elderly. But the roots of her interest are also deeply personal. Extremely close to her own grandparents—particularly her maternal grandfather, now ninety—and raised in a part of Buffalo, New York, where there was a large elderly population, Patty always drew comfort and support from the older people around her. When her own marriage ended in 1979 and her life seemed to be falling apart, she dove into her "project" with all her soul. In all, she donned her costume more than two hundred times in fourteen different states. Here is the remarkable story of what she found.

Columbus, Ohio, May 1979

Leaning heavily on her cane, Pat Moore stood alone in the middle of a crowd of young professionals. They were all attending a gerontology conference, and the room was filled with animated chatter. But no one was talking to Pat. In a throng of men and women who devoted their working lives to the elderly, she began to feel like a total nonentity. "I'll get us all some coffee," a young man told a group of women next to her. "What about me?" thought Pat. "If I were young, they would be offering me coffee, too." It was a bitter thought at the end of a disappointing day—a day that marked Patty's first appearance as "the old woman." She had planned to attend the gerontology conference anyway, and almost as a lark decided to see how professionals would react to an old person in their midst.

Now, she was angry. All day she had been ignored . . . counted out in   5
a way she had never experienced before. She didn't understand. Why didn't people help her when they saw her struggling to open a heavy door? Why didn't they include her in conversations? Why did the other participants seem almost embarrassed by her presence at the conference—as if it were somehow inappropriate that an old person should be professionally active?

And so, eighty-five-year-old Pat Moore learned her first lesson: The old are often ignored. "I discovered that people really do judge a book by its cover," Patty says today. "Just because I looked different, people either condescended or they totally dismissed me. Later, in stores, I'd get the same reaction. A clerk would turn to someone younger and wait on her first. It was as if he assumed that I—the older woman—could wait because I didn't have anything better to do."

New York City, October 1979

Bent over her cane, Pat walked slowly toward the edge of the park. She had spent the day sitting on a bench with friends, but now dusk was falling and her friends had all gone home. She looked around nervously at the deserted area and tried to move faster, but her joints were stiff. It was then that she heard the barely audible sound of sneakered feet approaching and the kids' voices. "Grab her, man." "Get her purse." Suddenly an arm was around her throat and she was dragged back, knocked off her feet.

She saw only a blur of sneakers and blue jeans, heard the sounds of mocking laughter, felt fists pummeling her—on her back, her legs, her breasts, her stomach. "Oh, God," she thought, using her arms to protect her head and curling herself into a ball. "They're going to kill me. I'm going to die. . . ."

Then, as suddenly as the boys attacked, they were gone. And Patty was left alone, struggling to rise. The boys' punches had broken the latex makeup on her face, the fall had disarranged her wig, and her whole body ached. (Later she would learn that she had fractured her left wrist, an injury that took two years to heal completely.) Sobbing, she left the park and hailed a cab to return home. Again the thought struck her: What if I really lived in the gray ghetto . . . what if I couldn't escape to my nice safe home . . . ?

Lesson number two: The fear of crime is paralyzing. "I really understand now why the elderly become homebound," the young woman says as she recalls her ordeal today. "When something like this happens, the fear just doesn't go away. I guess it wasn't so bad for me. I could distance myself from what happened . . . and I was strong enough to get up and walk away. But what about someone who is really too weak to run or fight back or protect herself in any way? And the elderly often can't afford to move if the area in which they live deteriorates, becomes unsafe. I met people like this and they were imprisoned by their fear. That's when the bolts go on the door. That's when people starve themselves because they're afraid to go to the grocery store."

New York City, February 1980

It was a slushy, gray day and Pat had laboriously descended four flights of stairs from her apartment to go shopping. Once outside, she struggled to hold her threadbare coat closed with one hand and manipulate her cane with the other. Splotches of snow made the street difficult for anyone to navigate, but for someone hunched over, as she was, it was almost impossible. The curb was another obstacle. The slush looked ankle-deep—and what was she to do? Jump over it? Slowly, she worked her way around to a drier spot, but the crowds were impatient to move. A woman with packages jostled her as she rushed past, causing Pat to nearly lose her balance. If I really were old, I would have fallen, she thought. Maybe broken something. On another day, a woman had practically knocked her over by letting go of a heavy door as Pat tried to enter a coffee shop. Then there were the revolving doors. How could you push them without strength? And how could you get up and down stairs, on and off a bus, without risking a terrible fall?

Lesson number three: If small, thoughtless deficiencies in design were corrected, life would be so much easier for older people. It was no surprise to Patty that the "built" environment is often inflexible. But even she didn't realize the extent of the problems, she admits. "It was a terrible feeling. I never realized how difficult it is to get off a curb if your knees don't bend easily. Or the helpless feeling you get if your upper arms aren't strong enough to open a door. You know, I just felt so vulnerable—as if I was at the mercy of every barrier or rude person I encountered."

Ft. Lauderdale, Florida, May 1980

Pat met a new friend while shopping and they decided to continue their conversation over a sundae at a nearby coffee shop. The woman was in her late seventies, "younger" than Pat, but she was obviously reaching out for help. Slowly, her story unfolded. "My husband moved out of our bedroom," the woman said softly, fiddling with her coffee cup and fighting back tears. "He won't touch me anymore. And when he gets angry at me for being stupid, he'll even sometimes. . . ." The woman looked down, embarrassed to go on. Pat took her hand. "He hits me . . . he gets so mean." "Can't you tell anyone?" Pat asked. "Can't you tell your son?" "Oh, no!" the woman almost gasped. "I would never tell the children; they absolutely adore him."

Lesson number four: Even a fifty-year-old marriage isn't necessarily a good one. While Pat met many loving and devoted elderly couples, she was stunned to find others who had stayed together unhappily—because divorce was still an anathema in their middle years. "I met women who secretly wished their husbands dead, because after so many years they just ended up full of hatred. One woman in Chicago even admitted that she deliberately angered her husband because she knew it would make his blood pressure rise. Of course, that was pretty extreme. . . ."

Patty pauses thoughtfully and continues. "I guess what really made an   *15* impression on me, the real eye-opener, was that so many of these older women had the same problems as women twenty, thirty or forty. Problems with men . . . problems with the different roles that are expected of them. As a 'young woman' I, too, had just been through a relationship where I spent a lot of time protecting someone by covering up his problems from family and friends. Then I heard this woman in Florida saying that she wouldn't tell her children their father beat her because she didn't want to disillusion them. These issues aren't age-related. They affect everyone."

Clearwater, Florida, January 1981

She heard the children laughing, but she didn't realize at first that they were laughing at her. On this day, as on several others, Pat had shed the clothes of a middle-income woman for the rags of a bag lady. She wanted to see the extremes of the human condition, what it was like to be old and poor, and outside traditional society as well. Now, tottering down the sidewalk, she was most concerned with the cold, since her layers of ragged clothing did little to ease the chill. She had spent the afternoon rummaging through garbage cans, loading her shopping bags with bits of debris, and she was stiff and tired. Suddenly, she saw that four little boys, five or six years old, were moving up on her. And then she felt the sting of the pebbles they were throwing. She quickened her pace to escape, but another handful of gravel hit her and the laughter continued. They're using me as a target, she thought, horror-stricken. They don't even think of me as a person.

Lesson number five: Social class affects every aspect of an older person's existence. "I found out that class is a very important factor when you're old," says Patty. "It was interesting. That same day, I went back to my hotel and got dressed as a wealthy woman, another role that I occasionally took. Outside the hotel, a little boy of about seven asked if I would go shelling with him. We walked along the beach, and he reached out to hold my hand. I knew he must have a grandmother who walked with a cane, because he was so concerned about me and my footing. 'Don't put your cane there, the sand's wet,' he'd say. He really took responsibility for my welfare. The contrast between him and those children was really incredible. The little ones who were throwing the pebbles at me because they didn't see me as human. And then the seven-year-old taking care of me. I think he would have responded to me the same way even if I had been dressed as the middle-income woman. There's no question that money does make life easier for older people, not only because it gives them a more comfortable life-style, but because it makes others treat them with greater respect."

New York City, May 1981

Pat always enjoyed the time she spent sitting on the benches in Central Park. She'd let the whole day pass by, watching young children play, feeding the pigeons and chatting. One spring day she found herself sitting with three women, all widows, and the conversation turned to the few available men around. "It's been a long time since anyone hugged me," one woman complained. Another agreed. "Isn't that the truth. I need a hug, too." It was a favorite topic, Pat found—the lack of touching left in these women's lives, the lack of hugging, the lack of men.

In the last two years, she had found out herself how it felt to walk down Fifth Avenue and know that no men were turning to look after her. Or how it felt to look at models in magazines or store mannequins and *know* that those gorgeous clothes were just not made for her. She hadn't realized before just how much casual attention was paid to her because she was young and pretty. She hadn't realized it until it stopped.

Lesson number six: You never grow old emotionally. You always need to feel loved. "It's not surprising that everyone needs love and touching and holding," says Patty. "But I think some people feel that you reach a point in your life when you accept that those intimate feelings are in the past. That's wrong. These women were still interested in sex. But more than that, they—like everyone—needed to be hugged and touched. I'd watch two women greeting each other on the street and just holding onto each other's hands, neither wanting to let go. Yet, I also saw that there are people who are afraid to touch an old person . . . they were afraid to touch me. It's as if they think old age is a disease and it's catching. They think that something might rub off on them."

20

New York City, September 1981

He was a thin man, rather nattily dressed, with a hat that he graciously tipped at Pat as he approached the bench where she sat. "Might I join you?" he asked jauntily. Pat told him he would be welcome and he offered her one of the dietetic hard candies that he carried in a crumpled paper bag. As the afternoon passed, they got to talking . . . about the beautiful buds on the trees and the world around them and the past. "Life's for the living, my wife used to tell me," he said. "When she took sick she made me promise her that I wouldn't waste a moment. But the first year after she died, I just sat in the apartment. I didn't want to see anyone, talk to anyone or go anywhere. I missed her so much." He took a handkerchief from his pocket and wiped his eyes, and they sat in silence. Then he slapped his leg to break the mood and change the subject. He asked Pat about herself, and described his life alone. He belonged to a "senior center" now, and went on trips and had lots of friends. Life did go on. They arranged to meet again the following week on the same park bench. He brought lunch—chicken salad sandwiches and decaffeinated peppermint tea in a thermos—and wore a carnation in his lapel. It was the first date Patty had had since her marriage ended.

Lesson number seven: Life does go on . . . as long as you're flexible and open to change. "That man really meant a lot to me, even though I never saw him again," says Patty, her eyes wandering toward the gray wig that now sits on a wig-stand on the top shelf of her bookcase. "He was a real old-fashioned gentleman, yet not afraid to show his feelings—as so many men my age are. It's funny, but at that point I had been through months of self-imposed seclusion. Even though I was in a different role, that encounter kind of broke the ice for getting my life together as a single woman."

In fact, while Patty was living her life as the old woman, some of her young friends had been worried about her. After several years, it seemed as if the lines of identity had begun to blur. Even when she wasn't in makeup, she was wearing unusually conservative clothing, she spent most of her time with older people and she seemed almost to revel in her role—sometimes finding it easier to be in costume than to be a single New Yorker.

But as Patty continued her experiment, she was also learning a great deal from the older people she observed. Yes, society often did treat the elderly abysmally . . . they were sometimes ignored, sometimes victimized, sometimes poor and frightened, but so many of them were survivors. They had lived through two world wars, the Depression and into the computer age. "If there was one lesson to learn, one lesson that I'll take with me into *my* old age, it's that you've got to be flexible," Patty says. "I saw my friend in the park, managing after the loss of his wife, and I met countless other people who picked themselves up after something bad—or even something catastrophic—happened. I'm not worried about them. I'm worried about the others who shut themselves away. It's funny, but seeing these two extremes helped me recover from the trauma in my own life, to pull *my* life together."

Today, Patty is back to living the life of a single thirty-year-old, and   25
she rarely dons her costumes anymore. "I must admit, though, I do still think a lot about aging," she says. "I look in the mirror and I begin to see wrinkles, and then I realize that I won't be able to wash *those* wrinkles off." Is she afraid of growing older? "No. In a way, I'm kind of looking forward to it," she smiles. "I *know* it will be different from my experiment. I *know* I'll probably even look different. When they aged Orson Welles in *Citizen Kane* he didn't resemble at all the Orson Welles of today."

But Patty also knows that in one way she really did manage to capture the feeling of being old. With her bandages and her stooped posture, she turned her body into a kind of prison. Yet, inside she didn't change at all. "It's funny, but that's exactly how older people always say they feel," says Patty. "Their bodies age, but inside they are really no different than when they were young."

Suggestions for Writing and Discussion

1. Choose one of Barrett's episodes and summarize it. Then explain your response to this episode.
2. In paragraph 4 Barrett mentions a "gerontology conference" that Pat Moore attended. Check the meaning of *gerontology* in a dictionary. What is the origin of this word?
3. In this piece Barrett describes many specific incidents that took place when Moore was "old." From all of these, which one did you find most touching? Which made you the angriest?
4. Do you think Barrett paints an accurate picture of what it's like to be old in America today? Can you think of any other approaches she might have used in writing this article? Please explain.
5. After reading this essay, do you think you will be more aware of elderly people and their problems? Why or why not?
6. Interview an elderly person you know to discover how aging has affected this person. Write a report describing what you discovered through your interview. As you write, keep members of your class in mind as the audience.
7. Practice being a careful and astute observer. Go to a location that attracts all kinds of people and search out and observe an elderly person in that situation (grocery shopping, a restaurant, church). Do your observations support any of the seven lessons in this piece? Do any contradict these lessons?

Suggestions for Extended Thinking and Writing

1. Write an essay in which you explain how it feels to live in a stage of life other than old age (for instance, early childhood, adolescence, or middle age). Use anecdotes and dialogues to show your reader the responses of those outside the group you are describing to those who are members of that group.

2. In a recent magazine or newspaper, find a current article that deals with the problems or strengths of senior citizens. Write an essay that provides a brief summary and your response to the article.

THOMAS JEFFERSON

The Declaration of Independence

> *American revolutionary leader and political philosopher, Thomas Jefferson was the third president of the United States. Jefferson was born in 1743 in Virginia and was raised as a member of the wealthy, well-educated Southern aristocracy. His father owned a prosperous plantation and his mother belonged to the Randolph family, which was prominent in colonial Virginia. After graduating from William and Mary College, Jefferson studied for and was admitted to the Virginia bar and was elected to the Virginia House of Burgesses (an early legislative body) in 1759.*
>
> *Jefferson read deeply in seventeenth-century English history, political theory, and law. Drawing on this background, Jefferson and a group of fellow revolutionaries drafted the Declaration of Independence in June 1776 for the Second Continental Congress. The declaration argues that the acts of tyranny perpetrated by the British government gave the colonists the right to declare themselves free of the "political bands" that had tied them to their mother country.*

Pre-Reading and Journal-Writing Suggestions

1. Explore the meaning of *independence* for a few minutes. Then freewrite on how much independence you have in your own life right now.
2. Imagine that you are in charge of setting the rules for a completely new nation. What five basic rights would you consider most important and why?

> *In Congress, July 4, 1776*
> *The Unanimous Declaration of the Thirteen*
> *United States of America*

When in the Course of human events, it becomes necessary for one   *1* people to dissolve the political bands which have connected them with another, and to assume among the powers of the earth, the separate and equal station to which the Laws of Nature and of Nature's God entitle them, a decent respect to the opinions of mankind requires that they should declare the causes which impel them to the separation.

We hold these truths to be self-evident, that all men are created equal, that they are endowed by their Creator with certain unalienable Rights, that among these are Life, Liberty and the pursuit of Happiness. That to secure these rights, Governments are instituted among Men, deriving their just powers from the consent of the governed. That whenever any Form of

Government becomes destructive of these ends, it is the Right of the People to alter or to abolish it, and to institute new Government, laying its foundation on such principles and organizing its powers in such form, as to them shall seem most likely to effect their Safety and Happiness. Prudence, indeed, will dictate that Governments long established should not be changed for light and transient causes; and accordingly all experience hath shown that mankind are more disposed to suffer, while evils are sufferable, than to right themselves by abolishing the forms to which they are accustomed. But when a long train of abuses and usurpations, pursuing invariably the same Object, evinces a design to reduce them under absolute Despotism, it is their right, it is their duty, to throw off such Government, and to provide new Guards for their future security. Such has been the patient sufferance of these Colonies; and such is now the necessity which constrains them to alter their former Systems of Government. The history of the present King of Great Britain is a history of repeated injuries and usurpations, all having in direct object the establishment of an absolute Tyranny over these States. To prove this, let Facts be submitted to a candid world.

He has refused his Assent to Laws, the most wholesome and necessary for the public good.

He has forbidden his Government to pass laws of immediate and pressing importance, unless suspended in their operation till his Assent should be obtained; and when so suspended, he has utterly neglected to attend to them.

He has refused to pass other Laws for the accommodation of large   5
districts of people, unless those people would relinquish the right of Representation in the Legislature, a right inestimable to them and formidable to tyrants only.

He has called together legislative bodies at places unusual, uncomfortable, and distant from the depository of their Public Records, for the sole purpose of fatiguing them into compliance with his measures.

He has dissolved Representative Houses repeatedly, for opposing with manly firmness his invasions on the rights of the people.

He has refused for a long time, after such dissolutions, to cause others to be elected; whereby the Legislative Powers, incapable of Annihilation, have returned to the People at large for their exercise; the State remaining in the mean time exposed to all the dangers of invasion from without, and convulsions within.

He has endeavored to prevent the population of these States; for that purpose obstructing the Laws for Naturalization of Foreigners; refusing to pass others to encourage their migration hither, and raising the conditions of new Appropriations of Lands.

He has obstructed the Administration of Justice, by refusing his Assent   10
to Laws for establishing Judiciary Powers.

He has made Judges dependent on his Will alone, for the tenure of their offices, and the amount and payment of their salaries.

He has erected a multitude of New Offices, and sent hither swarms of Officers to harass our people, and eat out their substance.

He has kept among us, in times of peace, Standing Armies without the Consent of our legislatures.

He has affected to render the Military independent of and superior to the Civil Power.

He has combined with others to subject us to a jurisdiction foreign to   15 our constitution, and unacknowledged by our laws; giving his Assent to their Acts of pretended Legislation: For quartering large bodies of armed troops among us: For protecting them, by a mock Trial, from punishment for any Murders which they should commit on the Inhabitants of these States: For cutting off our Trade with all parts of the world: For imposing Taxes on us without our Consent: For depriving us in many cases, of the benefits of Trial by Jury; For transporting us beyond Seas to be tried for pretended offenses; for abolishing the free System of English laws in a neighboring Province, establishing therein an Arbitrary government, and enlarging its Boundaries so as to render it at once an example and fit instrument for introducing the same absolute rule into these Colonies; For taking away our Charters, abolishing our most valuable Laws and altering fundamentally the Forms of our Governments: For suspending our own Legislatures, and declaring themselves invested with power to legislate for us in all cases whatsoever.

He has abdicated Government here, by declaring us out of his Protection and waging War against us.

He has plundered our seas, ravaged our Coasts, burnt our towns, and destroyed the lives of our people.

He is at this time transporting large Armies of foreign Mercenaries to complete the works of death, desolation and tyranny, already begun with circumstances of Cruelty & Perfidy scarcely paralleled in the most barbarous ages, and totally unworthy of the Head of a civilized nation.

He has constrained our fellow Citizens taken Captive on the high Seas to bear Arms against their Country, to become the executioners of their friends and Brethren, or to fall themselves by their Hands.

He has excited domestic insurrections amongst us, and has endeavored   20 to bring on the inhabitants of our frontiers, the merciless Indian Savages, whose known rule of warfare, is an undistinguished destruction of all ages, sexes, and conditions.

In every stage of these Oppressions We have Petitioned for Redress in the most humble terms: Our repeated Petitions have been answered only by repeated injury. A Prince, whose character is thus marked by every act which may define a Tyrant, is unfit to be the ruler of a free people.

Nor have We been wanting in attention to our British brethren. We have warned them from time to time of attempts by their legislature to extend an unwarrantable jurisdiction over us. We have reminded them of the circumstances of our emigration and settlement here. We have appealed to their native justice and magnanimity, and we have conjured them by the ties of our common kindred to disavow these usurpations, which would inevitably interrupt our connections and correspondence. They too have been deaf to the voice of justice and consanguinity. We must, therefore, acquiesce in the necessity, which denounces our Separation, and hold them, as we hold the rest of mankind, Enemies in War, in Peace Friends.

We, therefore, the Representatives of the United States of America, in General Congress, Assembled, appealing to the Supreme Judge of the world for the rectitude of our intentions, do, in the Name, and by Authority of the good People of these Colonies, solemnly publish and declare, That these United Colonies are, and of Right ought to be FREE AND INDEPENDENT STATES; that they are Absolved from all Allegiance to the British Crown, and that all political connection between them and the State of Great Britain, is and ought to be totally dissolved; and that as Free and Independent States, they have full Power to levy War, conclude Peace, contract Alliances, establish Commerce, and to do all other Acts and Things which Independent States may of right do. And for the support of this Declaration, with a firm reliance on the protection of Divine Providence, we mutually pledge to each other our Lives, our Fortunes, and our sacred Honor.

Suggestions for Writing and Discussion

1. The eighteenth-century language in this document may cause some problems in reading. To understand the issues and concerns here, rewrite the first two paragraphs, translating what is said into modern English.
2. The document is structured in four parts: the Preamble, the Declaration of Rights, the Bill of Indictment, and the Statement of Independence. Where does each part begin? Why do you think the authors organized this document in this way?
3. In paragraph 2, the authors write that people have certain rights, such as "Life, Liberty, and the pursuit of Happiness." Name another right that you feel is as important as the three named here. Explain your choice. As you write, keep in mind Thomas Jefferson and the other writers of the Declaration. Explain to them why you think they should have included your "right" as part of the original document.
4. Summarize all of the grievances the Declaration expresses against the king using just one sentence. To do this, you'll need to identify a central principle that all the listed grievances exemplify.
5. From your knowledge of American history, explain some of the reasons people emigrated from England and settled in what they called the New World.
6. Considered one of the greatest documents in history, the Declaration of Independence, among other things, states that when people have been treated unfairly or denied certain rights, they have the right to overthrow their oppressors. With this thought in mind, what groups in American

society today could use this premise as a reason for revolting against an oppressive group in this country?

Suggestions for Extended Thinking and Writing

1. Using the Declaration of Independence as a model, write your own document arguing that you (or a group to which you belong) should be free of governance and rules that you consider to be unfair and oppressive.
2. Consider any of the selections in this section in the light of the freedom demanded by the Declaration. Write an essay that shows how you think the writers of the Declaration would respond to the selection you have chosen.

AUDRE LORDE
Power

> *Audre Lorde, a poet and scholar of West Indian descent, was born in New York City in 1934. After completing graduate school at Columbia University and working for several years as a librarian, she became a teacher of creative writing at Tougaloo College in Mississippi and John Jay College and Hunter College in New York. She published seven volumes of poems, nearly all of which embody her deep commitment to social justice issues, particularly racism and sexism. She concentrates on love between women, racism in the women's movement, and heterosexism in black communities. In a 1983 interview, she advised young black women "not to be afraid to feel and not to be afraid to write about it. Even if you are afraid, do it anyway." Her works often embody themes and figures from traditional African myths and contemporary African writing. Describing her own writing, Lorde said, "There are very few voices for women and particularly very few voices for black women. . . . I feel I have a duty to speak the truth as I see it and share not just my triumphs, not just the things that felt good, but the pain, the intense, often unmitigating pain. It is important to share how I know survival is survival and not just a walk through the rain" (*Utne Reader, March/April 1993). After a fourteen-year battle with breast cancer, during which she published* The Cancer Journals, *she died in 1992.*

Pre-Reading and Journal-Writing Suggestions
1. How much control do you feel you have over your life? Too much? Enough? Not enough? Please explain.
2. If you could change any one thing about your life right now, what would it be and why would you choose it?
3. For one reason or another, most of us have stereotypical views when it comes to people outside our own experiences. Freewrite about one group of people toward which you have certain biases.

The difference between poetry and rhetoric   *1*
is being
ready to kill
yourself
instead of your children.   *5*

I am trapped on a desert of raw gunshot wounds
and a dead child dragging his shattered black
face off the edge of my sleep
blood from his punctured cheeks and shoulders

is the only liquid for miles and my stomach   10
churns at the imagined taste while
my mouth splits into dry lips
without loyalty or reason
thirsting for the wetness of his blood
as it sinks into the whiteness   15
of the desert where I am lost
without imagery or magic
trying to make power out of hatred and destruction
trying to heal my dying son with kisses
only the sun will bleach his bones quicker.   20

The policeman who shot down a 10-year-old in Queens
stood over the boy with his cop shoes in childish blood
and a voice said "Die you little motherfucker" and
there are tapes to prove that. At his trial
this policeman said in his own defense   25
"I didn't notice the size or nothing else
only the color," and
there are tapes to prove that, too.

Today that 37-year-old white man with 13 years of police forcing
has been set free   30
by 11 white men who said they were satisfied
justice had been done
and one black woman who said
"They convinced me" meaning
they had dragged her 4'10" black woman's frame   35
over the hot coals of four centuries of white male approval
until she let go the first real power she ever had
and lined her own womb with cement
to make a graveyard for our children.

I have not been able to touch the destruction within me.   40
But unless I learn to use
the difference between poetry and rhetoric
my power too will run corrupt as poisonous mold
or lie limp and useless as an unconnected wire
and one day I will take my teenaged plug   45
and connect it to the nearest socket
raping an 85-year-old white woman
who is somebody's mother
and as I beat her senseless and set a torch to her bed
a greek chorus will be singing in ¾ time   50
"Poor thing. She never hurt a soul. What beasts they are."

Suggestions for Writing and Discussion

1. Read this poem silently to yourself. As soon as you finish reading summarize, in one sentence, the central idea Lorde's words convey.
2. Reread the poem one more time, this time concentrating on the pictures you see. Describe the pictures that remain in your head after reading this poem.
3. Look at the images you have written and write your reactions or feelings about each image.
4. What emotions and ideas does Lorde express in this piece? Give specific examples of images that suggest the emotions and ideas you have listed.
5. Like Lorde, most of us find a way to deal with our emotions. Write an essay in which you explain how you deal with disturbing thoughts, feelings, or fears.

Suggestions for Extended Thinking and Writing

1. What does it mean to be powerful in America today? Write an essay in which you attempt to answer this question by referring to at least two of the selections in this text.
2. Create your own metaphor for your writing process; then use this metaphor as the basis for a poem.

SUGGESTIONS FOR MAKING CONNECTIONS

1. Choose four characters from this section to participate in a conversation regarding the following statement: "We don't need any laws in this country and we don't need the constitution. All we need to do is treat people with respect."
2. Choose four pieces from this section and analyze what each one reveals about democracy in America.
3. Write a conversation among Bigler, Keath, and Shilts about a person's basic rights.
4. What makes an effective argument? To answer this question, choose one piece that you feel moved or convinced you the most and one that had little or no effect on you. Compare these two pieces to analyze what elements of writing appeal to you the most as a reader.
5. America was built on the power of the individual to rule and govern his or her own life. By referring to several readings in this section, analyze how much a specific group (your choice) in this country has benefitted from democracy and how much democracy still limits this group.

6. Analyze the ads in a current popular magazine or newspaper whose audience is, in general, the American public (*Time, Newsweek, U.S. News and World Report, People,* or *U.S.A. Today,* for example). Note how many times minorities, women, men, old people, young people, handicapped people, and so on, appear in the ads. If you find the ads omit a certain group or culture, write a letter to the publishers explaining your observations.

7. Study the Declaration of Independence and imagine a forum in which four of the following people are allowed to ask Thomas Jefferson three questions that relate to their lives today and to the purpose of the framers' original document: Greg Keath, Randy Shilts, Katherine Barrett, Audre Lorde.

8. Argue for or against the following proposition: On-going education is essential if all humans are to achieve equal rights. Refer to several sources in this section as you write your argument.

12
Questions of Language

Previews: QUESTIONS OF LANGUAGE

After I was married and had lived in Japan for a while, my Japanese gradually improved to the point where I could take part in simple conversations with my husband and his friends and family. And I began to notice that often, when I joined in, the others would look startled, and the conversational topic would come to a halt. After this happened several times, it became clear to me that I was doing something wrong. But for a long time, I didn't know what it was.

From: *Conversational Ballgames,* NANCY MASTERSON SAKAMOTO

Reading programs taught in English to children with Spanish as a first language waste their acquired linguistic attributes and also impede learning by forcing them to absorb skills of reading simultaneously with a new language.

From: *Bilingual Education: The Key to Basic Skills,* ANGELO GONZALES

Foreign-language acquisition is one thing for the upper-class child in a convent school learning to curtsy. Language acquisition can only seem a loss for the ghetto child, for the new language is psychologically awesome, being, as it is, the language of the bus driver and Papa's employer. The child's difficulty will turn out to be psychological more than linguistic because what he gives up are symbols of home.

From: *Bilingual Education: Outdated and Unrealistic,* RICHARD RODRIGUEZ

The first time it happened to me I was nine years old. Cornered in the school bathroom by the class bully and her sidekick, I was offered the opportunity to swallow a few of my teeth unless I satisfactorily explained why I always got good grades, why I talked "proper" or "white."

From: *What's Wrong with Black English?"* RACHEL L. JONES

NANCY MASTERSON SAKAMOTO

Conversational Ballgames

> *Nancy Masterson Sakamoto is a professor of American studies at Shitennoji Gakuen University, Hawaii Institute. After working as a teacher trainer in Japan, she coauthored* Mutual Understanding of Different Cultures *(1981) and* Polite Fictions *(1982), from which this essay is taken.*

Pre-Reading and Journal-Writing Suggestions

1. Do you think you are a better speaker or a better listener? Please explain.
2. Write about a time when the communication between you and another person broke down. Why do you think this happened?
3. Write about the person with whom you feel most comfortable talking and write a brief dialogue that shows the two of you talking together.

After I was married and had lived in Japan for a while, my Japanese   1
gradually improved to the point where I could take part in simple conversations with my husband and his friends and family. And I began to notice that often, when I joined in, the others would look startled, and the conversational topic would come to a halt. After this happened several times, it became clear to me that I was doing something wrong. But for a long time, I didn't know what it was.

Finally, after listening carefully to many Japanese conversations, I discovered what my problem was. Even though I was speaking Japanese, I was handling the conversation in a western way.

Japanese-style conversations develop quite differently from western-style conversations. And the difference isn't only in the languages. I realized that just as I kept trying to hold western-style conversations even when I was speaking Japanese, so my English students kept trying to hold Japanese-style conversations even when they were speaking English. We were unconsciously playing entirely different conversational ballgames.

A western-style conversation between two people is like a game of tennis. If I introduce a topic, a conversational ball, I expect you to hit it back. If you agree with me, I don't expect you simply to agree and do nothing more. I expect you to add something—a reason for agreeing, another example, or an elaboration to carry the idea further. But I don't expect you always to agree. I am just as happy if you question me, or challenge me, or completely disagree with me. Whether you agree or disagree, your response will return the ball to me.

And then it is my turn again. I don't serve a new ball from my original   5
starting line. I hit your ball back again from where it has bounced. I carry
your idea further, or answer your questions or objections, or challenge or
question you. And so the ball goes back and forth, with each of us doing
our best to give it a new twist, an original spin, or a powerful smash.

And the more vigorous the action, the more interesting and exciting
the game. Of course, if one of us gets angry, it spoils the conversation, just
as it spoils a tennis game. But getting excited is not at all the same as getting
angry. After all, we are not trying to hit each other. We are trying to hit the
ball. So long as we attack only each other's opinions, and do not attack each
other personally, we don't expect anyone to get hurt. A good conversation
is supposed to be interesting and exciting.

If there are more than two people in the conversation, then it is like
doubles in tennis, or like volleyball. There's no waiting in line. Whoever is
nearest and quickest hits the ball, and if you step back, someone else will hit
it. No one stops the game to give you a turn. You're responsible for taking
your own turn.

But whether it's two players or a group, everyone does his best to keep
the ball going, and no one person has the ball for very long.

A Japanese-style conversation, however, is not at all like tennis or
volleyball. It's like bowling. You wait for your turn. And you always know
your place in line. It depends on such things as whether you are older or
younger, a close friend or a relative stranger to the previous speaker, in a
senior or junior position, and so on.

When your turn comes, you step up to the starting line with your   10
bowling ball, and carefully bowl it. Everyone else stands back and watches
politely, murmuring encouragement. Everyone waits until the ball has
reached the end of the alley, and watches to see if it knocks down all the
pins, or only some of them, or none of them. There is a pause, while
everyone registers your score.

Then, after everyone is sure that you have completely finished your
turn, the next person in line steps up to the same starting line, with a
different ball. He doesn't return your ball, and he does not begin from where
your ball stopped. There is no back and forth at all. All the balls run parallel.
And there is always a suitable pause between turns. There is no rush, no
excitement, no scramble for the ball.

No wonder everyone looked startled when I took part in Japanese
conversations. I paid no attention to whose turn it was, and kept snatching
the ball halfway down the alley and throwing it back at the bowler. Of
course the conversation died. I was playing the wrong game.

This explains why it is almost impossible to get a western-style conversation or discussion going with English students in Japan. I used to think
that the problem was their lack of English language ability. But I finally came
to realize that the biggest problem is that they, too, are playing the wrong
game.

Whenever I serve a volleyball, everyone just stands back and watches it fall, with occasional murmurs of encouragement. No one hits it back. Everyone waits until I call on someone to take a turn. And when that person speaks, he doesn't hit my ball back. He serves a new ball. Again, everyone just watches it fall.

So I call on someone else. This person does not refer to what the previous speaker has said. He also serves a new ball. Nobody seems to have paid any attention to what anyone else has said. Everyone begins again from the same starting line, and all the balls run parallel. There is never any back and forth. Everyone is trying to bowl with a volleyball.

And if I try a simpler conversation, with only two of us, then the other person tries to bowl with my tennis ball. No wonder foreign English teachers in Japan get discouraged.

Now that you know about the difference in the conversational ballgames, you may think that all your troubles are over. But if you have been trained all your life to play one game, it is no simple matter to switch to another, even if you know the rules. Knowing the rules is not at all the same thing as playing the game.

Even now, during a conversation in Japanese I will notice a startled reaction, and belatedly realize that once again I have rudely interrupted by instinctively trying to hit back the other person's bowling ball. It is no easier for me to "just listen" during a conversation, than it is for my Japanese students to "just relax" when speaking with foreigners. Now I can truly sympathize with how hard they must find it to try to carry on a western-style conversation.

If I have not yet learned to do conversational bowling in Japanese, at least I have figured out one thing that puzzled me for a long time. After his first trip to America, my husband complained that Americans asked him so many questions and made him talk so much at the dinner table that he never had a chance to eat. When I asked him why he couldn't talk and eat at the same time, he said that Japanese do not customarily think that dinner, especially on fairly formal occasions, is a suitable time for extended conversation.

Since westerners think that conversation is an indispensable part of dining, and indeed would consider it impolite not to converse with one's dinner partner, I found this Japanese custom rather strange. Still, I could accept it as a cultural difference even though I didn't really understand it. But when my husband added, in explanation, that Japanese consider it extremely rude to talk with one's mouth full, I got confused. Talking with one's mouth full is certainly not an American custom. We think it very rude, too. Yet we still manage to talk a lot and eat at the same time. How do we do it?

For a long time, I couldn't explain it, and it bothered me. But after I discovered the conversational ballgames, I finally found the answer. Of course! In a western-style conversation, you hit the ball, and while someone else is hitting it back, you take a bite, chew, and swallow. Then you hit the ball again, and then eat some more. The more people there are in the conversation, the more chances you have to eat. But even with only two of you talking, you still have plenty of chances to eat.

Maybe that's why polite conversation at the dinner table has never been a traditional part of Japanese etiquette. Your turn to talk would last so long without interruption that you'd never get a chance to eat.

Suggestions for Writing and Discussion

1. In your own words, summarize Sakamoto's main point in this essay.
2. Explain what Sakamoto means when she says she acted "instinctively" (paragraph 18).
3. Do your own experiences with conversations support or contradict any of Sakamoto's findings? Please explain.
4. Sakamoto uses the metaphor of tennis to explain how Americans talk with one another. Brainstorm for other metaphors that explain how any three of the following specific groups talk with one another:
    - a man and a woman on a first date
    - a parent and a two-year-old
    - a parent and a teenager
    - an adult child and an elderly parent
    - an employer and an employee
    - a teacher and a student
    - a patient and a doctor

    After you find metaphors you like, use them to explain to the groups of people you've chosen how they can learn more about communicating with each other.
5. Become an avid eavesdropper and listen in on a conversation between any two people you know. After listening in for a minute or two, how would you characterize this conversation? In what way does this conversation reflect the relationship between these two people?
6. After reading this piece, which way of conversing do you admire most? Why?

Suggestions for Extended Thinking and Writing

1. Using your own experiences as well as selections from this text, explain how people isolate or play games with one another without using words.
2. Write an essay in which you analyze your ability to communicate through speaking and listening. Support your analysis with examples from your home life, school or work relationships, personal relationships, and casual or distant relationships.

ANGELO GONZALES

Bilingual Education: The Key to Basic Skills

> *Angelo Gonzales is the educational director of ASPIRA, an organization that promotes awareness and advocacy of issues related to Hispanic Americans. This essay and the essay by Richard Rodriguez (p. 319) appeared as companion pieces in the* New York Times *educational supplement. Together these essays suggest the complexity of the bilingual education question.*

Pre-Reading and Journal-Writing Suggestions

1. If you moved to a foreign country and had the choice of attending either a school where classes were taught in your native language or one where classes were conducted in the foreign language, which one would you choose? Based on your answer, what problems might you encounter in the school of your choice? What might you learn or fail to learn?
2. Write about a particular class in your educational experience in which you didn't learn as much as you wanted to. What factors came into play in this experience? How might you have learned more in this situation?

If we accept that a child cannot learn unless taught through the language he speaks and understands; that a child who does not speak or understand English must fall behind when English is the dominant medium of instruction; that one needs to learn English so as to be able to participate in an English-speaking society; that self-esteem and motivation are necessary for effective learning; that rejection of a child's native language and culture is detrimental to the learning process: then any necessary effective educational program for limited or no English-speaking ability must incorporate the following:

- Language arts and comprehensive reading programs taught in the child's native language.
- Curriculum content areas taught in the native language to further comprehension and academic achievement.
- Intensive instruction in English.
- Use of materials sensitive to and reflecting the culture of children within the program.

Most Important Goal

The mastery of basic reading skills is the most important goal in primary education since reading is the basis for much of all subsequent learning.

Ordinarily, these skills are learned at home. But where beginning reading is taught in English, only the English-speaking child profits from these early acquired skills that are prerequisites to successful reading development. Reading programs taught in English to children with Spanish as a first language waste their acquired linguistic attributes and also impede learning by forcing them to absorb skills of reading simultaneously with a new language.

Both local and national research data provide ample evidence for the efficacy of well-implemented programs. The New York City Board of Education Report on Bilingual Pupil Services for 1982–83 indicated that in all areas of the curriculum—English, Spanish and mathematics—and at all grade levels, students demonstrated statistically significant gains in tests of reading in English and Spanish and in math. In all but two of the programs reviewed, the attendance rates of students in the program, ranging from 86 to 94 percent, were higher than those of the general school population. Similar higher attendance rates were found among students in high school bilingual programs.

At Yale University, Kenji Hakuta, a linguist, reported recently on a study of working-class Hispanic students in the New Haven bilingual program. He found that children who were the most bilingual, that is, who developed English without the loss of Spanish, were brighter in both verbal and nonverbal tests. Over time, there was an increasing correlation between English and Spanish—a finding that clearly contradicts the charge that teaching in the home language is detrimental to English. Rather the two languages are interdependent within the bilingual child, reinforcing each other.

Essential Contribution

As Jim Cummins of the Ontario Institute for Studies in Education has 5 argued, the use and development of the native language makes an essential contribution to the development of minority children's subject-matter knowledge and academic learning potential. In fact, at least three national data bases—the National Assessment of Educational Progress, National Center for Educational Statistics–High School and Beyond Studies, and the Survey of Income and Education—suggest that there are long-term positive effects among high school students who have participated in bilingual-education programs. These students are achieving higher scores on tests of verbal and mathematics skills.

These and similar findings buttress the argument stated persuasively in the recent joint recommendation of the Academy for Educational Development and the Hazen Foundation, namely, that America needs to become a more multilingual nation and children who speak a non-English language are a national resource to be nurtured in school.

Unfortunately, the present Administration's educational policies would seem to be leading us in the opposite direction. Under the guise of protecting the common language of public life in the United States, William J. Bennett, the Secretary of Education, unleashed a frontal attack on bilingual education. In a major policy address, he engaged in rhetorical distortions about the nature and effectiveness of bilingual programs, pointing only to unnamed negative research findings to justify the Administration's retrenchment efforts.

Arguing for the need to give local school districts greater flexibility in determining appropriate methodologies in serving limited-English-proficient students, Mr. Bennett fails to realize that, in fact, districts serving large numbers of language-minority students, as is the case in New York City, do have that flexibility. Left to their own devices in implementing legal mandates, many school districts have performed poorly at providing services to all entitled language-minority students.

A Harsh Reality

The harsh reality in New York City for language-minority students was documented comprehensively last month by the Educational Priorities Panel. The panel's findings revealed that of the 113,831 students identified as being limited in English proficiency, as many as 44,000 entitled students are not receiving any bilingual services. The issue at hand is, therefore, not one of choice but rather violation of the rights of almost 40 percent of language-minority children to equal educational opportunity. In light of these findings the Reagan Administration's recent statements only serve to exacerbate existing inequities in the American educational system for linguistic-minority children. Rather than adding fuel to a misguided debate, the Administration would serve these children best by insuring the full funding of the 1984 Bilingual Education Reauthorization Act as passed by the Congress.

Suggestions for Writing and Discussion

1. In your own words and in one sentence only, summarize Gonzales's central point in this essay.
2. Read paragraph 2 and explain what Gonzales means when he says that English-speaking children come to school equipped with the "prerequisites to successful reading development."
3. List the specific sources Gonzales uses to support his thesis. How credible do you find these sources? Do they seem reliable? How varied or up-to-date are they? As you discuss these questions, imagine that your audience is a group of teachers who have many students for whom English is a second language. Your purpose is to explain to them why they should or should not take Gonzales's points seriously.
4. In this essay, Gonzales chooses to appeal to the reader's sense of logic, for the most part. Why do you think he adopts this approach, and for what

specific readers might this approach be most effective? Please explain your answers.

5. Gonzales claims that "children who speak non-English are a national resource to be nurtured in school." However, he does not explain specifically how this should be done. If you were an elementary school teacher, what specific things could you do to nurture these children?

6. Gonzales writes that bilingual education is not a matter of choice: It is a matter of rights. On what main reason does he base this claim? Do you agree or disagree with his position here? Explain your answer.

Suggestion for Extended Thinking and Writing

Call several schools in your area to learn whether bilingual education is a concern. If it is, discover how they approach this issue. Talk with a variety of people connected to the schools, including teachers, principals, and students. Also research your state and local school offices to discover the existing policy on bilingual education. Write a report on your findings and share it with your class.

RICHARD RODRIGUEZ
Bilingual Education: Outdated and Unrealistic

> Born to Mexican immigrant parents in 1944, Richard Rodriguez experienced painful conflicts between speaking Spanish—his "home" language—and English—the "public" language expected from him at school. He resolved these conflicts by speaking, reading, and writing English nearly exclusively from his elementary school years onward. After graduating from Stanford University, he earned a graduate degree from the University of California at Berkeley and later became a professor of Renaissance literature at Berkeley. Rodriguez is best known for his autobiography, Hunger of Memory (1982), where he describes the impact of schooling on his life and his opposition to such policies as bilingual education and affirmative action. Hunger of Memory won several awards, including the Gold Medal for nonfiction from the Commonwealth Club of California, the Christopher Prize for Autobiography, and the Ansfeld Wolf Prize for Civil Rights from the Cleveland Foundation. A recipient of a 1992 Frankel Award, given by the National Endowment for the Humanities, Rodriguez was nominated for a 1993 Pulitzer Prize in nonfiction for his most recent book, Days of Obligation.
>
> Currently Rodriguez is an associate editor with the Pacific News Service in San Francisco, an essayist for the "MacNeil/Lehrer News Hour," and a contributing editor for Harper's magazine and for the "Opinion" section of the Los Angeles Times. He has produced two documentaries for the BBC, and has published widely in magazines, journals, and newspapers, including the Wall Street Journal, American Scholar, Time, Mirabella, Mother Jones, New Republic, and U. S. News & World Report.

Pre-Reading and Journal-Writing Suggestions

1. Have you ever experienced a conflict between what you learned at home and what you encountered in the classroom at school? If so, describe the conflict and explain how you resolved it or discuss why you believe the conflict remains unresolved.
2. If you are bilingual (or multilingual), explain the benefits as well as any drawbacks you see in knowing more than one language. If you are not bilingual (or multilingual), talk with someone who is, asking this person about the advantages and disadvantages he or she sees in knowing two or more languages. Explain your response to what you have learned. As you write, consider your fellow students to be your audience. Your purpose is to provide a point of view on this topic that is not offered by either Gonzales or Rodriguez.

How shall we teach the dark-eyed child *ingles*? The debate continues much as it did two decades ago.

Bilingual education belongs to the 1960's, the years of the black civil rights movement. Bilingual education became the official Hispanic demand; as a symbol, the English-only classroom was intended to be analogous to the segregated lunch counter; the locked school door. Bilingual education was endorsed by judges and, of course, by politicians well before anyone knew the answer to the question: Does bilingual education work?

Who knows? *Quien sabe?*

The official drone over bilingual education is conducted by educationalists with numbers and charts. Because bilingual education was never simply a matter of pedagogy, it is too much to expect educators to resolve the matter. Proclamations concerning bilingual education are weighted at bottom with Hispanic political grievances and, too, with middle-class romanticism.

No one will say it in public; in private, Hispanics argue with me about   5
bilingual education and every time it comes down to memory. Everyone remembers going to that grammar school where students were slapped for speaking Spanish. Childhood memory is offered as parable; the memory is meant to compress the gringo's long history of offenses against Spanish, Hispanic culture, Hispanics.

It is no coincidence that, although all of America's ethnic groups are implicated in the policy of bilingual education, Hispanics, particularly Mexican-Americans, have been its chief advocates. The English words used by Hispanics in support of bilingual education are words such as "dignity," "heritage," "culture." Bilingualism becomes a way of exacting from gringos a grudging admission of contrition—for the 19th-century theft of the Southwest, the relegation of Spanish to a foreign tongue, the injustice of history. At the extreme, Hispanic bilingual enthusiasts demand that public schools "maintain" a student's sense of separateness.

Hispanics may be among the last groups of Americans who still believe in the 1960's. Bilingual-education proposals still serve the romance of that decade, especially of the late 60's, when the heroic black civil rights movement grew paradoxically wedded to its opposite—the ethnic revival movement. Integration and separatism merged into twin, possible goals.

With integration, the black movement inspired middle-class Americans to imitations—the Hispanic movement; the Gray Panthers; feminism; gay rights. Then there was withdrawal, with black glamour leading a romantic retreat from the anonymous crowd.

Americans came to want it both ways. They wanted in and they wanted out. Hispanics took to celebrating their diversity, joined other Americans in dancing rings around the melting pot.

Mythic Metaphors

More intently than most, Hispanics wanted the romance of their dual   10
cultural allegiance backed up by law. Bilingualism became proof that one

could have it both ways, could be a full member of public America and yet also separate, privately Hispanic. "Spanish" and "English" became mythic metaphors like country and city, describing separate islands of private and public life.

Ballots, billboards, and, of course, classrooms in Spanish. For nearly two decades now, middle-class Hispanics have had it their way. They have foisted a neat ideological scheme on working-class children. What they want to believe about themselves, they wait for the child to prove, that it is possible to be two, that one can assume the public language (the public life) of America, even while remaining what one was, existentially separate.

Adulthood is not so neatly balanced. The tension between public and private life is intrinsic to adulthood—certainly middle-class adulthood. Usually the city wins because the city pays. We are mass people for more of the day than we are with our intimates. No Congressional mandate or Supreme Court decision can diminish the loss.

I was talking the other day to a carpenter from Riga, in the Soviet Republic of Latvia. He has been here six years. He told me of his having to force himself to relinquish the "luxury" of reading books in Russian or Latvian so he could begin to read books in English. And the books he was able to read in English were not of a complexity to satisfy him. But he was not going back to Riga.

Beyond any question of pedagogy there is the simple fact that a language gets learned as it gets used, fills one's mouth, one's mind, with the new names for things.

The civil rights movement of the 1960's taught Americans to deal with 15 forms of discrimination other than economic—racial, sexual. We forget class. We talk about bilingual education as an ethnic issue; we forget to notice that the program mainly touches the lives of working-class immigrant children. Foreign-language acquisition is one thing for the upper-class child in a convent school learning to curtsy. Language acquisition can only seem a loss for the ghetto child, for the new language is psychologically awesome, being, as it is, the language of the bus driver and Papa's employer. The child's difficulty will turn out to be psychological more than linguistic because what he gives up are symbols of home.

Pain and Guilt

I was that child! I faced the stranger's English with pain and guilt and fear. Baptized to English in school, at first I felt myself drowning—the ugly sounds forced down my throat—until slowly, slowly (held in the tender grip of my teachers), suddenly the conviction took; English was my language to use.

What I yearn for is some candor from those who speak about bilingual education. Which of its supporters dares speak of the price a child pays— the price of adulthood—to make the journey from a working-class home into a middle-class schoolroom? The real story, the silent story of the immigrant child's journey is one of embarrassments in public; betrayal of all that is private; silence at home; and at school the hand tentatively raised.

Bilingual enthusiasts bespeak an easier world. They seek a linguistic solution to a social dilemma. They seem to want to believe that there is an easy way for the child to balance private and public, in order to believe that there is some easy way for themselves.

Ten years ago, I started writing about the ideological implications of bilingual education. Ten years from now some newspaper may well invite me to contribute another Sunday supplement essay on the subject. The debate is going to continue. The bilingual establishment is now inside the door. Jobs are at stake. Politicians can only count heads; growing numbers of Hispanics will insure the compliance of politicians.

Publicly, we will continue the fiction. We will solemnly address this   20
issue as an educational question, a matter of pedagogy. But privately, His-panics will still seek from bilingual education an admission from the gringo that Spanish has value and presence. Hispanics of middle class will continue to seek the romantic assurance of separateness. Experts will argue. Dark-eyed children will sit in the classroom. Mute.

Suggestions for Writing and Discussion

1. Summarize the basic difference between Rodriguez's central idea and Gonzales's main point.
2. Read paragraph 5 and explain what Rodriguez means when he says, "Childhood memory is offered as parable." What is a parable? How does Rodriguez's use of the word relate to your understanding of its definition?
3. Gonzales appeals primarily to the reader's reason. Find five specific words, phrases, or passages that demonstrate his approach and go on to explain how each phrase affected you as a reader.
4. Gonzales's use of local and national test results seems convincing, and yet Rodriguez claims that we still don't know whether bilingual education works. Why isn't he convinced by these statistics? Do you agree with him? Explain.
5. Although both Rodriguez and Gonzales are descendants of Hispanic culture, their goals for the education of Hispanic children differ. List the goals that each writer promotes and draw some inferences about the core of their disagreement.
6. In a public school, should a child be entitled to his or her native language in the classroom? Support your position with three convincing reasons, and address opposing viewpoints as part of your argument. As your au-dience, imagine the school committee of a community that has recently had an influx of families who do not speak English.
7. After reading both Rodriguez's and Gonzales's essays, which approach do you feel would be most effective for residents in your community or

in a community nearby that has a significant bilingual population? Explain how several specific points the author makes might connect with the characteristics specific to your community.

Suggestion for Extended Thinking and Writing

Several countries, for example, Belgium, Holland, and Switzerland, have more than one official language. In many other countries students learn at least one other language (often English) in addition to their country's official language. Do you think that the United States should require everyone to learn a second language? After considering the pros and cons, argue for or against the following proposition: Every student in the United States should be required to become fluent both in English and in at least one other language.

GLORIA NAYLOR

A Question of Language

> *Born in 1950 in New York City, Gloria Naylor felt, from her grade school years on, "most complete when expressing [herself] through the written word." She notes that, as a child, she "wrote because I had no choice," but she kept her writing private and hidden. After high school, she followed in her mother's footsteps and worked as a telephone operator, continuing to write, but not for publication. In 1968–1975, she traveled in the South as a missionary for the Jehovah's Witnesses. The crucial moment in her life as a writer came when she returned to school (Brooklyn College CUNY) and discovered the works of Toni Morrison. After reading Morrison's* The Bluest Eye *in 1981, Naylor tried her hand at writing a novel,* The Women of Brewster Place, *which was published in 1982 and won an American Book award. Following this early success in the publishing world, she earned a graduate degree in Afro-American studies from Yale University. Her later books include* Linden Hills *(1985) and* Mama Day *(1988). Naylor has worked as a columnist for the* New York Times *and has been visiting professor and writer in residence at Princeton University, New York University, the University of Pennsylvania, Boston University, and Brandeis. "A Question of Language" was first published in the* New York Times *in 1986.*

Pre-Reading and Journal-Writing Topics

1. What do you think has had more influence in your life: the spoken word or the written word? Explain by using specific incidents from your past that support your answer.
2. In your household, what topics were or are taboo as far as children are concerned? Explain.

Language is the subject. It is the written form with which I've man-   1
aged to keep the wolf away from the door and, in diaries, to keep my sanity.
In spite of this, I consider the written word inferior to the spoken, and
much of the frustration experienced by novelists is the awareness that whatever we manage to capture in even the most transcendent passages falls far
short of the richness of life. Dialogue achieves its power in the dynamics of
a fleeting moment of sight, sound, smell, and touch.

I'm not going to enter the debate here about whether it is language
that shapes reality or vice versa. That battle is doomed to be waged whenever we seek intermittent reprieve from the chicken and egg dispute. I will
simply take the position that the spoken word, like the written word,

amounts to a nonsensical arrangement of sounds or letters without a consensus that assigns "meaning." And building from the meanings of what we hear, we order reality. Words themselves are innocuous; it is the consensus that gives them true power.

I remember the first time I heard the word *nigger*. In my third-grade class, our math tests were being passed down the rows, and as I handed the papers to a little boy in back of me, I remarked that once again he had received a much lower mark than I did. He snatched his test from me and spit out that word. Had he called me a nymphomaniac or a necrophiliac, I couldn't have been more puzzled. I didn't know what a nigger was, but I knew that whatever it meant, it was something he shouldn't have called me. This was verified when I raised my hand, and in a loud voice repeated what he had said and watched the teacher scold him for using a "bad" word. I was later to go home and ask the inevitable question that every black parent must face—"Mommy, what does 'nigger' mean?"

And what exactly did it mean? Thinking back, I realize that this could not have been the first time the word was used in my presence. I was part of a large extended family that had migrated from the rural South after World War II and formed a close-knit network that gravitated around my maternal grandparents. Their ground-floor apartment in one of the buildings they owned in Harlem was a weekend mecca for my immediate family, along with countless aunts, uncles, and cousins who brought along assorted friends. It was a bustling and open house with assorted neighbors and tenants popping in and out to exchange bits of gossip, pick up an old quarrel or referee the ongoing checkers game in which my grandmother cheated shamelessly. They were all there to let down their hair and put up their feet after a week of labor in the factories, laundries, and shipyards of New York.

Amid the clamor, which could reach deafening proportions—two or three conversations going on simultaneously, punctuated by the sound of a baby's crying somewhere in the back rooms or out on the street—there was still a rigid set of rules about what was said and how. Older children were sent out of the living room when it was time to get into the juicy details about "you-know-who" up on the third floor who had gone and gotten herself "p-r-e-g-n-a-n-t!" But my parents, knowing that I could spell well beyond my years, always demanded that I follow the others out to play. Beyond sexual misconduct and death, everything else was considered harmless for our young ears. And so among the anecdotes of the triumphs and disappointments in the various workings of their lives, the word *nigger* was used in my presence, but it was set within contexts and inflections that caused it to register in my mind as something else.

In the singular, the word was always applied to a man who had distinguished himself in some situation that brought their approval for his strength, intelligence, or drive:

"Did Johnny really do that?"

5

"I'm telling you, that nigger pulled in $6,000 of overtime last year. Said he got enough for a down payment on a house."

When used with a possessive adjective by a woman—"my nigger"— it became a term of endearment for husband or boyfriend. But it could be more than just a term applied to a man. In their mouths it became the pure essence of manhood—a disembodied force that channeled their past history of struggle and present survival against the odds into a victorious statement of being: "Yeah, that old foreman found out quick enough—you don't mess with a nigger."

In the plural, it became a description of some group within the com- 10
munity that had overstepped the bounds of decency as my family defined it: Parents who neglected their children, a drunken couple who fought in public, people who simply refused to look for work, those with excessively dirty mouths or unkempt households were all "trifling niggers." This partic-ular circle could forgive hard times, unemployment, the occasional bout of depression—they had gone through all of that themselves—but the unfor-givable sin was lack of self-respect.

A woman could never be a *nigger* in the singular, with its connotation of confirming worth. The noun *girl* was its closest equivalent in that sense, but only when used in direct address and regardless of the gender doing the addressing. *Girl* was a token of respect for a woman. The one-syllable word was drawn out to sound like three in recognition of the extra ounce of wit, nerve or daring that the woman had shown in the situation under discussion.

"G-i-r-l, stop. You mean you said that to his face?"

But if the word was used in a third-person reference or shortened so that it almost snapped out of the mouth, it always involved some element of communal disapproval. And age became an important factor in these ex-changes. It was only between individuals of the same generation, or from an older person to a younger (but never the other way around), that "girl" would be considered a compliment.

I don't agree with the argument that use of the word *nigger* at this social stratum of the black community was an internalization of racism. The dy-namics were the exact opposite: the people in my grandmother's living room took a word that whites used to signify "worthlessness or degradation and rendered it impotent. Gathering there together, they transformed *nigger* to signify the varied and complex human beings they knew themselves to be. If the word was to disappear totally from the mouths of even the most liberal of white society, no one in that room was naïve enough to believe it would disappear from white minds. Meeting the word head-on, they proved it had absolutely nothing to do with the way they were determined to live their lives.

So there must have been dozens of times that the word *nigger* was 15
spoken in front of me before I reached the third grade. But I didn't "hear" it until it was said by a small pair of lips that had already learned it could be a way to humiliate me. That was the word I went home and asked my

mother about. And since she knew that I had to grow up in America, she took me in her lap and explained.

Suggestions for Writing and Discussion

1. Naylor begins this piece by stating, "Language is the subject." What, then, is the major problem that this subject confronts? Summarize Naylor's main point about this subject.
2. "Words themselves are innocuous; it is the consensus that gives them true power." Explain the words *innocuous* and *consensus* as Naylor uses them here. Do you agree with her claim? Explain.
3. When, according to Naylor, can language be powerfully effective? When can it be powerfully destructive?
4. In your own words, what are the different connotations of the word *nigger* when Naylor heard it used among her own people, in her own household? Why wasn't she puzzled by the meaning of *nigger* at these times in her life?
5. Why does Naylor condone black people using the word *nigger* but find it derogatory when used by others? What gives one group a "right" to a word while the use of it by an outside group is considered wrong? As you write, consider that your audience is a group of college officials who must develop a definition of what comprises acceptable and unacceptable language in public forums on campus.
6. At the end of this piece, when Naylor's mother takes her on her lap to explain what the white boy meant by the term *nigger,* what do you think she says? Consider writing your response in the form of a dialogue between mother and daughter.

Suggestion for Extended Thinking and Writing

Each of the words in the following list contains various levels of meaning. Choose one word from this list and interview fifteen people, asking each for his or her definition of the word. Have those you are interviewing use each word in a sentence to clarify its meaning, and feel free to ask any questions based on the meaning they have assigned to the word. Take careful notes during each interview, and then write an essay in which you synthesize the various meanings people associate with the word.

foreign	polite
dominance	duty
clever	politician
ambition	glamorous
culture	habit
feminist	masculine
feminine	progress

RACHEL L. JONES

What's Wrong with Black English?

> *When Rachel Jones was a sophomore at Southern Illinois University, she wrote this essay, which originally appeared in* Newsweek's *"My Turn" column.*

Pre-Reading and Journal-Writing Suggestion

Explain how you change your way of speaking depending on the person or persons to whom you are speaking, the place, and the circumstances. Try to write about a specific incident that happened this past week.

William Labov, a noted linguist, once said about the use of black English, "It is the goal of most black Americans to acquire full control of the standard language without giving up their own culture." He also suggested that there are certain advantages to having two ways to express one's feelings. I wonder if the good doctor might also consider the goals of those black Americans who have full control of standard English but who are every now and then troubled by that colorful, grammar-to-the-winds patois that is black English. Case in point—me.

I'm a 21-year-old black born to a family that would probably be considered lower-middle class—which in my mind is a polite way of describing a condition only slightly better than poverty. Let's just say we rarely if ever did the winter-vacation thing in the Caribbean. I've often had to defend my humble beginnings to a most unlikely group of people for an even less likely reason. Because of the way I talk, some of my black peers look at me sideways and ask, "Why do you talk like you're white?"

The first time it happened to me I was nine years old. Cornered in the school bathroom by the class bully and her sidekick, I was offered the opportunity to swallow a few of my teeth unless I satisfactorily explained why I always got good grades, why I talked "proper" or "white." I had no ready answer for her, save the fact that my mother had from the time I was old enough to talk stressed the importance of reading and learning, or that L. Frank Baum and Ray Bradbury were my closest companions. I read all my older brothers' and sisters' literature textbooks more faithfully than they did, and even lightweights like the Bobbsey Twins and Trixie Belden were allowed into my bookish inner circle. I don't remember exactly what I told those girls, but I somehow talked my way out of a beating.

"White Pipes"

I was reminded once again of my "white pipes" problem while apartment hunting in Evanston, Ill., last winter. I doggedly made out lists of available places and called all around. I would immediately be invited over—and immediately turned down. The thinly concealed looks of shock when the front door opened clued me in, along with the flustered instances of "just getting off the phone with the girl who was ahead of you and she wants the rooms." When I finally found a place to live, my roommate stirred up old memories when she remarked a few months later, "You know, I was surprised when I first saw you. You sounded white over the phone." Tell me another one, sister.

I should've asked her a question I've wanted an answer to for years: *5* how does one "talk white"? The silly side of me pictures a rabid white foam spewing forth when I speak. I don't use Valley Girl jargon, so that's not what's meant in my case. Actually, I've pretty much deduced what people mean when they say that to me, and the implications are really frightening.

It means that I'm articulate and well-versed. It means that I can talk as freely about John Steinbeck as I can about Rick James. It means that "ain't" and "he be" are not staples of my vocabulary and are only used around family and friends. (It is almost Jekyll and Hyde-ish the way I can slip out of academic abstractions into a long, lean, double-negative-filled dialogue, but I've come to terms with that aspect of my personality.) As a child, I found it hard to believe that's what people meant by "talking proper"; that would've meant that good grades and standard English were equated with white skin, and that went against everything I'd ever been taught. Running into the same type of mentality as an adult has confirmed the depressing reality that for many blacks, standard English is not only unfamiliar, it is socially unacceptable.

James Baldwin once defended black English by saying it had added "vitality to the language," and even went so far as to label it a language in its own right, saying, "Language [i.e., black English] is a political instrument" and a "vivid and crucial key to identity." But did Malcolm X urge blacks to take power in this country "any way y'all can"? Did Martin Luther King Jr. say to blacks, "I has been to the mountaintop, and I done seed the Promised Land"? Toni Morrison, Alice Walker and James Baldwin did not achieve their eloquence, grace and stature by using only black English in their writing. Andrew Young, Tom Bradley and Barbara Jordan did not acquire political power by saying, "Y'all crazy if you ain't gon vote for me." They all have full command of standard English, and I don't think that knowledge takes away from their blackness or commitment to black people.

Soulful

I know from experience that it's important for black people, stripped of culture and heritage, to have something they can point to and say, "This is ours, *we* can comprehend it, *we* alone can speak it with a soulful flourish." I'd be lying if I said that the rhythms of my people caught up in "some serious rap" don't sound natural and right to me sometimes. But how heart-warming is it for those same brothers when they hit the pavement searching for employment? Studies have proven that the use of ethnic dialects decreases power in the marketplace. "I be" is acceptable on the corner, but not with the boss.

Am I letting capitalistic, European-oriented thinking fog the issue? Am I selling out blacks to an ideal of assimilating, being as much like white as possible? I have not formed a personal political ideology, but I do know this: it hurts me to hear black children use black English, knowing that they will be at yet another disadvantage in an educational system already full of stumbling blocks. It hurts me to sit in lecture halls and hear fellow black students complain that the professor "be tripping dem out using big words dey can't understand." And what hurts most is to be stripped of my own blackness simply because I know my way around the English language.

I would have to disagree with Labov in one respect. My goal is not so   *10* much to acquire full control of both standard and black English, but to one day see more black people less dependent on a dialect that excludes them from full participation in the world we live in. I don't think I talk white, I think I talk right.

Suggestions for Writing and Discussion

1. Summarize Jones's view of black English.
2. Define the phrase "capitalistic, European-oriented thinking" as Jones uses it in her essay (paragraph 9).
3. In what ways might Jones's position as a college student affect the way readers view her main premises?
4. Why does Jones include her family background in this piece? How would the essay be changed if this information was excluded? Explain your answer.
5. How does Jones's preferred choice of dialect connect her to or disconnect her from other cultures?
6. Why does Jones include the language used by famous black leaders and writers in America, past and present? What does she gain by using these specific people as examples? Can you think of any influential black people who do not fit into her category? As you write, imagine that your audience is a group of school children. You will be speaking to them at a celebration of Martin Luther King's birthday.

Suggestion for Extended Thinking and Writing

Listen carefully to the dialogues of a television sitcom in which the main characters are black. Do these characters conform to Jones's white

English dialect, or do they use the black English she describes? How do you think Jones would react to the way language is used in this show? How do you react?

———————

KITTY TSUI

Don't Let Them Chip Away at Our Language

Kitty Tsui was born in Kowloon, Hong Kong, in 1952. She grew up in England and Hong Kong and moved with her family to the United States in 1969. In addition to being an actress and competitive bodybuilder, Tsui is an acclaimed artist and is the author of a collection of poetry, The Words of a Woman Who Breathes Fire *(1983).*

Pre-Reading and Journal-Writing Suggestions

1. Complete the following statement, and freewrite for five or ten minutes: "The one thing about my community, state, or country that really makes me angry is . . . ."
2. Why do you (or why don't you) get actively involved in community, state, or national issues that make you angry?

haa-low, okay,   1
dank que, gut bye.

the only words
my grandmother knew.
the only words of english   5
she spoke
on a regular basis
in her rhythm of
city cantonese
mixed with   10
chinatown slang:
du pont guy,
low-see beef,
and, you good gel,
sic gee mah go,   15
sic apple pie
yum coca co-la.

a few proper nouns
were also part of
her vocabulary.   20
ny name, kit-ee
san fan-see,

pete gid-ding
her favorite
weatherman on tv,   25
say-fu-way
where she would
stock up on
rolls of toilet paper,
sponges and ajax.   30
on sale, of course.

in the spring of 1985
a republican assemblyman
proposed a bill
to make english   35
the official language
of the state.
his rationale:
we're no longer
going to let them   40
chip away at our language.
if they can't
understand english
they shouldn't be here
at all.   45

we first came
in 1785, three seamen
stranded in baltimore.
later we were
merchants and traders,   50
cooks and tailors,
contract laborers hired
to work in the mines,
in construction,
in the canneries,   55
hired to do what no man would:
hang from cliffs in a basket,
endure harsh winters
and blast through rock
to build the iron horse.   60

we became sharecroppers
growing peanuts,
strawberries,
cabbage and

chrysanthemums.   65
opened restaurants
and laundries,
worked in rich homes,
on ranches and farms
tending stock,   70
cleaning house,
cooking and ironing,
chopping firewood,
composing letters home
dreaming of a wife, a son.   75

we are tong yan,
american born
and immigrants
living in l.a., arizona,
brooklyn and the bronx,   80
san mateo and the sunset.
we eat burgers and baw,
custard tart and bubblegum.
we are doctors, actors,
artists, carpenters,   85
maids and teachers,
gay and straight.
we speak in many tongues:
sam yup, say yup, street talk,
the queen's english.   90

please don't let them
chip away at our language.

Suggestions for Writing and Discussion

1. Summarize the conflict this poem describes.
2. Explain how the title relates to the central idea of the poem.
3. Tsui chooses to use only lowercase letters in this poem. Why do you
   think that is? Would the poem have been changed for you if she had used
   capital letters in the conventional places? Explain.
4. Analyze the English words that the speaker's grandmother knew (lines
   1–31). What parts of American culture does she relate to? From what
   parts is she excluded? Why does Tsui bother to include the specific
   products that the grandmother uses? What do these details add to the
   poem?

5. Compare the responsibilities of the first Chinese settlers (lines 46–60) with those in later years (lines 61–75). What conclusions can you draw about this group of people?

6. Explain the last two lines of this poem. How are these lines different from lines 39–41?

Suggestions for Extended Thinking and Writing

1. Research the contributions of your ancestors to America. Write an essay, or perhaps a poem, using specific images to explain these contributions. As your audience, consider the readers of a magazine published by a local historical society. Your purpose is to draw their attention to the special contributions of your family.

2. Write a letter of thanks in which you acknowledge the specific ways in which past family members have contributed to who you are today.

SUGGESTIONS FOR MAKING CONNECTIONS

1. Write an essay in which you argue that language should belong to the people who speak it. Use the experiences and insights you find in at least three sources in this section to support your argument. You may, of course, use other sources as well.

2. Write an essay in which you argue for or against the following proposition: The rules of standard American English ought to be followed by all writers and speakers in our society. Refer to as many supporting sources in this section as you can.

3. Write a conversation that might take place between two of the authors in this section. The viewpoints do not necessarily have to be contrasting for this conversation to be effective. For example, you could pair up Gonzales and Rodriguez or Jones and Rodriguez.

4. Write an essay on sexism or racism in the language of advertising. Use examples from current ads and commercials, as well as the arguments of several authors in this section.

5. Compare the language in three different types of popular music today: perhaps the language of a white female country-western singer, of an urban black rapper, and of a white rock idol. How do the lyrics, messages, and syntax compare with what the authors in this section have told us?

6. Write an extended metaphor that shows how sexist or racist language affects you or someone you know well. You may choose the format of an essay or a poem for this topic.

7. Considering your own observations, as well as what you have discovered from the selections in this section, write a speech in which you try

to convince local high school or college students that our language creates and maintains sexist myths. Propose several suggestions that may help change this situation.

8. Write an essay in which you examine the power of a single word, based on the sources in this section.

9. Choose a racial, national, sexist, or religious insult and analyze the possible implications of this slur. See if you can discover where the term originated, and how the term has changed in meaning today.

10. Can people from one culture ever really understand a person from a different culture? Rely on your own experience as well as the information in this section in order to answer this question.

11. Does what we say really reflect what we think? Write an essay in which you explore this question in terms of your own life as well as the lives of the authors you have met in this section.

12. Write a paper in which you examine how television comics and sitcom characters create humor from racial, religious, gender, or age stereotypes. Is the humor harmless? What do you think? What would other authors in this section think?

ACKNOWLEDGMENTS

Text Credits

Paula Gunn Allen, from *The Sacred Hoop.* Copyright © 1986, 1992 by Paula Gunn Allen. Reprinted by permission of Beacon Press.

Maya Angelou, from *I Know Why the Caged Bird Sings.* Copyright © 1969 by Maya Angelou. Reprinted by permission of Random House, Inc.

Paul Aronowitz, "A Brother's Dream," January 14, 1988. Copyright © 1988 by The New York Times Company. Reprinted by permission.

Katherine Barrett, "Old Before Her Time," *Ladies' Home Journal,* August 1983. Copyright © 1983 Meredith Corporation. Used with the permission of Ladies' Home Journal magazine.

Eric Bigler, "Give Us Jobs, Not Admiration." Originally published in *Newsweek.* Reprinted by permission of the author.

Gloria Bonilla, "Leaving El Salvador," from *You Can't Drown the Fire: Latin American Women Writing in Exile,* ed. by Alicia Portnoy, 1988. Reprinted by permission of Cleis Press.

Judith Ortiz Cofer, "*Casa,*" reprinted with permission of the publisher of *Silent Dancing: A Partial Remembrance of a Puerto Rican Childhood.* (Houston: Arte Publico Press–University of Houston.)

Jacques d'Amboise, "I Show a Child What Is Possible" from *Parade,* August 6, 1989. Reprinted with permission from *Parade* and the author. Copyright © 1989.

Harry Dolan, "I Remember Papa," in *From the Ashes: Voices of Watts,* ed. by Budd Schulberg, 1968.

Michael Dorris, "Indians in Aspic." February 24, 1991. Copyright © 1991 by The New York Times Company. Reprinted by permission.

Nora Ephron, from *Scribble, Scribble.* Copyright © 1978 by Nora Ephron. Reprinted by permission of Alfred A. Knopf, Inc.

Nicholas Gage, "The Teacher Who Changed My Life," from *Parade,* December 17, 1989. Reprinted with the permission of *Parade* and the author. Copyright © 1989.

Bernard R. Goldberg, "Television Insults Men, Too," March 14, 1989. Copyright © 1989 by The New York Times Company. Reprinted by permission.

Angelo Gonzalez, "Bilingual Education: The Key to Basic Skills," November 10, 1985. Copyright © 1985 by The New York Times Company. Reprinted by permission.

Patricia Hampl. Copyright © 1986 by Patricia Hampl. First published in *The Graywolf Annual.* Permission granted by Rhoda Weyr Agency.

Lawrence E. Harrison. Copyright © *The National Interest,* No. 28, Washington, D.C. Reprinted with permission.

Sue Horton, *Los Angeles Times Magazine,* October 16, 1988.

Rachel L. Jones, "What's Wrong with Black English," *Newsweek*, December 27, 1982. Reprinted with permission of the author.

Lewis P. Johnson, "For My Indian Daughter," from *My Turn* column, *Newsweek*, September 5, 1983.

Greg Keath, "Abortion Is Not a Civil Right." Reprinted with permission of *The Wall Street Journal*. Copyright © 1989 Dow Jones & Company, Inc. All rights reserved.

Audre Lorde, "Power," reprinted from *The Black Unicorn, Poems by Audre Lorde*, by permission of W. W. Norton & Company, Inc. Copyright © 1978 by Audre Lorde.

Deborah Marquardt, from *Ms* Magazine, May, 1987.

Mark Mathabane, from *Kaffir Boy in America*. Reprinted with the permission of Charles Scribner's Sons, an imprint of Macmillan Publishing Company. Copyright © 1989 Mark Mathabane.

Grace Ming-Yee, from *Ms* Magazine, July 1988. Reprinted by permission of *Ms* Magazine, © 1988.

Toshio Mori, "The Woman Who Makes Swell Doughnuts," from *Yokohama, California*. Reprinted by permission of The Caxton Printers, Ltd., Caldwell, Idaho 83605. "Abalone, Abalone, Abalone" from *The Chauvinist and Other Stories*. Copyright © 1979 Asian American Studies Center, UCLA. Reprinted by permission.

David Morris, "Rootlessness," from May/June 1990 issue of *The Utne Reader*. Reprinted by permission. David Morris is Vice President of the Minneapolis and Washington, D.C., based Institute for Local Self-Reliance.

Gloria Naylor, "A Question of Language," February 20, 1986. Copyright © 1986 by The New York Times Company. Reprinted by permission.

Tran Thi Nga, "Letter to My Mother," from *Shallow Graves: Two Women and Vietnam, 1986,* by Tran Thi Nga and Wendy Wilder Larsen. Reprinted by permission of Schecter Communications Corp.

Charles Osgood, from *Nothing Could Be Finer Than a Crisis That Is Minor in the Morning*, by Charles Osgood. Copyright © 1979 by CBS, Inc. Reprinted by permission of Henry Holt and Company, Inc.

Grace Paley, from *The Little Disturbances of Man*, Viking: New York, 1959. Copyright 1959, 1994 by Grace Paley. Reprinted by permission of Grace Paley. All rights reserved.

Bernice Johnson Reagon. Reprinted by the permission of the author, copyright 1976. Originally published in *Sing Out!* magazine, 1976.

Ishmael Reed. Reprinted with permission of Atheneum Publishers, an imprint of Macmillan Publishing Company, from *Writin' is Fightin'* by Ishmael Reed. Copyright © 1988 by Ishmael Reed.

Richard Rodriguez, "Bilingual Education: Outdated and Unrealistic," November 10, 1985. Copyright © 1985 by The New York Times Company. Reprinted by permission.

Mike Rose. Reprinted with the permission of The Free Press, an imprint of Simon & Schuster, from *Lives on the Boundary: The Struggles and Achievements of America's Underprepared*. Copyright © 1989 by Mike Rose.

Joanna Russ, from *Again, Dangerous Visions*, by Harlan Ellison. Reprinted by permission of Joanna Russ. Copyright © 1972 by Joanna Russ.

Jim Sagel, "Sandra Cisneros," from *Publisher's Weekly*, March 29, 1991. Published by Cahners Publishing Company, a division of Reed Publishing USA. Copyright © 1991 by Reed Publishing USA. Author of 12 books of bilingual poetry and prose, Jim Sagel is the recipient of the Premio Casa de las Americas, one of the most important literary awards in Latin America.

Nancy Masterson Sakamoto, "Conversational Ballgames," from *Polite Fictions: Why Japanese and Americans Seem Rude to Each Other*, by Nancy Sakamoto and Reiko Naotsuka.

Randy Shilts, "What's Fair in Love and War." From *Newsweek*, February 1, 1993. Copyright © 1993, Newsweek, Inc. All rights reserved. Reprinted by permission.

Cathy Song, "The Youngest Daughter," from *Picture Bride*, 1983. Reprinted by permission of Yale University Press.

Brent Staples, "Just Walk on By: A Black Man Ponders His Power to Alter Public Space." Copyright © 1986 by Brent Staples. Reprinted by permission of the author. Brent Staples writes on politics and culture for The New York Times Editorial Board. His memoir, "Parallel Time: Growing Up in Black and White," is published by Pantheon Books (1994).

Amy Tan. Reprinted by permission of G.P. Putnam's Sons from *The Joy Luck Club* by Amy Tan. Copyright © 1989 by Amy Tan.

Miguel Torres, "From Mexico 1977," in *American Mosaic: The Immigrant Experience in the World of Those Who Lived It*, by Joan Morrison and Charlotte Fox Zabusky. Copyright © 1980, 1982, 1992 by Joan Morrison and Charlotte Fox Zabusky. Currently available from University of Pittsburgh Press.

Kitty Tsui, "Don't Let Them Chip Away at Our Language," from *An Ear to the Ground: An Anthology of Contemporary American Poetry*, by Marie Harris and Kathleen Aguero (eds.).

Alice Walker, "The Right to Life: What Can the White Man Say to the Black Woman?" from *Her Blue Body Everything We Know, Earthling Poems, 1965–1990*, copyright © 1991 by Alice Walker. Reprinted by permission of Harcourt Brace & Company.

Photo Credits

Page 60 (top), © Ulrike Welsch/PhotoEdit; (bottom) © Ellis Herwig/Stock Boston. **Page 61,** © Topham/The Image Works. **Page 116** (top), © Joel Gordon 1986; (bottom), © Peter Menzel/Stock Boston. **Page 117,** © H. Armstrong Roberts. **Page 154** (top), © Joel Gordon 1991; (bottom), © Frank Siteman/Stock Boston. **Page 155,** © Charles Harbutt/ Actuality, Inc. **Page 200** (top), © Hazel Hankin/Stock Boston; (bottom), © Jonathan A. Meyers/JAM Photography. **Page 201,** © Jim Sheldon/ Sygma Photo News. **Page 232** (top), © Jane Scherr/Jeroboam, Inc.; (bottom), © David M. Grossman/Photo Researchers, Inc. **Page 233,**

© Topham/The Image Works. **Page 268** (top), © Mike Mazzaschi/Stock Boston; (bottom), © David Jennings/The Image Works. **Page 269,** © Mark Antman/The Image Works. **Page 308** (top), © David Jennings/The Image Works; (bottom), © Charles Kennard/Stock Boston. **Page 309,** © Joel Gordon 1991.

INDEX